Tribal Studies and Beyond

Dhirendra Nath Majumdar, at the Department of Anthropology, c. 1955–6

Tribal Studies and Beyond

Contributions of D.N. Majumdar to Indian Anthropology

H.S. SAKSENA

RAWAT PUBLICATIONS
Jaipur • New Delhi • Bangalore • Guwahati • Kolkata

ISBN 978-81-316-0909-5

The publication of this book was financially supported by the ICSSR. The responsibility for the facts stated, opinions expressed, or conclusions reached, is entirely that of the author and that the ICSSR accepts no responsibility for them.

ICSSR Consultant:
Professor Yogesh Atal, D-224, Sushant Lok Phase I, Sector-43, Gurugram.

Published by
Prem Rawat for **Rawat Publications**
Satyam Apts, Sector 3, Jawahar Nagar, Jaipur 302 004 (India)
Phone: 0141 265 1748 / 7006 Fax: 0141 265 1748
E-mail: info@rawatbooks.com
Website: www.rawatbooks.com

New Delhi Office
4858/24, Ansari Road, Daryaganj, New Delhi 110 002
Phone: 011 2326 3290

Also at *Bangalore, Guwahati* and *Kolkata*

Typeset by Rawat Computers, Jaipur
Printed at Nice Printing Press, New Delhi

Contents

Foreword

Students of disciplinary history have to attend to two tasks. First, they have to explore collective orientations among like-minded scholars, whether they are self-consciously a 'collective' or 'school', formally so designated, or only informally thus referred to. Many examples come to mind, such as (to mention only a couple) the 'Subalterns Collective' in India among historians, or the 'Frankfurt School' in Europe among philosophers and social scientists. The second task, complementary to 'collectivization' is 'individuation' or the high lighting of the work of an individual scholar as if he or she stands alone, an island unto themselves. Actually, no scholar ever stands alone: there always are predecessors, contemporaries, and successors. Put otherwise, one usually has had teachers, and has colleagues and students. Both the methodological approaches have their uses as well as limitations, and these must be recognized by the researchers. Analytical presentations are not merely factual expositions but include interpretations.

One of the instances of a 'school' in India in the field of social sciences is the Department of Economics and Sociology at the University of Lucknow during the 30 years, 1921 to 1950, from its inception to the process of disaggregation which began with the establishment of the Department of Anthropology in 1950 and later, in 1953, the carving out of the Department of Sociology from the parent group, leaving the economists by themselves in the Department of Economics.

Even before this process of disaggregation began, the contribution of D.N. Majumdar always stood apart as he was the lone anthropologist among the teaching faculty of the Department. Majumdar explicitly emphasized the distinctiveness of anthropology from economics and sociology, even when the former discipline was presented as *comparative* economics to accommodate traditional economic systems such as that of India. Majumdar remained steadfast in his conception of his subject as having two essential dimensions, namely the physical (or biological) and the socio-cultural (For a detailed discussion, see my edited volume *Sociology at the University of Lucknow: The First Half-Century*, OUP, 2013).

A general indifference towards disciplinary history among social scientists in India has resulted in the absence of a significant body of historically grounded work focusing on groups of scholars or individuals. The situation has begun to change, it seems, and we now have intellectual biographies of at least two founding fathers of sociology, Swapan Kumar Bhattacharya's *Indian Sociology: The Role of Benoy Kumar Sarkar* (University of Burdwan, 1990) and S.K. Pramanick's *Sociology of G.S. Ghurye* (Rawat, Jaipur, 1994). Most recently we have a nuanced discussion of aspects of the contributions of Radhakamal Mukerjee, *The Quest for Indian Sociology* (Indian Institute of Advanced Study, Shimla, 2014) by Manish Thakur. I have already mentioned the book of select short texts and editorial commentaries, *Sociology at the University of Lucknow*. As for anthropologists, there is no study devoted to any one of the founders, notably A. Aiyappan, K.P. Chattopadhyay, B.S. Guha, and Irawati Karve.

Hari Sahai Saksena's present book is, to the best of my knowledge, the first full length study of the work on an Indian anthropologist. To write about a 'general' anthropologist such as D.N. Majumdar, in our times of specialization is, needless to emphasize, a daunting task. It is highly commendable that Dr Saksena decided to accept this challenge, and, what is more important, achieved noteworthy success in his endeavour.

Inevitably, there is a primary emphasis in Saksena's book on Majumdar's contributions to cultural-social anthropology than to biological anthropology. Saksena himself belongs to the third batch of students who completed their studies leading to the Master's degree (MA) in 1954 at the recently established Department of Anthropology at the University of Lucknow. The prescribed courses of study comprised 'papers' in cultural anthropology, physical anthropology, and prehistory, with an additional outside-the-Department 'paper' in sociology. The second year provided for specialization in either cultural-social anthropology or physical anthropology.

Saksena specialized in the former area. Soon after receiving his MA in 1954, he joined the Lucknow-Cornell Project on the study of rural communities, and this took him to Cornell University, Ithaca, NY, as a Research Associate for a year. The following year (1956–57) he worked as a lecturer in cultural anthropology in the University of Lucknow. He then joined the organization of the Commissioner for Scheduled Castes and Scheduled Tribes in New Delhi. He retired in 1988 from the position of Director, National Commission for Scheduled Castes and Scheduled Tribes. In the discharge of his official duties, he engaged in ethnographic investigations and survey research, and produced studies in these areas as also on policy formulation and implementation. Subsequent to his retirement, he has been closely associated with various academic programmes of the Ethnographic and Folk Culture Society in Lucknow, including responsibility as an editor of *The Eastern Anthropologist*, the internationally well-known journal established by D.N. Majumdar in 1947. He was, thus, well qualified to undertake a study of the contributions of D.N. Majumdar as teacher and researcher in the fields of cultural anthropology, sociology and biological anthropology.

Awarded a two-year Senior Fellowship by the Indian Council of Social Science Research (ICSSR) in 2012, Saksena finished his assignment within the prescribed period, and the present book is the outcome. I now welcome its publication.

The book is primarily expositional in character, which is of course the right way to begin in the presentation of the work of a scholar. The important questions of how it may be evaluated and by which criteria arise only after we first describe what its scope is and locate it in its place and time. As such an expository study, Saksena's *Tribal Studies and Beyond: Contributions of D.N. Majumdar to Indian Anthropology* is comprehensive in coverage and accessible in style. When a reader will have completed his or her perusal of it, he or she will have a fairly clear picture of Majumdar's contributions.

Saksena presents in this book Majumdar's contributions to tribal ethnography, covering communities from a wide range of habitat, cultural and economic life, and social organization, from what were in his time of fieldwork the provinces or states of Bihar and Uttar Pradesh and are now Jharkhand, Uttarakhand, and Uttar Pradesh. He also considers Majumdar's post-1947 studies of caste social structure and dynamics, rural development problems and programmes, urban settlements, composition of the working class, and emerging problems such as unemployment among the educated. While in his earlier studies of tribal communities, Majumdar had improved upon available methods of ethnographic description and analysis, Saksena shows that in his later village studies he clearly was one of pioneers. He also brings in Majumdar's anthropometric and serological surveys of select groups in Bengal, Gujarat, and Uttar Pradesh. The contributions in the field of physical anthropology are understandably presented in less detail.

Altogether, Hari Sahai Saksena's book is an exemplary work of exposition and, as such, it is significant contribution to the history of anthropology in India. It is a pleasure to commend it to the attention of all interested readers. One hopes that other scholars will take up from where Saksena leaves the work to both produce further studies of Majumdar's work and also the contributions of his Indian contemporaries.

T.N. Madan
Doc. Hon. Causa (Paris, Nanterre)
Emeritus Professor (Sociology)
Institute of Economic Growth (University of Delhi)
Distinguished Senior Fellow (Adjunct)
Centre for the Study of Developing Societies, Delhi

Acknowledgements

This study has been made possible only with the active help and cooperation from several institutions and individuals. It is now my privileged duty to express my gratitude and thank them.

The work was inspired by my former teacher, Professor T.N. Madan, more than a decade back. His concern about its progress, and advice has been generously there, all along. Moreover, he has been kind enough to add a 'Foreword'. I can never thank him enough.

The Indian Council of Social Science Research granted me a Senior Fellowship (2012–2014) for the project. Dr Harish Sharma, Deputy Director, dealing with research fellowships, helped me at every stage for which I express my gratefulness. The affiliating institution for the Senior Fellowship, Giri Institute of Development Studies, Lucknow, its former Director Professor A.K. Singh and present Director Professor Surinder Kumar, facilitated my work, including visits to Sonbhadra, Kolkata and Delhi. Their staff was always prompt and considerate. The ICSSR helped in the publication with their publication subsidy and I am obliged to the officers concerned, as also Yogesh Atal to whom the manuscript was sent for evaluation.

Availability of the library in the Ethnographic and Folk Culture Society and its staff was forthcoming throughout, thanks to its librarian, and former General Secretary, Professor Nadeem Hasnain and the present one, Professor Sukant K. Chaudhury. The Society also provided financial help to enable me to visit Cambridge, when I was in England in 2005. Keen interest of friends, Nadeem and Sukant, in my work is reflected in many ways including books lent from their rich personal collections and in sparing time to go through my drafts and making valuable comments. They also made books available to me from the Departments of Anthropology, and Sociology, respectively and also the Tagore Library, Lucknow University. Nadeem was kind enough to organize a one-day symposium on Prof. Majumdar's work in the Department of Anthropology in February 2013 at my request. Other friends at Lucknow who were of help are

Professors J.M.S. Verma and D.R. Sahu, and Chandra Sen. Among the other institutional libraries which provided the reference materials are GIDS Lucknow, Delhi University, Jawaharlal Nehru University, Guwahati University and the Indian Statistical Institute, Kolkata. I am grateful to their librarians for active support.

Senior anthropologists and sociologists, all of them my old friends, who spared me a good deal of time for personal discussions and correspondence, are many. Their views and suggestions benefitted me immensely. Prof. N.S. Reddy, Prof. Yogendra Singh, Prof. Ajit K. Danda, Prof. R.K. Jain, Prof. Binod Agrawal, Prof. Yogesh Atal, Prof. Soumendra Patnaik and C.B. Tripathi were the most helpful. My sincere thanks to them. Unfortunately, some others – Prof. S.K. Srivastava, Prof. K.N. Sharma, Prof. Ghaus Ansari, Prof. Dharani Sinha, Prof. B.K. Roy Burman, Prof. Gopala Sarana, Prof. Sunil Misra and Prof. I.P.S. Monga have since passed away. I remember them and cherish my association with them. My young friend, Subhu Ray, Department of Anthropology, Calcutta University, took care of me when I visited the University and various institutions in Kolkata, and I am beholden to him.

As always, Manorama, relieved me from the stress of household worries and allowed me to indulge fully in this pursuit. And the family also provided assistance for this sustained work in different ways. Alka, my daughter-in-law, arranged to send me some reference materials from the University of Michigan, USA, during 2013–14, and Amit and Jaya often saved my running to different institutions outside Lucknow. Similarly, Soumitra and Anju ran errands for me at Delhi. Tarun Khanna was, as ever, the man in my need.

And lastly, this work, just, could not have progressed without the competent stenography of Mukesh Mourya, and his skill in searching relevant materials on the Internet and systematic filing of the voluminous papers.

Pranit Rawat, has to be thanked for promptly accepting the publication and giving it the excellent shape in which it is there before the readers.

Lucknow

H.S. Saksena

1

D.N. Majumdar

His Life and Work

Researching on a person, his life and his academic reach, one usually has to explore the biographical or autobiographical sources about him, archival material relating to the correspondence and other such personal writings, the person's own academic or general works which may sometimes reflect the person of the author, and discussions and interviews with his colleagues, friends, students, family members and any other contemporaries.

Majumdar was born in June 1903, more than 111 years ago and he passed away on the night of 31 May 1960 suddenly due to a cerebral haemorrhage. At the time of his death, his friend, Dr S.K. Chakrabarty, was with him but his efforts to remedy the attack failed. Actually, it was his long standing practice to invite his postgraduate students of both previous and final class (who were passing out), along with colleagues and friends for a get together on the last day of every academic session at the university. However, in 1960 it was a dinner hosted by the then Vice-Chancellor after which came the stroke.

It seems, he never planned or could write any biographical or autobiographical article or book about himself. And his anthropology, which was in fact dearer to him than anything else, except perhaps his only child, always engaged him completely. Going through his writings which are copious, more than 200 papers and more than a dozen books, one hardly ever gets a glimpse of Majumdar as a person though his empathy and understanding of the people among whom he was working, and the quality of rapport is remarkably noticed – the thoroughness of his ethnography has been widely commented upon. In the days when Majumdar was most active, the common and almost the only medium of communication was through letters, and he did carry out a substantial correspondence with his academic contacts and friends as well as his students. However, this author's search for his papers provided him with almost no material in the Department of Anthropology, University of Lucknow, which he had founded in 1951 and the Department of Economics and Sociology in which he worked as a faculty member continuously from 1928.

Vidyarthi (1961), under the title, 'Academic Career of the late Professor D.N. Majumdar', writes:

> On my request Professor Majumdar was kind enough to prepare this biographical note in the year 1959 for my use. Certain changes have been made here and there to make the information up to date-editor.

The two-page details here appear to be the only source which can be attributed to Majumdar himself. Most of the other biographical and academic details can only be sourced from a few obituaries written by his students and friends in academia and also a few letters he had written which were made available by some of his prominent students. His wife and Promilla, his only child, have both passed away.

D.N. Majumdar was the eldest son of Mrs Kusum Kumari and Mr Rewati Mohan Majumdar. He was born in Patna, Bihar (then Bengal), on 3 June 1903. His student career was brilliant at the Dacca Government College and the University College, Calcutta. He did his matric and intermediate science in first division and BA with distinction. In his post-graduation in anthropology from the Calcutta University, he stood first class first in the year 1924. S.C. Roy was a visiting lecturer to the newly established Department of Anthropology, Calcutta University, and he initiated Majumdar in field work in Chhota Nagpur in 1923 (Sarkar, 1991: 24). Subsequently, on Roy's suggestion Majumdar took up the study of the Ho tribe in Kolhan and Roy even accompanied him to the Kolhan region to acquaint him with his field, and also provided Majumdar with some of his own notes. Majumdar always regarded S.C. Roy as his mentor with a great sense of gratitude for this early training in comprehensive ethnography. L.K. Anantakrishna Iyar too was one of his teachers in the university (Danda and Chakrabarti, 1989: 2). While working among the Ho, he was a Premchand Roychand scholar of the Calcutta University. This scholarship was awarded only to the most brilliant students engaged in original research and it used to be a coveted honour those days. In 1928, he was selected by Prof. Radhakamal Mukerjee as a lecturer in primitive economics in the Department of Economics and Sociology, University of Lucknow. The department had been started by Mukerjee in 1921. Another great honour came his way the next year when he was awarded the Mouat Gold Medal by the University of Calcutta.

In the University of Lucknow, Majumdar was entrusted with the teaching of non-monetized primitive economic systems and also, sometimes, banking and fiscal management. He found the latter not of much interest. But his lectures on primitive economics, which were anthropological, soon attracted his students and within a couple of years he had started the practice of taking post-graduate students for field work and even making them his co-authors in papers presented in the Indian Science Congress. This was the beginning of his popularity and the close life long relationship with his students.

In 1927, he married Madhuri Guha, daughter of the late Mrs and Mr Prafulachand Guha of Calcutta. Kumkum was their only issue and she was married long after Majumdar's death to Himeshchandra Mukherjee, a lawyer at Siliguri in West Bengal. Kumkum passed away in 2008.

In 1933, Majumdar went to the Cambridge University where he studied social anthropology with Prof. T.C. Hodson, a former civil servant who had worked among the tribes of North-East India. In May 1935, he submitted his Ph.D. dissertation at the Cambridge University, entitled, 'A Changing Austric Culture'. This was the outcome of his work among the Ho which was later published under the title, *A Tribe in Transition – A Study in Culture Pattern* (60: 1937). The thesis in its appendices included some anthropometric data – Frequency Curves of Stature, Nasal Index, Cephalic Index and Arm's Reach – which were excluded from its published version. While at Cambridge he was also appointed to deliver a course of lectures and he was the first Indian to get 'such a distinction in Anthropology from any English University' (Sarana, 1961: 106), and *The Cambridge University Calendar (1935–36),* sourced by this author in 2005. It also records that besides Hodson there were six other professors who were the examiners for his thesis, and he was the only Indian awarded a doctorate in 1935.

While in England, he also received advanced training in physical anthropology from Prof. G.M. Morant, and studied serology with Prof. R. Ruggles-Gates and worked in the Galton Laboratory, London. Apart from these distinguished professors in physical anthropology from whom Majumdar learnt the latest in the subject, he also attended the seminars of Professor B. Malinowski in the London School. Thus, he made himself abreast of the latest in social anthropological approaches and was oriented thoroughly into the 'functional' approach. He was deeply influenced by Malinowski. In his own classes he always discussed Malinowski's functional theory and his contributions to social anthropology feelingly, and regarded him as his teacher. In fact, retrospectively remembering Majumdar as a teacher it seems that he followed Malinowski in ways more than academic orientation.

Kuper (1973: 34–35) has described Malinowski's charisma and his relationship with his students as follows:

> Malinowski would recruit people from all over to attend these seminars, and perhaps, to be converted; and those students who did attach themselves to him soon became an integral part of his world. A Chinese student once remarked, 'Malinowski is like an Oriental teacher – he is a father to his pupils. He has us to his home; he gets us to run messages for him; sometimes we even cook for him. And we like to do these things for him.' When he moved ... in the summer some students would go with him ... taking part in informal seminars in the evening ... he demanded their complete loyalty. He came increasingly to see himself as engaged in a battle for truth ... .

This reminds us, who were his students, of Majumdar's relationship with his own students in more ways than one. Majumdar's own relationship with his promising students was like a devoted parent's concern for their work and career. He was appreciative of the 'loyalty' of his students and it is reflected in his dedicating *The Matrix of Indian Culture* (1947) 'to my pupils of the M.A. final class in anthropology, 1947 whose love and loyalty I sincerely reciprocate'. And, D.P. Mukerji, his friend in the University of Lucknow, saying:

> ... he succeeded in enlisting them for the different colleges and universities of India, and also for his journal, I think very few men in India have produced a better set of research workers than he had done. He was a friendly man and his students were devoted to him .... I have hinted above that he was a fighter, but he fought for causes, for the principles he cared for .... (1962: 10)

And, therefore, it is not surprising that no less than three festschrifts were posthumously published in his honour, as noted by Peter Burger, a Dutch anthropologist who has worked in India, in a personal communication to this author. Also, the first three scholars selected for the prestigious fellowship in the Australian National University initiated in early 1950s were his students.

The years after his Cambridge tenure brought some mentionable academic distinctions. In 1936, he became a Fellow of the Royal Anthropological Institute of Great Britain and Ireland. He was also invited to deliver a series of lectures on Indian culture at Vienna. Thus, his visit to the UK in mid-1930s was a focal 'point of his career in anthropology' (Sarana, 1960: 106). In both physical and social anthropology, he oriented himself during this period in the latest developments and continued his efforts to keep himself acquainted with the developments in both the branches of anthropology till the end was initiated.

Soon after his return to India, he was elected to preside over Anthropology and Archaeology Section of the 26th Session of the Indian Science Congress at Lahore in 1939. His presidential address to the Section reflects how his academic thinking, particularly relating to culture change among tribal communities, began to focus on the processes of 'acculturation' and 'trans-culturation' which remained a focal issue in his writings in the subsequent decades. Concluding his presidential address, Majumdar avers:

> The contacts between social groups have led to miscegenation of cultures. A group which has not lost its interest in life and possesses vitality must adopt traits from other groups. This adoption of alien traits is usually selective and it is on the nature of this selection that the future of the group depends. The process of selective adoption may be called acculturation. (73: 1939: 41)

And, as Madan (1983: 10) comments:

> Soon we find him writing about social change, particularly in situations of culture contact. This was to become, as I will try to show, a life-long interest, and even more than that, a lifelong concern.

Majumdar was also perceptive enough to see that this process of development was not, however, an easy one (ibid.: 10). Towards the close of 1930s, Majumdar had two of students working under his supervision for their Ph.D. Kunwar Indrajit Singh who was from Akaltara, a Gond princely state of the then Central Provinces, was working on the 'Gondwana and the Gonds'. He completed his work in early 1940s and his book was published in 1944 under the title, *The Gondwana and The Gonds (A Study in Primitive Economics)*. Dr Singh describes Majumdar as his:

> teacher and friend who initiated me into the methods and techniques of firsthand field surveys and had accompanied me in several ethnographic tours

in the Gond country to equip me with the scientific pre-requisite of intensive anthropological studies.

This statement is indicative of how Majumdar guided intensively his doctoral candidates. The other research scholar working under him was Y.S. Parmar of Sirmur (Nahan) in Himachal Pradesh. Parmar later became the first Chief Minister of Himachal Pradesh. Thus, it is apparent that Majumdar started attracting students from different parts of the country. Parmar wrote his thesis on 'The Marital Life of Trans Giri Tract', a polyandrous community across the Yamuna from Jaunsar-Bawar, Deharadun. Parmar's book was published much later in 1975 under the title, *Polyandry in the Himalaya.* Jaunsar-Bawar was the area where Majumdar had started his intensive study of polyandry. The practice was first mentioned to Majumdar by Malinowski in his seminars and Majumdar had then assured Malinowski that he would make a study thereof (1960: viii–ix).

II

During 1940–50, a number of distinctions and achievements came his way. The decade saw Majumdar getting settled as a leader in professional anthropology. In 1941, he was elected Fellow of the National Institute of Sciences (India), and in the same year the Census Commissioner of the United Provinces (now Uttar Pradesh) invited him to undertake an anthropometric and serological survey of the Provinces. Majumdar, further, planned an ethnographic survey of the tribes and criminal tribes in the province. For the anthropometric and serological survey, Majumdar measured about 4000 persons belonging to 21 social groups, castes and tribes, and collected blood group data in respect of 5000 persons. Next year, in 1942, he was invited by Sir Theodore Tusker, Supervisor of the Indian Civil Service Training Centre at Dehradun, to deliver a course of lectures on Indian anthropology, a new initiative in the field of Indian anthropology. These lectures were later published in 1944 under the title, *Races and Cultures of India*. The book has since been revised and reprinted three times. Probably, it is Majumdar's best known published work. Majumdar had associated with Prof. P.C. Mahalonobis, Director of the Indian Statistical Institute, Calcutta, for the analysis of the statistical data relating to the anthropometric and serological survey of the United Provinces. Then, in 1945, Mahalonobis invited him to undertake an anthropometric, serological and health survey of Bengal.

The University of Nagpur invited him in 1946 to deliver the Sri Mahadeo Hari Wathodkar Memorial lectures. These lectures were published in 1947 under the title, *The Matrix of Indian Culture*. The Gujarat Research Society also approached him to undertake an anthropometric and serological survey of Maha-Gujarat in 1946 and this Society awarded him the Gujarat Research Society Medal for outstanding contributions to Indian physical anthropology, in 1950. These three surveys have been discussed at length in another chapter.

The journal, *Man in India,* founded in 1921 by S.C. Roy, appointed him as one of its Honorary Editors in 1949, a position from which he resigned in 1955. He, however, remained the founding Editor of *The Eastern Anthropologist*, the quarterly journal published by the Ethnographic and Folk Culture Society, till his death.

This decade was also the period when he was able to get an integrated syllabus in sociology and anthropology adopted at the post-graduate level in economics which he taught along with Radhakamal Mukerjee and D.P. Mukerji. It was designated as 'Economics B group'. Thus, in the words of one of his distinguished students he was able to take social anthropology from a couple of questions in one paper of economics to an integrated group of papers as an alternative course in MA (Economics). At the under-graduate level also 'sociology and anthropology' now formed a full paper along with two papers in economics. In 1950, Majumdar was offered the position of Director, Tata Institute of Social Sciences, Bombay, and he had almost made up his mind to leave the University of Lucknow. The then Vice-Chancellor, Acharya Narendra Dev, persuaded him to continue at Lucknow and a personal professorship was created for him.[1] He had become a Reader in the Department of Economics and Sociology earlier, in 1946. In early 1950s, as Madan (2013: 29) recalls:

> Majumdar was still on his own as the only anthropologists there responsible for teaching and research supervision. This obviously was a very heavy work load. He was an energetic person and a conscientious teacher, very popular with students generally, primarily because he was readily accessible and his lectures were sharply focused on the syllabus.

III

In 1951, an independent department of anthropology was created, with him as its Head. Thus, in one decade Majumdar through his untiring efforts succeeded in setting up an Anthropology Laboratory, and Department of Anthropology in the University of Lucknow, and the Ethnographic and Folk Culture Society as also its quarterly journal, *The Eastern Anthropologists,* which almost from the very beginning acquired an international readership, with C. von Furer-Haimendorf as its foreign editor. The department began to attract students from different states like Orissa, and the North-East from the very beginning.

The Wenner-Gren Foundation, New York, organized an International Symposium on anthropology at New York in mid-1952. This symposium was intended to assess accomplishment of anthropological science and to solicit answers on what directions future research would be likely to take. Some 80 anthropologists from all over the world were invited to this Symposium, in which Majumdar represented India, Pakistan and Ceylon. He also co-chaired a session with Julian H. Steward. Subsequently, he was also a Visiting Professor of Far Eastern Studies at the Cornell University, Ithaca, New York, and here he planned a research programme for village studies in Uttar Pradesh as a collaboration between the Lucknow University and the Cornell University. Prof. M.E. Opler was its co-director and the programme was launched in 1953 for a period of three years. It was financed by the Ford Foundation in India.

In the year 1953, he was elected Fellow of the American Association of Physical Anthropologists. In the ensuing year, he was a delegate, appointed by the United Nations to the World Conference on Population held at Rome, where he was elected as a member of the International Union for the Scientific Study of Population. During the same year, he also attended the International Sociological Congress at Paris, as a delegate.

In 1955, he presided over the Anthropological Section of the First All-India Sociological Conference held at Dehradun and was elected General President of the Second Conference which was to be held at Patna in 1956. The Indian Sociological Society had been founded by Prof. G.S. Ghurye and Majumdar was one of its oldest members. The next year, in 1957–58, he was a Visiting Lecturer in Asian Anthropology in the School of Oriental and African Studies at the University of London. In that very year, he was awarded the Annandale Gold Medal by the Asiatic Society of Bengal for contributions to Asian Anthropology. In 1959, he made his last visit abroad, lecturing at the Institute of Social Science, the Hague, and visiting Britain and France.

He came to be closely associated with the Planning and Evaluation Programme of the Government of India from 1955 onwards. He was appointed member of the Standing Committee of the Research Programme Committee (Planning Commission). In 1955 and in 1958, he was made a member of the Central Advisory Board of Anthropology. In the same year, he was invited by the Indian Council of Medical Research to be a member of its governing body.

In 1960, he was appointed as Dean of the Faculty of Arts at the University of Lucknow and in the same year came his sudden demise.

The general reputation that Majumdar enjoyed among his students and in the university was that he was deeply involved in Anthropology and was a charismatic teacher. Thus, it is apparent that Majumdar had started attracting students from different parts of the country to the Department of Economics and Sociology in the university.

In order to know more about him and his relationship with his students some of the most prominent ones were requested to write about their personal relationships with him. Many of his students had come to occupy the highest positions in their departments and also much prominence in the subject. I was told that one of his students from the Department of Anthropology, Delhi University, said in the 1980s that at least 8–10 departments of anthropology in the country as well as abroad, then, were headed by Majumdar's students. His relationship with these students was almost in the *guru-shishya* traditions of Hindu learning. He always treated his promising students as his 'sons and daughters' and made them a part of his family.

IV

The late Professor Ghaus Ansari, the then Chairman, Institute of Social and Cultural Anthropology, University of Vienna, remembered him warmly in his Urdu autobiography (*Umre Rafta*, 2002) thus:

> Gradually I became more interested in anthropology. The chairman of the department of anthropology was the well known anthropologist Professor D.N. Majumdar. His magnetic personality and interest in the subject, impressed me

> so much that I decided to pursue anthropology in my higher studies .... In those days student professor relations in the university were so distant that undergraduate students would not dare approach a senior professor or a head of department. Contrary to this practice Professor Majumdar always encouraged us to approach him directly without any hesitation anywhere inside the class, in his room or even in the corridors.[2]

Ansari refers to DNM as his most affectionate teacher who always provided some kind of a warmth and security to him. He also talks of the interest which this 'affectionate teacher' took in the publication of Ansari's thesis as a book by the Ethnographic Folk Culture Society and laments that the binding of the book was completed after his death.

N.S. Reddy was one of the seven research scholars who had completed their Ph.D. under Majumdar. He has retired as a professor from the Central University, Hyderabad. He writes:

> I did my M.A. in the late forties and my doctoral research in the early fifties, was during what may be described as the golden age of Lucknow University. It was my good fortune to have been associated with stalwart teachers like Dr D.N. Majumdar and Professor Mukerjee (Dr Radhakamal Mukerjee was mostly away on some assignments at that time) .... If any one asks me the question as to why I became a teacher my simple answer is that it was my teacher Dr D.N. Majumdar who was solely responsible for it. Dr Majumdar was not just a teacher, but he was also a preacher and a proselytizer. Whenever he discovered promising students, he would go all out to baptize them and ensure that they would carry forth his scholastic torch. He belonged to the noble tradition of teachers whose ambition was to be excelled by their own pupils.[3]

And, a letter, dated 12 November 1957, to R.K. Jain, Emeritus Professor, Jawahar Lal Nehru University, New Delhi, further highlights his concern for his students. He was a visiting faculty in the School of Oriental and African Studies in London and writing to Jain in mid-November 1957, he says:

> ... trying to finish my work by February, so that I may come back a month in advance of your examinations – I do not think, my presence would have benefited you all for most of the time I am out of Lucknow, but as you have said, it would give you some satisfaction to be with me. I am always thinking of you all and I shall always do, and you know, nothing does please me better than the achievements of my pupils. I did not have all the opportunities you have of books of library, and the advance(d) knowledge that anthropologists today can command, and I grew like wild exotic creeper– I have my limitations, but also I possess an optimism and love for work .... .

Late Dharani Sinha who made a name for himself in exploring anthropological dimensions of management studies as a professor in IIM Calcutta, before he became Director, Administrative Staff College, Hyderabad, described his former teacher thus:

> D.N. Majumdar was a general anthropologist in the true sense of the term ... believed anthropology was a holistic discipline and he demonstrated it in his

> own scholarly work … . Majumdar was a rare breed of professionals having contributed to different facets of anthropology … . D.N. Majumdar believed that anthropology has to be relevant, it has to assist in planned social change. Village studies contributed to this challenge … demonstrated that it was necessary to understand social fabric of even an urban conglomerate in order to bring about planned change … . Majumdar positioned anthropology as an applied discipline … . This stance of his brought me intellectually close to him … . Majumdar taught me the art of participant observation, the skill of meticulous and vivid description … when I shifted from anthropology to management, this basic approach lived with me and gave me my identity as a management professional with anthropological perspective.[4]

Sinha pointedly mentions a very salient aspect of Majumdar's personality which combined in him an anthropologist stressing fieldwork and ethnography and a teacher. Several of his students who worked with him on the projects which he conducted during the 1950s, shared a feeling that Majumdar became a 'changed person' in the field, informal, friendly and caring. He helped his field workers in every way but at the same time got annoyed whenever he found them leaving the field without any adequate reason. In this context this author would like to mention that Majumdar strongly felt that the young students should not marry before they complete their stretch of field work, specially if it was for a Ph.D. He got upset when he heard that one of his promising students, who was preparing for fieldwork under a prestigious fellowship, had married. However, the news was only a rumour. When the father of this author went to invite him for the wedding of his son, his first reaction was to tell him that 'he would have preferred if he could have finished his doctoral work before marrying'. Thus, he always had a fatherly concern for his students. But at the same time tolerated no diversions and compromise in the quality of ethnographic fieldwork.[5] Late Prof. Gopala Sarana said that 'his concern for his students was immense and touched one's heart … .

Here, this author would also like to recall the advice that Majumdar gave, when he was preparing to join the central services. Majumdar had asked him to remember two things – one, that he should always remain in touch with his seniors as well as juniors from the department and treat them like elder or younger brothers and two, to continue his interest in anthropology and keep himself abreast with its development, even if one was in some administrative job. These points go a long way to show how his students always felt an affinity with the fellow students of Majumdar and the Department. And, then, it also extended the reach of anthropology, 'converts' to use Kuper's phrase. Majumdar also took interest in the work of younger anthropologists from other departments as well. Later day eminent anthropologists, like B.K. Roy Burman, I.P.S. Moga and Yogesh Atal, warmly recounted their contacts with Majumdar, when this author discussed him with them. In fact, Roy Burman had remarked that had Majumdar been selected to head the newly created Department of Anthropology, University of Delhi, the entire scenario of anthropology in the country would have undergone a change.

V

Majumdar's Vision for the Institutions

As detailed earlier, in 1940, when the Superintendent of Census Operations in Uttar Pradesh was preparing for the 1941 Census, Majumdar was associated with the Census to plan an ethnographic survey of the Province. This extensive work provided Majumdar with an opportunity to set up Anthropology Laboratory in the University of Lucknow and to analyse this data. Its statistical processing was carried out in collaboration with P.C. Mahalonobis in the Indian Statistical Institute, Calcutta. The Laboratory was the first institutional centre for anthropology, headed by Majumdar and it became a part of the Department of Anthropology a decade later.

The Ethnographic and Folk Culture Society for Northern India was his subsequent vision which took shape in 1945, though as was his usual practice, he credits its creation to 'a handful of young postgraduate student of Lucknow University' (96: 1946: 1). In this context his long term vision was:

> The birth of a cultural society like the one of ours is an event of more than passing interest as the study of ethnology and ethnography which include folk culture as well, has not yet received recognition ... and has not filtered into the curricula of University courses in northern India. A limping attempt has been made at Lucknow by including anthropology as a part of the study of economics and sociology, a procedure which on the face of it must be regarded as of doubtful expediency. Yet science today owns no frontiers and the deeper we go into the details of a discipline, the more we are likely to find out its ramifications which are vital to its existence and functioning. Gone perhaps are the days when economics was regarded as the dismal science of wealth. It is today the science as well as the art of social life, of social welfare. The roots of our wants, of our wealth-getting and wealth-spending habits must be sought in the traditional patterns of culture, in customs and mores of the people and a knowledge of the latter is to be regarded as indispensable for a proper evaluation of the role of economics in social life. (ibid.: i–ii)

Starting with its series of publications on folklore, the Society started taking shape and with its quarterly journal, *The Eastern Anthropologist,* being founded about two years later in 1947 the identity of this institution came to the fore in the growing world of anthropology in India and abroad.

The creation of a separate Department of Anthropology came a few years later in 1951, in spite of stiff opposition from Mukerjee.[6] The Department with only three faculty members became a busy centre for teaching and research, both in physical and social anthropology and publications provided professional work to a large number of young scholars. Anthropometric survey of the United Provinces, Racial, Serological and Health Survey of Gujarat, Anthropological Study of Growth among School Children being some of the earliest studies in the Department. After his participation in the Wenner-Gren Foundation symposium on anthropology in New York to which he was the only invited Indian anthropologist and his visiting professorship at Cornell University, Majumdar initiated in the Department, the Cornell Lucknow Research Project of Rural Studies with funding from the Ford Foundation in 1953. This was, perhaps, the largest research project in the field of anthropology and sociology in India till then. All these department-centred academic programmes brought a number of foreign scholars and research students to the University of Lucknow. Justifiably, Furer-Haimendorf found that it 'has for many years been the most active department of anthropology in the whole of south Asia' (Sarana, 1960: 112).

Majumdar's relationship with Radhakamal Mukerjee, it seems, had by now soured further. About the same time, the Cornell Lucknow Project also ended due to Majumdar's differences with M.E. Opler. But Majumdar was able to continue the research studies he had undertaken under that programme, with funds from the Research Programme Committee, Planning Commission. With Mukerjee as Vice-Chancellor, another outstanding project which was offered to Majumdar was scuttled by the university administration. Under the programme for the development of Scheduled Tribes, the Government of India was interested in creating a centre for imparting orientation in tribal culture and development leading to a diploma in tribal development. The course was offered to the Department of Anthropology, Lucknow University, but the University administration did not agree to take it up.[7] In the closing years of the 1950s may be as a premonition, Majumdar was seriously concerned 'about the fate of Anthropology Department of Lucknow University and the EFCS after he was gone' (Ansari, 2002). And, as Ansari further comments:

> Regretfully, it so happened that after his sudden demise in 1960 the ugly tussle for the succession of the headship of the department (Anthropology) began ... Majumdar had farsightedly involved some eminent persons of the city in the organizational structure of the Society, who did not have any personal ambitions; thus it kept the Society free from personal strife ... .[8]

VI

Majumdar's Public Anthropology and Use of Hindi

Public anthropology has come in use as a term denoting the process of popularizing what are the basic concepts in anthropology to the general public. Such a move means not only widening the base of knowledge about the subject in general but also the way in which its applied aspects can be expanded. Majumdar came to Lucknow after doing his post graduation in anthropology from the Calcutta University and a stretch of field work among the Ho in Bihar (now the area is in the state of Jharkhand). United Provinces had a very small population of tribals which was located in the fartherest corners in the south and north of the Province. In the central areas however there were a large number of tribes, 'then labeled as criminal tribes'. As he was lecturer in primitive economics that is non-monetized economics, the academic area that he had to explore for his teaching was a comparative study of the institutions connected therewith. Anthropology, as it was then – with its blending of socio-cultural anthropology with physical anthropology mainly as a study of racial traits and composition and some archaeological anthropology – was almost unknown to UP and almost the entire central and northern India.

In this scenario, one has to see how he created a place for anthropology not only in the academic world but also in the public mind and in the administration, during only three decades of his life and work. He, in his own inimitable manner, used to convey this situation to his students through an anecdote. He used to tell them, emphasizing the importance of field study methods in anthropology, that when he first proposed taking his post-graduate students of economics and sociology for a field trip 'to some far off place, perhaps 'Singbhum', the then Vice Chancellor who was a big Talukdar asked him as to why he had chosen to take his students to such a remote place 'to see a field when there were vast areas of fields', say, in the former's own *talukdari*. As Madan and Sarana (1962: 7) say, 'therefore, only to be expected that he should have taken a particular interest in the peoples and cultures of this state', and his first paper relating to the Korwa, a primitive tribe in Southern UP came out in the *Man in India* in 1929 and thereafter a regular chain of papers on the ethnographic scenario of UP followed. Unlike some of his contemporaries in sociology and anthropology, he never wrote in Bengali and in the true spirit of cultural interaction pleaded and took active steps for 'anthropology in Hindi medium'. By the early 1940s he had contributed about a dozen articles in Hindi for the four volumes of *Hindi Vishwa Bharti*, a pioneering encyclopedic work in Hindi published from Lucknow. In 1945 when he founded the Ethnographic and Folk Culture Society he again emphasized the need for taking anthropological knowledge to the public through their own language; and in 1947 in his brief editorial to the inaugural number of *The Eastern Anthropologists* he wrote:

> And we know as well the handicap natural to presenting our knowledge through the medium of a foreign language. We believe we should be able to fulfil our obligation in this respect by publishing our results of study and research in the language of the Province. This requires .... (*The EA*, 1: ii)

Thus, in spite of his not being able to write in Hindi, Majumdar's strong feeling for popularizing anthropological knowledge made him actively participate in getting such material published. In the 1960s, he contributed twelve articles in Hindi to the *Hindi Vishwa Bharti*. The contents of these articles covered a wide range of anthropological knowledge regarding the tribes of various provinces and the criminal tribes of Uttar Pradesh. These were brief cameos running into five to 10 pages, well suited for school-going adolescents. Thus, he presented scientific anthropological knowledge about the life in tribal India, their economic and social conditions, language, etc., in an easy-to-understand style. This author himself remembers reading these articles with great interest during his school days in mid-1940s. This publication was well illustrated and produced. In fact, in those days little was known about the tribal world of India in the United Provinces and thus, Majumdar's participation in this outstanding venture in Hindi publication rendered a valuable service. No other social scientist of his time had written anything for publication in Hindi. Some other contemporary social scientists who wrote in any Indian language were Radhakamal Mukerjee, N.K. Bose and D.P. Mukerji, and may be a few others from West Bengal, in Bengali. Anthropological material in Hindi by S.C. Dube and L.P. Vidyarthi mainly came much later.

Subsequently, Majumdar also initiated the publication of the *Prachya Manav Vaigyanik* (126: 1949; 141: 43: 1951), a sister journal to *The Eastern Anthropologist* in Hindi in 1949. This journal is still being published by the EFCS as *Manav*. Moreover, he contributed articles to other popular Hindi journals like *Aajkal* (147: 1952) and *Samaj* (175: 1955; 180: 1956; 186: 1957; 191: 1958).

Majumdar's long association with another Hindi-speaking state, Bihar, is also mentionable in this context. Vidyarthi (1961: v) has with much feeling described his association with Bihar, starting from early 1920s. Majumdar had during the 1950s, contributed a number of papers to the journal in Hindi published by the Department of Anthropology, Ranchi University, and also continued his association through visits to Patna and Ranchi.

Furthering this endeavour to popularize anthropological knowledge, in 1958 he published *Bhartiya Sanskriti ke Upadan* with an aim to familiarize the educated public with the fundamentals of science of anthropology, as it would also advance the utilization of such knowledge and the services of anthropologists in social development (189: 1958: 7). He strongly felt that spreading scientific knowledge regarding cultural diversities and the ways to avoid any conflict due to intolerance was the key to a 'civilized living' in our country. Thereafter, he published one of his most significant village studies first in Hindi – *Chhor Ka Ek Gaon* (222: 1960) – which, unfortunately, came out posthumously and could never appear in English. This work has been discussed elsewhere.

In the light of Majumdar's contributions to popular writings in Hindi magazines and journals, as also his contributing substantial articles to the most popular English journals of his times, like *The Calcutta Review* and the *The Modern Review*, the observations of Srinivas and Panini that 'Indian sociologists do not seem to be sufficiently aware of the relevance of their discipline for popular education' and 'one of the obstacles' being their 'inability to shed jargon' (1986: 52) appear to be ill-founded.

VII

Around 1940, he was able to establish his anthropological laboratory in the University, as he was preparing to undertake a large serological and anthropometric survey in Uttar Pradesh. This major step taken in the advancement of public anthropology in Lucknow was initiated by him through this laboratory. Subsequently, the newly created department of anthropology began organizing exhibitions related to the different fields of anthropology. Here would be displayed various charts and pictorial depictions of genetics and other aspects of physical anthropology as also the artifacts and material culture of the different tribes in UP and elsewhere. The exhibitions were organized in the university itself. After 1945, the Ethnographic and Folk Culture Society became an instrument for popular anthropological education. Under its auspices he directed the presentation of a stage play, 'The Descent of Man', which attracted the attention of intellectuals, literati, and political leaders of the day. Incidentally, Sampurnanand, the then education minister of UP, who was the chief guest for the show, sanctioned a recurring grant to the EFCS on his own (Sanwal, 2005: 113) which came as a much needed financial support for the Society. Some of the reminiscences of his students who participated in this effort highlight its impact in general. Late Prof. K.N. Sharma recalled this event of December 1950 as follows:

> Looking back at the preparation for the drama, I think the preparation of script based on physical anthropology and designing of scenes of the environment of each anthropoid were difficult tasks. They required not only facts but also ingenuity and imagination to put a dry subject before the audience in an interesting and absorbing manner. These tasks were performed by Professor Majumdar with the help of Mrs Kusum Dar. I played the role of Neanderthal .... Finally, the drama achieved tremendous success .... [9]

A pivotal part in this drama, that of the professor making introductory comments on each anthropoid was performed by C.B. Tripathi, an undergraduate student, whom Majumdar found the most suitable for such a key role.[10]

In fact, the Department of Anthropology and the EFCS continued with their role in popularizing anthropological knowledge and the specific aim of introducing 'diversity of cultures' to the people even later through their active participation in all the cultural events in Lucknow, exhibitions and festivals (*Mahotsava*) which gave impetus to tourism and revival of interest in some of the tribal handicrafts, such as Tharu appliqué work on garments and artistic basketry and also their performing arts. This kind of effort, two or three decades later, became a part of the all-India and state cultural scenes. K.S. Mathur, who succeeded Majumdar as Head of the Department and General Secretary, EFCS, in 1962 played a very important role in this endeavour.

Any discussion on Majumdar's tireless efforts to popularize anthropology and to bring anthropological knowledge in the public realm cannot be completed without describing the chain of events related with human skeletal remains discovered in the lake of Rupkund situated at an altitude of more than 18,000 feet in Garhwal, Uttarakhand (then part of Uttar Pradesh). The news about the discovery of these remains were flashed by the news media and radio all over the country. It sparked off controversies as to the origins of these remains. Majumdar got involved with this episode rather reluctantly because some of the specimen brought by Mahesh Chandra of *The Statesman* landed in his laboratory for examination. These were collected by a forest officer on the direction of N.S. Bhandari, the then Deputy Minister of Forests, who had been Majumdar's student. Attempts were made to reach the site by parties of anthropologists and non-anthropologists by the summer of next year but failed to succeed due to extreme weather. Majumdar was provided with a grant by the government of UP to explore the site but his team too could not reach Rupkund because of the inclement weather conditions. Taking the criticism of the press and the public in this regard very seriously, Majumdar decided to embark upon a second trip, taking its entire financial and academic burden on himself. He was accompanied by a team of six members. He was able to reach Rupkund during this trip in September 1957 and returned with a large collection of 'skeletal as well as artifactual materials'. 'He wanted to succeed .... He did succeed'. Though later he remarked, 'Was a fool to risk the life of you all in this venture' (Singh, 1999: 313). Collected material was listed under 38 heads with dozens of specimens each and studied under his supervision and direction in the anthropology laboratory of his department. Realizing the potential of this material, he wanted all the needed time and resources for studying it. And, in the process, he approached J.B. Griffin, Director, Museum of Anthropology, and M.R. Cane of the Radio Carbon Laboratory, Ann Arbor Michigan for their findings. 'Unfortunately a full report could not be published because of his sudden demise' (ibid.: 314). Majumdar also documented the folklore prevalent among the Garhwal people about Rupkund. The folklore indicated that there was a narrow pass leading to Tibet near Rupkund in those times. His other finding was that the skeletal remains were about 650 years old. The people who had perished were of the same racial stock and resembled the people of Swat and Hunza Valleys of the North-West. They had no resemblance with the local people. It is likely that they were on a pilgrimage as there were hardly any weapons and the party included women as well. Majumdar was of the view that a further exploration was called for. Historically, he also connected some of the remains to a small army unit sent to Tibet by Muhamad Tuglak, the then Emperor of Delhi (Majumdar, 1958: 94–106). His findings about Rupkund were tentative and the article referred to above was published in the *Prachya Manav Vaigyanik*.

The way in which Majumdar used to attract and 'capture' young students for anthropology may be quoted here. Leela Dube reminiscences, thus:

> ... as his (S.C. Dube) lone pupil in anthropology, I listened to his descriptions of Bizzare customs and to his discourses on the conceptions of human birth imparted by anthropology, he also talked to me about those scholars, Indian and foreign, who had impressed him. In the winter of 1945–46, I met one such scholar, D.N. Majumdar, when he came to Nagpur to deliver the Wathodkar memorial lectures. I heard him speak on Khasa polyandry, and suffered a mild culture shock .... I was thus being ushered into a world of cultural diversity, undreamt of by me, through my contact with anthropologists and the so called primitives. (1975: 158)

The depth and thoroughness of Majumdar's fieldwork and his devotion to the anthropological methodology as basically formulated by Malinowski is well known (Madan, 1984, 2011, 2013). Mukerji (1961) describes him as 'fundamentally a field anthropologist who had strayed into general anthropology ... .'

In harmony with his professional personality he had made plans for his post-retirement engagement. Having worked intermittently for long among tribals of Dudhi, southern UP, his plans were:

> For many years I have been thinking of a suitable plot of land ... situated as near Rihand Dam site as possible without the risk of the area being acquired by the

government or being flooded by the Rihand Dam ... acreage of the spot should be such that I can grow a little produce for consumption, and be also near the tribal people to carry on my field work side by side .... (Letter to Chandra Sen, Supervisor of the Dhanaura research team, dated 19 January 1957)

Vidyarthi (1961: v), however, reveals:

Bihar was not only his first field research, he also planned Bihar his last field. He was to join at Patna as the Director of A.N. Sinha Institute of Social Science.

VIII

Majumdar's Promotion of Academics in Anthropology

Majumdar, as the first generation of formally trained anthropologists in India had to play a pivotal role in developing academic studies in anthropology and as a branch of knowledge along with conducting extensive field researches in different branches of anthropology. He always described himself as a 'general anthropologist' and, thus, expressed his interest in almost all the branches of anthropological studies. Moreover, since he had moved away from his centre of origin, Department of Anthropology and Ancient Indian History, Calcutta University, and came to be a part of the Economics and Sociology Department at Lucknow he, perhaps, strongly felt that he had to assume several roles – as a teacher of primitive economics; creating almost from a scratch anthropological literature based on his extensive fieldwork as well as to develop an active centre for anthropological studies, as distinct from the field of economics of which he was then a part. This latter role implied a responsibility to write and develop textual material for students at graduate and post-graduate levels as also for the benefit of public workers particularly administrators and the general public. Further, his acute awareness and a sense of responsibility for a role in ameliorating the conditions of tribal people and other marginalized sections made him write extensively on anthropology as a branch of knowledge for a variety of readership.

In the fulfillment of these responsibilities, he contributed three books, two of which were developed as textbooks. Two of them were based on two sets of lectures he had delivered while the third and the last one, in co-authorship with T.N. Madan, as a concise and extremely readable text book both for the beginners in social anthropology as also for any general reader interested in acquainting himself with this field. Of course all the three had a focus on the people of India. The first two books (*The Matrix of Indian Cultures* and *Races and Cultures of India*) were published in 1940s, after Majumdar had become a reputed anthropologist. The latter book which was more of a text book was revised by him and substantively enlarged through three later editions and it is still current as a source book in anthropology. It was also translated as *Bhartiya Sanskriti Ke Upadan* published in 1958. The third, *An Introduction to Social Anthropology*, published in early 1955 is still being widely circulated for students appearing in the university and competitive examinations.

Races and Cultures of India has developed out of a course of lectures which Majumdar delivered for 'ICS probationers and the minor chiefs who received their training at Dehradun' in April 1942. This can be called a significant event in the history of anthropology in India as being probably the first systematic course of lectures to introduce the probationers of the 'steel-frame' of the government to the 'entire field of Indian anthropology in the light of the latest materials, particularly regarding primitive cultures in India and the racial composition of the Indian population. In his 'Preface' to the first edition of this book, Majumdar highlights the importance and relevance of a knowledge of 'problems of acculturation and decay arising from the clash of cultures and contact of races', and the 'problems of administration of primitive and backward communities under the political control of European peoples'. He also takes note of the usefulness of 'certain aspects of biological evidence' and how it can contribute to 'mitigate caste and communal antagonism as well as untouchability' if it is widely known to the public. In this context, Majumdar also points out how the anthropological theories regarding man's cultural development have been undergoing revision and that a civilizational approach is far from adequate in the Indian conditions, as:

> A knowledge of customs, practices, art, religion, morality and law is of great practical importance to those who deal with people in the course of their multiple contacts with them. A study of civilization is not enough, for while the records of our achievements are available, those of the savage and semi-savage groups are only orally transmitted from generation to generation (page, ix).

Thus, emphasizing the significance of oral history as a vital part of the narrative – what decades later, came to be known as subaltern narratives.

A mention has already been made about Majumdar's vision for the need to publish anthropological material in Hindi which he initiated through first contributing popular articles. Subsequently, he also came to realize that there should be textbooks covering different branches of anthropology for the university students as the universities in Uttar Pradesh as well as in other Hindi speaking states had begun adopting Hindi as the medium of instructions.

In order to fulfil this need and to give a concrete shape to his vision, he along with a group of his students capable of writing in Hindi prepared a programme to get such textbooks written under his own direction or getting his writings in English rendered into Hindi under his close directions. This programme was initiated by him in early 1950s.

The first such Hindi book was a rendering of his *Races and Cultures of India* into Hindi in which several of his students participated along with a well known Hindi author. *Bhartiya Sanskriti ke Upadan* was the result of this effort which according to Majumdar, in his *Prastavana* of the book, was to serve a double purpose– presenting the basic material relating to anthropology for the general readership as well as for use by the students. Majumdar remarks that the first purpose was more important for him than the second one (189: 1958: 07).

Sarana was the co-author of the original textbook on *Pragitihas* (pre history and early man). The book was first published in 1964 and its second revised edition came in 1990. The manuscript of this book was ready for the press just before Majumdar's demise (223: 1964: vi). In his *Prastavana* to the second edition, Sarana (226: 1990: vii) is appreciative of Majumdar's liberal approach to language (Hindi) and his foresight for the need for textbooks in Hindi, fully realizing its importance. It is mentionable that when these two books were written, no standardized scientific terminology in Hindi had been prepared and Majumdar, his co-authors and his friends had to make sustained effort to suitably express the scientific and technological terms used in anthropology. Needless to add that these were the very first books in social anthropology and prehistory and even in 1990 when its second edition was prepared there was no book in this branch of anthropology. This edition, however, adopted the standardized scientific terminology prepared at the initiative of the Government of India, as far as possible. A book on physical anthropology and anthropometry had also been planned but it came well after Majumdar's death under the authorship of R.D. Singh.

Pragitihas, comprehensively and concisely covers the entire field of prehistory. It is divided into three parts – fundamental principle of prehistory, the European prehistory and the Indian prehistory.

Thus, it is evident from the above narration and analysis how Majumdar became one of the pioneers and doyens of professional anthropology through his vision of expansion of the discipline in general and institutions like the Department of Anthropology and the Ethnographic and Folk Culture Society in particular. Subsequent chapters will be a testimony to his works on various aspects of Indian society.

Notes

1. Sanwal recalls that Dr Sampurnanand, the then Education Minister of UP overruled the negative views of his department over this proposal and noted that anthropology as a subject deserved a separate department for itself and Majumdar a professorship (Sanwal, 2005: 113, 123). Both of these proposals were strongly opposed by Radhakamal Mukerjee.
2. Translated excerpts enclosed with Ghaus' letter, dated 25 January 2005, to the author.
3. Letter dated 1 September 2012 to the author.
4. Letter dated 23 March 2005 to the author.
5. Madan (2011: 178–82) has made some interesting comments in this regard and tells us that Roy compared fieldwork to meditation (*dhyan*) or 'of self-forgetting absorption'. And one would like to add that Roy was Majumdar's mentor and guide. And, also, Srinivas 'went as far as to suggest that the best fieldworkers are single individuals without family obligations' (ibid., 245).
6. See note 1.
7. As this author was working with the Commissioner for Scheduled Castes and Scheduled Tribes, a Constitutional authority, these developments came to his personal knowledge. The scheme was taken up by Prof. B.H. Mehta in the Tata Institute of Social Sciences, who went on to organize a training-cum-action and

research centre under it at Chhindwara. Visiting this centre in 1956, this author found that skills in growing flower gardens and horticultural knowledge was being imparted there.

8. Notably, Sir Sita Ram as its founder President and Haikarwal, an educationist and B.D. Sanwal, ICS in its executive committee. They maintained life-long interest in the activities of the Society.
9. Letter dated 14 January 2005 to the author.
10. Mentioned in his personal reminiscences communicated to the author.

2

Majumdar's Tribal Ethnography

Majumdar is known for his ethnography of Indian tribes and his interpretation and comments on the dynamics of culture change through contact. As different kinds of problems emanate from such contacts and also certain benefits, his views on what was needed for bringing a better future for the tribal people of India and how anthropologists could play a positive and helpful role in this national endeavour are very significant. Since the anthropology of his time had its colonial overtones, 'tribe' as a category, as defined in the Census operations, from time to time, was almost unquestioningly accepted by social anthropology as also sociology. The tribes as such were conceptualized as the earliest inhabitants of the sub-continent and perceived in the evolutionary theoretical model. Majumdar's major work on the Ho and other writings on the Tharu and Korwa have been, broadly, taken into account here for the analysis of tribal ethnography.

Use of Social Categories

Majumdar in his ethnography has used the social categories which were largely contributed and developed through the Census by the colonial administrators, and missionaries who were writing on Indian people. He observes that 'tribe, caste, sect and class are the various categories of social stratification in India'. He defines a tribe which is 'a collection of families or groups of families' by spelling out its characteristics as: bearing a common name, occupying the same territory, speaking the same language and observance of taboos regarding marriage, professions and occupations. Further, 'a well assessed system of reciprocity and mutuality of obligations' are also seen. Endogamy as a unit, several clans constituting it and the basis for clans, is seen as a belief in kinship based either on totemic division, territorial contiguity or common residence. A tribe is also a political unit with a political organization ruled by hereditary kings or chiefs with a council of elders and hereditary headmen (221: 1944: 367). Majumdar, however, subscribes to the view that 'the distinction between tribe and caste, particularly between the tribes and the castes on the lower rungs of the Hindu social ladder is difficult to establish' (ibid.: 368). Thus, tribes preceded the formation of castes and, of course, class.

Thus, it is notable that Majumdar while using these categories in his ethnographic descriptions always critically looked at them and pointed out how the category salience of these terms as developed by the colonial power, were not empirically tenable in India. In this context, he particularly examined how the Indian situation of culture contact, 'acculturation' and 'trans-culturation' which were always focused by him, differed from those elsewhere. He was of the view that these processes of contacts between tribes, tribes and castes, and the castes were unique in a way to the Indian scenario. Diffusion of 'traits' and evolution of cultures could be observed through these situations, in a scientific field work. He used scriptural sources infrequently and also the observations of indologists in a very limited way as he believed that he could discern and observe the process in the everyday life of the communities under study. And, here his use of history too, was very limited perhaps because of the Malinowskian influence. Unlike African Studies, in India, even inter-tribal contact situations were observed by him to have changed and unleashed acculturative forces apart from the patterns adopted from the mainstream community – the Hindu castes. Even the limited recorded history by colonial officers which generally did not go beyond two to three hundred years could be used in this context. It can be recalled that the postmodern approach and other currents of ethnography in its wake changed the language, focii and the designs of ethnographic narratives around 1970s and thereafter.

Apart from these categories, Majumdar has also frequently used some loaded terms like 'savage', 'uncivilized', etc., located in the evolutionary, missionary or colonial narratives. This usage is more of a stamp of the anthropology of his times than connotative. But his reviewers are critical about the use of such terms (Leach, 1946: 67; Berreman, 1968: 1158–60).

Elsewhere he has also felt that 'the tests which we have indicated above can be easily applied and a new list of tribes can be drawn up ... will reduce the number of tribes needing care and leveling up' (Naik, 1968: 87). This is with reference to the scheduling of tribes under the Constitution of India and the planned government action to ameliorate the conditions thereof.

The first three papers written by him and which were published in *Man in India* during 1923 dealt with 'Custom of burning human effigies', 'Kalinauch' and 'Customs and Taboos connected with pregnancy and child birth' were all about the people of Eastern Bengal, now part of Bangladesh, which was Majumdar's native province. These papers were basically descriptions of cultural traits connected with the customs and practices reported therein. One can even say that their contents were simply recapitulation of exotic customs and rituals for which anthropology was then known.

Subsequently, however, from 1924 onwards, Majumdar began presenting his comments on contact situation among a tribal people, the Ho, he had taken up for in-depth study under the advice and guidance of Roy. Roy had by then established himself as a reputed ethnographer of the tribal communities in Chhota Nagpur and had published *The Mundas and their Country* in 1912, and also started his journal, *Man in India*, in 1921. This journal and also the *Journal of the Royal Asiatic Society of Bengal* were then the medium for the publication of papers relating to anthropological researches, which were mainly being done at that time by colonial administrators and some public men. Needless to point out that Majumdar was among the first generation of professionally trained anthropologists.

An analytical review of Majumdar's writings in the field of tribal ethnography in India indicates that in Chhota Nagpur, he studied the Ho, an austric culture intensively. His publications on the Ho starting from 1924 and up to 1937 included more than 30 papers before he prepared his Ph.D. thesis in the Cambridge University and subsequently published it as a *Tribe in Transition* (1937).

Among these papers more than 25 were devoted to different aspects of Ho culture – institutions, beliefs and practices – while six were devoted to their anthropometry, serology, etc. The thesis, he submitted at Cambridge in May 1935, was entitled 'A Changing Austric Culture'. Its main contents running into 28 chapters were all related to the socio-cultural aspects of the Ho ethnography, but one of its appendices contained anthropometric data– frequency curves of stature, nasal index, cephalic index and arm's reach. Other appendices included folktales and folksongs from Kolhan.

This thesis as published in 1937, eliminated anthropometric data, and carried the imprint of Majumdar's later orientation in anthropological theory and methodology which he had probably imbibed at Cambridge, and through Malinowski's seminars in London. He also acknowledged the new approach to the study of culture propounded by Ruth Benedict.

The publication of 1937 was followed by *The Affairs of a Tribe* (131: 1950) based on his revisits among the Ho of Kolhan. Keesing (1953) mentions it as below:

> Redfield demonstrated the methodological importance of documenting stability and change by revisiting a group periodically, a field work practice by now being done by a number of the pioneers in acculturation studies (50–120). Majumdar in India, for example, resurveys what in 1937 he called 'A Tribe in Transition' (50–97). (Keesing, 1953: 61)

Significantly, Redfield's work referred to here studies changes for progress in a village, a pioneering village study from Mexico; an interest which Majumdar keenly took up a little later in early 1950s through his village studies.

Madan had delivered the D.N. Majumdar Memorial Lectures for 1980 under the auspices of EFCS in January 1982. EFCS had initiated these lectures earlier. The first of Madan's two lectures, entitled, 'Development of Cultures' is perhaps the first attempt by any scholar to explore the writings of Majumdar on culture, contact, acculturation and so on; extensively explored and analyses facet of Majumdar's ethnography, his own fieldwork, and his comments on the views of a few other scholars, mostly western, on the subject. An exploration of this theme in Majumdar's work right from 1923 onwards also reveals the theoretical moorings of Majumdar and his most significant contributions to this field.

Madan has very aptly titled his first lecture as 'Development of Cultures' wherein he presents an outline of Majumdar's views on 'the relationships of culture and development' (Madan, 1983: 5). Therein Madan hopes to bring forth 'the flavours of the hopes and aspirations and of the sense of national responsibility which informed the work of many Indian social scientists of Majumdar's generation' (ibid.: 5). The second lecture debates on the relationship of culture and development as it has evolved over the years. It presents a discussion on the progress of a culture of development as perceived by Madan, specially 1950s onwards.

Madan traces the development of Majumdar's approach or thought from his initial three papers (1923) which reflect his interest in the study of 'culture traits' and not with cultures as 'wholes' and the 'phenomenon of social change', 'but soon we find him writing about social change, particularly in situations of culture contact ... a lifelong interest, and even more than that, a life long concern' (Madan, 1983; 2013: 32).

Majumdar's papers on various aspects of Ho culture began appearing from 1924 and two of his papers published in 1925 – 'Cry of Social Reforms among the Aboriginies' and 'Some Ethnographic Notes on the Hos of Kolhan', clearly initiate Majumdar's 'concern'. The paper first mentioned documents significant needs for change (in the Ho culture) as felt by the leaders of the community and voiced through a number of resolutions passed in their meetings held in March 1924 and later. The opening part of this paper indicates how Majumdar, who probably witnessed these events when he visited the Ho area as a postgraduate student under the guidance of Roy and L.K. Ananthakrishna Iyer, perceives the situation:

> The social progress which we meet within different parts of India suggests to the most casual observer a warning which every anthropologist in the land should beware of. The influence of social culture has reached the most neglected nook of our land and it is no wonder that the aboriginal people who supply us a clue to the evolution of primitive society and who even now present us with a culture more or less stagnant and traceable to the very early period of their existence should receive the light of culture to some extent. By this I mean that the so called uncivilized non-Aryan people, call them Dravidian or pre-Dravidian as you please, are fast lighting the candle of civilization and with the help of Christian missionaries, they are trying to dispel the darkness and misunderstanding that so long shaded them. (9A: 1925: 285)

Thus, Majumdar has clearly discerned the contact situation he was witnessing between a primitive culture and advanced ones, the *diku* or Hindus living in the area and the large number of missionaries. It has to be noted that this article, which also includes a brief description of the Ho culture had appeared in the *Modern Review* (March 1925), then a very widely read English monthly published from Calcutta.

Thus, Majumdar took to a study of culture and social change almost from his very initiation into anthropology. He 'anticipated' the formulation of the nature of the dynamics of culture change by Bronislaw-Malinowki (2013: 32). However, Keesing in his epitomical reference source, *Culture Change: An Analysis and Bibliography of Anthropological Sources to 1952* (Committee for Anthropological Research, Stanford University, 1953) variously documents Majumdar's abiding interest in the dynamics of culture process, as a student of Malinowski. Keesing observes (1953: 30–31):

> Malinowski's students went particularly into the British African areas ... mostly including a strong acculturation emphasis and often applied anthropology dimensions. But others worked elsewhere, e.g. Firth and Piddigton in the Pacific area, Fei in China and Majumdar in India.

Contextually, Keesing mentions along with Firth, Perham, and Eggan, Majumdar working on culture change situations in India as presenting rich and varied materials on cultural dynamics. Chronological Bibliography therein makes repeated mention of Majumdar's publications– *Transition* (37–37: 178), his Presidential Address to the Section of Anthropology, Indian Science Congress (1939), entitled 'Tribal Culture and Acculturation' (39–57: 184), and *Fortunes* (44–58: 200), as also several articles contained in the festchrift presented to S.C. Roy, edited by Mills, Majumdar et al., (1940). Grigson, Hutton and Majumdar are the only scholars in India who find repeated mention and references in Keesing (1953).

Some other aspects of salience in Majumdar's perception may also be noted. First, there is an unquestioning acceptance of 'tribe' as a construct while 'caste' represents a culturally different conglomerate. Then, secondly, the identity or the boundaries of a tribe are seen in terms of an emphasis on its racial origins and features and their differences from the other contiguity along with its culture. Thirdly, the 'cultural traits' which Majumdar had been observing and reporting in a number of papers published from 1924 to 1928 about the Ho, such as their songs, games, lifecycle rituals, kinship terms, beliefs and attitudes, have all been more or less subsumed into a 'culture contact situation' as detailed in 'cry' of social reforms from within. Thus, Majumdar reflects, on the one hand, his study of 'traits' in an 'evolutionary-diffusionists' frame, but delineates social change as well, and also some role for an emerging leadership– the meetings for adopting resolutions being presided over by a Manki, the traditional leader, who was then a Member of the Bihar and Orissa Legislative Council. His published papers during this period also include Ho anthropometry (4: 1924; 9: 1925; 15: 1925 and 24: 1926).

Ho Ethnography: Ho Environment/Their Country

The Kolhan Government Estate was a part of the Singbhum district of Bihar when the fieldwork was carried out. It is the south-western border area of Bihar and now forms a part of the Jharkhand state, while the district is now West Singbhum.

The Hos are concentrated in the Kolhan which is partly an area of flat and open lands and also hills and valleys which used to have thick forests in the western and southern parts. Though there are a number of rivers, these are small streams except in the rainy season and therefore do not provide much scope for irrigation. The forests have a large variety of flora and fauna. The area is very rich in mineral wealth and iron ore was being extracted by two companies, Bengal Iron and Tata Iron. This industrial activity has revolutionized the economic life of the people. There is also a cement factory near Chaibassa, the district headquarter which employs a big labour force. The mining activity and the possibility of other kinds of deposits have led to the extension of railway line and a network of roadways in the area.

History indicates that the Ho were not the earliest settlers in Kolhan. They had eliminated the original settlers (*Khuntkattidars*). They came to the area from north or north-west and perhaps displaced Bhuiyas and also Mundas. The name of villages and hills indicate this. The Ho had trouble with the ruling chiefs in the area and the latter approached the British for help. The area was taken over by the British in 1821 but in 1931 the Hos joined the rebellion of the Mundas against the colonial power. As a result the British took over Kolhan under their direct management in 1830, and the first settlement was carried out in 1838–39. The revenue was fixed per plough, but the definition of the area under one plough was changed from time to time.

The general principle of tenure of land for cultivation in Kolhan is that the land is at the disposal of the community, subject to the control of the hereditary headman. No alienation can be made and outsiders brought in as cultivators without the permission of the Deputy Commissioner.

The history of forest administration dates back to 1892 before which all the forest was village forest. The forests were declared protected forests without taking the rights of the people into consideration. In 1909, an enquiry into the rights and the recording of such rights was carried out but no action was taken on the basis of these records of rights. An inequitable distribution of forest based lands among the villages and the abrogation of customary rights of the Ho which resulted into a shortage of food and other problems was thus initiated with the setting up of forest administration.

Administration

The Kolhan administration has some unique features. The object of the administration was to keep the Kolhan for the Ho and to govern them through their communal system which was implemented through the control over traditional Mankis and Mundas by the Deputy Commissioner. Thus, it was a system of indirect rule where the Deputy Commissioner or the Superintendent of *Estate* had a pivotal role. The offices of Manki and Munda were neither purely elective nor strictly hereditary. They had to surrender their political power and there was a gradual weeding out of hereditary village headmen. Their position was further weakened by the introduction of *thana* system of policing. Due to such a situation *benami* transfers were taking place and gradually the jurisdiction of the Mankis and Mundas in civil and criminal cases was being delimited. Broadly, it is seen that the spirit of indirect rule was not being followed from the very beginning though formally it was in vogue.

The People and their Historical Background/Character and Attitude

The Ho dislike being called as Kol by which name they are known to the outside world. In appearance, the males do not seem to have a very robust and strong physique but the women are graceful and good looking. There is a discussion on whether the excessive use of rice bear by men harms their health and generally lowers the average longevity. From the earlier reports, it is also noticed that the people have lost their qualities of head and heart. System of indirect rule as prevalent in Kolhan has drawbacks which have brought many vices among the Ho. This is compounded by cultural contacts with inferior castes.

Majumdar proceeds to present the distribution of Austric speaking people in India. The Austro-Asiatic family includes the Munda speaking tribes which are the Munda, Ho, Santal, Bhumij, Juang and other tribes, including Bhil and Korwa. They are the most widely known primitive people in northern India and they have been migrating to far off places.

A discussion on the physical features, as seen in the anthropometric data available so far for the people in the area follows. Majumdar compares the measurements collected by him with the earlier series. He finds that there does not appear any significant difference between three groups, viz., Ho, Bhumij and Munda. Therefore, from historical and cultural evidence, supported by anthropometric evidence, these people are believed to have had the same or very similar origins and also, there is a close similarity between their physical types which does not suggest any Mongolian infusion. The Ho and other tribal groups, however, show significant difference from caste groups like Brahmans and Kayastha. An anthropometric study of Ho boys (104) between 7 to 15 years reveals that a Ho child normally is well cared for. They go along with their parents to the fields and forests to help themselves with the produce of the forest or hunt.

Material Culture/Village Settlement, Clothing and Decoration, Food and Food Taboos, Economic Life

Typical Ho houses are built on high ground or ridges. They are generally situated away from the roads and railway line and surrounded by forests. Now, villages are settled on the banks of rivers or by the side of hill streams. A boundary line of fixed stones slabs is found, and at the threshold of the village is the cemetery (*sasan*). Since every *killi* of the village has a separate *sasan*, the villages with multi-*killi* residents have several *sasans* surrounding it. In the *sasan*, graves also have stone slabs over them. These are known as *sasandiri*. There now seems to be no superstition or religious respect for the ancestors' graves. The village is divided into *tolas* and the *tola* at the centre which is generally that of the original settlers has the village *Akhara* adjoining it. Dormitories are now rarely found except in the west and north west areas. Every village has a grove (*jahira*) which is presided over by old spirits.

The houses can be classified into three categories according to the status of the people as there are 'classes' among them now. It has a verandah, a sleeping room and a dining room including kitchen. This room also has *ading* where the ancestors of the family are 'carefully sheltered' and offerings are made to them when the food is cooked. The kitchen is sacred to the Ho as it is a part of the *ading* and none but members of the family and *killi* are allowed to enter it as the family *bongas* reside in the *ading*.

During the last 30 years, there has been a growth of population and government control over the forest has tightened. This has changed the Ho economy from hunting and fishing supported by agriculture and shifting cultivation to employment in the industries and mines. However, their spirit, 'cooperative activity' and the concept of 'joint ownership of land and joint efforts' are still manifest in their daily activities and celebration of various festivals. Since there are certain areas like agricultural production over which the Ho have no control, the Ho still believe rather strongly in the magical rites, ancestor worship and propitiation of the innumerable *bongas* with prayers, chants and sacrifices.

The communal control over the land is exercised through the *Munda* and the land passes from father to son. A Ho cannot dispose of this land as it does not belong to him absolutely (now this legal position has been amended). All the sons have a right over the land but the eldest son receives the largest share. However, this practice is not uniformly followed. The unmarried daughters have usufructuary rights over their father's land.

Theoretical Bases of Approach to Ho Ethnography

Transition (1937) and *Affairs* (1950) present comprehensively a description of Ho culture, the ethnic and historical affinities of the Ho with other Munda tribes. However, the anthropometric and serological data about the tribe, which was a part of his original thesis, have been totally eliminated from the first monograph. Misra (1987: 21) who studied the Ho living in the adjoining Mayurbhanj district of Orissa describes Majumdar's contribution as 'no doubt outstanding to the study of Ho culture in Kolhan which is an entire lifetime dedicated research on the tribe'.

The introductory sections of both the books carry a very detailed discussion of the methodology and theoretical underpinnings as followed by Majumdar in his study of the Ho. In the later volume, he also presents his conceptual frame for the study of the principal factors involved in the functioning of a culture and how their interplay results into culture change. This formulation argues how the factors MARC function to create the base of a culture (1950: xi–xxii). This approach has to be discussed thoroughly along with what he had commented earlier as his adaptative methodology rooted in the different schools or approaches to the study of culture as these emerged historically in the advance of anthropology as a science of man and his environment, physical and social.

In *Transition* (1937: i–iv), Majumdar writes about 'several new approaches to the problems of social anthropology'. He discusses Rivers and his study of similarity of cultural traits leading to diffusion and blending of cultures.

Radcliffe-Brown and Malinowski claimed that the function of the anthropologists was: 1. to deduce and formulate general laws governing the structure of primitive society; 2. give an accurate picture of the individual in the whole complex of the society; 3. discover the role of specific customs and rites; 4. as culture is a complicated piece of machinery, it has to be appraised, not through individual traits but to reveal its coordinated working as a living system. As Malinowski puts it, anthropology does not look at the details of culture in order to appraise them as details, but examines to see how and why they work, how they fit into the whole pattern, what is the motive behind them, and then, finally, to reveal how these are coordinated in a working and living system? Therefore, it calls for a change in methods of anthropological field investigations and this need has contributed to recent developments in the techniques of observation, particularly participant observation, as shaped by Malinowski's own fieldwork.

Following the brief discussion on evolutionary, diffussionist and functional approaches, as mainly developed by the British anthropologists, Majumdar holds out that the new approach to the study of culture as formulated by Ruth Benedict, an American anthropologist, could also be profitably used in his study. At the same time, he points out certain shortcomings of this approach along with its strength. Benedict's gestalt based approach can yield better results in describing and analysing a culture than the functional one because it stresses more on the development, through socialization of individual personality in a social framework 'rather than on the scaffolding' (Majumdar, 1937: ii). In the search for 'patterns' in a culture as manifest in the personality of the individuals constituting it, this approach delves deeper into the attitudes, inhibitions and fulfillments which are the springs of individual action and, thus, reveal the ethos of the culture as it aims to control and determine individual and group behaviour. Benedict calls the genius of culture as configuration. This configuration is 'no doubt a stable element so long as the tribe or culture is a closed group' (ibid.: iii); and here lies its limitation in this approach. According to Majumdar when this approach is contextualized in the scenario of tribal cultures in India, the configuration or pattern may not be found to be 'a stable element' and, therefore, difficult to discern or may even be absent in the situations of continuous change or transformation– the case with the Ho culture. As he explains:

> The composite culture-complex emerging out of the blending of different cultures depends on the relationships of hostility or comradeship between the tribal groups, on inertia or adaptability, or again, on the dominating role of leaders in different cultures.
>
> The present field study of the culture pattern in the Chota Nagpur plateau amply illustrates this. The configuration of Munda culture here undergoes striking changes, as the different branches of the Munda linguistic group are not closed units and interpenetration of culture traits has been easy. Whatever traits have been borrowed have been woven into the general texture of life through a process of assimilation of which the methods and technique are of great interest to anthropologists. (ibid.: iii)

Further, elucidating the contact situations, Majumdar points out that several tribes belonging to the Munda linguistic group have experienced, what he calls, overlapping of cultures which has led to blending while some ethnic groups have lived in segregated units, thus, preserving their pristine elements of the uniform Munda culture. Moreover, the migrations of Munda people and their employment in industrial and mining complexes have led to their picking up traits from a new and standard type of culture slowly. When the industrial or mining complex is away from their habitat, the effects are less disintegrating but when such complexes are in the midst of tribal area they attract a mixed population recruited from different levels of cultures which create a profound effect upon the tribal cultural pattern. 'The one supreme value of the concept of a pattern or *gestalt* is that it enables us to fix upon a selective agency for new traits' (ibid.: iv). The stability of the pattern enables us to determine the traits imbibed later. Majumdar advances the view:

> The difference between Malinowski and Benedict's methodology consists in a difference of emphasis. Whereas the first is concerned with the functional adaptation both inside and outside a scheme of culture, the latter is primarily interested in its ethos. This does not create any great difference in the technical method of observation, nor in the fundamental purpose of study, which is that of the individual living in active association of give and take with his group and its mores. A synthesis of these two approaches has been my ideal in the present enquiry. In the following pages I have attempted to give a general description of the Munda cultural pattern, not only as a closed group, but also as an open one willing to change under pressure of alien influences but not violently departing from its norms. The resultant blending gives us the picture of the living Munda culture of to-day. (ibid.: iv)

Keesing's review of the period 1940–52 on social change (1953: 39–40) states that:

> Studies in the area of culture change, culture contact, and acculturation are being given increasingly the more general label of 'cultural dynamics,' … . On the theoretical side, 'evolutionism,' apparently long since dead … was now being used again somewhat by some scholars for the generalization of history … . In the United Kingdom a few scholars, notably Childe, still tend to use the old terminology of 'savagery' and 'barbarism', along with 'evolution' … dominant theory, now that extremes of 'diffusionism' are moribund, is a 'social structure' approach in which concepts and ideas from both Malinowski and Radcliffe-Brown have tended to fuse … . For long critical of the 'configurational' and varied 'psychological' approaches rampant in American theory, British scholars tend themselves to shift in the latest years toward more psychologically oriented interests.

Thus, it is apparent that the theoretical approach of a synthesis between functional and configurational methodologies which, Majumdar argued, as being more suitable for the study of the process of 'cultural dynamics' among the Indian tribes in *Transition* (1937) was adopted by British scholars in later years.

In *Transition*, Majumdar attempts to develop and follow a methodology combining the functional and *gestalt* approaches to add to the richness as also analytical sharpness with reference to the cultural traits of the Ho undergoing a transition as documented in his ethnography, thus:

> We shall describe in the body of the book how a particular tribe, within this area, viz., the Ho has preserved its pattern and how it has reacted to changes. Primitive culture is dynamic, and changes and modifications are natural; but how these changes occur, who are responsible for introducing them, and what are the chances of survival of these introduced traits, we shall attempt to discuss in the pages that follow. (ibid.: x)

A few descriptive paragraphs summarizing the important common elements of Munda culture in the given geographical area, particularly the traits which are obviously indigenous to it, close the introduction.

The introductory section of *Affairs* (131: 1950) carries this discussion on the different schools of thought further. Referring to a number of studies carried out by Firth, Audry Richard, Lucy Mair and others, Majumdar points out that the integral approach of the functionalism enabled a researcher to appraise traits with reference to their role in the institutional frame and a total cultural situation; and functionalism is neither anti-historical nor anti-distributional as it attempts to view a 'culture' rather than cultures, and, thus, 'does not expose the fieldworkers to the temptation of working out fantastic evolutionary schemes or of gleaning fictitious and unreal similarities to map distribution of cultural traits'. Majumdar also underlines how the essentiality of objectively documenting a culture, at work, in the field needs trained and competent field researchers, having knowledge of the dialect or language of the community they are studying as also a prolonged stay among the people. He goes on to mention some of the vital parameters to be documented carefully in such studies. In its latest phase, functionalism had now emphasized the functional analysis of relation between biological, psychological and culture determinism and the linking up of the various types of cultural responses with the system of needs – biological, derived and integrative. However, Majumdar observes some constraints to this approach:

> But under the stress of dynamic changes, when cultures impinge, one on another, dominate or disintegrate, the functions may accrete, attenuate or lose their significance in the context of change. (ibid.: vii)

Majumdar is also critical of Malinowski's approach to the study of social change in Africa because it takes into account only the Euro-American or Western influence determining change but ignores the inter-tribal contacts which also contribute to various levels of social change. And, this is also the case with tribal India. In this context, he observes that the three column approach for the study of social change charted out by Malinowski (1945: 37) 'ignores some of the most important two ways sources of culture change' (ibid.: 8) in his essay.

In the Indian context, according to Majumdar, the transition or change has been a two-way traffic between the advanced Hindu culture and the primitive and simple tribal cultures. Therefore, he favours the use of the term 'trans-culturation' as suggested by Ortiz, a Cuban scholar, rather than 'acculturation' which may seem to imply only a one-way adoption from a higher level culture to a primitive culture.

Further, analysing the Indian context, Majumdar points out that the process of trans-culturation/acculturation which has been going on in India for centuries is a 'selective process' as all traits are adopted selectively and even adapted and reinterpreted in terms of traditional patterns. Thus, Majumdar's methodology also incorporates Benedict's configurational approach. In his words:

> This is why, one culture may appear to be distinct from another even if both are found to share the same environment enjoying the same levels of progress. The diversity of cultures as shown by Benedict, results from the fact that every culture does not capitalize all possible interests 'provided either by the human age-cycle or by the environment or by means of various activities'. The identity of a culture depends upon the selection of interests, not all the interests. Cultural institutions are selected for the emphasis particular culture puts on some aspect or other of the range of potentialities of human behaviour. (ibid.: ix)

Analysing the contact situations of the Indian tribes more closely, Majumdar points out that:

1. There are many tribes who have gradually and intensively merged into castes. In this process of assimilation, they have come to occupy the position of exterior castes.
2. There are some other tribes who are adaptive, and these are either commensalic, symbiotic or acculturative. Commensalic tribes are cooperating with Hindu castes in common socio-economic pursuits and adopting their material culture while the core of their tribal beliefs and practices still remain healthy.
3. The third group which are acculturative, adapt to a changed cultural situation through selective adaptation of traits. Significantly, this process has not been one of unmixed benefits and gives rise to a hostility or 'contra-acculturation'.

In fact, apart from the tribes mentioned at two and three above even the tribes who have preferred to remain in isolation are also facing discomforts or even extinction. Thus:

> It is not only that acculturation has failed, but isolative groups have also suffered by isolation, their discomforts have mounted with the result that to-day many of the latter groups are becoming extinct or are in the process of such extinction. Neither has assimilation of tribes solved the problem of the tribes so assimilated, for they have a degraded social status in the hierarchical set up of the caste structure. (ibid.: x)

Under these circumstances an urgent need for cooperation between the social groups and different levels of cultures has arisen. But, such a cooperation needs a basis – consciousness of a homogeneity either in race or in culture or in religion as such common interest alone creates strong bonds of cooperation and consolidation. This analytical appraisal of contact situations clearly holds out the field for application of anthropology and the role for activist organizations and NGOs. Thus, Majumdar's approach foreshadows what Singh (2011: 114–5) attributes to have been triggered by 'critical theory' in sociology and social anthropology after 1980s.

Theoretical Frame for Dynamics of Contact and Change

This critical discussion of the situation, which exists not only among tribal groups but also the caste groups residing in these areas, makes Majumdar formulate a theoretical framework regarding 'contact of cultures of unequal levels of elaboration or growth' and compounding his views on the 'contribution that anthropology could make to easing the tensions inherent in such situations' (Madan, 2013: 33).

Contact situations demand the achievement of a state of equilibrium which has to be achieved through adjustment between human organism and the external environment. The external environment subsumes two categories, namely, human beings and external forces and objects and there is constant interaction between the two. The relations between needs and responses on the part of the organism, produces institutions, etc. But, the external or terrestrial factors contribute to the determination of these responses which can be called the basic postulates of a culture or cultures.

Several elements which are themselves variable, make up the basic postulates. Majumdar identifies these elements as Area, Resources, Man and Cooperation, detailed as below:

1. Area is terrestrial and in the case of a tribe or community it can shrink or expand both quantitatively and qualitatively, in response to the needs and requirements, for example shifting cultivation, nomadism and so on.
2. Resources of the Area are animate and inanimate and these also undergo change.
3. Man is the determinant factor in this ecological set-up.
4. Cooperation between the units of the social groups for maximum exploitation of available Resources in the Area inhabited is essential for the *survival*, *health* and *progress* of Man.

The four factors mentioned above contribute to determine and maintain the Base of a culture. Thus, MARC can be postulated as an interdependent functional unit of these value determinable factors. These four factors have been put in their logical order and Man is the dominant factor. Majumdar avers that MARC can be used as an elastic concept to figure out the Base of a culture. Further, its elasticity lies in the context of changes because any change in one of the factors would effect a corresponding change as determined by the direction of the resultant. Since, the base of a culture is function of MARC, Majumdar presents this relationship as:

Base = K (Resultant) = *f* MARC (ibid.: 13)

Majumdar, however, admits that 'it may not be possible to apply rigorous statistical enquiry into the variability of the factors that constitute the MARC', which means that 'K remains indefinite'. But, it can be possible, Majumdar argues to indicate the possible range of a culture without determining K in absolute measures. Thus:

> The attitudes that determine achievement or define the limits of a culture in the context of MARC result from what may be called the 'density' of culture. As in the drosophila experiment, at a certain low density, population does not increase fast, at a higher density there is a rapid increase of population till it reaches the asymptotic level, so also in the density of culture. At a low density, ideas and attitudes do not find ready acceptance, so that they are not important; as the density of a culture increases through interpenetration of ideas within the culture, due to the increase of cooperation between members of the group and the borrowings that are initiated by personality reactions, the attitudes take shape rapidly till all the possible ones are formed to make the configuration asymptotic with regard to the attitudes. At this point we reach the concept of *Gestalt* or configuration. Thus MARC is the base on which culture is built up in its final form; a culture is limited by attitudes and the various parts of the culture become linked and interlinked as the density of a culture rises to a saturation point. In this sense, no culture is superorganic, no culture is mere organic, but interpenetrative and linked but limited by the base or MARC. (ibid.: xiii–xiv)

Explaining the working of these concepts further, Majumdar points out that when Base changes, as it must, the direction of MARC varies or intensifies in the shape of technology and institution making and, thus, 'the original institutional setup realigns itself to the institution base' (ibid.: xiv). Thus, a certain level of density of culture (or equilibrium) is attained. However, when a new density arises, the forces of MARC may change its direction 'either converging to the original base, in which case there is a cultural revivalism or diverging towards disintegration of cultures'. A stagnation of the Base can also occur:

> When the institutions work in unison, aim at integration and succeed in effecting the same, whether in response to the old base or the new, a stagnation results, for every factor of MARC has a functional limit, as for example, in the fulfillment of desires, or satiation of hopes and ambitions. (ibid.: xiv)

In postulating the concept of Base, Majumdar makes use of the *gestalt* or configurational approach, as he says: '... in the MARC we merely regard the factors as forces, which cooperate to produce a resultant direction or the Base of a culture'. These forces cooperate optimally in a close but integrated culture when it is not affected by contacts. This is a state of culture where mutuality, reciprocity and a chain of lifelong duties and obligations develop a homogeneity and consciousness of kind. Say, in the case of a hunting tribe, the Base is so small that the saturation density with regard to its population and possible cooperation would minimize discomforts and maximize satisfaction. However, it also devises ways like infanticide to continue the balance with the Base. Similarly, when the Base for a tribe or clan expands, say with the discovery of new resources, it may devise new institutions and thereby work out a new solidarity. Demographically, the size of a group responds to their productive techniques and 'the complexity or density of a culture may increase in proportion to the degree of cooperation between the MARC factors' (ibid.: xvi). As the Base has already widened in this context of a changing culture, it reaches a level where assimilations become possible. But:

> So long as assimilation is not effected there may still be responsiveness in cultures which makes cultures adaptive. An adaptive culture as mentioned before, may be mere commensalic. The two extreme processes are 'isolation' and 'assimilation' and in between we meet with cultures that develop a symbiotic relationship or acculturate. In an isolative culture, the base remains narrow and limited and therefore incapable of adjusting to new situation either by changing or mutating. In the adaptive culture the base expands slowly, there is an ease with which the basic needs are met, there is more leisure, and therefore scope for learning and for trial of new ideas and beliefs. No change of attitudes is necessary, yet cultures respond and become hospitable. At first such hospitability refers to superficial or inconsequential elements of other cultures, but in course of time the accommodation provided to such traits increases the overall capacity of the culture and makes it possible for the culture to accept and assimilate complex and vital traits of other cultures. (ibid.: xvi–xvii)

However, in a different scenario:

> When a culture reaches saturation density with regard to traits, indigenous and borrowed, and the base still remains narrow, it may show signs of intolerance, become isolative, or the base may show cracks or fissures, resulting in a cultural *malaise.* In such cases, detribalization, disintegration of beliefs and practices and economic maladjustment, tear up the existing base, and put the culture out of gear. (ibid.: xvii)

Discussing the situation in Chhota Nagpur, Majumdar says that in most of this region, the Base has increased in proportion to the demographic accretion through industrialization and opening up of the Area. This has made it possible for the tribals to adapt and acculturate. Though the outlets provided for transfer of population by these expanded economic activities have found ready acceptance with some sections of the tribal people, yet the Base of Munda culture have not kept pace with needs, with the result that the acculturative process that was at work is not functioning as it did, and today the tribes are showing an intolerance towards adoption of traits from the advanced neighbours. This intolerance is expressed in suspicion, hatred and a conscious effort at consolidation of the tribal cultures. In reality the political consciousness of the *Adibasis*, which stands for a revivalism and integration, is a direct result of contra-acculturation or intolerance against adoption of foreign traits, tools and techniques, though these have stood them in good stead in the early decades of the present century and before (ibid.: xviii).

Examining the Ho culture, Majumdar observes that today it 'has become dense, fully integrated with regard to its base and ... has developed a pattern. But, this pattern is not what Benedict has described ... viz., a more or less consistent pattern of thought and action with characteristic purposes that stabilize behaviour and consolidate experience' (ibid.: xviii). According to Majumdar, Hos have acculturated to Hindu culture, represented by the lower castes in their neighbourhood they have reacted to it, but, this 'reaction is informed rather than Ho style'.

Summing up this conceptual and analytical approach to the study of cultural change, Majumdar reiterates that every culture is to be studied in the context of its cultural dynamics irrespective of whether the forces affecting it are Euro-American, technological or indigenous. Comparing with the earlier situation in their contacts with Hindus and their civilization, Majumdar observes:

> In earlier days the base did not change suddenly, for the forces that make for such change did not gather sufficient momentum due to low density of culture or absence of speed or alarming tempo. Technological advance has helped to widen the base and transport and communications have made transfer or dispersal of population easy, so that no longer do the tribal people to-day need be confined to their settlements. Technological advance is retarded if the area diminishes, the size of population grows small, the degree of cooperation between the people is leveled down, or the resources become scarce or shy. But there is no inherent defect in the people, however low the levels of achievement they possess, that would militate against the absorption process that is essential for ushering in a technological civilization. All that is needed is a change or expansion of the base or a culture by proper planning. (ibid.: xviii–xix)

There is no inherent incompetence among tribal people to absorb or assimilate technological advance. The problem actually 'rests fairly and squarely on the inadequacy of the Base'. Majumdar advances, in this context of determining the inadequacy of the Base and the reasons therefore factorized as per MARC, a role for anthropological studies as follows:

> The structure of a society is a basic postulate in the context of MARC and attitudes only shape in a dense culture reaching the saturation or asymptotic level in a logistic sense. If we find structural, configurational and themal approaches fully satisfied in a concept of the base and the superstructure resting on it, anthropologists must evaluate culture with regard to the K or the base and thus present his findings as dynamic facts in an everchanging milieu. The base is changing continuously and discontinuously. Variation of cultures result from continuous change far more than it does from the discontinuous change, the scope of which is limited. What is known as culture-heredity or continuity can be understood only with reference to the base or of MARC and personality and attitudes are functions of this base. It is in the context of the discussion above that the Ho culture receives illumination and appraisal. (ibid.: xxii)

It is apparent from the above discussion that his formulation of the concept of MARC is an overreaching kind of approach which is basically functional but with emphasis on factorizing both *gestalt* and its patterns and their constituents into a formula. Furthermore, it also attempts to suggest a more definitive but preliminary and rather too synoptic a methodology for quantifying the trends and measuring the extent of 'acculturation'. The consequent methodology of MARC also, thereby, implies how the likely ill effects of 'acculturation' and 'trans-culturation' can be avoided or modified by introducing planned changes through the application of anthropological knowledge. Thus, MARC also visualizes to explore the scope for application of anthropological knowledge in a more well defined direction by basing it on some statistical measurement of the process of change. This at any rate would seem to have been Majumdar's expectation.

This entire approach or strategy for defining, measuring and directing, to some extent, the process of 'acculturation' has not however been spelt out or elaborated by him anywhere in the *Affairs*. A couple of years later, however, he had while commenting on Ralph Beals' paper on 'acculturation' at the International Symposium on Anthropology at New York observed:

> Acculturation studies must be correlated with the time factor or mobility. Indians once looked to the West for traits which they incorporated into their culture; today, the terminals and voltage are both changing. The Chhota-Nagpur tribes, Santhals, and Mundas, who live in compact blocks of millions, have not acculturated much, while the scattered tribes have detribalized. A quantitative approach to acculturation would be possible if we could develop a technique of ethnometry, of measuring ethnographic phenomena, and we are trying to develop formulas .... (Sol Tax, 1953: 126)

Here, Majumdar's reference to our 'trying to develop formulas' or a technique of ethnometry is presumably a reference to the then ongoing effort at the Indian Statistical Institute, Calcutta, to apply the D^2 multi-variate formula in statistics developed by Mahalonobis to the task of various 'problems and issues in social research ... for which it could be pertinent' and this includes assessing the 'process of change by a chosen list of quantitative parameters' (Mukherjee and Bandyopadhyay, 1964: 270).

In this discussion, the suggestive explication of a formula to measure the capacity of a culture to absorb changes and lead to progress through a 'larger conceptual scheme', in Keesing's review of *Affairs*, is relevant (1952: 392). Describing the study as 'documentation of cultural dynamics' and 'delineations of the further impact of modern civilization upon these hitherto isolated village groups', Keesing observes Majumdar as having started 'with the older ethnological traditions' but 'also not afraid to strike out on his own'. And, here he mentions Majumdar's earlier attempt in *Fortunes*, where in the concluding chapter he brings up 'a theoretical approach to culture as a social vigilance schema built of conscious and unconscious factors'; and, then, about the 'Introduction' in *Affairs* where he:

> Offers a useful brief critique of 'acculturation' theory, and also a larger conceptual scheme, summarized in the formula $B = K = f\ MARC$, in which M is man, A is area, R is resources, C cooperation. Together they form 'an

interdependent functional unit', providing B, the 'base of a culture', and K, the 'resultant' of the interplay of variable and dynamic factors. Such grand schemes, which perennially rear up in this country like bomb bursts to disturb and contaminate the slow theoretical work of peaceful specialists in their own well fenced disciplines, probably have their usefulness. But the book will serve best the purposes of those who wish to examine carefully gathered case materials on traditional Indian village life and its contemporary modification .... (Keesing, 1952: 392)

Concluding Discussion

Majumdar's ethnography is not simply problem-oriented. It also carries strains of not only his theoretical orientations, but also through its descriptions, interpretations and comparisons, indicate the development of his own theoretical approach. This may be in connection with the social change and the process of transition, in the Ho case, or degeneration of culture and resultant loss of interest in life and decimation in the case of Korwa, or the factors creating a syncretic Hindu festival in Bastar. Similarly, his own theoretical orientations received from Malinowski and other British anthropologists and the *gestalt* approach of American anthropology is reflected in his attempt to interpret the functional importance of institutions, practices and beliefs and simultaneously indicating any cultural patterns which he could discern. A dominating pattern can be seen in the case of Korwa's pessimism for their future which guides their attitudes and action; the gender relationship among Tharu rooted in their historical narratives and the patterns of magical practices of their women of which even the non-Tharus have a dread; and the patterns of Ho life largely determined by their changing religious beliefs under the influence of the mainstream culture, education and the location of industrial and mining activities in their areas.

While Majumdar has been simply described as a 'functionalist', by and large, his ethnography does not stick to one single theoretical frame and goes even beyond the tenets of the different British schools and American schools of culture and personality as he makes use of his rich ethnographic data and arrives upon his own formulations covering the nature and impact of contacts of cultures. He also draws his generalizations and comparisons on the basis of a few case studies as also occasional use of some statistical data which he can find. It needs no emphasis that Majumdar has repeatedly stated his experience and conviction with regard to the then existing theoretical frames in his two empirical studies on the Ho and also what he subsumed under the title of 'modern trends in social anthropology', particularly relating to the study of tribal groups in India (66: 1938: 168–174).

It will not be inappropriate to point out that Majumdar's difficulty with regard to anthropological theories of the times, and their use as the bases for empirical studies or ethnography, has been experienced by others as well. To mention illustratively, Murphy 'finds orthodox theories inadequate and was forced to turn to new and innovative works and to return to older bodies of social thought that shared my outlook' and therefore his thought-provoking 'alarms and excursions in anthropological theory' was reflective of the 'mood of profound social unrest and pessimism that began in the mid-1960s. Murphy too finds the difference between British social anthropology and American cultural anthropology 'not of great magnitude though they may overwhelm the specialist who are emerged within them' (Murphy, 1971: 15–16). This is almost what Majumdar had said in his introduction to *Transition*; that the difference ... consists in emphasis (60: 1937: iv). Murphy further observes that 'culture and social structure are often used in exactly the same way and to refer to the same things ...'. This has been 'recognized by' Fortes also (1953: 21), as below:

> social anthropologists study what others call 'culture' but from the perspective of social structure. What are called 'structural principles' by one may be called 'values' by the other, just as one may prefer the word 'agnatic' to another's 'patrilineal.' In most cases the choice of words makes little differences to the analysis, but they are significant because of differential loyalty .... (ibid.: 16)

Delving into this rather contentious issue, this author has attempted to look into some other later approaches as well. The 'Grounded Theory approach to qualitative research and analysis' strikes one as being resonant here. O' Reilly (2005: 200–01) observes that Strauss and Corbin's 'Grounded Theory' is based 'on a methodology with the following salient angles:

- 'A way of thinking about and studying social reality' that does see theory as being grounded in data without a simplistic adoption of inductive reasoning.
- There is an interplay between researchers and the data, where the researcher is not afraid to draw on his/her own experiences when analysing, because 'these become the foundations for making comparisons and discovering properties and dimensions' (Strauss and Corbin, 1998: 5).
- The theories that are produced are seen as modifiable, qualifiable, and open in part to negotiation, but, because these theories are grounded in data, researchers are confident about their validity.
- It is helpful if the researcher is flexible and creative, and open to criticism and debate.
- The research is essentially inductive: theoretical ideas have value but researchers are skeptical of them until they are grounded in data.
- Most grounded theory researchers hope their work has relevance for other academic and non-academic audiences (so research and intellectual endeavour are not divorced from people's daily lives).

Thus, O' Reilly interprets it as being 'not at all prescriptive about methods ... there may be some use of statistics, but qualitative research is essentially non-mathematical and interpretive which does not stand in contrast to scientific. Indeed grounded theory is more objective and therefore scientific because it enables the research participants to set the agenda or to have a voice independently of the researchers' (2005: 201).

Hence, a likely appraisal in this regard is that Majumdar though exposed to the several theoretical models and methodology of his times tried to develop his own frame of approach for collecting, analysing, comparing and drawing conclusions from his materials in the veracity of which he had confidence. This is a notable feature of the work of this first generation professional anthropologist, who also wanted to make his anthropology reach non-academic audiences as also had a strong nationalistic urge to make his intellectual endeavour useful to the country's colonial problems and subsequently the post-colonial policies to reform and develop the society. Whether his work can be explicated under the Grounded Theory framework is an issue for further debate.

In fact, in the context of the foundations of Ho religion, he pointedly mentions that he had differed from S.C. Roy, his teacher, 'because of my theoretical leaning', which Roy did not encourage; he was so full of facts, that he would not like to commit'. Majumdar adds that he 'had nearly carried him with me – about the Ho religion' (1954: 349).

Interestingly, writing on 'theory and ethnography in the 'modern anthropology of India', Berger (2012) while critically outlining the theoretical strands and discussing various frames comes to cover a stage, about which he observes that, 'if read critically, older ethnographies, although perhaps framed in out-dated theoretical perspective, are a valuable source of information. Quite obviously this view of ethnography as the necessary and reliable basis of anthropological generalization is worlds apart from Dirks' indictment of the same practice' (ibid.: 349)

Further, Berger comments, of course in the context of Indian anthropology, that most anthropologists, 'do not follow any single theoretical paradigm or methodology but pick and choose whatever helps them make sense of their research problems' (ibid.: 349). Thus, Majumdar can be judged as one of the finest ethnographers who used multiple theories depending on the context.

The discussion about Majumdar's findings on culture change in the next chapter further strengthens what has been observed here in looking critically into his ethnography.

3

Anthropological Perspective on Primitive Religion

The importance of religion in human society can never be over valued. In fact anthropologists discussing the modern trends in something of a loss of interest and faith in religious practices, specially in western societies, too have stated in their conclusion that the hold of religion does continue and even gets more of strength (Firth; Evans-Pritchard). Firth finds that religion is one of the great driving forces in human activity both individually and socially. It gives rise to elaborate institutional organization and gives sanction for a wide range of conduct relating to almost the entire gamut of social and economic relations, as is obvious in the conditions seen around the world today.

Majumdar had studied a number of tribal communities in the country and also villages inhabited by tribes, and both tribes and castes. The ethnographic accounts elaborate the culture of the people as all villages were treated and studied as 'little communities'. The Ho of Kolhan, Singbhum district and several tribes of UP, namely the Korwa, the Tharu, and the Khasas, were the tribal communities studied by him in detail. His work among Ho is the most important one as he had done his fieldwork there for long. A theoretical frame for the religious-cum-magical practices among them has been presented by him in both the books on the Ho, specially the later one, together with a salient paper, 'Bongaism' in Roy's festschrift, edited by him and others (79: 1940: 60–79). Therefore, it would be appropriate to present in more details and analytically comment on his views regarding the Ho religion, first, along with his perspectives on other tribes.

Ho Religion and Bongaism

Majumdar observes that in monographic delineation of culture, theoretical interpretation of any aspect of it is considered out of place and this explains the absence of any systematic effort to analyse and interpret the tribal cultures of the Chota Nagpur plateau (ibid.: 60). He had, however, attempted to explain the religious experience of the Ho, along with other aspects of culture in *Transition* and his paper on 'Bongaism' (ibid.: 60) in order to elucidate the points at issue. Elsewhere (165: 1954) he informs that I know the views of the Late S.C. Roy .... If I had differed I had done so because of my theoretical leanings, which my teacher (Roy) did not encourage; 'he was so full of fact that he would not like to commit, although I can tell in confidence that I had nearly carried him with me (on Ho religion)'.

The Ho religious beliefs and their entire bases are derived from their belief in Bonga, and therefore Majumdar has called it 'Bongaism'. The roots of Bongaism lie in the very beliefs of the Ho in the creation of the world and the origin of the human race. In both the versions (Tickell's early account and the later one) of the legend connected therewith, Sing-Bonga is self-created and he created the earth. He also made it habitable by creating all kinds of flora, fauna and its topography. Then he created man out of the egg of a bird. The story goes on to tell us how Sing-Bonga was offended and destroyed the mankind. Thereafter Nage-Bonga or the water deity came with a pair of living souls which she had kept under water. These, brother and sister, under influence of *Handia* (rice-beer) also created by Sing-Bonga, copulated and the human species was born again.

The belief system of the Ho broadly makes out the Sing-Bonga to be their supreme god and creator. Then, there are just a few other Bongas who are among the beneficent Bongas. These are Nage-Bonga (river goddess and wife of Sing-Bonga), Disauli (god of the Hatu) and Marang-Bonga (god of the ancestral home). The other category of Bongas, malignant and mal-efficient is practically innumerable and they differ according to locality. A list of such Bongas in the area where fieldwork was carried out is given. Noticeably, most of the malignant Bongas are not indigenous to Ho, but have their counterparts among the neighbouring Oriyas, as their names indicate this borrowing. Even though beneficent Bongas can chastise or punish persons who break the tribal code, it is not done malevolently by them.

Explaining the meaning of Bonga, Majumdar refers to Roy and Bodding and observes that 'Bonga is a generic name and it is applied indiscriminately to refer to gods and spirits. The real meaning of Bonga is a power, a force and the religion of the Hos may be called 'Bongaism' and Sing-Bonga is a power, a very big power which pervades all space, as it were; Bonga has not got any shape or form'. It can take any form or shape. A hierarchy of power is also recognized among them. Though this conception is not essential to Bongaism proper, it is something which has evolved in the course of their association with the different manifestations of this power. It might have been established by a process of trial and error. What was only a vague and mysterious power became identified later on with the thing, or object from which it derived its name.

The term 'Bonga' is used indiscriminately to signify man, animal, plant and even material objects. The power possessed by animal or plant is derived from the impersonal force, Bonga. This belief has the function of regulating social conduct and individual behaviour and also to explain any phenomenon or moving object the mechanics or technology behind which is not known to the Ho. The difference in the authority wielded by different persons can also be explained through this concept as a difference between the degrees of power possessed by them. Comparing certain practices among the Ho as also in the relationships between Brahman and untouchable castes in South India, Majumdar concludes that 'such precautions are found necessary in mutual interest and the origin of this practice is explained by the belief in *mana* or an impersonal force, which I should think forms the substratum of primitive religion everywhere ...' (131: 1950: 273).

Certain other aspects of Bongaism are that Sing-Bonga is neither named in rituals nor worshipped while the marriage of Sing-Bonga with Nage-Bonga is ritually celebrated. The most commonly propitiated Bonga is Disauli and sometimes Marang-Bonga is worshipped along with Disauli. Thus, a significant aspect of the coherence of their belief in Bongas is that as a collectivity, the Bongas 'do not excite as much concern as when a particular Bonga is mentioned'. Even though after the Maghe festival the Ho 'annually drive away their Bonga out of their village so that they may not be required to pay constant attention to their needs and aspirations' (ibid.: 270), the naming of *Disauli* the *Marang-buru* or even the *Nage-eras* must not be suggested for that would surely bring calamity to them. Thus, the *Deuri* exercises caution in naming any Bonga and usually refers to the places where they are believed to reside. To a certain extent, it can be said that anthropomorphism in case of the Bongas among the Ho is rather vague except for their power to dominate the life of the Ho and any questions regarding the 'personality' of these Bongas are evaded by the *Deuri*. Though they feel the sure and certain influence of the Bongas, they consider them as manifestations of a power, which can chastise or punish them and also give them plenty, a power which they have attempted to control and manipulate but which has always overpowered them in all spheres of life.

The symbolic conception relating to the Bongas in some form is provided only in glimpses in their dreams. *Disauli*, the most powerful Bonga after Sing-Bonga and believed to be his assistant, makes its symbolic presence felt that is forerunner of future events, in the dreams of *Deuri* or *Manki* or the *Munda*.

We can now turn to discuss the typical social situations which give a base for religious action (Firth, 1951: 220) which is goal-oriented and value governed, thereby determining relationship in social living. The belief in Bonga conceptualizes two categories of Bongas – beneficent and maleficent – and hence different situations of life and social living call for solutions in this context. These solutions are offered by magic, witchcraft, prayers, propitiation and sacrifices which are determined diagnostically by the different agents of the supernatural world, namely the *Deonwa* and the *Deuri*, through interpretation of dreams, utterances when possessed as a result of the incantation and other rituals and various practices of divination. The different situations calling for such magico-religious interventions can be categorized as below:

(i) For ensuring plentiful crops, hunt, fishing and other such productive activities.

(ii) Prevention and cure from calamities like disease, epidemics and other adverse circumstances brought about by either category of Bonga as a result of transgressing social and moral codes, magic and other processes initiated by outsiders, *Diku*, etc., both individually and by the community.

(iii) For the enforcement of traditional codes of conduct or laws relating to crime, anti-social actions, etc.

Productive Activities

The disposal of the main agricultural crop, paddy, begins with ceremonial thanks giving to the Bongas for which it is placed in a corner of the *ading*. Then, before the family partakes of the new crops, ceremonial offerings are made to Sing-Bonga, *Disauli* and ancestral spirits sheltered in the *ading*. For fishing, which is always done in groups, the owner or the lessee of the *dab* (pond) propitiates the *Nage-Bonga* or the river spirit. The village *Deuri* offers a hen, a couple of eggs and a white hair-comb to the *Nage-Bonga* after which all the people assembled for fishing sprinkle water over themselves. And, fishing activities begin thereafter and continue for several days.

Disease and Calamities

The belief is that affliction on the Ho is caused by malignant Bongas who are really gods of alien people and the witches and sorcerers who are usually anti-social members of the tribe. In case of all diseases, they try both the indigenous and modern medicine as also other methods of diagnosing the disease by the *Deonwa* and its remedies by way of propitiation. Herbal medicines are also prescribed by the *Deonwa*. Apart from the belief in witches and sorcerers and malignant Bongas, another dangerous method of inflicting disease by an enemy is *najom* or administering of poison by witches or sorcerers. The *Deonwa* has also the competence to find out the effects of *najom* and medicines therefor. Malignant Bongas are also believed to cause disease to the cattle. *Sing-Bonga* and the *Nage-Bonga*, being the supreme beneficent spirits, are questioned by the *Deonwa* to find out the source or malignant Bongas and spirits responsible for the disease. The *Deonwa* uses a variety of incantations and *mantram* to identify the source which is often times found in its abode in a forest and a propitiation has to be carried out there. In cases of epidemics, the villagers approach the *Deuri* to undertake propitiatory measures. The placation is done collectively by the villagers and their leaders after a cooperative endeavour for collecting all the material necessary for the worship and sacrifice. The propitiation is offered to *Disauli* and worship is offered to the *Sing-Bonga*. Here, in this process the collective effort and solidarity of the community is ensured. Significantly, it is followed by individual action in each family by way of cleaning the *ading* and the house and utensils.

Tribal Code

Taboos which are also regarded as a part of the religious belief system regulate a large range of human action. Taboos are meant to protect women, children, etc.

in a vulnerable state like pregnancy, child birth, young children and babies which may attract envious action from malignant spirits, magic, etc. On the other hand, there are taboos to prohibit incest, mischief and such other anti-social acts. As there is no Mundary word equivalent in meaning to taboo, the word *Bonga* is commonly used to explain the source of all prohibitions (131: 1959: 235). Broadly, the actions tabooed fall into two categories – serious ones and those which are not so serious. The second category may attract only ostracism while the serious ones, generally relating to food and sex and marriage, are taken note of by the *Killi* and attract drastic steps like *Kajomasin* i.e. a total boycott of a person by the members of the tribe. The readmission of a *Kajomasin* to the *Killi* is through expiation. This involves some religious rituals like sacrifice to the *Sing-Bonga* with prayers and incantation by the *Deuri*, visit to certain specified sacred places by the person who had been a *Kajomasin* and a feast for the *Killi* and other elders. Incest taboos, if violated, bring maximum religious-cum-social sanction and invite elaborate expiation. The feeling of guilt is oftentimes very serious. Majumdar reports in detail a case witnessed by him in *Affairs,* where a young man stated that he had brought death on himself by committing incest, and he actually died a few days later of fever. Food taboos also spell a kind of protection to individuals and the community from the actions of alien people, witches and sorcerers. Ordeals and oaths which are also based in religious beliefs do not find a mention in the Ho ethnography while their importance has been saliently documented among other tribes studied by Majumdar.

The tribals of Chota Nagpur have been in close contacts with the Hindu communities specially the lower castes since long. However, among the five important tribes of the area, the Ho, particularly those residing in the Kolhan government estate have been the least affected through these contacts because of a comparative isolation and an indirect rule introduced in the area by the colonial powers. This has also meant that the influence of Christianity resulting into conversion has no roots among the Ho. In 1931 Census, there were 248 Hos per thousand who returned themselves as Hindu while the Christians were only four. The comparative figures among Oraon, in the same Census, were 349 and 228 and among the Kharia 353 and 436. Thus, Munda tribes other than Hos have been greatly influenced by contacts with Hindus and Christianity, but the Hos have experienced the least effect. Therefore, *Bongaism* as seen among the Ho conceives of least anthropomorphism as stated earlier. At the same time, though, the Ho pantheon too has come to include some gods and goddesses from the Hindu pantheon. Hence, Majumdar has analysed the contents of hymns and prayers addressed to the *Bongas* during the principal worship festivals of the Ho and finds that the 'impersonal character of the Bongas may be gathered' from these texts. In the case of the gods of the Hindu pantheon, the hymns and prayers addressed to them convey ideas about the shape, form and nature of the divinities but in contrast, no such details are found in the prayers for the Ho *Bongas*.

In support of this conclusion, the prayers for propitiations spoken by the *Deuri* on occasions like *Maghe parva*, *Oteili*, *Baha*, *Hero*, *Batauli* and *Jomnama* have been documented (79: 1940: 79). These texts use supplicatory terms addressed to *Disauli*, the second most important *Bonga*. These are, 'serve you', 'worship you', and the 'sacrifices or offerings like red cock, brown hen, etc. and certain kinds of grains and seeds'. The prayer is intended to make *Disauli* and other *Bongas* to restrain tigers, snakes, etc. from making the Ho people their prey when they go into the forest for various purposes. In another prayer the hierarchal order of the *Bongas* has also been projected and then the supplication is addressed to them collectively.

In the *Oteili* prayer, the ancestors' spirits are expected to save the Ho as also their cattle from various diseases as a result of the worship. Similarly, a request to secure them from tigers, etc is made in the context of the Ho collecting or eating *mahuva* and *sarojom* flowers and drinking as well as during visits to the forests. In certain other prayers, the ploughed and planted fields of the Ho are to be protected from any decay and rot and to yield in plenty.

Religion and Change

Durkheim observes, 'religion as very useful institution ... better adopted than any other institution ... to show us essential and permanent aspect of humanity' (Malefijt, 1968: 59). And, Majumdar's empirical studies made him believe that it provides the primitive groups with a lease of vigour in life, and with tools of adaptation through changes in their religious attitudes, manner of worship, the indigenous pantheon and in general religious beliefs (79: 1940: 61). The Mundari speaking tribes have shown this kind of elasticity in no small measure. This 'elasticity' has allowed introduction of innumerable gods and spirits in their pantheon today thereby bringing their tribal religion nearer to popular Hinduism. In the process, the religion of the lower castes of Hindus has also incorporated many tribal gods. This trans-acculturative process sort of invigorates the Ho to a better cohesion and an ability to adjust to the changing economic and social milieu around them.

The Korwa Religion

Majumdar had begun studying the Korwa, a small tribe, declining in population, residing in Mirzapur district (now Sonbhadra district of U.P.) at around the same time that is in 1920s (see 30A: 1929). It would be interesting to examine the religious life of the Korwa in order to make a comparative analysis. Majumdar observes:

> Tribes like the Korwas who are on evil days still claim allegiance to their great clan god Raja Chandol, but their interest is more concentrated on propitiating the evil spirits they know by the legion, or those whom their shrewd neighbours force on them in order to exploit them with their help. (90: 1944: 60)

The Korwas have lost the traditional beliefs in their indigenous pantheon and they say that times have changed and the powers that their tribal priests or the Baigas possessed have weakened. The gods have become apathetic. This atmosphere of despondence and fear among them encourages adoption of some alien gods and spirits which the Baigas, who belong to a different tribe, Chero, advise them to propitiate. This has proved to be an exploitative step. Thus, there is no trans-acculturation here and no adaptation to the borrowed religious traits. The Korwas 'have ceased to think about them (the adopted gods and goddesses of the Hindu) and merely follow prescriptions without expecting any spectacular results' (ibid.: 62). It can be said that this tribe, which also belongs to Munda ethnic group, had earlier believed in an impersonal mysterious force, *Bonga*, like the Ho. But subsequently their pantheon changed without adaptations and 'genuine incorporation' and now it has 'tended to become nebulous slowly thinning out to become a vague power, uncertain in its attitude and uncanny in its relations with them' (ibid.: 63). The Korwa live in an atmosphere of mortality as is natural for a dying tribe. A case observed by Majumdar shows how even the news of his son's death did not produce any disquietening change in the father who continued with his task at hand, and not leaving in haste to see the dying or dead person. However, the Korwa of an adjoining area, Sarguja district, presented a different picture. This leads to a conclusion that imposition of alien gods and goddesses without adaptation and interchange of rituals and beliefs with the neighbouring alien castes or tribes lead to a loss of confidence and faith in a culture. This creates what Majumdar calls, 'a tranquil despair', disorganized social structure which may lead a tribe to decimation, even extinction.

The Tharu Religion

The Tharu, a tribal community living in the *tarai* area of Uttar Pradesh, is both geographically and ethnically distant from the Ho or Korwa. Majumdar began his study of this tribe in mid-1930s and *Fortunes*, which was a part of his studies relating to the 1941 Census in the state, includes a detailed essay on them. The Tharu believe that they are the descendant of Rajput women and their servants with whom they had to flee due to enemies. However, anthropometric and serological data collected by Majumdar indicate that there is no scientific evidence of Rajput origins of the Tharu women. The traditional high status of the women among them is attributed by him to a likely matriarchal matrix of Tharu culture, noticeable among women in the cis-Himalayan region.

The Tharu have been in constant contact with their Hindu neighbours and Majumdar's observation as well as earlier reports on Tharu culture highlight changes in their culture as a result of contacts with Hindu neighbours and also, later on, with Muslim traders like *Banjara*. Obviously, therefore, it is difficult to present any historically authentic earlier account of their religious beliefs. A recent study (Maiti, 2004) observes: 'culture contact has brought about a change of views among the Tharu towards supernatural elements. It is not easy to understand the complicated pantheon of Tharu deities and spectral beings, their modes of worship, system of offerings and their categorization. Very often even the elders among them falter and get confused while providing details' (ibid.: 45).

Majumdar finds even the influence of Arya Samaj, a widespread reformatory religious movement of the early 20th century among the Hindus, as a part of the cross currents influencing the Tharu religious beliefs. Majumdar's accounts as well as the later accounts agree that the Tharu believe in Bhumsen (Bhauiya or Bhumia) to be their patron deity, the one presiding over the village. Raksha is taken by the Tharus as their patron saint. Then, their cattle are protected by Nagarhi or Darchandi who is worshipped by the village in the Pradhan's house. Each Tharu has a mound in the centre of the courtyard or in front of the house with a wooden peg fixed to represent these goddesses and other gods as well. Offerings to the village deity are goats, meat, fish and *gur*. Since the Tharu are agriculturists and prosperous agriculturist, by and large, because of the fertile lands of the *tarai*, they make sacrifices and propitiations to the gods and spirits in which they believe, at every critical stage in the progress of the crop. The *Bharara*, who is a medicine man and priest-cum-magician of the Tharu, performs the religious as well as magical rites and rituals. He plays a very prominent role in placating and propitiating the spiritual beings controlling and influencing the destinies of human beings.

A significant aspect of the Tharu life is that their neighbouring Hindu communities believe that the Tharu, specially Tharu women, are powerful magicians and excel in such practices which enables them to control men or even turn them into their pets. And, on their part, the Tharus also believe that they are not immune from the evil eye, evil tongue, and evil acts of their neighbours as well as witches and sorcerers among them.

Since the Tharu pantheon now includes a number of Hindu gods and goddesses like Krishna, Mahadev, Kalka, etc. their *Bharara* have also considerably added to their range of propitiatory action. Furthermore, if the *Bharara* can divine the cause for any crisis or calamity and yet his remedies do not bear results, the Tharu also call *Pahari* Brahmans, like the Bhoksa which is a cognate tribe almost completely Hinduised. In fact, the latter 'live under his (*Pahari* Brahman) spiritual hegemony. The *Pahari* Brahman families ... have divided the whole of Buxar (area of the Bhoksa) between themselves' (Hasnain, 1979: 87). The *Pahari* Brahmans have come to considerably influence the Tharu cultural life though they are not generally publicly introduced as a part of their religious organization. Thus, there is a rather placid co-existence of religious practices inclusive of borrowed elements as well as a belief in magic and sorcery with its own range of remedial action by the *Bharara*. Similarly in the matter of cause for various diseases or epidemics they have faith both in their *Bharara* as also in the modern medicine and doctors. In their cycle of festivals, they have now incorporated quite a few days of fasting as observed among their Hindu neighbours and festivals like Janamashtami and Shivratri are being celebrated. The Brahmans have also introduced the worship of Satyanarayan and his *katha* has become quite popular. Holi was traditionally a very important spring festival among Tharus. On Dushahara, they have now taken to sacrificing cocks and pigs to propitiate the *Devi* who is often confused with *Mata*. But the tradition connected with Diwali, which was observed for propitiation of ancestral spirits, has undergone a change and it is celebrated with both the traditional and Hindu elements of lights and worship.

Majumdar's account does not include the contents of any devotional or religious songs or utterances. However, in her later account, Maiti observes that their traditional *sakhi*, the devotional songs calling upon the deities for their blessings now include prayers to a number of Hindu gods and goddesses and Muslim saints as well (2004: 248–49). Majumdar's conclusion about the Tharu culture is:

> While in other parts contacts with advanced cultures have disintegrated tribal cultures, among the Tharus a careful process of selective adoption of traits and customs from neighbouring cultures has secured for them a stability, while they have emphasized the useful element of the indigenous cultural pattern. (90: 1944: 65)

Firth describes this phenomenon as 'primitive externalization of evil'. This concept or approach creates the firm beliefs in malignancy of neighbours and their magic, presence of ghosts and witches, and it also makes outcome of propitiatory action uncertain; and one can add here to the incorporation of alien gods and goddesses, largely benevolent into the pantheon of the community.

Srivastava's study focusing on the dynamics of cultural change of the Tharu in Nainital Tarai was conducted during 1948–1950 and as such he has focused most on the change in different aspects of Tharu culture, including religion. Srivastava observes that the Tharu 'conception of Supreme Deity appears to have become more refined and alleviated than it might have been before' (1958/2011: 218–19) and he is considered too high for 'direct and intimate communion' with the Tharus, and this characteristic is akin to Sing Bonga as discussed earlier. In Majumdar's words this would be 'un-worshipped god'. The Tharu, according to their original beliefs, categorized the deities and spirits into benevolent and malevolent. The benevolent have to be approached with prayers and supplications and offerings while the malevolent ones have to be controlled, averted or exorcised by spell, threats and other methods of white or black magic. Some of them also receive regular offerings such as the ancestor's spirits. Srivastava's observations give an impression that the process of incorporation of Hindu gods, Muslim *pirs* and even Sikh *gurus* and beliefs has been going on. The Muslim *pirs* and Sikh *gurus* are imbued with beneficence and Tharus look to them for personal favours and gains (ibid.: 218)

A recent discussion of the Tharu living in Bihar *Tarai* reaffirms the view. Srinivashan and Ranjan (2006: 108–9) observe that community 'interaction and interrelation with Hindu society over a long time has not eventually resulted in the Tharu becoming Hinduised ... have of course adapted some components of Hindu way of life, just as local society have adapted some of their .... Worship of Shiva, Hanuman, Satya Narayan, Kali, Durga, Brahma ... say they are positively oriented towards the Hindu social order but do not accept that they are Hindus ... make a sharp distinction between themselves and non Tharus'.

Thus, the Tharu have adapted and adopted features from the neighbouring society, including Buddhism in Bihar *Tarai* (ibid.: 110) and in the process, as Majumdar observes, have relaxed practices like tribal endogamy, allowed bringing women from the outside and, thus, infuse 'ethnic mixture and strength'.

The Khasa Religion

Majumdar's attention to the fraternal polyandrous society in Jaunsar-Bawar and adjoining areas began from certain remarks about it made by Malinowski in one of his seminars in London. After his return to India, Majumdar started his field work in Jaunsar-Bawar and the adjoining Rawaain areas, publishing his first paper on 'Sex and Marriage in the Doon District' (72: 1939). He has observed that the Khasa culture in the area has been deeply impressed by contact with Dom the aboriginal elements who are of Austric extraction, while the Khasa claim to be Hindus, fast adopting Hindu names, beliefs and practices, etc. to bring their identity close to the Hindus of the plains. However, practices like remarrying widows, polyandry, legal recognition of divorce traditionally place them apart. Because of their geographical location, the Khasa have lived in comparative isolation. Majumdar describes in a comparative manner (220: 1962: 250) the various elements of Khasa beliefs regarding cosmos and other phenomenon with the Munda (Australoid) and the Hindu beliefs in the plains and concludes:

> Their religion is a curious blend of Hindu and tribal beliefs and practices and a functional analysis of these, is sure to provide interesting material ... magic and religion closely interlaced ... magic plays an important role ... giving them confidence in danger and crisis as well as day to day life ... importance of the evil eye and evil tongue ... oaths and ordeals have significance. (ibid.: 250)

In their beliefs, magic, sorcery and evil eye, etc. the role of *Baki* (diviner) in propitiating the spirit/god responsible is important. At the same time *Baki* is also the medium of 'possession by the Mahasu *deota* who is their chief deity or their real *deota*. Mahasu originally belongs to Kulu and the Pandavas are believed to have established the most important Mahasu temple at Hanol in Jaunsar-Bawar which was originally a Vishnu temple. The Mahasu religious complex carries historical antiquity reflecting, cultural traits diffused from outside and assimilated in the local culture' (ibid.: 257). The Hanol temple is a place of pilgrimage for the entire Jaunsar-Bawar and also the people from many other places in Himachal Pradesh and Garhwal. Mahasu also tops a hierarchy of a number of spirits, gods and goddesses of an inferior order.[1] These fall in two categories, *Birs* who attend on Mahasu and those who do not attend or serve Mahasu. The organization of his 'cult' also perpetuates and supports a variety of rules of conduct for the few different castes found in the area. It has assigned roles and duties for them wherein the Kolta is a menial, viewed as defiled and untouchable with a peripheral role, though unavoidable (Bhatt, 2010: 362).

Baki are only from the Rajput and Brahman castes and they become *Baki* on the basis of some intuition, dream or vision and begin sacrifices to the *deota* which 'opens his tongue and thus this person comes to be regarded as a seer/diviner'. Jaunsaris also believe in *bhut* or *chudail* as the forms which the spirits of certain dead persons take. Majumdar is of the view that the origins of various spirits and their power lie in the environment of the people, which generated such beliefs. In this area, the high hills, dense forests and dark and stormy nights constantly reinforce such beliefs.

The customary system of the enforcement of cultural code included an important place for ordeals. However, this practice is not common any more, though swearing by gods or before Mahasu on oath is common and it is practised even in formal law courts.

The festivals which the Khasa observe are inter-village and inter-*khat* affairs, buttressing their social solidarity and reinforcing the caste hierarchy and the lower status of the Dom and Kolta (Hasnain, 2012: 80–85). Mahasu *deota* is worshipped along with some local beliefs and faiths. A great deal of social cooperation is needed because the festivals are celebrated on a large scale for days together. The four important festivals are *Magh*, after rabi crop has been sown; *Bissu*, in the month of April which is celebrated in the name of Mahasu and Shilguru the god of sheep; *Mond* a festival in May–June which is celebrated across *Khat* boundaries for fishing and cutting of *timur* tree for collecting its bark; and *Pahari* Diwali another important festival during which the dances and mimicry performed include demonstrating the lower position of the Kolta and Bajgi. Thus, these festivals and the ritualistic dances, etc. which form their part contribute to the structural specifics of the area, reasserting the superior and power position of the Khasa vis-à-vis the lower castes. Majumdar's ethnography of the religion and festival of the Khasa does not, however, fully document the Kolta related aspects of the Jaunsari society.

Dasserah in Bastar

The foregoing brief presentation of Majumdar's observations on the religious life in different tribes, a tribe-caste village and a region bring out how he was constantly interested and concerned with study of religion as it functions in a human collectivity and how the religious practices and changes therein affect various aspects of the life of the concerned community. In this context we can also refer to how he viewed a very important yearly celebration of a Hindu festival in a multi-tribal context. Majumdar's Presidential Address, Section of Anthropology, Indian Science Congress at Lahore (73: 1939), entitled 'Tribal Cultures and Acculturation', deals with, inter alia, the rituals and other practices connected with the celebrations of Dasserah in Bastar which continues for about a fortnight.

Bastar was a princely state during colonial times headed by the Raja of Bastar. The family which ruled, as the legend goes, was established there by the grace of goddess Danteshwari whose main temple is situated in Dantewada, south Bastar. The state, a part of the colonial Eastern States Agency, was a large and important state before its merger after Independence and inclusion in the reorganized state of Madhya Pradesh. It was heavily forested and inhabited by a number of tribes and castes. The Dhakar is regarded as the highest caste or Chhatriyas with Halbas next to them. The tribal groups are Murias, Marias, Dhurvas and Gadvas sharing a common culture with minor variations. In religious worship and other practices, the Halba and Dhakar cultural pattern 'is an open one and which is very much build upon an aboriginal foundation' (73: 1939: 12). 'Tribal groups are coming together as sharer of a common cultural existence, except the Marias of Abujmarh hills'. Majumdar stresses that the culture of other castes of Bastar like 'Kurukhas, Kewats or Dhimar, suggest (that) ... its caste system essential characteristics which favoured its growth and persistence were most probably of tribal origin' (ibid.: 16). Anthropometric evidence collected by Majumdar does not show much variation between the different castes and tribal groups in Bastar. Majumdar goes on to describe two institutions of Bastar, *Ghotul* an indigenous cultural institution and then an institution of the advanced culture, the Dasserah festival. The observations on *Ghotul* discuss the functions that this institution performs in the tribal life.

> The Dasserah festival on the other hand has a different tale for it has been introduced by the ruling family and participation of all tribes and castes of the state is regarded as more or less obligatory'. (ibid.: 33)

Danteshwari is the family goddess of the founder of Bastar family. The Dasserah festival is held in her honour and except perhaps the Maria of Abujmarh, all other groups participate in the festival including the Marharas a Hinduized untouchable caste of weavers, and they are the traditional priests in the temple of Kachin where the ruling chief has to pray before he undertakes to perform the ceremonies connected with Dasserah. The cycle of worship has different shrines and the end of 15 days celebration in the Danteshwari temple located in the palace compound of Jagdalpur, as well as the bringing of Danteshwari *Devi* from her main temple in Dantewada on a palanquin, the movement of the Raja in two chariots (*raths*), large and small, and the pulling of these chariots by large crowds of different tribes who assemble, abdication by the Raja of his secular position of the ruler to the Diwan, and his assuming the position, behaviour, dress, etc. of an ascetic, as also substituting a chosen Halba for the required penance instead of himself, all have the various tribes and castes as participants. The roles they assume include priestly duties, helping hands in the worships, bringing different kinds of objects and material required, chariot construction with sal wood and pulling these chariots are all taken up by different castes and tribes including Brahmans and Chhatriyas during a period of 15 days. The festival ends with the Raja reassuming his secular duties. For this ceremonial assumption the Raja is brought in a chariot pulled by the Dandami Marias who reside in the entire area. It shows 'how far the different tribes cooperate among themselves in social, economic and religious life' (ibid.: 38). Majumdar observes that in southern India where also various castes and tribes have been assigned duties in the organization of temple worship. The two prominent racial groups, Australoid or Pre-Dravidian and the Aryan, share duties which do not bring them together into close contact as the worships are done by the members of the entire castes.

> In Bastar, however, the cooperation between the various cultural groups which do not appear to have maintained their ethnic identity is more real and the inferior cultural groups have not been denied important roles in the organization and performance of the worship .... In Bastar the fact of their cultural difference has been forgotten and there is one festival for all in which rites and customs of primitive and advanced cultures have blended together. (ibid.: 39–40)

Analysing this process in Bastar, where like Dasserah examples of reciprocal relationship and interdependence in economic and social spheres is seen,

Majumdar examines whether the biological concept of 'symbiosis' as used by Nadel explains such 'group contact and consequential reaction'. Majumdar doubts whether symbiosis would be a suitable concept for the process. He opines that what Nadel called a symbiotic relationship is connoted by the process of acculturation and we have seen how reciprocity and mutuality of obligations between the various social groups of a culture area have led to acculturation which has linked section with section and produced an interesting culture complex (ibid.: 41).

Religion in a Tribe-Caste Village

Chitaura, a village studied by Majumdar in Sonbhadra district of UP, is an area where tribe and caste populations come together and live in mixed villages. This village is inhabited by five tribes and 12 castes. The religious practices here include regular worship of Shiva in the five *deosthans*, out of a total of six such places of worship. The Shiv *deosthan* were constructed in the village about 100 years ago. Mondays are specially regarded as the days for Shiva worship and both castes and tribes participate in the *kirtan* that take place there on Mondays. However, the tribal participants do not sit on the raised platforms of the *deosthan*. A very important place where both tribes and castes make offerings is the *deosthan* or platform where Nanku Manjhi, the original tribal settler of this village and its official *supurdar*, and his wife were buried. Even Brahmans make offerings there. On the day of the main worship which is held once in three years, offerings of he-goat, pig, cock, seven bottles of country liquor, sweets, areca nuts, tobacco and hemp are made. The Baiga conducts the ritual and also performs a *havan*. The spirit of Nanku Manjhi is invoked, and makes him the medium for answering the questions put by the people regarding their problems. After the worship and *havan* at this place, people led by the Baiga go to the *deosthan* of *Mahadani*, a spirit ruling the village. *Havan* is performed there as well and *Mahadani's* spirit makes the Baiga her medium to answer questions. During this ritual the Baiga goes on uttering the words, '*deota*, come and take your *prasad* and protect us'. This fair and ritual offering at Nanku Manjhi's *chabutara* is continuing even now and it has in fact become more elaborate and better participated with the *chabutara* built into a walled place with sacred flags (Saksena, 2013: 13–14).

The Baiga also conducts a number of rituals connected with agricultural seasons, for instance, the *tod pooja* conducted before the sowing of *rabi* crop and then again ritual and offerings made in every field before planting paddy. The Baiga also performs a *havan* in the name of *Mahadani* and makes offerings when a plot is taken up for agriculture for the first time.

The people of Chitaura believe in two types of magic – beneficial and malevolent. *Ojha* are the magicians who perform beneficial magical practices while female *dains* and male *daiya* are believed to control evil spirits for malevolent purposes. The beneficial magical practices cure snake bite, evil eye, several types of diseases, and diseases of cattle. The *Ojha* invokes the spirits of ancestors or his *gurus* to counter *dains* or *daiya* who perform these practices. A documentation of several cases of the two types of magical practices is from both the tribe and caste families.

The belief in omens, good and bad days and time, two kinds of dreams that forewarn of good and bad events and other omens are widely believed in by both the tribal and caste groups. If the dreams are forewarnings of bad events, then the person consults the *Ojha* and the remedy suggested include sacrifice to some evil spirits or offerings to some god.

Among life cycle rituals, the Hindu castes follow their traditional practices while among the tribal groups there is the practice of a ritual to determine whether the dead person would be reborn in the family or not. This practice is common among Munda tribes and Ho as well.

Discussion

The six short notes from the ethnographic presentations in Majumdar's writings presented in previous sections, cover a very extensive range of human societies in India. From a small and very backward tribe facing a crisis of existence, to medium sized and large tribal societies who have adapted healthily to the impact of another more advanced culture, to a mixed rural community, to an isolated regional society with two distinct strata of ethnic and cultural stock, we find how religion as well as magic function in these cultures. As already mentioned, Majumdar frankly states that theorizing on religion has not been much of his aim and its detailed ethnography actually aims at, if we use Evans-Pritchard's (1965: 120) words, 'religion is what religion does, for the social anthropologists'. As such, there have been theories about primitive religion and its origins but a definition has been rather difficult. The closest that Majumdar attempts as a definition is when he says: 'Then there is religion; it is the human response to the apprehension of something, or power, which is super natural and supra-sensory. It is the expression of the manner, and the type of adjustment effected by people with their conception of the super natural' (177: 1956: 151).

Study of Religion – Methodology

Majumdar in his study of *Bongaism* has also repeated his observations which he has made at several other places, viz. the impact of a dominant culture like Hinduism makes on tribal cultures. And, in the context of primitive religions, the changes resulting from such an impact have to be very carefully handled by the investigator. Spelling out the proper methodology therefor, he observes:

> It is therefore necessary to handle our field material on primitive religion very carefully. The blending of cultures in tribal areas has produced a complex cultural life even among the most unsophisticated of the primitive groups. Many ideas are new, the old ones have been put forward in new garb and questions regarding the authenticity of recorded statements when put to tribal people, today, elicit answers in accordance with their interpretation of the motive of the person making such inquiries. (79: 1940: 62)

The careful analysis of Munda beliefs and rites 'collected firsthand by trained ethnographers' would provide some evidence about 'religion *as it was*', and nothing perhaps is more important to the history of religion than beliefs and practices which claim an antiquity and are regarded with sanctity by the people concerned. Three types of evidence can be discerned about the religious life of the Munda Tribes:

- the testimony of writers who have given detailed and meticulous accounts of Munda religion;
- the dream experiences of the people through which even today they regulate their religious life;
- the hymns and prayers of the people addressed to their tribal gods which in all religious worships detail the roles of the gods and discuss their nature and personality if there be any (ibid.: 63).

In the backdrop of this approach to study of religion, Majumdar's ethnography primarily documents the social functions that religion performs along with magic, witchcraft, prayer, sacrifice, propitiation and so on in the given human societies. He sums up this view:

> Failures of magic are corrected by further magic and thus .... In course of time magic must be reinforced by supplicatory rites, for the essence of magic is coercion and when it fails approach to the higher powers can be effected only through prayers and prescriptions which define the role of gods and deities or superior powers .... When spell is transformed into prayer, magic yields to religion .... Both magic and religion are 'tools of adaptation' .... Yet magic plays its role in society and in its extremely differentiated form it hinges on beliefs in a mystical impersonal force called *mana*, *wakua* or *bonga* .... Magic also assumes a uniformity of nature and this brings it in line with science .... (221: 1961: 418–19)

Majumdar propounds the view that in all primitive religions in India there is a belief in a mystic super power. However, the belief is that this power extends to both animate and inanimate objects and forces of nature as well as the spirit or soul or *mana* in individuals. Different primitive cultures, however, attribute anthropomorphism to this force or power in different ways. In some societies hardly any anthropomorphism has developed while in other cultures this process may have concretized the 'force' to different extents. He, however, thinks that in the more primitive societies the extent of anthropomorphism is the least.

Since the Ho, Majumdar's first ethnographic field, are a Mundari tribe and it was suggested to him for study by S.C. Roy, the influence of Roy's writings and thought should obviously be there. Roy (1912, 1995: 296) makes the following observations regarding the religious beliefs of the Munda:

(i) Munda believe in a supreme deity, Sing-Bonga, whose blessings they invoke before every important religious ceremony, he has indeed no specific worship except in cases of serious general calamities when he is invoked and a white fowl is sacrificed.

(ii) The other Bongas are the spirits of his dead ancestors and presiding deity of the village. They are *mana-ting* Bongas, gods who have to be worshipped.

(iii) Then, there are malevolent spirits who require to be acquiesced or propitiated, the *Banita* Bongas, some of them are spirits of persons who die unnatural death. The *Pahan* (village priest) does not propitiate them. This is done by *deonras*, often a non-Munda.

(iv) The fourth class of spiritual entities are nature gods, including *Nage-era*; they stand midway between the beneficent and malevolent spirits.

(v) Mundas also believe in guardian angels of particular families and classes like married women, the *achrael* Bonga.

Over these inferior classes of powers and spirits rules the great Sing-Bonga by whose appointment they hold their places and perform their functions. On death of a Munda, his *rowa* or soul is carried away by the *Jomraja*. The belief in rebirth is 'yet in a rudimentary stage'.

In the notes on religion based on Majumdar's ethnography, his developing the concept of Bongaism on the basis of his observations of the basic theme of Ho religious beliefs as well as practices has been of great significance. Sarana (1961: 8–9) describes it as the Indian parallel to the Melanesian term *mana*. Bonga is a conception of power, impersonal and omnipresent, beneficial and vague. This power, though it has no anthropomorphism, condenses itself and thus can be identified with things or objects of the Ho surroundings or environment. Read with what we have noted above of Roy's writing on Munda religion, at least a quarter century before Majumdar's *Transition*, we can see the way Majumdar has conceived of what he describes as 'roots of primitive religion' and religion 'as it was' (79: 1940: 63–64), and from this hypothesis emanates his basic thinking that a belief in such a force or power forms the substratum of primitive religion everywhere.

The discussion on Bongaism in *Affairs* attributes a base for this belief in the *gestalt* psychological approach as well. Bongaism, thus, springs from 'a general emotional attitude towards the entire primitive milieu of the tribal people. The total tribal environment and the objects therein are psychologically felt to be a part of himself, by the tribal man to which he is well adjusted; except when he has to find ways to remedy a difficult situation when because of the introduction of the adverse forces he perceives it to have become 'strange'. This psychological state of fear sets in because the primitive man cannot 'view his personality as distinct from the environment'. Therefore, he has to not only find an explanation but also the remedies in the form of magic, religion, rituals, prayers, supplication, etc. Sarana (1961: 10) has described Majumdar's explanation as 'a good example of a 'conscious model' constructed by an anthropologist to interpret a social phenomena'.

Significantly, Sing-Bonga, the supreme Bonga, Majumdar observes, is 'an un-worshipped god' though his blessings are sought at the time of various propitiatory rites and making offerings to the lesser Bongas in the hierarchy as well as the *eras*. The elaborate description and discussion of the Ho pantheon also brings out the presence of two distinct agents or ministers who carry out the propitiatory and other rites intended to address the hierarchy – the *deuri* and the *deonwa*. The *deonwa* is the hereditary priest of the village and is always a Ho, while the *deuri* can be from non-Ho tribes or a caste. 'The *deuri* is entrusted only with the worship of benevolent deities like Sing-Bonga, Nage-Bonga, *Disauli* who are few in number'. *Deonwa* deals with 'a legion of spirits, malevolent and mischievous ... most of the spirits which the *deonwa* has to propitiate are of a foreign origin, and new ones are created' (131: 1950: 258–59). Earlier, Majumdar has already observed that most of the malevolent spirits or Bongas in the Ho pantheon have been incorporated from alien culture generally the Oriya Hindu culture in the neighbouring areas. This dichotomy of agents of ministration for the indigenous pantheon and borrowed pantheon in the primitive religion is not unique to the Ho. We find it among other tribes too, like the Tharu, the Khasas and the Gonds (Singh, 1944: 154–55). Thus, in a way, the entry of alien gods and spirits often associated with the kind of human problems not known in the past to a tribal society and which have to be appeased because of the new and different kinds of calamities opens up the entry for their ministers/agents belonging to the impacting culture.

Another remarkable feature traceable to alien influence in the death rites of the Ho is connected with *Sasan-diri*, the stones placed on the graves of dead ancestors in the burial ground (*Sasan*) in the village. In the 'advanced villages, there is no superstition for these funerary slabs, and no religious respect for the remains of the ancestors ... in many villages men and women sit, eat their meals, tell stories and indulge in various other pastimes'; even though some of the stones are anointed with oil and vermilion occasionally (131: 1959: 44). This is a clear instance also of 'sacred' being turned into 'profane'.

The concept of Bongaism as put forward by Majumdar also attracted some comments from R.R. Marett. Writing about 'Bongaism', Marett (1938) had observed that, 'the Ho religion is at the pre-animistic level when gods and spirits have little and no individuality and all turns on securing the aid of Bonga or a wonder working power, by means of any one vehicle or other that may be handy'. The term 'Bongaism', as Majumdar later explains, 'has been coined by me in describing the religion of the Hos. The power of Bonga has also been compared by him to the belief in *mana* among Melanesian people. Marett (1938) had further 'evolved a special form of animalist theory which he called *manaism'* which is born out of their belief in a certain understandable, impersonal, non-material and un-individualized supernatural power which takes abode in all the objects, animate and inanimate ...' (177: 1956: 155–56). Certain other attributes of this 'animalist' power are that it is more or less beyond the reach of the senses, may differ in intensity of the degree in which it is present in a person or an object, which may explain the differences and position of power and status of persons as well. Thus, 'Majumdar's description and analysis of the conception of Bonga ... falls in line with Marett's theory of primitive religion' (ibid.: 156). However, Majumdar through his ethnographic studies on different tribes in India appears to correlate his concept of Bongaism also to the facts of cultural change brought about by the influence of Hinduism as well as intertribal contact situations. But, he asserts, the concept of Bongas with its emphasis on the impersonal character of the Bongas, as gathered from the hymns and prayers addressed to the Bongas, points out to its essentially being a substratum and rather original feature of tribal religion because, according to him:

> In the hymns and prayers addressed to the gods of the Hindu pantheon, we get ideas about the shape, form and nature of the divinities. The features of the Hindu divinities, are faithfully portrayed in them, but, no such reference is found in the tribal hymns and prayers; the latter are protective formulae, which refer to the dangers to which the Hos are exposed, and supplications to the Bongas to protect their life and property form their main theme ... these are addressed to the Dessauli, which represents the supernatural power of their habitat and as such does not possess any shape, size or complexion. It is either the power of this village, that village or of a group of villages. The higher the number of villages in a group, the greater is the power of the Dessauli and the Diuri who serves the Dessauli gains his status in the village in accordance with the effectiveness of his rendition of these hymns and prayers. (79: 1940: 72–73)

As a part of the study of Ho religious beliefs, Gautam Sankar Ray, Department of Anthropology, Calcutta University, along with G. Chattopadhyaya and B. Banerjee (1954: 288–300), made some basic criticism of the concept of Bongaism and the belief in Bonga as put forth by Majumdar in *Transition* and *Affairs*. Essentially, Ray, on the basis of this study of Ho residing in the adjoining state of Saraikella (Orissa), contended that the Ho beliefs in Sing-Bonga *was anthropomorphic* as also were the beliefs relating to certain other Bongas; the hierarchy of Bongas and eras among the Ho of Sarikella was rather different or even absent; the place of abode of certain Bongas as indicated by Majumdar's studies were incorrect; and Majumdar's recognition of 'a world of Bongas' was contradictory to the idea of a supreme power as held out by him. Ray et al. observed:

> In conclusion we beg to suggest that there is still a possibility of reconstructing the basic form of Ho religious beliefs and practices by further field work among the different sections of the Ho people, and by comparing their ideas with those of allied tribes like the Munda, Kharia, Birhor and Santal before they lose all their past traditions under pressure of a rapidly changing economy.

Majumdar comments on this critique (164: 1954: 346–350) contesting the issues raised therein primarily on three grounds. First, the critic's field work among the Ho of Saraikella was of a short duration and it was not conducted in the Ho language while Majumdar himself did his fieldwork in the language spoken by the tribe. Secondly, the terms and the beliefs thereby connoted may differ somewhat in the two areas in question; and thirdly the influence of Hindu neighbours has been bringing about changes in the beliefs and practices of the tribal people and this impact may differ from area to area. Ray et al. had also quoted from a review of *Transition* appearing in *Man in India* which according to them was presumably written by S.C. Roy, wherein Majumdar's views were not agreed to. In this context, Majumdar quoted the same review wherein the reviewer had said that, 'the kind of Ho customs and beliefs appears to be in general fairly accurate and the inferences drawn up by the writer are on the whole probable'. It may be added here that we have already brought out the similarities between Roy's description of Munda religion (1912) with Majumdar's findings and his conceptual frame of Bongaism.

The concept of Bongaism, that is a belief in a supreme being, the Creator of the world and also its destroyer, at least once, an un-worshipped God otherwise, but approached in situations of deep crisis and the One who is at the apex of a hierarchy of gods and deities, who ordains, which Majumdar has described in his ethnography can be compared to similar beliefs of Hinduism. However, Majumdar has argued convincingly that the concept was indigenous to tribal India particularly the tribes of Munda origins, including Korwa. Bose commenting on the deep interest of Majumdar in the religions of primitive Indian tribes observes:

> In some of his writings there is an indication that he also thought that many of the superior ideas in Hindu religion were already present among our brethren inhabiting the mountains and jungles of India. (1961: i)

The discussion above highlights how Majumdar tried to study both the original or 'as it was' features of tribal religion as also the changes which had been occurring in both its basic thoughts as well as pantheon, manner of placation, etc. because of the growing influence of Hinduism primarily, as generally practised by the lower castes living around the tribal areas, the religion of other tribes in the neighbourhood, and also Christianity. Since, Majumdar in his ethnography was particular about documenting changes his methodology for the study of religion obviously emphasizes this, broadly from the functional viewpoint. Bose's comment, quoted above, clearly picks up this aspect and tries to connect it with Hindu religion.

To conclude, it can be said that the brief notes on religious thought, beliefs and practices of the tribes, in a focused way, bring out some common features:

- His analysis of *Bongaism* underlines how certain 'superior ideas in Hindu religion were already present' there.
- Anthropomorphism, multiplicity of gods and goddess in pantheon and their functional role in assuaging crisis situations of individuals or society and hierarchy among the pantheon can be seen as some of the features which have been making their way into tribal religions.
- Underrunning some of the changes in tribal religion is a psychological state of disquiet, anxiety and fear from the other dominant cultures and government, and this has contributed substantially to the changes in beliefs and practices, in order to face or counter it.
- This situation has contributed to changes in religion by way of incorporation of new gods and goddesses with their Hindu names and qualities, adoption and adaptation of modified Hindu gods and their names, eg. *'Jomraja'* for *'Yamraj'* (god of death), and nascent adoption of ideas of rebirth and retribution.
- Borrowings are not just confined to beliefs and pantheon but also to the engagement of religious and magic functionaries for servicing them, eg. *Deuri* from lower castes among the Ho, Pahari Brahmans among the Tharu

and Ojha among the Korwa. These functionaries help the tribals in placating the effect of malevolent gods, spirits, magical practices, etc., and some benevolent ones for averting natural calamities.

The process, as concisely put forth by Majumdar, has been:

> If anything provides the primitive groups with a lease of life, with tools of adaptation, it is the change in their religious attitudes, in their mode and manner of worship, in the personalities of their indigenous pantheon and in general religious beliefs. It is not, however, necessary that their religious life should undergo a transformation, or a metamorphosis. What is needed is an elasticity in their attitude to religious beliefs and prescriptions, and the Munda speaking tribes show such elasticity in no small measure. (79: 1940: 61–62)

Another very important conclusion which Majumdar has drawn up clearly from his studies of a variety of tribal religions is, as he says, in the *Affairs*:

> Analyzing tribal religion further it is seen that in the field there does not exist any distinction between animism and popular Hinduism. Elwin found that the distinction between tribal religion and Hinduism or the previous classification into animism and Hinduism is meaningless. Both tribal people and Hindus are always willing to worship a few more gods for advantages. From this angle the tribal religion represents today, marginal religion, and even an elaborate tribal religion that of Gonds of central India can hardly be distinguished from the religion obtained among the lower castes of Hindus. The latter have incorporated many tribal gods. Similarly, tribal religion has been permeated with Hindu ideas, rites and rituals, very similar to popular Hinduism. (131: 1950: 269)

Such a conclusion has not come from Majumdar alone. In fact Majumdar himself quotes Elwin in this regard and also Hutton and Risley.

On the other hand, the catholicity of Hinduism particularly the practices and beliefs of the lower and middle level Hindu castes is also patent. And as Sarana (1961: 11) has quoted Radhakrishanan's famous statement that, 'Hinduism absorbs everything that enters into it, magic or animism, and raises it to a higher level' as 'Hinduism is not a movement, not a position; a process not a result; a growing tradition, not a fixed revelation'.

It may be observed from the above description that how Majumdar passionately analysed religions aspects of various comments and almost proved that religion is a part of the holistic structure of tribal life.

Note

1. Bhatt (2010), in his study, in depth, has pointed out that Mahasu is not the God or the Supreme Being. He is a *deota*, deity/god, and not 'exclusively sacred .... Carries prominent traits of profanity, for beside being *deota*, Mahasu is also Raja (ruler) to the followers of the cult' (ibid.: 1). Mahasu *deota* and his cult is dubbed as 'tribal', but basically it is Hindu. It is not 'Brahmanical' .... Intricately has its own organizational trait (ibid.: 31). The belief system shows Mahasu as a divine crusader against injustice, tyranny and *Rakshasi* deeds ... divine administrator of justice and security ... symbol of hope and a safety valve against familial and other conflicts (ibid.: 180).

4

Culture Contact and Culture Change

Majumdar's Presidential Address to the Section of Anthropology, Indian Science Congress 1939, is entitled, 'Tribal Cultures and Acculturation'. By then he had published his monograph on the Ho (1937). Apart from the Ho, Korwa, a small tribe, living in Mirzapur district of UP had received his attention and he had published more than half a dozen papers on various aspects of the Korwa culture. As pointed out earlier, his interest in social change or change in tribal cultures came to elicit a new focus on the basis of what he perceived of the culture change among the Korwa. He refers to it in this presidential address along with other issues connected with the kind of decline in the culture of tribes coming into contact with advanced and 'active' cultures. Around this time, the tribes of Central Provinces specially the most important one, the Gond, had also drawn his interest, and he had made field trips in the area specially Bastar which was then a princely state, largely with tribal population belonging to several tribes, all 'known to belong to the Gond race'. Moreover, 'the foreigners and migrants who have settled in the state are believed to have freely mixed with the native population' (73: 1939: 5). Thus, the situation of cultural contact and resultant changes in this area presented a scenario ideal for studying the processes and impact of contact between Hindus and tribes.

In his opening remarks, Majumdar stresses that the ethnographic approach of studying one tribe or caste in a particular area and producing a monograph on it had its advantages. He, however, felt that there was one inherent drawback in this monographic delineation of cultures:

> A defect which becomes increasingly vital as we proceed to describe cultures which have been penetrated by other cultures. The monographic method in amateur hands has invariably failed to separate the native warp from the foreign woof, and has failed also to evaluate the importance of the role of diffusion in cultural progress. In India most of the tribal groups have come in contact with higher social groups and rites and customs introduced from

> highly organized societies have blended with those of a primitive or infantile character. (ibid.: 1–2)

Under the circumstances, this highly scientific method has to be pursued differently so as to estimate 'how far social life has deflected from tribal norms under pressure of alien cultures'. And, this has:

> Made me undertake a comparative study of the social institutions of a number of groups living in a particular geographical area, in order to estimate the role of cultural contacts in primitive social life. Analysis has shown significant are the effects of such contacts, how social groups are adapting themselves to changed socio-economic conditions, also how maladoption is leading to tribal extinction or absorption into more dynamic and vital cultures. (ibid.: 2)

Developing his presentation with the aforesaid objective, Majumdar proceeds as follows:

- He identifies '12 groups' living in Bastar in the order of social precedence. Dhakars and Halbas are at the top while hill Mariyas are at the 'bottom of the social ladder'. In addition, there are five functional groups, numerically not very large, and they are of indigenous origins. This is confirmed by their physical features. They intermarry with the tribes when they live in their areas and they are small, scattered all over the state.
- Cultural differences between the various groups are not very sharp or well defined and, importantly, the transition from one group to the other is indeed difficult to discern except the groups at the extremes of the scale which differ significantly.
- Linguistically the common dialect is Halbi which is a mix of Hindi, Oriya and Marathi, akin to Chhatisgarhi spoken in the wider area. The tribals also speak different dialects of Gondi language and the tribes like Mariyas of Abujmarh hills who remain isolated speak a purer Gondi.
- Though, the state can be divided into linguistic zones, the frontiers of language are uncertain and show influence of each other as also the language in the adjoining provinces.
- Majumdar also makes a comparison of 16 absolute somatic characters of 10 main groups and works out the crude coefficient of racial likeness (CRL) earlier used by Morant which is not, however, a very reliable indicator as per the authorities quoted. However, Majumdar still presents the analysis of the data, he had personally collected.
- The conclusion, he draws, which seems to be rather too general, is:

> It may be suggested that the inter-relation between the various cultural groups in Bastar indicate an ethnic miscegenation and groups speaking the same or allied languages are more intimately related than those speaking different tongues .... .
>
> In most of the characters, the Halbas show the highest standard deviations while the Parjas come next to the Halbas. This is expected as both the Halbas and Parjas are recruited from various tribes and castes and they represent only cultural patterns and not ethnic groups. (ibid.: 10)

The cultural groups and their ethnographic descriptions are interesting. The narration traces how a small group of Kshtriyas came to occupy this area inhabited almost solely by tribals and how the migrant group was numerically strengthened through the dictates of the Raja. He introduced widow remarriage among the four higher castes but marriages with tribal women also went on because of a shortage of women. Dhakars and Halbas were the two higher castes, after Brahmans and Kshtriyas who occupy fertile tracts in the midst of tribal groups and marriages with tribal women among them still goes on. This mixed settlement has made it possible for the Muriyas and Mariyas 'who adapt many of their alien traits' while the Halbas themselves 'have confirmed consciously or unconsciously to the prevailing tribal pattern of culture – a similar material culture and belief in sorcery. Thus, the Halba, whose dialect is spoken throughout Bastar, is a group 'which is very much built upon an aboriginal foundation with an open cultural pattern'.

- As regards Dhurvas, they have assimilated many of the customs and practices of the higher cultural groups whose language they speak now. But their own beliefs and practices have not been abandoned, though sometimes attenuated.
- The Bhatras are a little higher in social scale than the Parjas, they have come to have some subgroups claiming distinct social status as a result of Hinduization. The Hinduized sections put on sacred thread and consider themselves higher than those who 'still adhere to tribal prescription'. They practice permanent cultivation as is the case with Parjas.

The tribal villages in Bastar are almost self-sufficient. Usually, there is a family of blacksmith or other artisans which provide services to its village and also some adjoining villages. This artisan element also comes probably from a tribal substratum. These artisan groups are similar to those among Saoras of the adjoining Andhra areas (Arisis, Kundals, and Lohars). Some of them now constitute separate endogamous castes though marriages with Saoras are still not barred.

The above tribe-caste dynamics as seen in Bastar and its adjoining areas and also among Saoras of Orissa suggests:

> A plausible solution of the origin of caste. The caste system in its present form may be a post-Aryan development, but its essential characteristics which favoured its growth and persistence were most probably of tribal origin. The Kurukhs, Kewats or Dhimar who live by fishing in Bastar affords an example on this point. (ibid.: 16)

The Kurukhs are fisherman and they are indispensable to the social economy of the Mariyas' country. The same is the position about the Rawats of Bastar who tend cattle of the people. The process looks like that 'a clean caste was created among the unclean aboriginals' and given recognition as such by the Rajas. According to Grigson:

> A large number of the persons returned as members of the Hindu functional castes, the graziers, potters, fishermen, weavers, blacksmiths and others, are in

> reality members of the primitive tribes speaking their language and only differentiated from them by their occupation. There is nothing in their appearance to distinguish these persons from other aboriginals, they follow their tribal religions whether enumerated as such or as Hindus. (ibid.: 17)

The material culture of the people, both castes and tribes, is very simple and the wants of the people are not varied. However, certain artistic items like ornaments, combs and metal work are commonly made by different groups. There is no industry worth the name in the area and the 'wild tribes' are still accustomed to their nomadic lives in the forest, with an economy of hunting, collection and shifting cultivation.

Agriculture is now the mainstay, and permanent cultivation goes on among all the castes and tribes except for those living in forests and hills. However, irrigation and other better agricultural practices are not common. Where greater security of crops has been achieved through knowledge of agricultural practices, there has been a change in rituals connected with agriculture– sacrifices or magical practices have been replaced by thanksgiving services and ceremonial partaking of the new crops. Competition, though not so acute as yet, has replaced custom in some form and also multiplied the wants. The requirements for money for bride price and satisfying other needs become difficult to meet even now, and this has meant debts and a resultant system of bonded labour, *kabadi*. The system is met mostly in settled areas where alien settlers are there. Often a *kabadi* has to live in the outhouse of his master. Vigorous attempts to eradicate the system, declared illegal this year, have not succeeded much.

In the concluding section of this address, Majumdar presents his views on acculturation as a process. He argues that 'evolution (from many simple and isolated cultural groups) of a complex cultural solution or fusion could be marked into stages' (73: 1939: 40). Two case studies of cultural institutions – one indigenous viz. *gotul* or youth dormitory and the other of advanced culture, the Dusserah festival – precede this argument to support it.

Gotul – An Indigenous Cultural Institution

The case of *gotul* has been presented because in Bastar it is the pivot of social life, where found, and has often obscured the tribal and clan organization. Majumdar's approach in presenting the ethnographic account of *gotul* is a synthesis of evolutionary – diffusionsist and functional – configurational frame. The discussion on *gotul* basically argues that the origins and the mechanism connected with the *gotul* are significantly functional; though, its origins among widely distributed tribes and areas not only in India but abroad may be accidental inventions connected with the needs for security and protection among hunting and nomadic tribes. To quote:

> The origins of an institution, a custom or a religious rite may be an accident, as inventions usually are, but the complicated machinery of social formation that we have inherited today has gathered its complexity and momentum in course of its career .... The principles which underlie the survival of social institutions

> are indeed numerous ... . A cultural trait borrowed or indigenous, remains unchanged if it cannot be fitted into the existing structure of the society or if any change in form leads to maladjustment. Again an institution may be put to several uses. (ibid.: 31)

The dormitory, a youth organization, may have its origins in the needs of a hunting and nomadic community but in course of time it has become a vital venue for communal activities, socialization and training of youth and inculcation of discipline. It also ensures tribal endogamy. The configurational approach is reflected in the following statement:

> The social solidarity found in the dormitories reflects to a great extent on the tribal life and this perhaps accounts for the spontaneous discipline that characterizes the conduct of primitive life. (ibid.: 25)

The Dusserah Festival – An Institution of Advanced Culture

This festival, 'on the other hand, has a different tale to tell'. It has been introduced by the ruling family and 'participation of all tribes and castes of the state is regarded as more or less obligatory'.

The traditional observance of this festival has grown out of a legend narrating how an ancestor of the present ruling family fled from Warangal (Andhra Pradesh) as advised by his family goddess, Dhanteswari, in a dream and founded the present Bastar state. Annamdev, the founder, was a Rajput and he was accompanied by his priest and some representative Rajput families. The sword of Dhanteswari is worshipped as a symbol of the goddess in her temple at Jagdalpur, the capital of the state.

The festival is in honour of Dhanteswari and it is celebrated for 15 days, with a different programme of ceremonies each day. According to Majumdar:

> The peculiarity of this celebration is that it has brought together the various cultural groups in Bastar as sharers of a common heritage, for even the lowest of the castes has not been denied its share in the communal worship. Along with Dhanteswari a host of lesser powers and spirits, some indigenous, others borrowed ... are prayed to and propitiated by the people, which, however, bring animistic tribes and the many Hindu castes in a common religious fold ... . The totemistic Maharas had perhaps been responsible for the worship (of *Kachin*, perhaps a tortoise) but the clever adoption of this deity by the ruling family has solved the problem of incorporation of the Maharas in the Hindu community. (ibid.: 33–34)

The festival starts after making offerings to the souls of the ancestors, and the people living in Jagdalpur and neighbouring villages gather at the palace where the Raja heads the ceremonies. In the process of the festival both men and women from different castes and tribes fulfil their assigned roles including the priests connected with different deities in different temples. The Raja has to give up his royal duties and become a *Jogi* (ascetic) and resumes these secular duties after nine days. Interestingly, on the eleventh day, 'a kidnapping ceremony takes place ... by the Mariyas in a palanquin to a spot away from Jagdalpur where he has to encamp in Muriya settlements. On the occasion, the 'tribals also go for hunt in the forest and the game is offered to the Raja as a part of his food'. The Raja returns in the 'big chariot' guarded by Bhatras with bows and arrows. The Raja too carries a bow and arrows in his hands. Well organized arrangements are made for providing food and camping facilities to the villagers coming to Jagdalpur and the expenses are shared by the state and the contributions often as animals meant for sacrifice. Majumdar observes that:

> An analysis of the customary division of labour obtained during the Dusserah festival will show how far the different tribes cooperate among themselves in social, economic and religious life .... The respective importance of the various groups may be gauged by the duties each is required to perform, so that there is a well-assessed division of labour based on the numerical strength and cultural stage of the group concerned. The Bhatras parade armed with bows and arrows which are less effective than swords owned by the Halbas .... In some sense, however, the existence of the various groups as independent units has become difficult and inter-communication between them and reciprocity in their economic undertakings has become more real than before. (ibid.: 38–39)

On the basis of the above analysis Majumdar adds a comparison between the Dusserah festival in Bastar and the organization of the temple worship all over the South. He finds that in Bastar, 'cooperation between the various cultural groups, which do not appear to have maintained their ethnic identity, is more real and the inferior cultural groups have not been denied important roles'. On the other hand in South India, the 'arrangements and duties correspond to racial affiliation (australoid substratum and the 'Aryan speaking invaders')'. In the South 'the economic partnership between primitive and backward groups has been regarded as essential but no serious attempt has been made to bring together the different groups into a common religious fold. In Bastar the fact of their cultural difference has been forgotten and there is one festival for all in which rites and customs of primitive and advanced cultures have blended together (73: 1939: 40). At the end of his address, Majumdar observes:

> We have seen how reciprocity and mutuality of obligation between the various social groups of a culture area have led to acculturation which has linked section with section and produced an interesting cultural complex. (ibid.: 41)

He is of the view that the process of selective adoption (of traits) from other groups 'may be called acculturation'. All contacts between social groups lead to 'miscegenation of cultures'. Any group possessing vitality, as against loss of interest in life (which Majumdar had observed in his ethnographic study of the Korwa of Mirzapur) must adopt traits from other groups, of course selectively as the future of the adoptive groups would depend on the judicious selection of traits in the process of adoption.

As mentioned earlier, Majumdar visualizes that an 'evolution (from any simple and isolated cultural group) of (to) a complex cultural solution or fusion' (ibid.: 40) involves several stages of cultural change when the different cultural groups come in contact. He delineates these stages as, first associating temporarily for mutual benefit; secondly, as the bonds get closer groups associate permanently for mutual benefit (though the groups remain distinct) and; thirdly or finally, the distinctive characters of the different constituent cultural groups are lost. The case studies of one indigenous institution (*gotul*) and one of the advanced culture (the Dusserah festival) documents, to a certain extent, the stages in which the different cultural groups (tribes and castes) exist at the time of the study. Thereby, Majumdar presents his conceptualization of the process of acculturation through the Bastar scenario – the tribal groups which still retain the indigenous institution in strength, are in an earlier stage and the others are in the next stage, even when these 12 cultural groups do not show well pronounced somatological, linguistic and other cultural features.

Majumdar's theoretical orientations, particularly just before he had worked on this address, were from the British social anthropologists. In social anthropology, then, the evolutionary approaches derived from organic contexts were the sources for borrowing technical labels to describe social processes and institutions. And, he argues:

> If we have to borrow any biological concept to interpret such group cooperation and identity of interests, social commensalism would be more appropriate from both the anthropological and biological standpoints. (ibid.: 41)

This argument is necessitated by Majumdar's reference in the concluding part of his address entitled 'Symbiosis and Acculturation', to Nadel's use of the term social symbiosis in the context of a study of the culture of 'four different tribal sections originally distinct, separate cultural groups' who have migrated into their present domicile (Nadel, 1938). Majumdar describes the position of these four tribal groups as under:

> Today there exists between the separate localities and migrant strata the closest cooperation which is the fruit of a far-reaching adjustment. The social, economic and religious activities of these groups are shown to represent a reciprocity and interdependence linking section with section in the framework of a larger embracing social group unit, that is, as Dr Nadel calls, a symbiosis which represents the possible origin of clanship and is one of the three possible developments in attaining a social equilibrium between diverse cultural groups, cooperation, symbiosis and complete fusion. (ibid.: 40)

And, further on, Majumdar observing that the 'reciprocal relationship and interdependence in economic and social spheres' in Bastar 'presents a similar picture', he would like to examine whether the biological concept of symbiosis used by Nadel, could justifiably be borrowed. Examining the merits of the suitability of such a borrowing, Majumdar concludes that if, in any case, one has to borrow a biological term, 'social commensalism' would be more appropriate for the Indian situation. This term would describe the stages of contact and acculturation better. Therefore, the three possible stages given by Nadel (cooperation, symbiosis and complete fusion) would be cooperation, social commensalism and fusion. Majumdar's argument is:

> The idea of symbiosis would be applicable only if the groups of men were so completely dissimilar as to resemble different species of animals and secondly if there could be an organic union or internal partnership between the various cultural groups constituting the symbiosis, for symbiosis means an organic union or internal partnership between organisms of different species, so intimate that it can only be severed by death. Even if we replace organisms by cultural groups, as Dr Nadel suggests, and 'death' by discontinuance of continued cultural existence the analogy fails to answer other essentials of symbiosis. (ibid.: 41)

However, Nadel subsequently (1953: 179–80) states that he introduced the term 'symbiotic' to express this close, subjectively absolute and unalterable, interdependence which causes every section, as section, to assume specific duties (religious, political, etc.) on behalf of the community at large, i.e. on behalf of every other section.

And, further on, Nadel brings up a different kind of relationship, 'diacritical behaviour', which he distinguishes from symbiotic, thus:

> As we have said, any 'apportionment' of tasks to the groups segments also may be diacritical in that it serves to mark them off from one another. But it must be stressed that purely formal differences in behaviour between segments shade over into differences which have symbiotic importance. (ibid.: 179)

If we recall the pattern of assignments of different tasks to the participating cultural groups in the Dusserah festival of Bastar, it seems to this author that the pattern is one of 'diacritical behaviour'. And, this kind of significance thereof is further underlined by the fact that it was the state (Raja of Bastar) who is believed to have organized the festival in consultation with his priest, and assigned functions and duties to the different cultural groups residing in the area of Bastar, where he was trying to buttress the foundations of his rule. Thus, the entire scheme which bases itself on the allocation or 'apportionment' of roles or functions in a more or less egalitarian manner is 'diacritical', ordained by the state, and the state continues to play a determinant role in the entire celebrations. Probably, in its long history, the 'culture complex' has evolved its pattern or configuration with a firm set of beliefs among the participant groups. With the violent end of the dynastic sway this allocation or apportionment has also lost its rigour after 1960s.

Historically, the Kakatiyas kept Bastar under their rule for 20 generations and insulated for 400 years (Joshi, 1967). The post-1947 events in Bastar indicate that the then ruler came to believe in 'divine right of Kings' which was 'built upon their (the subjects) loyalty'. He, therefore, wanted to avoid its merger in the Indian Union. The merger eventually came in January 1948, but the ruler, Pravin Chandra Bhanjdeo, was set upon a course of confrontation with the Government of Madhya Pradesh which ended in his death during 1966 while he was making an effort to revolt against the state administration, supported by tribals (Joshi, 1967). The tribals were highly discontented as a result of the changed governance. In fact, certain parts of Bastar are today one of the main areas of violent movement under Naxal extremism.

Interestingly, in this context Ghurye (1943: 18) quotes Majumdar, in support of his argument on aborigines 'so called', without referring to Majumdar's analysis through two institutions and states, thus:

> Dr D.N. Majumdar has shown how the twelve main social groups are moderately differentiated in their cultures so that the transition from one to the next in order is not easy to discern, though the difference between the two groups at the extreme ends appears to be great. He has further illustrated the mutuality and cooperation of the various groups in the State festival of the Dasara. This feature of the socio-religious life of the Bastar he calls acculturation, which has linked section with section and produced an interesting culture complex.

This integration of tribes and a limited number of caste groups and the pattern of their limited loyalty to the Kakatiya state as also the connected religious beliefs and rituals have been perceptively commented upon by Nandini Sundar in her anthropological history of Bastar 1854–2006 (2007). Tracing the foundations and consolidation of Bastar state, which was ruled by a Kshtriya dynasty from the 13th century onwards, she observes:

> It is notable that the chariot processions and the celebration of Dusserah in Bastar coincided with the introduction of Brahmans, as two aspects of the process of achieving greater legitimacy ... . Contemporary descriptions of popular relations with the king revolve primarily around the issues of corvee and the Dusserah festival. Hegemony, it seems, was primarily achieved through two mechanisms– the ritualization of corvee as both a right and an obligation and the materiality of ritual within Dusserah – the integration through labour of different groups within the kingdom, and the integration of their Gods. Through the various rituals of Dusserah, the political history of the kingdom was expressed – the defeat of the various zamindaris and other territorial groups, as well as the fragility of Kakatiya rule and the king's dependence on the people. (ibid.: 55)

Sundar finds that the 15-day-long annual Dusserah festival is critical to the understanding of the Bastar polity. It also provides an alternative history, the one not laid out in 'linear time, but as several co-existing and contestary stories; one that subsume in a single event the dialectically produced relations between subalterns and sovereigns'. It also defines individual and collective identity.

As regards religious and ritual contents of Dusserah, she argues that even though Dhanteswari is one of the many goddesses, it is worshipped locally only because the king was able to establish and maintain his political power and 'gradually assimilate Dusserah and the worship of Dhanteswari to local festivals'. Significantly, she comments:

> Dhanteswari's position has to be seen through a hall of mirrors I mean that the rulers adopt 'tribal' gods and change them, and the tribals in turn adopt these changed gods and change them ... and so it goes on in endless mimesis. What is 'tribal' here, and what is 'Hindu'? Contra Ghurye, who used the phrase 'backward Hindus' for aboriginals, we might equally see the Hindus as

> overdetermined aboriginals. For the same reason, the concepts of 'Sanskritization', 'Kshatriyzation' and the newer variant, 'Hinduization' ... are not adequate to capture the nature of mutual appropriation and the resultant contradictions that co-exist in popular religion. Paraphrasing Sontheimer, one might instead use the term 'religious (re)configuration'. (ibid.: 62–63)

Sundar also concludes:

> Under colonial rule, there were accretions to the festival which reflected British modes of legitimation. This reworked Dusserah proved the ideal form for the ritual display of indirect rule ... . Thus empire was translated into local rituals, and indigenous rituals now added to the greater glory and diversity of empire.
>
> The 'Muria Durbar' was first begun in 1906 as part of the Dusserah programme as a means of communication between the administration and the public. Since then, it has served as the real microcosm of the polity. (ibid.: 73)

Surjit Sinha's study of tribal polities and state system in eastern India during pre-colonial times (1987) found the specific features seen in the Bastar polity and the Dusserah festival, generally present in the Eastern Indian principalities as well as North-East India. He delineates the following common features:

- The heads carried an aura of sacredness enacted through exemplary rituals and festivals. They were even regarded as 'moving gods' ruling on behalf of the presiding deities of their lineages.
- The exemplary rituals not only emphasized the role of the king as the blessed one but also as a mediator between the divine beings and the subjects thereby ensuring their welfare and prosperity.
- Some of these rituals, including the king's coronation, included a special role for the tribal chiefs and tribal subject.
- The heads of these principalities were always conscious about not disturbing the norms of indigenous tribals and other ethnic groups from whom they accepted only token tributes.

Synoptic View of Majumdar's Findings on the Tribal Situation

Transition (60: 1937) presents Majumdar's study of the Ho, which was initiated in mid-1920s and subsequently followed up in late 1940s and the publication of *Affairs* (131: 1950). In mid 1930s, the Bastar study which resulted into his presidential address (1939) on tribal culture and acculturation was conducted. Thereafter, he had carried out an ethnographic survey of the United Provinces in early 1940s as a part of the 1941 Census, which is partly contained in *Fortunes* (90: 1944). This wide spectrum of work, both in time and geographical area, documents through its rich ethnography, of course in the pattern of the ethnographic tradition of his times, and throws up various aspects of change perceived among the tribes of Chhota Nagpur, Central India and Central North India into focus under a whole range of factors initiating and determining the course of these changes. Now, we make an attempt to synoptically view this scenario of colonial times turning into earlier post-colonial years, and also examine them in the light of the later post-colonial developments.

Since his ethnographic account of the people of Uttar Pradesh was connected with the 1941 Census, in his introduction to *Fortunes* he has voiced the difficulty with exact categories into which the people can be ethnographically dealt with. He says that:

> The three categories, into which the people of India are ethnographically classified for *census purposes* and also in *popular parlance*, are 'race', 'caste' and 'tribe' though these are not mutually exclusive. Anthropologists ... are greatly handicapped by an absence of an exact terminology. A caste or a tribe is distributed over great areas, from province to province, the same caste in different areas do not intermarry and anthropometry often fails to affiliate them racially .... There has been a transition from tribe to caste, and examples of such social mobility are numerous. The same people have once been classed as a tribe, at another time they have formed a caste ... the strength and influence of caste organizations are often the determining factors in establishing caste claims, and thus new castes and sub-castes have received the sanction of the census which has transformed many an interbreeding community to inbred ones. (90: 1944: ix)

The issue of 'interbreeding' and 'inbred' communities leads him to dwell upon the complex issues related to the racial classification of the Indian population and summarizing, generally speaking, 'the raciology of India', he concludes:

> Thus, India contains all the racial types we meet in the world to-day, and innumerable sub-types ... the dovetailing of these groups in the peculiar economic structure of the country has produced a complex social life with a rigid code of ceremonial conduct, hypergamy, taboo and social incompetence. (ibid.: xiii)

The difference between the tribal groups and the caste structure lies 'in their (tribes) territorial affiliation, and in their freedom from economic interdependence'. However, such distinctions are not absolute as tribes have migrated from one part of the country to another, changing their languages and also taking up particular occupations. The case for tribal identity, thus, rests on a territorial base, therein, absence of economic interdependence and a social organization having clans and other features. But, all these boundaries have been undergoing changes and:

> There are innumerable cases of vertical mobility of the tribes to caste status, so that the distinction between tribe and caste is more academic than real. (ibid.: xiv)

This situation had perhaps led Risley to describe the seven types of castes which, however, admit of regrouping.

We can now turn to examine how these changes are ethnographically dealt with in these three works and also to see whether it has any relevance to the post-colonial tribal cultural scenario and its emergent issues.

Xaxa (2008) presented such issues in post-colonial India. Xaxa argues that anthropologists have seriously misconstrued the consequences and implications of the changes which the tribes (scheduled) have been undergoing for nearly a century, as their discourse on tribes has been couched primarily in terms of tribes being transformed into castes. Actually, new castes are no longer being formed, whether by the transformation of tribes into castes or by any other means in spite of the fact that the tribes have become peasants and have also been socially differentiated.

After examining the views expressed by Bose, Dube, Vidyarthi and others regarding the changing tribal society, Xaxa concludes that all the analyses in this regard correlate the tribes to the civilizational context of Hindu society whereas the correct frame to study a tribe would be as 'whole society' and therefore the frame for comparison has to be other 'groups or communities' such as 'regional communities', for example Gujarati, Bengali, etc. (ibid.: 26). The scriptural literatures have also described them as *jana* which means a 'people'. Xaxa states:

> The counterparts of tribes are not castes or peasants, as has been the case so far in tribal studies, but communities or societies incorporating castes and peasants, for the latter are not the whole society but only an element of the whole. A tribe, on the other hand, is a whole society like any other society, with their own language, territory culture, customs, and so on. Hence as societies, tribes must be compared with other societies and not with castes, as has been the case in sociological and anthropological writings. (ibid.: 26)

Discussing tribal dynamics, Xaxa further argues that a tribe is seen primarily as a 'stage and a type of society' that lacks the positive traits of modern society. These features may change on account of education, modern occupation, technology, etc. and then it is not considered tribal. However, there is a fallacy in this approach because the society (tribal) does not in this process change its basic identity which is essentially related to their habitats and social system, etc. and consciousness of being a part thereof. As in most of the areas where the Indian tribes live, viz., eastern, central and western parts, they have a history of being the earliest settlers even though they might have migrated to such areas, and thus:

> What remains uncontested is the fact that they have developed special relations with the territory in question. The communities in question considered these territories as their own against the claims of other communities. They considered themselves as having prior and preferential, if not exclusive, rights over the territory in which they lived, either on account of their prior historical settlement or their numerical dominance (ibid.: 37–38) ... and even Ghurye who otherwise talks of tribes as backward Hindus refers to them as aborigines. (ibid.: 31)

Xaxa compares this tribal identification with land or territory with the 'son-of-the-soil' theory 'raised from time to time by the dominant regional communities in India'. However:

> Paradoxically, whereas such privileges and rights are freely recognized with respect to these communities, the same is denied to tribal communities in

> India. In the process, they are being dispossessed of their control over resources (land, forest, water, minerals) in their own territory and are being subjected increasingly to misery, injustice, and exploitation .... In the absence of such powers and rights, a new form of identity, namely the identity of adivasis or indigenous people, is crystallizing among tribes in different parts of India. (ibid.: 38)

In fact, this 'crystallization' of identity as *adivasis* has grown into a bond for different groups, which as a category had taken on political overtones in many parts of the country even in the colonial days. Thus, the status of tribals as per Xaxa's analysis calls for an approach for ensuring minority empowerment and rights to them rather than the mainstream civilizational approach of acculturation/integration, and the issues thereof as viewed since the colonial times.

The contemporary tribal situation in most areas where the tribal people have a concentration, though no more dominance everywhere can be treated as a frame to examine how Majumdar views the situation, broadly, and the issues connected therewith. This may be done with reference to Majumdar's main ethnographic accounts of the Ho as well as other contexts of acculturation he has dealt with.

The Issues among the Ho

Majumdar (1950) concludes the situation as it emerged from his restudy in the last two chapters, entitled 'The Hos as They Are Today (Responses to Contact)' and 'The Prospect'. The first one briefly summarizes the salient changes in the Ho culture and social organization with the changing time and contacts. The next chapter portrays how Majumdar views the outcome of these trends, the issues arising therefrom and, of course, a remedial path in the perspective of application of anthropological knowledge and the approach envisaged in the Indian Constitution.

The Hos had come into contacts with other castes and tribes from very early times. They had migrated to this area perhaps to escape the alien landlords. In Kolhan they live with castes like *Tantis*, *Goalas* and *Kumars*. In some villages, they have ousted aliens while in others they are sharing the land and its resources. They have adopted rites and cultural traits from the more advanced communities and some of their own practices have been diffused outside. Material aspects of their life have undergone a great change by way of houses, furniture, etc. Now, the bamboo combs are disappearing and men have discontinued the use of bangles and ornaments, so is the case with women's ornaments and dress. In urban centres there is no difference between their dress and the dress of Christians. Soap, oil and toilet material is commonly used and women from families of Mankis and Mundas avoid outdoor work and even observe *parda*. Other household objects have also undergone changes. Young men and boys prefer to dress in shorts and shirts, while white saris are giving place to gaudy and bordered saris. Global war has put fabulous money in the hands of the tribal women' as their labour is required by the army. Hos have also become disease conscious and more appreciative of public health, asking for medical aid, but the priests still have an important role to play in moments of difficulty and crisis. However, cases of causing injury and death to suspected witches happen, even now and sometimes cause concern.

Mining and the setting up of a cement factory is exercising tremendous influence on the life and labour of the Ho. Their ancestors knew iron smelting and their attitude is not averse to working in mines. However, the mining companies are still not using modern machinery and security systems. The technical and higher staff is from outside and this causes discontent among locals. In order to ensure better employment for Ho and other local people, there is need for taking certain measures on the following lines:

- Organizing and training skilled local labour to encourage better opportunities.
- Improving the living conditions in the adjoining villages so that a share in the profits from these undertakings flows to people.
- Ensure equitable wages between male and female labour and local and outside labour.
- Ensure better living conditions, healthcare, etc. for tribal labour in labour colonies.
- Exploitation of tribal labour through contractors, manipulated prices of food stuffs and liquor should be eliminated.

Hos have now started participating in labour unions and there is a political awakening among them. Discussing the social and other problems related to tribal labour, Majumdar mentions how tribals still do not have a correct appreciation of the value of money. Moreover, they generally remain temporary labour because they come to the mines when they need cash for repaying debts, revenue taxes or other expenses connected with festivals and ceremonies. But at the same time, the managers of the mines find tribal labour better learners and workers. In this connection, Majumdar also suggests that tribal labour should be encouraged to migrate in families with provision for better living as is the case in tea plantation.

The influence of Hindu religious practices has been discussed and it has been pointed out that Hos have been effortlessly adapting Hindu deities with practical sagacity and there has been a transition from their indigenous faith, as they think it would avoid crises in their lives. The Christian missionary influence in Kolhan has, however, been insignificant perhaps because the type of administration that Kolhan has does not provide the reasons for better acceptance of change in faith. In fact, the opinion is against any missionary activities and there is now a desire on the part of the educated Ho to take over and manage the educational institutions set up by the missionaries.

There is a general breakdown of tribal solidarity and group activities are becoming difficult to organize. A substantial upper class has come up. They are adopting new food and living style and also visit eateries in the city. A taste for vegetables is also developing and therefore their kitchen gardens are now better looked after. Their games, both indoor and outdoor, are being abondoned and hockey and football are becoming popular. Hos are now entering district and states teams. Their attitude to outsiders seems to have changed as they are growing in awareness along with becoming sophisticated. There is an intolerance of strangers and suspicion of other people, and Hos have even banned 'commensally' with the '*Diku*'. They 'realize today that hardly any good can come from contacts with the Diku and they are often bitter and sarcastic in their parleys and conversations' (ibid.: 285). They are bilingual with a number of people going out to Assam and Bengal and are fast picking up Bihari. But, significantly, their attitude is of insisting on their own dialect when they interact with the *Diku*. The channels of contacts 'with civilization' are many. Mankis and Mundas come into contact with administrative staff and frequently visit Chaibasa or Jamshedpur. So is the case with common people who are better informed today. In *Transition* this range of growing contacts, bothways, has been presented through a sociogram (1937: 181).

There is a system of indirect rule in Kolhan but in recent years a lot of disaffection against the decisions of the hereditary tribal officers and village leaders has been noticed. Crime and law suits also 'show a phenomenal increase'. The data from the registers maintained by the Kolhan Superintendent for the years 1930–31 and 1933–34, and for three years 1946–47 to 1948–49, bears this out. It is observed that many of these cases could have been avoided from being placed before the Kolhan Superintendent had there been a more judicious handling by village leaders through arbitration. But, the tribal officers have also learned many vices from touts and litigatants and there are cases of corruption among them. This can also be attributed to the dependence of their position on the administration and not on the goodwill of the people. Moreover, they are adopting a standard of living higher than they can afford. A role is also played in this regard by the Hos who have lived outside and have a little education or some knowledge of law. They take advantage of people's ignorance and motivate them to avoid panchayats and take to litigation and thereby exploit them.

Such protracted litigations ruin the tenants financially. Moreover, an unhappy situation exists today in Kolhan as the Superintendent as well as Welfare Officer and their subordinates are ignorant of the Ho dialect and Ho culture. Therefore, the only way to remedy this situation is to strengthen the tribal organization and make the tribal officers really responsible to the people.

Looking at 'The Prospect', Majumdar briefly mentions the provisions relating to the administration of Scheduled Areas in the Constitution of India. Majumdar hopefully highlights here the key provisions relating to centre's powers to give direction regarding tribal welfare and administration and the role of Governor in the administration of the Scheduled Areas. And, in retrospect it has emerged that, by and large, several such provisions in the Constitution were ignored in practice (*Scheduled Areas and Scheduled Tribes Commission Report* Vol. I, 1960–61: Chapter 5, 6, and 7). A reference is also there of the various measures 'meant to cater to the needs of tribal rehabilitation' and 'linking of development plans with tribal welfare'. This 'carries a voice of hope' the 'voiceless millions of India' are badly in need of today. There is also a word of praise for the pattern of administration adopted for tribals in Hyderabad State (where Christoph von Furer-Haimendorf was the Advisor) as 'indications that anthropologists must welcome'.

A discussion on emergent trends with some suggestions which follows are insightful and based on the Ho ethnography:

- It is noticed that even where disintegration of tribal life has taken place, a new cement has been found in political interest and the Adivasi populations in some parts are awakening. The need of the hour is to assess with *competence and sympathy* the problems of tribal adjustment and welfare. In this context, the element of growing tribal consciousness and their strength and importance of their front against exploitation has to be tackled. A *note of warning* in this connection would be that tribal problems may assume 'hydra-headed proportions' if distress flourishes due to the administration's ignorance and lack of sympathy, and already 'the cup of tribal life is full of miseries'.
- The failure of the tribals to escape derision at the hands of non-tribals has developed an inferiority complex among them. This has made them fall back upon their own systems of beliefs, values and creates a revivalism specially among the advanced sections. This also encourages growth of tribal solidarity and political consciousness or something of a 'sub-nationalism'. However, even though there may be some realization on the part of Dikus about it, prejudices die hard and this may cause reactions on their part and of course a cycle of reaction. Majumdar hopes that the educated tribals would not be highly suspicious like the people from the other class and 'will help to achieve what the administration should stand for, namely, all round tribal progress and welfare'.
- Certain laws like the criminal law, etc. must be viewed in a different perspective if they treat certain people as criminals for their customary practices. The officers working in the tribal areas will have to be sympathetic and understanding and not trying to have power for selfish and personal ends.
- The process of industrialization which has been coming about without considerations of local or territorial conditions and planning has also to be regulated and adapted in keeping with the conditions of the tribals in such areas. The policy of special treatment for tribal labour and the manner in which skills can be developed among them is again stressed. A few more suggestions to bring about improvement in the conditions of employment and providing facilities have been made. It has also been pointed out that the tribal labour is being engaged through contractors and not directly by the mining companies which leads to more exploitation and discontentment.
- A tribal culture has to be seen in the light of its historical and social background and its dynamics by way of pace and level of accepting change and, therefore, their problems have to be viewed specifically for each different group. Plans for tribal rehabilitation must recognize the cultural levels of the tribals and they should not be drawn on any set formula as is

being done. The priorities in problems for being taken up should be the economic front and education. In respect of education there is a need for a wide range of adaptations and reforms in different tribal areas.

- Tribal response to cultural dynamics depends upon personalities, and group mores can be changed only through personality development, a process which should be the most vigilant concern to those who have the tribal welfare at heart and work for it.

This concluding section, thus, discusses the issues and problems faced by the Ho by way of a summing up. The discrete issues like that of land alienation at the hands of money lenders and other *Dikus*, denial of traditional forest rights or access due to the colonial forest laws, community control over other natural resources; and the likely results of the rising awareness and solidarity, even sub-nationalism, and multifaceted effects, both positive and negative of the changes in the pattern of culture, personality, beliefs, attitudes, and so on are amply documented in the ethnography. The analysis by way of 'prospects' reflects shape of the events which overtook the area at least three to four decades later. It carries a marked prescience and anticipation, arrived at in an inductive manner by Majumdar. It reveals in a nascent manner the contentions and volatile issues which developed later, as they were in the times of his study. A note of forewarning is also patent therein as well as the need to prioritize tribal policies and proper administration. A historical retrospective resume of the demand for Jharkhand and growth of other tribal movements in Chhota Nagpur, Jharkhand as well as other parts of central Indian tribal belt is hardly necessary here.

Later studies of such movements during the early colonial times and, then, in the first half of the 20th century in this area (ref. Ekka, 1972; Fuchs, 1992; Sachchidananda, 1978; Singh, 1982, 1993; Shah, 1990 among others) have observed a continuity in the factors triggering the movements in the course of almost two centuries as reactions to tribals' loss of control over resources and a variety of cultural factors, even though some movements are categorized into different types. By and large, the earlier tribal struggles were mostly violent, termed as 'rebellions' or 'uprisings', etc. by the colonial government while subsequently they assumed different complexions like Reformatory movement or Sanskritization, later on spanning cultural identity, autonomy and in the recent decades the violent extremist naxalism for 'liberation'.

Interestingly, Fuchs (1992) refers to two Messianic or Bhagat movements pioneering religious reformation, Sanskritization or Hinduization in 1930s and late 1950s among the Ho. However, the movements were short-lived because the difficulties in access to natural resources and shortage thereof in the Ho areas then was not as severe. Majumdar has also referred to this comparatively happier position of the Hos though the Haribaba and Lakh Bodra movements documented by Fuchs and others do not feature as such in Majumdar's account.

These Bhagats worshipped Hanuman, abstained from flesh food and alcohol, wore the sacred thread, took frequent baths, grew the sacred plant of *Tulsi*, and discarded and attacked vigorously the beliefs in *bongas*. However,

Haribaba was arrested in 1931 and the movement soon died out. Thus, 'another hope of the tribals for liberation from oppression and want for self rules was lost' (ibid.: 72).

The other movement of a slightly different type was started by LakhBodra about 20 years later around Jhinkapani, an industrial centre in Kolhan. Bodra called his organization as Adi Samaj and developed its own prayers and ethical values (*Adi Sanskriti*) bearing the imprint of Hinduism. He also developed a Ho script and wanted it to be the medium for Ho education. One of his disciples later provided a different direction. He claimed to have been inspired by Singbonga, the Ho Supreme God. The aim was to organize the Ho society through a new religion as the society was 'disorganized'. The followers observed simplified ceremonies of the lifecycle, abstained from liquor and recited simple prayers. These movements also died out within a decade even though both Haribaba and Bodra had developed links with the nationalist movement, Mahatma Gandhi and Congress. Bodra also meddled in politics. Xaxa (2008: 52) reinterprets[1] such movements differently in seeking 'solution not in terms of changing the relations between tribes and non-tribes but by initiating change within their own societies.'

Issues of UP Tribes

The *Fortunes of Primitive Tribes*, as mentioned earlier, was connected with the 1941 Census in the United Provinces. It presents cameos on ethnography and anthropometry of the Korwa of Mirzapur district and the Tharu of Tarai, followed by the one on the polyandrous Khasa – the two upper castes, Rajputs and Brahmans – in Jaunsar-Bawar region; as also a combined presentation on the more important criminal tribes of UP and their specific problems. A short essay at the end provides a comparative and analytical insight on the general tribal situation particularly in the context of contacts with a few other tribal groups and the mainstream Hindu population. The essay on criminal tribes promises a full-fledged work on them because of their substantial presence in the state. This, however, never came up perhaps because he had later on taken up a study on two criminal tribes and might have based the promised work on its findings.

The title of the concluding essay envisages discussion on 'tribal economy and social vigilance' but its contents are somewhat wider.

Discussing tribal economy, Majumdar stresses the adaptations necessary to enable a tribe live contentedly and grow in the area it inhabits:

(i) This would involve relations of interdependence with the fauna and flora of the habitat.

(ii) Adjustment to the forces of environment which would provide security and thus a scope for progress.

(iii) Developing an organization of its entire group mind and group behaviour channelizing efforts of individuals properly and for maximum success.

This reflects Majumdar's initial thinking on the conceptual approach, MARC, which he developed in *Affairs* (1950), which was basically functional along with a search for patterns in their culture.

Majumdar illustrates in a comparative manner how the institutions initially evolve and then change in accordance with the exigencies of the adjustments attempted by the people when there are changes in the environment, habitat and the peoples' access to them.

Urgent needs of adjustment may compel a tribe to choose a wrong plan of conduct, practices, and institutions. For instance, Korwas' use of roots and berries to countenance famine may have caused physical maladjustments. In certain tribes, the institution of *Gotul* exercises not only control over morals but also inculcates discipline and proper educative socialization. Annual festivals and ceremonial rituals are spontaneous responses and even though the tribes today know that the traditions can be violated, following them adds to a solidarity and orderly existence. Similarly, a strong group organization ensures the regulation of sex and marriage in the socially approved manner and contributes to prevent tribal disorganization due to a likelihood of disturbed ratio of sexes, or onslaught of outside elements. Certain taboos and other codes of conduct which are universal features in tribal culture, observed spontaneously due to beliefs in divine retribution may also weaken and consequently call for judicial and legal prescriptions implying fresh problems.

Next, Majumdar stresses how the tribal way of life constitutes 'one single life pattern' and therefore an acquaintance with it would be possible only through a holistic appraisal, and any piecemeal view would miss its meaning. Any interference with the important features of tribal culture and efforts to create another cultural scheme would lead to chaotic conditions unless the tribal society readjusts itself and readapts. This adoption to changed conditions is made in one or more of the following ways:

(i) By gradual substitution, as for example, by religious conversion in the case of the Sonthal and the Munda of Chhota Nagpur, who were faced with wholesale exploitation and expropriation of their rights to land by the alien landlords.

(ii) By a process of acculturation, by slowly absorbing culture traits from their neighbours.

(iii) By injecting into their culture customs and institution, new dress and newer luxuries or new mode of life The new situation brought about by contacts with civilization, for example, is likely to interpose into the general scheme of primitive life and routine producing a slow but sure deterioration. Again a tribe may develop a sort of cultural 'nomadism' which disintegrates traditional beliefs and practices and substitutes opportunism for stability, expediency for social values (90: 1944: 212).

An example in this regard from Chhota Nagpur is of army camps replacing thick forests which have disturbed tribal life though a lot of money is injected into the economy. Institutions like youth dormitory have been totally disturbed. The Korwa, cut off from their natural resources now face a stratified society whose influence has permeated every aspect of tribal life. Lack of adjustment to this situation has brought about a harsh struggle and loss of faith in tribal traditions and even confidence in themselves, a kind of social neurosis, loss of fertility, anxiety and so on. In contrast, the Tharu present an adaptive culture. Majumdar is of the view that the dominant position of women among Tharus has contributed much to an adjustment with the changed environment. The women have practised witchcraft and their reputation in this regard has shielded the tribe from its neighbours and also ensured that the menfolk become domesticated and subservient. Changes in their culture have been consciously adopted through the initiative of women.

The Khasa have developed an elaborate social organization on a feudal basis. They are immigrants into their present habitat and appear to have superimposed their culture on a tribal matrix. The adjustment is reflected in the role of a low caste tribal functionary who assists the *Sayana* and is recognized as such by the administration. This case is similar to Oraon of Chhọta Nagpur who are immigrants into the Munda country and they have left the duty of propitiating the spirits and deities to the latter. Among Khasas the need for organized defence against attackers like the Sikhs has created the institutions of *Thokdars* who organize security. The need for organizing younger members for this purpose has perhaps given rise to fraternal polyandry. The Khasa culture has not been greatly influenced by contacts because of remoteness of their habitat. The Khasa culture also presents a lack of repression in sexual matters which has contributed to their happy disposition in the face of adverse environment. A comparative picture of the three cultures is presented in the following words:

> The feudal structure of the Khasa society, the hardship of life experienced in the inhospitable mountains or in the ravenous valleys, the scarcity of women and the instability of domestic life engendered by the laxity of the marital code, all have produced a fatalistic trend of mind among the Khasas so that superstitious beliefs about life and the environment they live in, find ready reception among them. While the magic of the Tharu women have contributed to the adaptation of the Tharus, the magic of other tribes have forced the Korwas into seclusion, the superstitious beliefs and traditional rites and rituals have protected the Khasas from disintegration and thus in spite of cultural changes in the neighbourhood the Khasas have clung to their polyandry and to their marital code and have maintained their feudal rights and obligations. (ibid.: 217)

This delineation of the observed patterns of tribal culture reveal the interlacing of beliefs and customs and the contents of culture can be grouped into spheres of social life. A harmonious balance is essential for survival. However,:

> Under ordinary circumstances even where there are contacts between two or more cultures, the configuration of each does not change much. It is more or less abiding or stable. But when the impacts are violent between a dominant culture and a decadent one the latter may be largely reactivated by new needs and emotional appeals. The decadent culture can hardly stem the advance of ideas, and can only secure survival by surrendering their values and even identifying completely with the dominant culture. Such identification, however, is taking place in some areas in India and the effect on their patterns of life and living requires to be assessed before a final verdict is pronounced. (ibid.: 219)

Majumdar categorizes beliefs and customs which constitute a major element of culture into dominant ones (which are manifest in live customs and rites) and others (which are not seriously regarded and so they languish). He designated these two categories as 'critical' and 'sub-critical beliefs and customs'. Critical beliefs shape the attitude of the society to customary conduct and form the vital part of the apparatus by which a society maintains itself. As a community passes through various levels of cultural developments, its system of social security undergo changes and:

> Gradually the development of personality and growth of knowledge diffuse the intensity of beliefs, and (as) their sanction is derived from supernatural powers, gods and spirits, and oaths and ordeals reinforce obligations socially approved. When these fail to elicit compliance with customary conduct, social prescription or legal enactment assumes responsibility for conformity to traditional pattern of life and all that it stands for. (ibid.: 221)

This view is reinforced by a number of examples from the beliefs and customs of Naga, Oraon, Ho, Khasa and Khond.

In this context Majumdar draws a very interesting parallel with Henry Head's discovery of a system of Aphasai of control exercised by higher centres of the nervous system over the lower centre and holds out that this principle can also be applied on a social scale. He supports this view with examples from the cultures described, Khasa and Criminal Tribes, and concludes:

> Culture, primitive or advanced, from this point of view is a vigilance schema built out of conscious and unconscious factors. When such schema form a well-knit pattern so that we may not interfere with any aspect without interfering with the system as a whole, we call it a unitary culture pattern. When, however, we have several schema instead of one, some with respect to marriage, some with respect to food, others with the various material needs and requirements, we have a heterogeneous system. We should suspect in these cases a long process of trial and error, a process of building and rebuilding of vigilance. A unitary vigilance schema implicates either a stereotype set of factors or the operation of a higher conscious and rational factor. Thus both the 'natural' and 'cultural' peoples may have a unitary vigilance schema, it is only among the peoples in the transitional stage who exhibit a heterogeneous vigilance schema. A detailed discussion on social vigilance is reserved for a later publication to follow. (ibid.: 227)

Cultural Contacts and Change

Majumdar's focus, almost from the very beginning of his anthropological journey, on the study of contact situations and cultural changes, including a gestalt approach as a lifelong concern (Madan, 2013: 32), has been mentioned earlier. The recognition to his outstanding contributions in this field came internationally when he co-chaired the Session, Problems of Process: Results, considering papers related to the themes of acculturation, culture, personality and society, and national character in the International Symposium on

Anthropology, sponsored by the Wenner-Gren Foundation for Anthropological Research at New York in June 1952. Julian H. Steward, an acknowledged authority on the South American situations of culture contact and culture area approach, was the Chairman of this Session. The participants in the Symposium were some 80 selected scholars from all over the world, who discussed 50 papers written by experts. Majumdar's remarks on Ralph Beal's paper on 'acculturation' and some other papers in this Session reflect his insight into this area of study. Majumdar observed:

- Indian anthropology, although inspired by British anthropology, has not developed along British lines but rather along the lines that you find in the United States. This may be a case of selective acceptance or convergent development.
- India has a unique scope for the study of cultural dynamics. The Constitution of India provides for the gradual transition of 30 million tribal people to rural status, and 60 million of backward castes are waiting to be levelled up.
- Beal shows the processes and the possibilities of the study of cultural change or acculturation, and says that the full acceptance of acculturation, which he equates with cultural contact, is quite recent.
- However, in India, systematic study of cultural change had been initiated as early as 1931, under the auspices of the decennial census, and the Indian literature too abounds with references to cultural change and cultural contact. This literature in vernacular finds no mention in Western publications.
- Pointing to the significance of Beal's emphasis on the need for precise definition of terms like 'assimilation', 'adaptation', 'acceptance', 'symbiosis', 'commensalism', 'acculturation and trans-culturation' and 'for reduction of the processes into standard categories', Majumdar pointed out that his (Beal's) stages were adaptation, syncretism and reaction in varying degrees. Majumdar was of the view that adaptation was not a process of acculturation for acculturation was a grafting process like the grafting of tissues. Therefore, this process if effected without complete knowledge of 'clinical conditions' would increase tension potential and produce friction. 'A toxic effect of acculturation' is evident in many parts of India today as contra-acculturation. How prophetic!
- Although, theoretically, acculturation may be both one or two-way traffic, it is in practice the passing of traits from a higher culture or conquest group to a backward or conquered group. For example a 'native people in contact with technological civilization will acculturate or perish but contact with a non-conquest group may lead to trans-culturation (and not acculturation).
- Acculturation studies must be correlated with the time factor or mobility. Moreover, 'a quantitative approach to acculturation' is also called for. For example in Chhota Nagpur, tribes who live in compact blocks of millions have not acculturated much, while the scattered tribes have detribalized. Majumdar felt that if we could develop a technique of ethnometry or measuring ethnographic phenomenon, quantitative approach to

acculturation could be more effectively used. He added that, 'we are trying to develop formulas' in this direction.

- Beal's response to Majumdar was positive: 'one of the questions that Mr Majumdar raised about the size of groups having some relationship to the rate or character of acculturation immediately struck me as raising some very important problems, one of them having reference to the job of acculturation that was done by 20 thousand Spaniards in the first 80 years of the postconquest history of Mexico – a very extensive and very rapid acculturative process (Sol Tax et al., 1953: 131).
- Commenting on Hallowell's paper, 'Culture, Personality, and Society', Majumdar made the observation with culture, personality, and society 'can be postulated as completely independent variables. We have to deal with two types of personality: First, the personality of the culture; second, the personalities within a culture. The second help asses the first; but has the first no significance with respect to the second?' (ibid.: 126).
- With reference to Mead's paper on 'National Character' Majumdar questioned how such studies could be of national character when the word 'nation' is not today an anthropological concept. We have seen the processes of fission and fusion of national groups: 'Would it not be better to use regional types for nation'. Mead explained: '... that any people of any race who are for long enough time members of a political nation, will display certain characteristics. It is the exact opposite of racism' (ibid.: 139).

Cultural Change among the Indian Tribes

The studies of cultural change, followed on the basis of some theoretical leads in the study of change, were provided to the first generation of trained anthropologists when they studied in British Universities. Aiyappan, Chattopadhyay, Ghurye, Majumdar, and subsequently Srinivas methodically studied change as a part of their ethnography. However, earlier, the methodology was influenced by the diffusionist-evolutionist approach as seen in Chattopadhyay and also his student, N.K. Bose. Majumdar's study of Hos (1937) is regarded as a pioneering study both by way of a study in cultural change as well as the first problem oriented study of an Indian tribe. Moreover, its significance lies in the fact that his approach was basically functionalist with a combination of the configurational approach developed by the American anthropologists, particularly Benedict who first attempted to discern dominating patterns in the culture of a community. In this discussion, we will also follow up this approach as seen in his subsequent studies related to the U.P. tribes– Korwa and Tharu– and Gond and other central Indian tribes of Bastar (Vidyarthi, 1978, Vol. 1: 438–39).

Vidyarthi, while discussing cultural change, among tribes observes that:

> The study of the two major cis-Himalayan tribes the Khasa by D.N. Majumdar, and Tharu by S.K. Srivastava also establish that both the tribes, though originally they had tribal matrix and continued to have certain distinctive tribal traits, have now been accepted as the Kshatriyas ... . From his study of the

> culture of the Khasa it becomes clear that they have modeled their ways of life after the Rajputs and the Brahmans of the neighbouring plain area. With their fast adoption of the Hindu surnames and social connections with the Rajputs and Brahmans of the plains, they declare, themselves as Rajputs and Brahmans respectively. (ibid.: 441)

This does not, however, seem to be a correct interpretation of what Majumdar has written:

> As regards racial affiliation, the High castes show general resemblance to their equals in the plains, with the characteristics popularly known as 'Aryan' features. They claim to have immigrated from Kashmir or the north-west in ancient times, though some immigrant families from the neighbouring districts or states can also be found. The lower castes, especially the Bajgis and Koltas, have been regarded as aboriginals or belonging to an earlier wave of immigrants. They often have the features which may be regarded as derived from the Proto-Australoid strain, though mixed features are not uncommon .... We may add here that, whatever origins may be attributed to various groups of people in this area, they seem to have been isolated from the people of other areas to a great extent and for quite a long time. They themselves, therefore, formed an integral multi-caste community, with defined relative status, mutual relationship and interdependence. They also established among themselves certain peculiar customs and usages in matters of social organization, including the systems of family and lineage and the village organization, occupational pattern, etc. as well as of socio-religious rituals, supernatural beliefs, and festivals. It appears that when this community came into contact with outsiders, the latter often ridiculed them on account of their curious customs. There seems to have been much misunderstanding or lack of understanding of the local culture pattern.
>
> It is also noticed that cultural contacts have from time to time brought about changes especially in the border areas and in the area near the Chakrata Cantonment. (220: 1962: 24)

Majumdar's lectures in the Nagpur University were delivered towards the end of 1946 only a few months before the country got its Independence. Part two of the published version of these lectures (98: 1947) reviews quite in detail the tribal situation including effects of tribal contact with more advanced people and the issues connected with tribal 'rehabilitation'. After describing the channels of tribal contacts with non-tribal people and cultures, Majumdar goes on to classify the tribal population broadly into three groups, these are:

1. Primitive tribes outside the pale of Hindu influence, the so-called 'real primitives'.
2. Primitive tribes who have adopted Hindu customs, beliefs and practices, have shown a degree of association with the Hindu castes and have attained some cultural progress, but who are not yet recognized as forming the exterior castes.

3. Primitive tribes who are Hinduized but maintain social distance from the clean castes, though some of them are indistinguishable from the inferior ranks of the caste order, exterior or clean.

   The first group is numerically small indeed; they live in inaccessible hills and virgin forests and little is known about their life and habits except the materials that occur in monographs on primitive and aboriginal peoples in India while a very thin partition divides the third group from the lower castes 'depressed' or otherwise. There is no tribe today which may be taken to mark the zero point of culture contact. Even the most isolated culture of today is a 'blended' one, in which rites and practices from highly developed cultures have got mixed with those of a primitive and 'infantile' kind (ibid.: 131–32).

This three-fold classification still carries some validity in the tribal policy of the Government of India. It came to recognize a distinct group of scheduled tribes as 'primitive tribal groups' (P.T.G.) and in addition finds that many of the scheduled tribes have evolved into two, more or less, distinct groups– those who have been able to take advantage of the protection and benefits extended to them and others whom such programmes and protection have failed to reach.

Significantly, while specifying this classificatory approach, Majumdar has emphasized that the tribes in India during the historic period continued to retain their 'units of highly integrated political systems' and also in 'economic transactions'. He, however, adds that the tribal organization of some of the 'primitive tribes' show 'unmistakably signs of alien influence', now. These observations point out to the tribes being in ancient India and even later autonomous communities with their own polity, compared with Xaxa's (2008) critique of the ambiguity of tribe as a category and the need to treat them as *jana* or autonomous collectivities. However, Majumdar also points out to the myriad problems arising out of fast changing situations like Second World War touching and influencing the tribal areas like the North-East and even Chhota Nagpur which have resulted into inabilities of the tribal polity to deal with.

A discussion of this situation, further, leads Majumdar to examine the system of indirect rule as followed by the colonial government in tribal areas. It may be mentioned that the system was not uniform and had varied in different areas due to the exigencies, historical, political, as well as tribal reaction to the colonial rule. Quoting Hutton's adverse comments on indirect rule in Assam hills, Majumdar says, 'while we admit the evil effects of indirect rule, there exists a strong case for it among the savage and non-savage people all over the world' (98: 1947: 138). Then, he goes on to discuss his ethnographic notes relating to the prevailing political and administrative system among the Chhota Nagpur tribes in order to distinguish the conditions in India when compared to other parts of the world under colonial rule. He spells out how the 'recognition of the indigenous tribal organization by the government' has not achieved, what is held out to be the advantages of indirect rule. By and large, he has found that the tribal leadership under this system is not responsive enough to the needs and expectations of their people and, thus, 'brought this system of indirect rule amongst the Indian tribe into conflict with tribal patterns of life and living' (ibid.: 142). The situation has been further complicated by a new class arising among the tribals 'whose contacts with the outside world and their cash earnings ... have raised them in the estimation of the tribal people' who sought after their advice and greatly valued it (ibid.: 143). Thus, indirect rule has created situations of conflict in leadership.

Elsewhere, subsequently in 1958 (Vidyarthi, 1968: 105–06), examining the approaches to tribal problems and the resultant situation, he observes:

> There is a strong feeling of discontent and frustration among the tribals against the reform agencies. They want to do their own engineering and it should be the aim of the government to sponsor tribal leadership in matters of tribal reform. The examples of contra-acculturation we have in India, particularly in Bihar, which deliberately wean the tribes from levels of progress that might as well be targets of their achievements, make us doubt the efficacy of the reform approach. I would rather go in for nationalization of welfare activities, rather than leave the destiny of the tribes in the hands of erstwhile politicians. But, I also know that in exorcising ghosts, we often find that the mustard seeds that we use, may become ghosts themselves. That I would leave for a competent appraisal by anthropologists.
>
> The Planning Commission would do well to sponsor an expert committee of 3 anthropologists to assess and evaluate tribal problems in the light of experiences of tribal administration. It should be a fact-finding as well as a policy formulating Committee.

The frustration and contra-acculturation that Majumdar has stressed here in 1940s were only the early signs of extensive tribal unrest which also assumed violent manifestation from about 1960s in Andhra Pradesh later spreading out gradually.

Concluding Discussion

In the foregoing discussion on cultural contact and social change, Majumdar's observations and analyses regarding Ho, Bastar tribes and then regarding the comparatively smaller and rather extensively dispersed tribal communities of Uttar Pradesh have been highlighted at some length. All these ethnographic accounts were written on the basis of his field enquiries in the decades of 1930–40, along with some earlier papers. This chronological spread just touches upon the post-colonial period and the adoption of a Constitution for the Indian Republic in 1950. Subsequently, his observations mostly synoptic with some data of later years and rather anticipatory observations relating to the impact of the changed policies and the extensively adopted C.D. Programme, along with its modified projects. These were called Special Multi Purpose Tribal Blocks and taken up in selected tribal areas. Also a variety of schemes broadly falling under categories of educational, economic and communication, health, etc., which were taken up under the Five Year Plans. His writings after *Affairs* mainly are the revised and added portions in *Races and Cultures* (3rd and 4th edition), and some papers and Presidential Addresses.

Very briefly the entirety of his explications of the tribal vis-à-vis others, mainly Hindu castes situations provide the following impressions:

- Historical conditions of contact have been continuously changing the tribal cultures in varying degrees, complexion and nature.
- Tribes have been transforming into castes rarely higher castes and mostly into lower castes.
- Territorial concentration in certain areas by one or a few more tribes is also varied though affinities in identity and culture can be discerned.
- The changes in political and social organizations, institutions have been gradually occurring often undermining traditional institutions authority and leadership and even creating classes in an otherwise egalitarian communities.
- In some of the tribal communities there has always been a hierarchical and feudal system, the origins of which Majumdar has attempted to decode.
- A functional and configurational analysis of the cultures studied mostly revealed an equilibrium but it has been disturbed in varying degrees in certain tribes as a result of a variety of contacts – the neighbouring castes, missionaries, traders, government policies and its execution through personnel who are deficient in more than one ways.
- The situation as seen by Majumdar opens up ample scope for application of anthropological knowledge.
- In spite of many negative hues as revealed through his observations, Majumdar's remarks carry a strong positivism and hope though he has sounded very significant notes of warning alarms in the form of contra-acculturative forces, changing attitudes and so on and again hopes that these forces would not be allowed to go out of hand.

In this regard his classification of the tribal communities into three groups holds much significance. With some modifications it is accepted by others like Dube, Vidyarthi and even Elwin. Majumdar's critique of the colonial system of indirect rule and isolating areas also seems to be quite predictive if one takes into account the wide deficiencies reported in the findings of various governments reports subsequently. These findings resulted in adoption of a policy of funding which was first suggested by him, as discussed elsewhere, and emphatic reiteration of many of his suggestions by way of siphoning the impact of industrialization and raising up skills among the tribal youths in the affected areas. His strong nationalist and pro-development views and never going into the Marxist analysis and approach as also a faith in functionalism, however, often blunted the edge of his critique. It can also be recorded here that no anthropologist or sociologist observer of the tribal scene up to, say, early 1960s had foretold any violent reactions on the part of the tribal people in spite of their historical narration of the events and causes connected with a long chain of tribal revolts against colonial or feudal authority.

In 1960, the scheduled areas and the Scheduled Tribes Commission too had taken note of the fact that there were no less than 'four different layers, amongst the tribals'. They even thought of preparing a list of the Scheduled Tribes falling in these four layers with a view to recommending de-scheduling of some coupled with the suggestions for measures necessary for those lagging behind. They could not pursue the idea because of 'lack of data as stated in the Commission's Chairman's letter to President of India in this report' (Government of India, 1961).

It is interesting to examine Xaxa's analysis on the better development of some tribes compared to others and the likely factors which determine this kind of a dichotomy. He observes that differences among the Scheduled Tribes have been highlighted more in the drawing of such comparative pictures vis-à-vis the Scheduled Castes. However, he does proceed to identify certain scheduled tribal communities who have benefitted most from protective discrimination under the Constitution and the likely factors causing the condition. He identifies Minas, Oraons and in the North-East, the Mizo and the Khasi. Broadly speaking, he points out that all these tribes accepting Oraon had some structural features that explain their better performance. They constituted a fairly differentiated community with privileged sections like chieftains, ranks, status and linkages with more assets as compared to the commoners. These sections could, therefore, take better advantages of education and economic opportunities. Among the Oraon, though 'they were relatively egalitarian', the influence of missionaries opening up opportunities of education and awareness gradually came to develop social differentiation and the 'emergence of such groups fairly early helped communities such as Oraon to take advantage' more than others. The process of urbanization in certain areas perhaps brought about by industrialization, trade and communications also helped (2008: 98–99).

The trends of the developing tribal situation brought out by Majumdar and others (Dube, Vidyarthi– reports to Planning Commission) and Haimendorf (1982) and Xaxa (2008) are strongly indicative of the rising dissatisfaction and resentment among the tribes of certain areas. This situation first manifested itself in early 1960s in the Srikakulam district of Andhra Pradesh which was organized by the Naxalite activist from this movement in West Bengal. The earliest reports on the unrest, which was violent there, assigned it to the failure of the state to implement the protective laws effectively.

It would not be out of place here in the context of the implementation of the tribal policies that the situation of violent discontent first erupting in Andhra Pradesh has by now become quite widespread. It is claimed to be a 'revolution for liberating tribals of large tracts of contiguous districts' in Andhra, Chhatisgarh, Madhya Pradesh, Jharkhand, Orissa and Bihar, as well as the south-eastern districts of Uttar Pradesh. Some of the observations contained in the *Report of the Expert Group to Planning Commission* (Government of India, 2008) would be quite revealing and relevant to understanding the changing conditions, is quoted below:

- In general, the contradiction between the tribal community and the State itself has become sharper, translating itself into open conflict in many areas. Almost all over the tribal areas ... people seem to feel a deep sense of exclusion and alienation, which has been manifesting itself in different forms (ibid.: 8) ... with the paradigm shift of economic policy from 1991 all these other values of egalitarianism, equity, control of exploitation, social, economic and political justice lost their earlier priority (ibid.: 57).
- Apart from the physical and occupational displacement caused by large projects, in the case of the Fifth Schedule areas, unless the tribals are resettled in the same scheduled tract, they will face deprivation of the special rights that have accrued to them by virtue of the schedule (ibid.: 16).
- They have, therefore, little autonomy to act on their own in any matter. Adivasis, by and large, are distanced from dominant non-tribal communities and have considerable space to act autonomously (ibid.: 19) .... The political equality– is compromised in various ways.
- There is, however, a failure of governance, which has multiple dimensions and is not confined to the inefficiency of the delivery system only. It is not fortuitous that overwhelmingly large sections of bureaucracy/technocracy constituting the delivery system come from landowning dominant castes or well to do middle classes, with their attachment to ownership of property, cultural superiority, purity-pollution governed behaviour and a state of mind which rationalizes and asserts their existing position of dominance (ibid.: 22). There are remote areas in the country where there is hardly any governance (ibid.: 59).

Thus, the report also documents the failure of government to ensure 'raising the level of administration' in the Fifth Schedule areas for which the Constitution had made the Central government responsible both financially and by directing action through the state governments. The report goes on to examine the failure of both policies, governance and the personnel in different fields like the implementation of elaborate laws enacted to ensure autonomy, development, education and other services and freedom from exploitation, their land alienation, control over forest resources, low wages, etc. The report also suggests that:

> A strategy of constructive management of conflict requires two key measures. At its present stage, priority should be accorded to search out creative policies that bridge gaps between state interests and those of tribal communities. Tribes are not opposed to development. All that they want is to control its pace and influence, its pattern and direction so that they are enabled to prevent its damaging effects and enjoy some of its benefits (ibid.: 78).

This discussion brings up how the acts of omission and emission at different levels and indifference to the findings and warning of prominent anthropologists and sociologists have contributed to the creation of a serious situation across the tribal belt in the heart of the country. The movement has taken a course different from the introversion, as seen by Xaxa.

Note

1. Xaxa argues:

   There is no doubt that such movements have been active vehicles for Sanskritization. However, to describe them merely as that would be an over-simplification. Rather, these movements are more in the nature of a critique of their society. After all, tribes have been steadily losing control over their land and other resources, and they have had to face extreme exploitation. Although they have resisted these conditions from time to time through armed revolt, they have been unsuccessful in changing their current circumstances ... . Hence, tribals have sought a solution to their problems by directing attention towards their own societies.

5

Tribal Rehabilitation

The use of a term like 'rehabilitation' in place of other terms such as 'welfare', 'development', 'uplift', by Majumdar in most of his writings related to the need for amelioration or development work among Indian tribes may today sound like an anachronism. 'Rehabilitation' in its use during the past few decades or so has become contextualized with the displacement or uprooting of human populations due to the various kinds of developmental activities. Therefore, it carries an implication or connotation of 'shifting' to a different site and the rehabilitative measures appropriately needed by the affected people. However, if we study Majumdar's writings from the earliest, we can correctly gather why he uses this unusual term. As pointed out elsewhere, right from 1925 onwards, Majumdar had started gathering significant information on the changes he had perceived in the traditional patterns of living of tribal people through his intensive fieldwork which also included acquiring knowledge of language or dialect spoken by the tribe. The analyses of his observations made him conclude that the changes were often undermining the tribal cultures because of the impact of a variety of alien factors over which the tribals themselves had little control. The tribal cultures in India in constant contact, historically, with the mainstream, predominantly Hindu culture had been changing slowly with long term adaptations of the traits and institutions they had been adopting. In the process, they had even transformed into castes, generally the lower castes. However, with the advent of the colonial rule the scenario changed fast, and often suddenly, when the East India Company assumed actual administration of the areas inhabited by the tribes, as a result of the company's interventions into the domain of local rulers. The forces unleashed by this change resulted into some kind of shock for many tribal communities, disturbing the equilibrium of their life, specially economic and religious. Naturally, as a trained anthropologist of the first generation, Majumdar felt that the scientific studies of the tribes would lead to suitable measures being devised for meeting these crisis situations and thus, perhaps, came his use of a term like rehabilitation.

Idea of Development

Within the above broad framework, Majumdar's diagnostics and prognosis in respect of the Indian tribals developed from his earliest writings which I place in 1925, to the fourth edition of *Races and Cultures* (1961). And also a posthumously published paper in Vidyarthi's *Applied Anthropology* (1968: 98–100). His focused views on the Ho situation, the Korwa, Bastar tribes, and the Tharu are contained in his books (*Transition, Fortunes, Races and Cultures* – first edition; *Matrix*). Overall, one can say that his approach to tribal problem as a whole, and in respect of particular communities was derived more or less inductively from his widespread work on cultural contact situations in different contexts and also various formulations and changes in government policies from time to time ending in the provisions for 'Scheduled Tribes', 'Scheduled Areas' and 'Tribal Areas' as defined and declared as per the Indian Constitution. It is, however, noticeable that during the most part of the last decade of his academic work (1950–60) he did not write much on the tribal situation as, such, which was emerging as a result of the planned initiatives taken up by the government. But, it may be added that perhaps the most significant development in this area came about in the decade of 1960 after his death to which the most prominent anthropologists of his time made critical contributions.

Majumdar's appreciation of how the tribal culture, the Ho in this case, was undergoing changes particularly under the influence of Christian missionaries (Majumdar, 1925: 285–86) and what he perceived as an 'urge' for social reforms (change) emanating from the Ho themselves, has been commented upon earlier. His evaluation of the Ho situation, however, did not go beyond these limited observations at that time.

The Korwa, among whom he started his fieldwork after joining at Lucknow attracted his critical comments on the issues of conditions arising primarily out of contacts and hence 'a need for rehabilitation'. Referring to the past writings of William Crooke and from his ethnographic study of the Korwas, he concludes:

> Such an active and powerful tribe, much more interesting from the cultural point of view are the Korwas ... at present a dying tribe with little or no ambition in life; scarcely getting a full meal a day and always at the mercy of the money-lenders whose slaves they are for the debts of their forefathers as well as their own. (32: 1929: 149)

The conditions of the tribe are described and their problems like imported diseases, dwindling population, poverty and a shattered economy leading to almost constant famine like conditions are traced to the various environmental, administrative and cultural imbalances.

Motivations Determining Customs

Significantly, we find Majumdar trying to look at the customs prevalent in different societies particularly Ho and the Hindu society in Eastern Bengal, from a perspective which was not based on evolutionary or diffusionists approaches common to anthropology, then. Writing in 1925, Majumdar analyses the funeral ceremonies or death rites among Indian tribes – the Toda, Badaga, and the Chhota Nagpur tribes, including Ho. He points out that the Ho practise two sets of funeral rites for deaths, which he calls 'green funeral' immediately after the death, and 'dry funeral', a second ceremony held after the lapse of some period. Suggesting that the primitive beliefs hold that the final disposal of the remains of the dead should be held back in anticipation of the return of the soul to the body. The second ceremony came at a stage when such a return would not happen. But, in this perspective, he also views that the dry funeral ceremonies had an economic aspect too as these ceremonies were held for several deaths in the community as such. The ceremonies were linked to the comparative economic well-being of the community after the harvest time and, thus, had an economic aspect to be considered (12: 1925: 208–09). He also connects certain ceremonies related to the *pooja* festival in East Bengal as well to this motivation.

Subsequently, he contextualized the above perspectives in the functional approach of Malinowski with reference to the latter's *Crime and Custom in Savage Society* (1926). Majumdar argues that the 'savage' does not follow the customs due to some 'slavish, unwitting and spontaneous' reverence for tradition. He follows a certain custom because he has 'recognized its practical utility by experience or reason'. The second funeral among certain Indian tribes which is 'more important than the first and the funeral for all deaths in the village on one day', should be seen in this light. This avoids any economic stress as it is held after the harvesting season. Further developing this perspective, he observes that in Kolhan where contacts of the Ho with popular Hinduism are not very close, their customary practices in various other areas of social life also imply the economic motivations in a functional manner. The institution of dormitory among not only the Chhota Nagpur tribes but also the North-Eastern tribes is elaborately documented and discussed. However, he also concludes:

> The more primitive the society the greater is the consideration for the results or the economic benefits arising out of marriage. The Hindu conception of marriage for the purposes of reproduction can thus be taken as an earlier view where the results are more important than the actual union, the consummation is not in mating but in reproduction; this is the explanation of the popular conception that the son frees the father from eternal damnation .... The idea of economic benefit is responsible for the custom of bride price, which has been responsible for many of the ills. (36: 1930: 166)

Another graphic instance of Majumdar's functionalist interpretation, of the institution of polyandry in Jaunsar-Bawar, finds place in his first elaborate ethnography of the Khasa (Rajputs and Brahmins) of the area. Discussing their marital life, Majumdar observes:

> Polyandry is the common form of marriage among the people of the Himalayan region. It is so, as all the cultural groups in this region practice it. But it is also a fact that other forms of marriage are also practised along with polyandry ... so that monogamy, polygyny and polyandry and even group marriage are all practised side by side. Economic considerations have been suggested as the

> causes of polyandrous marriages ... . The Garhwalis today do not observe polyandry but the Jaunsaris do. Once I had a talk with a number of Jaunsaris on this subject. I wanted to know why the Jaunsaris still practised polyandry while their next door neighbours the Garhwalis had outgrown this practice. The answer was extremely significant. I was told that they did not envy the Garhwalis. The latter left their homes due to the disintegration of joint families. At first, land in Garhwal was measured by acres, then by roods, then by poles, then by yards and feet till they all left their villages and are today distributed all over the country as domestic servants. The Jaunsaris love their homes and do not want to repeat the experience of their neighbours. (80: 1940: 35–36)

And, further on, another factor which presumably contributed to polyandry is indicated in the Khasa being the people who sort of overwhelmed the indigenous community of Doms. Since there was a shortage of women in the course of the practice of hypergamy by the Khasa, they came to practice polyandry along with sexual relationships with the Dom women while prohibiting the marriage of Khasa women with the Dom.

Tribal Problems

By mid-1930s, Majumdar had formulated his views on tribal problems which he expressed in two papers (55–56: 1936), the first one discusses the declining conditions of the primitive tribes in India while the second one suggests his views on how the problem should be further studied scientifically and contains some very important practical suggestions. This paper is largely contextualized in the administrative provisions for the 'excluded and partially-excluded areas' envisaged in the Government of India Act 1935. It may be recalled that the continuance of the colonial policy of keeping certain areas, mostly tribal, out of the purview of the popularly elected provincial governments under this Constitution was strongly opposed by the Congress Party as being a step in furtherance of the British policy of 'divide and rule' and also promotion of an isolationist agenda for the tribal people.

In his paper (56: 1936), Majumdar discusses the formation of excluded and partially excluded areas intended to safeguard the interests of primitive and aboriginal tribes in the context of contact situations. Contacts have come about in a number of ways, namely due to existence of mineral resources, administrative activity, missionaries, vendors, development of transport and communication leading to filtration of alien traits, restrictions on forests and shifting cultivation and change in occupation through migration as plantation labour, etc.

Influence of caste system has caused the demarcation between popular Hinduism and tribal religion to become thin while Christianity has proved to be a 'great ally in tribes' by providing them secular benefits. Tribals have revolted from time to time against exploitation by the aliens, and missionaries often promise relief from it. The main features of the situation are:

1. Excise laws are another exploitative measure.
2. The displacement of tribal officers by those nominated by government.

3. Taking over of *jhum* lands as state forest.
4. Prohibition of quarrying stone, ore, etc. by owners of *jhum* land.
5. Ban on *jhuming*.
6. Marriage by capture being treated as an offence under IPC.
7. Exploitation in the transactions made in weekly *hats*.
8. The kind of education introduced in these areas being unsuitable to some extent.
9. Conflict between the complicated system of law and legal procedures and tribal customs or customary laws as well as imposition of British notions of individual ownership and ownership by crown.
10. A feeling of inferiority caused by missionary influences.
11. Introduction of venereal diseases through contacts.

Majumdar has commented on the decline of population seen among certain tribes between 1881 to 1931. These tribes are Toda, Asur, Korwa and Andamanis. Several other tribes find place in this list. Instances in this regard with reasons are: forest restrictions in the Korwa area, new diseases and epidemics among Khonds and some Assam tribes. Other factors which contribute are the limitations and inability of the indigenous herbs and medicines in curing new diseases, loosening of social control, new demands for products from outside and deterioration in the quality of food intake due to forest restrictions.

To conclude, Majumdar stresses the view that certain cultures provide proof of a wonderful capacity for acculturation without abandoning their indigenous cultural contents. In some areas, even where they have been subjected to ordinary laws and system of administration, the aboriginals have made progress 'entirely due to their association with advanced section'. Hence there is a need to assist various categories of tribals in their struggle for adaptation, as such.

Measures Necessary for Tribal Rehabilitation

Thus, Majumdar pleads for providing positive measures in matters relating to education, health, etc. and also a cautious 'mainstreaming'. He poses the question as follows:

> Whether exclusion will help the aboriginal tribes or special provisions in the Constitution by *ear-marking certain percentage of the Provincial revenues on the basis of population* for the development of the tribal areas and for welfare work among them would meet the situation is a matter of opinion. But it is imperative that the primitive tribes of India who form 7 per cent of the total Indian population and who even to-day *represent a vigorous and sturdy stock* capable of adjusting and adapting themselves under *careful supervision* should be protected from indiscriminate exploitation by advanced social groups and their rights and privileges should be adequately safeguarded till they can feel that they are a part of a larger political whole and are able to take their place by the side of their compatriots of the plains. (56: 1929)

The suggestion that a certain percentage of funds from the provincial revenues should be *earmarked,* on the basis of the tribal population *for the development of the tribal areas* and *welfare work* among them, demonstrates how Majumdar was way ahead of his times in planning of financial provisions for tribals. In fact, here he talks of *development* and welfare work in respect of the areas inhabited by the tribals and the tribal communities, rather than in his favourite idiom of 'rehabilitation'. No references from either anthropologists or social workers or administrators of those times, mid-1930s, contain any suggestions on these lines. Majumdar is also positive about the development of these areas which would of course imply communications, education and health services. Thus, he also spells out a strategy to eliminate isolation.

It may now be recalled that this suggestion was concretized much later in 1972 by the Planning Commission. L.P. Vidyarthi, one of the most distinguished students of Majumdar, was the Chairman of the Task Force on Development of Tribal Areas set up by the Planning Commission to thoroughly review the nature and level of development of tribals and tribal areas and to suggest a perspective of their development for the Fifth Plan. As the Task Force was also to indicate priorities, policies, programme and *outlays* for this sector, the Study Team suggested that:

> The State departments concerned should surrender a proportion of their budget provision, depending on the size of their tribal population in an area, to be merged with the special provision under Backward Classes sector.
>
> Task Force felt that a committee should be constituted at the State level to ensure flow of funds to the tribal areas at least in proportion to the tribal population in a district. (Home Affairs, 1975: 100)

Five Working Groups were also set up to facilitate the assignment of the Task Force for Identification of Tribal Development Areas and Less Developed Communities: Legislative and Administrative Setup; Tribal Development programmes based on Forest; General Programmes and Area wise Programmes of Infrastructure and Social Services in Tribal Areas; and Personnel Policy in Tribal Areas. Significantly, the identification and special programmes for Less Developed Tribal communities, subsequently called Primitive Tribal Groups, takes into account the three-fold categorization of tribal communities advanced by Majumdar, Dube and other anthropologists much earlier. A number of members of the Task Force, and the Working Groups were prominent anthropologists, and senior administrators advocating an anthropological approach who had long experience of working in the tribal areas.

The recommendations of the Task Force regarding flow of funds in tribal areas was adopted by the Planning Commission for all future Five Years Plans, both State and Central, through a strategy called 'Quantification of Funds for Scheduled Tribes' and the 'Tribal Sub-Plan Approach' from the Fifth Plan onwards.

Transition (60: 1937), as discussed elsewhere, was Majumdar's full-fledged problem oriented ethnography. Sachchidananda (1988: 180) observes that:

Majumdar (1937) was the first Indian anthropologist to concentrate attention on change in the study of the Ho in transition. Among the Korwa and Khasa as among the Ho, he was mainly dealing with the problem of culture contact under inspiration of Malinowski.

A combination of the functional approach from the British anthropology and *gestalt* from American anthropology was its theoretical frame. How the Ho has preserved their pattern of culture and how it has reacted to changes in the context of the social dynamics in the area and the problems of adaptation and adjustment connected therewith were the focal points. These problems, as commented upon in the concluding chapter, throw a light on the agents, and circumstances of contacts, such as administrative officers, law courts, high caste and low caste people, Christian Missions and other new institutions, mining and plantation in the area and communications network. Majumdar finds that the impact of the role of these agents of change is felt differentially among two classes of the Ho community – an upper class of Mankis, Mundas and substantial cultivators and the lower class of ordinary tenants and landless – which are emerging mainly as a result of the impacting forces. Overall, the evaluation of this emerging situation is that some new problems are being thrown up but, by and large, the Ho have 'held their own against heavy odds'. Their concentrations in a government state which provides certain protective measures as well have helped. Majumdar observes:

Their success in this respect, if success it may be called, may be traced to a number of more or less important elements in their culture, such as:

1. The compact area they live in.
2. The system of land tenure.
3. The conservative elements among the Hos.
4. The formation of new buffer class in Kolhan.
5. The social distance between the Hos and the Dikus, which has engendered a sense of rivalry and jealousy.

Kolhan is still the land of the Hos, in spite of the presence of the Dikus. They have occupied it and have maintained their occupation. The Hos are often encouraged to treat the Dikus as aliens. The land being inalienable, it has to be worked, as otherwise it passes on to the community (60: 1937: 195).

In addition, he concludes that:

The formation of classes in Kolhan has done much to soften the distinction between the aborigines and the higher caste people. The higher classes of the Hos form a sort of middle class, and thus bridge the gulf between two extreme sections of the people in Kolhan. This is contributing to a peaceful social progress. (ibid.: 196)

Thus, this study of the Ho spanning over a long period contributed to Majumdar's perceptive and empirical analysis of the tribal situation in Chhota-Nagpur which he used in a comparative manner to formulate his tenets of 'tribal rehabilitation' and his confidence in applying scientific anthropological studies for achieving that end.

Subsequently, we find him emphasizing the contribution anthropology could make to administration. Majumdar, in his paper (66: 1938) 'Modern Trends in Social Anthropology', mentions several such problems where anthropology can contribute, illustrated with the contact situation in different parts of Africa and how it is being studied by anthropologists to help administration. Majumdar concludes with a discussion on how anthropology has an important role to play in the areas inhabited by tribals in India.

In the same year, we find another piece of significant writing from Majumdar which raised a very sensitive aspect of tribal change, its problems and their likely remedies. It may be recalled that much earlier he had attributed rising awareness among the Ho for reformations in their social practices to their exposure to the teachings of Christian Missions in Chhota Nagpur (9A: 1925). In this paper (68: 1938), Majumdar analyses the rising numbers of Christian tribals in certain districts of Chhota Nagpur like Ranchi and Santhal Pargana and also the reason for the numbers of Christian population declining in the United Provinces, as per 1931 Census. He finds that the most important cause of the decline (in UP) is 'the comparative difficulty of providing economic assistance by the missionaries' (ibid.: 513). Therefore, groups, specially from among the lower castes which 'embrace Christianity for secular rather than spiritual benefits retrace their steps'. In the context of Chhota Nagpur, he points out to the following trends:

- In locations where the tribals live in compact areas and are numerically preponderant, and are also provided a protectionist administrative system, then, generally do not convert to Christianity.
- But, in areas where they are in a minority, they have either accepted Christianity or return themselves as Hindus.
- Detailing, the Munda case, Majumdar points out that after the establishment of colonial rule which introduced the policy of supporting Zamindars, restricting access to forests, taxation and entry of Hindu population in larger numbers in the areas, the tribals were in a rebellious mood. And then, Christian Missions came on the scene, promised to assist the Mundas in their fight against the Hindu landlords and, thus, the Mundas felt 'a great relief and show in Christian culture an escape' (ibid.: 514).
- The missionary organizations also on their own and with encouragement from the administration extended 'wonderful services for the aboriginal converts', and thus the number of Christian converts was on speedy rise.

In this backdrop, one would expect Christian tribals to be far more progressive, economically stable and educated. However, the actual conditions of the aboriginal converts now 'do not show a very high standard compared to their erstwhile brethren'. Their religious life and other practices also 'do not appear to be fundamentally different' (ibid.: 516), and so is the case with their living standards. Majumdar points out:

> A very reputed authority on primitive culture of this area has shown how animistic habits of thought have not been eradicated by Christianity and the basic ideas and fundamental beliefs of the Christian converts and the followers of tribal religion are largely similar. (ibid.: 516)

In spite of all these observations, Majumdar finds:

> But it is undeniable that the material advancement brought about by the Missions has more than compensated any lapse in this respect. (ibid.: 516)

The three papers (Sl. No. 56, 66, and 68) discussed here, as also his findings in *Transition*, amply document Majumdars' considered and a study-based scientific approach to the solution of the problems of the Indian tribes, particularly in the central zone where the largest number of tribals are concentrated. Almost all aspects of the situation have been commented upon and he does not fail to emphasize in different contexts that the Indian tribal scene has been changing. It has been in contact with the mainstream caste population which has created both positive and negative impact. Hence, this change has to be studied and monitored as also planned in a suitable manner keeping the conditions of the different tribes in view, 'avoiding any course of a flurry of imposition to which these communities may not be able to adjust' and adapt. In his Presidential Address to the Anthropology Section of the Indian Science Congress (1939), he brings up a brief ethnography of Bastar tribals and caste groups, showing how a tribal institution as well as a Hindu institution, *Dashahara* festival, are vigorously functioning. Concluding it, he analyses the various types of contact situations in which different tribal groups are seen or likely to face together with some diagnostic suggestions.

Contrarian Views, and Post-Colonial Scenario

A.V. Thakkar (Thakkar Bapa) a staunch follower of Mahatma Gandhi assumed the leadership of the plans and the implementation of the efforts of the Congress Party and Mahatma Gandhi on the tribal front from March 1922. He set up the Bhil Seva Ashram at Mirakhedi in Panchmahels for working among the Bhils of Gujarat (Shah, 1955: 148). The social services, he initiated, were in the field of education and subsequently cooperative societies. Thus, Thakkar Bapa's long stays in tribal areas and the services rendered by him and his lieutenants in Gujarat and other provinces, made them perceptive observers of tribal problems and they spelt out an approach for the 'uplift and welfare' of the tribal communities, the 'social workers approach'.

After the assumption of power by the Congress in several provinces on the basis the Government of India Act 1935, these provincial governments initiated new policies and programmes for the 'harijans and aborigines'. Thus, the problem of aborigines came to be discussed and debated on a variety of fora in the decade of 1930s. The vast data collected during the 1931 Census by Hutton and his writings, and various other reports provided rich material for these deliberations and debates.

The Problem of Aborigines in India by Thakkar (1941) came as a detailed presentation on the tribal populations in different parts of India, the problems they faced as perceived by Thakkar and the remedial measures he felt necessary were contained in this publication. It highlights restrictions on access to forest, making shifting cultivation illegal in many areas, the outcome of mining and other industrial activities in the tribal areas, indebtedness and bonded labour and land alienation. Further, excessive drinking, illiteracy and lack of education, health problems and imported diseases, lack of communications, problems connected with administrative and judicial system in tribal areas and lack of leadership were the other aspects discussed by Thakkar. In his concluding section, Thakkar, under the title 'Isolationism and Intervention', makes some comments about anthropologists.

Generally the government officials – particularly the English ICS officers – and the anthropologists do not favour the introduction of prohibition in aboriginal areas (Thakkar, 1941: 13).

Among those interested in the welfare of the aborigines there are two schools favouring two different policies, which are generally called 'Isolationism' and 'intervention'. Generally anthropologists and British members of the ICS and other government officers favour isolationism, which may be briefly explained as 'keeping the aborigines in their areas untouched by the civilization of the plains'. They fear that contact with the Hindus of the plains breaks the solidarity of the tribal society and brings many social evils into tribal areas, hitherto unknown there, like, for example, untouchability, early marriage and *purdah*. They are of opinion that the aborigines will try to imitate only the lower strata of the Hindu community of the plains and thus get demoralized and form another depressed community like the various Hindu Scheduled Castes. For example, Hutton writes:

> ... It is difficult for me to understand why these persons fear the contact with the Hindus and Muslims of the plains. It may be that in a few cases some social evils of the people of the plains are likely to be copied .... But to keep these people confined to and isolated in their inaccessible hills and jungles is something like keeping them in glass cases of a museum for the curiosity of purely academic persons .... In fact vast fields, concerning aboriginal life, still remain to be explored and there is plenty of work for anthropologists and other scholars .... What I mean to say is that a healthy comradeship should develop between the aborigines and the non-aborigines and each should profit culturally from the other and in course of time work hand in hand for the welfare of India as a whole .... Another charge leveled by some isolationists against indigenous social workers and nationalist politicians is that they are interventionists, that they approach the aborigines with the feelings of a morally and socially superior person approaching a degraded individual ... it is curious to note that these friends do not object to the Christian Missionaries' close and uncontrolled contact with them. Not only that, but they actively encourage them to spread Christian propaganda and even Roman script .... In fact it is unjust and wrong to call the indigenous social workers 'interventionists'. It would be proper to call them advocates of the policy of *assimilation* .... It

> is clear from the above that isolationists seem to doubt even the value of education so far as the aborigines are concerned. But at the same time it is encouraging to note that education is recognized at least as a weapon of defence against exploitation. (Thakkar, 1941: 23–25)

A discussion on the debate between 'isolationists' and 'assimilationists', particularly during 1940s cannot be complete without a reference to the works of Verrier Elwin. Thakkar Bapa's 'generally anthropologists' views quoted above, specifically the 'tribal contacts with the Hindus of the plains' and its effects, should be interpreted as an unnamed reference to a couple of foreign anthropologists, Verrier Elwin specially, who had by the beginning of 1940s come into sharp focus in this context.

Elwin who came to India in September 1927 as a missionary had subsequently changed into a disciple of Mahatma Gandhi and thereafter, almost giving up that life, set up an *ashram* in the Mandla district of Central Provinces (now Madhya Pradesh) to provide educational and medical services to the Gond and the Baiga. A prolific writer and a distinguished scholar in English literature from Oxford, Elwin at this stage started writing rich ethnography on the tribal communities among whom he was working. *The Baiga* (1939) was his first monograph. According to R.C. Guha (1999: 113), his appreciative biographer:

> When Elwin came to publish his ethnography of the Baiga, he had before him the example of Malinowski, ... Malinowski's work had given Elwin scientific sanction and a honourable precedent, the Pole was a dry-as-dust technician .... In contrast Elwin's account is animated and vigorous, illuminating through character and example what was for the tribe, is for him, 'the most important and enthralling thing in life.'

Baiga monograph was subsequently followed by a pamphlet, *Loss of Nerves: A Comparative Study of the Contact of Peoples in the Aboriginal Areas of the Bastar State and the Central Provinces of India* (1941) and, further on, with another pamphlet, *The Aboriginals* (1943) and its revised second edition (1944). In *The Baiga*, Elwin argued for the 'formation of a national park covering the wilder and inaccessible part of Mandla, where the Baiga would be sovereign, non aboriginals would be excluded ....' (Guha, 1999: 115).

And, this approach was further pursued in the two pamphlets. Elwin's views also enlisted the support of British ICS officers like W.G. Archer and W.V. Grigson who subsequently facilitated Elwin's appointment as Honorary Ethnographer and Census Officer of Bastar State. In 1940, Elwin moved to Bastar and thereby ensued his comparative study, *Loss of Nerves* (1941), *Maria Murder and Suicide* (1943), and the *Muria and their Gotul* delayed in its publication to 1947. The isolationists viewpoint came to assume its keywords like 'keeping the tribals in a zoo for anthropologists to study' and 'national parks for tribes' following the arguments contained in Elwin's Baiga monograph and the two pamphlets. It may be added that earlier in 1937 the Christian Missions' lobby as also the colonial administrators wanted to repatriate Elwin for his joining Gandhi's movement. He had then, in a statement for the India Office, said:

> On the other hand I myself consider the aboriginals to be pre-Hindu and that the adoption of Hinduism will be a major disaster for them; I welcome the Excluded Areas, and only wish that there were very many more of them; I consider that scientific anthropology should guide and regulate the administration of all primitive peoples and that they should not be handed over to elected politicians who have no knowledge of their special problems; and I think that the social and moral outlook of the Congress would cut the tap-root of vitality of aboriginal India. (quoted in Guha, 1999: 105)

However, in the course of his work in Bastar, Elwin's somewhat modified views on an affinity of tribal religion with Hinduism came to be formulated which finds an expression in the comparison contained in his pamphlet of 1941. Guha refers to this as follows:

> He now found to his surprise that he had to revise his opinion on another of the great faiths. Since he came to Mandla he had developed a strong dislike of Hinduism, for it was Hindus who– as moneylenders, landlords and officials– were the chief tormentors of his Baiga and Gonds. But in Bastar he discovered that Hinduism as a theological system was not that far removed from aboriginal thought. For the social life of the chiefdom revolved around the Dassera festival, when thousands of tribals from the hills descended on Jagdalpur to pay tribute to their king, whom they worshipped as the messenger on earth of Durga. The anthropologist concluded that the faith of the Bastar tribal 'was really closely related to Shaivite Hinduism. (ibid.: 137–38)

Majumdar had already documented the Dusserah in his Presidential Address of 1939 which is referred to by Guha as a 'classic essay' (ibid.: 366). Elwin's study on the Muria's ghotul also takes into account a 'functional account' of this institution in Bastar.

Majumdar in his review of the *Muria and their Ghotul* (111: 1948) has, while describing it as an outstanding publication, 'both from the points of view of its contents which have been skillfully handled, as also from the point of human interest he has brought to bear ...' (ibid.: 43) makes some critical comments relating to Elwin's methodology vis-à-vis the functional techniques of Malinowski. Also, mentioning the decline of this institution among several tribes, Majumdar argues that:

> If the very primitive Hill Marias do not have the dormitory or 'have it in embryo' the dormitory among the Murias as also among more advanced tribes, has acquired its status on the principle of 'graded utility'. The Muria gotul is a pathological development and no subjective evaluation or any amount of rationalization will help the Murias or any other tribe. Puritanism is no solution, neither a Dionysian philosophy of the gotul brand when contacts with civilization are producing 'loss of nerves' and social disequilibrium. A functional evaluation is the need for the Murias. The book by Elwin is a defence of a lost cause. A scientist must be objective, he fails in his mission if his sympathy becomes sentiment. (ibid.: 46)

Moreover, Majumdar also feels that photographs must be objective, meant for conveying what is true of the people. He adds, from his own observations in the area, that the Muria girls would not pose for nude photographs unless 'under threat or persuasion or extreme affection'. The review ends with the words:

> Anthropology is a science but can also be made subjective and idle curiosity. We do not want anthropology to be popular at such high cost. But whatever we may say, the book will be read and enjoyed by many, the descriptions will ring in the ear and the way of life that is doomed to extinction, will remain, 'forever young' in these pages as the Publishers have rightly said. The book is 'big' but we wish it were 'great' as well. (ibid.: 47)

Commenting on the richness of the documentation and the kind of photographs, Majumdar, as also the other readers of the book then, could not have been aware of how Kosi, Elwin's first wife who was a Gond from Mandla, had used a camera furtively and had been instrumental in winning over the Muria women folk in order to exchange confidences (Guha, 1999: 138–39). May be the Muria young men and women had valorized themselves to please the Englishman! Can we compare it to the quality of Mead's documentation of the Samoan youth and the 'making and unmaking of an anthropological myth'? (Freeman, 1983) Interestingly, 'Elwin hoped to enlist the aid to Jawahar Lal Nehru, 'the modern Hindu for reaching out a hostile public'.

Elwin's next book was *Bondo Highlander* (1950). Guha (1999: 208) describes it as, 'in some respects the most disappointing of all his books' being a conventional gazetteer like ethnography. Yet, Guha is vitriolic about some critical comments contained in Majumdar's review particularly about the way Elwin makes his writings popular reading and they sell. 'Handicaps that stifle anthropological research are inoperative in Elwin's case'. Basing his comments on letters and notings in some of Elwin's papers, Guha observes:

> Majumdar had reason to dislike Elwin. He had studied tribals, even tribals in Bastar, long before the Englishman. But Elwin's reputation quickly eclipsed his; worse, he thought Elwin's barbs at anthropologists who hurried in and out of the field were aimed especially at him. (Guha, 1999: 209)

Moreover, Elwin while reviewing S.C. Dube's, *The Kamar,* generously had 'wondered why the bright young scholar was keeping such dubious company' (reference to its publisher, The Ethnographic and Folk Culture Society), Guha's adverse comments, however, do not take into account some earlier reviews of Elwins' books by Majumdar. His, *Maria Murder and Suicide* (1943) was reviewed by Majumdar (93: 1944). The review is full of appreciation for this pioneering study in tribal crime and Majumdar has observed:

> Master technician characterized by deep humanity; fairness and sympathy for the aboriginal .... High standard and critical interpretation already familiar to us in his well known researches for which anthropologists feel deeply obliged ....

There is special appreciation for Elwin's suggestions underlining the need for understanding tribal customs which often clash with the criminal law, as they come from 'one who knows the aborigines well'. Subsequently, in 1947 Majumdar had reviewed Shamrao Hivale's biography of Elwin, *Gypsy Scholar*

(1946). Majumdar's review appreciates the book for its wealth of material, interesting quotes about Elwin's work through Bhumi Jan Seva Mandal and his concern for aboriginal tribes of India. The work, however, suffers from the defect inherent in one written .... By any fervent disciple and for not coming out enough with his own comments about the master. Thus, Majumdar was, in his reviews forthcoming with both praise and criticism. At one place Majumdar had also commented on the flow of Christian and Parsi charity for Elwin's work through his Mandal, because of the type of Elwin's popular work among the tribals of Central Provinces, and this was proved correct when JRD Tata and others discontinued their generous grants to the ashram when Elwin left the area to join as Advisor to Governor of Assam and Hivale wanted to continue the work (Guha, 1999: 297). Guha (1999: 179) too has described Gypsy Scholar as 'very much a commissioned work, with Sham the scribe, narrator and propagandist for various achievements.

This discussion on reviews was, however, diversive in our narration of the debate on 'isolationists' viewpoint. Elwin's own polemic, as voiced in *The Aborigines,* was moderated in the second edition of this pamphlet (1944) which Guha attributes to Elwin's understanding the 'value and purpose of the strategic retreat', in an India on the verge of Independence. The 'most combative paragraphs' from the first edition were dropped. Moreover, Elwin had done some rethinking of his own under attack from Ghurye and also Bose and others. It seems that the 'strategic retreat', was also rooted in Elwin suggesting to the India Office and ICS officers in November 1944 that a full-time advisor be appointed to advise the Government of India on aboriginal problems and the incumbent should be 'an Indian scientist of distinction'. Incidently, this was also the time when some British ICS officers and the India Office were trying to incorporate in the proposals for transfer of power a move to retain the tribal area of the North-East as 'crown colonies' under the control of the colonial power for at least a generation. Elwin's suggestion was passed on by the India Office to the Viceroy and in September 1946, Elwin was appointed Deputy Director in the newly set up Anthropological Survey of India with B.S. Guha as its Director.

On 31 August 1947, Elwin had testified before a subcommittee of the Constituent Assembly of India when he was working in the ASI. Here, he explained his position about his 'policy of isolation' in phrases 'nicely trimmed to the spirit of the age':

> Isolation, he told the committee, had once been advocated by him as a strictly temporary measure to protect the weaker tribes from the economic exploitation and psychic degradation that might result from uncontrolled contact. He had recommended it for the vast majority of tribals whom he called, in a very heavily trimmed phrase indeed, 'Hindus in the kindergarten class.' These had to be 'educated, developed and brought into the mainstream of modern Indian life as soon as possible.' Moreover, with a national and socialist government in place, Elwin saw that there was no place any more for isolation or exclusion. (Guha, 1999: 184–85)

Thus, after joining the Anthropological Survey of India, Elwin had 'trimmed' and phrased in a modified manner his views on the policy of isolation. Interestingly, his biographer (Guha, 1999) recounts several occasions when Elwin expressed his views on this acrimoniously debated aspect of tribal policy in India; and also how he had been making efforts to come to Jawaharlal Nehru's personal notice because he felt that Nehru was the only political leader who could appreciate the 'viewpoint on isolation, original or rephrased'. It was in 1945 that he got a chance to meet Nehru and discuss with him 'about tribal art' and 'art of living'. What followed was his appointment as Advisor to Governor of NEFA on tribes, and the policy and approach to development in that border area inhabited by a number of tribes which had till then remained in 'almost total isolation ... beyond the control of the Government of India ... with a political status different from most other parts of India ...' (Furer Haimendorf, 1982/85: 320). The policy drawn up and tried in NEFA was subsequently voiced by Nehru in the well known Tribal Panchshil and came to be accepted as guideline for tribal policy all over the country. NEFA and other tribal areas of Assam, declared as full-fledged states of the Indian Union in 1970s, had however formed an 'inner line' and therefore, were not open to any Indian visitors or academics, even from the Anthropological Survey of India without a permit administratively in Elwin's domain. Moreover, NEFA also came to be administered not by the Indian Administrative Service but by a service specially constituted and recruited by Elwin, the Indian Frontier Administrative Service. The Chinese invasion of NEFA in 1962 and its adverse outcome exposed it as a weaker, rather segregated, part of the country resulting into a long drawn phase of changes and its becoming a state, Arunachal Pradesh, with democratic institutions like any other state affirming the primacy of its tribal inhabitants.

The notable fact was that all the three papers which contained Majumdar's views on tribal problems as discussed above were not published in any scientific journal with limited readership but in the two widely circulated monthly magazines of the day. These magazines, then, reached the intellectuals, administrators, academics and others and, thus, we can presume that Majumdar wanted his views to become extensively known and debated. It was very much a part of his activism or public anthropology. It may also be added that by the beginning of 1940s, other anthropologists like Bose (1941) also had advanced the view that the tribals in India needed a well-studied and scientific approach for their welfare and development. Therefore, Thakkar's view that 'generally anthropologists favour isolationism' seems to have a patent bias or ignorance or deliberate omission of the well publicized views of prominent anthropologists of the day. Since Thakkar was the chosen 'beacon' of the Congress Party's work and policy exercises relating to tribals, his views and presence effectively kept all Indian anthropologists out of the Constitution-framing, policy planning, and the launching of new programmes for the Scheduled Tribes initially. A patent example thereof is that the very definition and process of recognizing tribal communities as Scheduled Tribes under the Constitution was, at its drafting stage, made administrative and legalistic, providing a good deal of scope for political considerations, by and large, of the executive and legislative wings at the Central and state levels. It eliminated any statutorily laid down scientific criteria for scheduling of tribes, which subsequently has given rise to inequalities, agitation and even violent movements. And so far only some processual contribution by the anthropologists in the system is being practised. However, these issues are out of the purview of this work.

Races and Cultures of India (91: 1944) was the revised version of a series of lectures which Majumdar had delivered to the ICS Probationers in 1942. These lectures were intended to provide the trainees a comprehensive introduction to people of India, their culture and various other aspects of their life and problems. The chapter 'Changing Canvas of Tribal Life' included in the part relating to Indian Social Organization and problems presents a view on tribal populations and the changes being brought about by their contact with the mainstream population and cultures.

There is no social group in India today with a zero point of cultural contact and, therefore, study of dynamics of culture change should be regarded as more important than monographic delineation of isolated tribal cultures. Broadly speaking, the changing economic environment has forced a new dynamics on the tribal people. Some tribal populations are facing bleak economic prospects in their own settlements and need a re-orientation of their economic life. It is also seen that some of the tribes, like those of Chhota Nagpur, because of the intense contact, have progressed at a tremendous pace, affecting in a few years changes which have taken centuries to achieve in other areas.

Majumdar has identified a range of factors directly responsible for what he called 'tribal discomfort' everywhere. These factors include the excise policies of the government, nomination by the government of tribal officers like Manki and Munda instead of hereditary ones, colonial forest laws restricting access to forest and banning of shifting cultivation, clash between some tribal customs and provisions of the Indian Penal Code, spread of new diseases, exploitation by money-lenders resulting in land alienation and mining and industrial activities in the resource-rich tribal areas. As a result of some of these factors several tribes have been declining in population.

The process of industrialization in the tribal areas which seems to have been introduced without considerations of local conditions and planning has also produced complications particularly in tribal cultures. Though it is a fact that many of the Indian industries depend entirely on tribal labour. Discussing tribal labour engaged in the mines and industries of Chhota Nagpur, Majumdar stresses that tribal labour from certain tribes are found to be efficient and quick in learning, and they have so far never added to the labour problems. But, this is no reason why their case should go by default; and their problems such as lower wages to contractual labour, lack of housing, health and educational facilities, etc. should not be solved. Majumdar makes out a very strong case for two long-term measures, viz., the training of tribals as skilled labour and opening of technical training centers as well as for assigning a certain percentage of the fabulous profits being made by the industry for rural welfare activities like schools, hospitals, drinking water wells, etc in the adjoining tribal areas.

Subsequently, Majumdar (1950: 292–98) has discussed the question of industrialization in tribal areas, particularly in the Chhota Nagpur context, elaborately and analytically. About tribal labour, he says:

> The managers tell us, that the tribal labourers are quick of perception and quite competent to follow instruction and their skill develop probably quicker than that of other communities, but what they acquire they lose in no time and most of the labourers end where they started, as coolies. The health of the people in the mines is never satisfactory. (ibid.: 295–96)

Moreover, since the management employs people from outside among their technical staff and high-paid labourers, the tribals are discontented. This may lead to labour unrest. The remedy, therefor, has been outlined by Majumdar. Tribal labour has also migrated to tea plantation and a comparison of their condition in mining industry with those prevailing in the tea plantation shows that the migrants to the latter have more opportunities of learning and incorporating new cultural traits. Majumdar has also stressed that the tribal labour would perform far better if their social environment can be secured. Thereby, the tribal communities will depend much more on the industries and this would encourage their specialization and acquisition of skills and also check detribalization.

This analysis of the situation and the well focused suggestions for action, coming in early 1940s and later in 1950 from Majumdar seem to be ahead of his times. The Task Force and Working Groups for the development of tribal areas and tribal communities during the Fifth Plan, mentioned earlier, had laid great emphasis on similar measures. B.D. Sharma, who was the officer in-charge of tribal programmes in 1970s, and later on Commissioner for Scheduled Castes and Scheduled Tribes, wrote:

> Therefore, the concept of industrialization will have to be some what broader and diversification of the tribal economy will have to be one of the important facets. Thus, assimilative capacity of the local community will be an important 'given condition' in the industrial planning of a tribal region. (Sharma, 1976: 5–6)

The issues, Sharma analyses in this context, include preparedness of the local community for a wide skill spectrum and diversification of tribal economy, building of entrepreneurship in the area and some adaptations in the industrial process itself to match the local socio-economic situation. A detailed strategy for ensuring healthy impact of industrial activity in the tribal hinterland, mutual appreciation of the needs of the industry and the people and advance planning to ensure better human resources and skills, infrastructure, etc., and also involving the traditional artisan groups in the area into the process have been suggested. These strategies were expected to be interwoven with the area-based tribal sub-plan starting mid-1970s.

The first number of the third Volume of *The Eastern Anthropologist* (September 1949) was a special tribal number. It contained papers on various aspects of the tribal life and their problems from a number of anthropologists and social workers, including A.V. Thakkar.

In his 'notes and comments', Majumdar points out how 'there has been considerable serious and non-serious scientific and sentimental writings relating to tribal or aboriginal problems'. Briefly mentioning the special provisions in this regard contained in the Draft Constitution of India, Majumdar points out that India, 'in her anxiety for coordinated social planning, we need a scientific attitude towards this vital problem', and further:

> Planning to be effective must be based on knowledge of tribal conditions in particular habitat and we need not have one tribal policy, but several. The motto of planning for tribal life, must be what Lord Raglan once said, 'we cannot be civilized unless we are all civilized'. It is the means or techniques that need competent appraisal and the articles in this issue will indicate the magnitude of the problem and the lines of approach from the angles of reform, science and welfare. (*The EA*, 3: 1: i)

Thakkar, in his leading article, discusses some pressing problems of primitive tribes and emphasizes that carefully planned schemes for protection of tribes, particularly the more primitive ones in great danger of becoming extinct, 'have to be prepared by the authorities concerned with the help of anthropologist and social workers' and, further stresses the need for specially trained workers. The contribution that non-official agencies with a missionary spirit can make in this field has also been emphasized with some details of the work planned by the Bhartiya Adimjati Sevak Sangh set up recently. Here, Thakkar seems to have shed off his earlier ire regarding anthropologists; and this is, perhaps, his first article in an anthropological journal. Majumdar in his article, 'The Changing Canvas of Tribal Life', puts forth his views on the ill effects of contacts with reference to particular agents of contact as also the positive aspects thereof, and hence the need for a careful scientific study of the dynamics of change in tribal culture so that the likelihood of developing a malaise can possibly be avoid. In this context, he also illustrates how administrative measures like introducing policing in Kolhan and nomination of unsuitable tribals as tribal officers can damage the whole process. Here, again, he emphasizes the need for upgrading skills of tribal labour and eliminating miseries the labourers are facing to avoid tribal 'ferment to the boiling pot'. Significantly, Majumdar has also thrown up what are now called gender issues. He points out that tribal areas have 'a contingent of able bodied, intelligent and hard working women' who for various customary reasons cannot expect to settle down in matrimony. This work force should not be wasted and they should be educated and trained to work usefully for the society as nurses, teachers, etc.

In 1946, Majumdar had delivered the Sri Mahadev Wathodkar Memorial Foundation Lectures in the University of Nagpur. One of these lectures was on, 'Tribal Rehabilitation' (Majumdar, 1947: 150–75). The lecture was mainly a review of his stand regarding the various aspects of contact situation among tribes. Briefly, he states:

The process through which the tribal cultures are usually transformed or modified may be one or other of the following:

1. Simple adoption or taking over.
2. Acculturation which involves,
   (a) acceptance and
   (b) adaptation.
3. Assimilation
   (a) Social commensalism
   (b) Plural Association (ibid.: 161).

Elaborating how anthropologists have analysed these different outcomes of the dynamics of change, Majumdar presents in the concluding section of the lecture, his vision of how our society which has such varied components should fare:

> A 'plural society' may exist as a confederation in which the constituent elements live their own lives though united for such resistance and aggression from outside, but having common territorial limits, without the means of secession even if the union is found to be intolerable. Such confederation is possible between different nations having common geographical boundaries, but culture has no such rigid frontiers, and various groups or tribes living together share common cultural traits though the patterns of their culture may be different. To me, it appears that the various groups of people sharing the same territory and forming parts of the same economic structure, can live, each its own life without fusion, having symbiotic or commensal relationship with one another, adopting desirable traits from one another and even acculturating on a generous scale, yet maintaining an identity of language and culture between the constituent elements or the group which must develop a consciousness of kind among the units– a sort of cultural federation, in which mutuality and reciprocity rather than submission and suppression would provide smooth working of the federal structure and adjustment of the various groups to one another without undue hardships or discomforts to the cooperating units. This if found possible, will do away with the necessity of ironing out cultural differences, at the same time produce a *modus vivendi* for cultural miscegenation. The significant cultural differences that we find today between the hill people on the one hand and the plains people on the other, between the tribes and castes, who need to be brought together for common good, may not pull the divergent elements in opposite directions, as contra-acculturation is likely to do. What is needed is mutual respect and understanding, and where the dominant or ruling groups has shown such respect and understanding cultural adjustment has been smooth and easy. It is I think possible for the tribes to-day to feel more secure and take greater share in the cultural progress of the country provided the attitude forced on the caste people by the numerical preponderance of the tribes and backward groups is not merely used for political expediency but as a sincere gesture towards a broad cultural movement seeking to absorb and assimilate the bulk of the primitive and backward substratum of population in the country. If the political leaders of the country fail to recognize the trends of political thought and aspirations surging in the minds of the newly conscious tribal groups and exterior castes, a

> possibility which however, cannot be ruled out as the indication goes, the future of India must be viewed with misgivings. (ibid.: 173–75)

Majumdar talks here of doing away with the necessity of ironing out cultural differences and achieving 'a modus vivendi for cultural miscegenation'. His viewpoint seems to be that such an approach would eliminate the 'contra-acculturative' trends among the tribal people. This idealistic situation has, however, never been elaborated by him nor has it been explicated how it can be made operationally processual. However, it sounds that it is somewhere akin to the multi-pronged 'inclusive' policies being pursued today which also implies rewriting or redefining of various laws which effect the 'other', so that policies and programmes on the ground adapt themselves more readily to the 'other'– and this is elaborately reflected in the recent anthropological writings (Xaxa, 2008; K.S. Singh on Identity and Ethnicity, 1993; Oommen, 1995 and others). This entire question has assumed vital importance in the context of the tribal policy combining a protectionist frame and area exclusion with safeguards as laid out in the Indian Constitution vis-à-vis demands for self-determination and rights to natural resources, as also the widespread extremist – Maoist movement for liberation in a very large number of districts having tribal populations and rich natural resources.

The politico-legal debate around the existing approach has been focusing on the observations that the concepts developed for advancing a colonial policy, woven through 'primitivism' and 'protectionism', were statutorily adopted by the British from the earliest days of the establishment of their rule in tribal areas; its history begins from the Scheduled Districts Act 1874 and the earlier Regulations evolving a 'paternistic system' of rule by selected British officers and subsequently elaborated by the British anthropologists and civil servants in colonized Africa. It is argued that 'primitivism' and its corollary a paternistic approach was developed as an ideology and, then, it was refined by the various Constitutional enactments by the colonial rulers till the Government of India Act 1935. As Chandra points out:

> Primitivism is a type of liberal imperial ideology of rule that has justified the subjugation of populations and places described as wild, savage or, simply, primitive. Primitive populations were, paradoxically, subjects of both *improvement* and *protection* in colonized societies (2013: 138).

The colonial reformers also incorporated the controverted concepts like 'tribes', 'castes, higher and exterior' and, thus, identified that the Indian society was stratified into three levels – caste Hindus, tribes co-existing with castes, generally exterior castes, and tribes living more or less exclusively. This culminated into an approach like that of Elwin – keeping them protectively in parks (excluded areas) which were typically backward tracts and even the idea of creating 'crown colonies', at least for a generation or two after the transfer of power.

It was rightly pointed out by the Congress at the time of the visit of the Simon Commission that this policy of exclusion of areas and communities had not achieved any liberally conceived growth or development for the tribes, not even educational – literacy rate among tribes was 0.7 per cent in 1931. It could never achieve any other positive results either.

A Congress pamphlet, titled, 'Excluded Areas under the New Constitution' (1937) lambasted 'the essentially reactionary nature of British rule in India', thus:

> That kept '15 million inhabitants of India ... preserved in a state of semi-barbarism, denied education, medical facilities and other amenities of civilized life' (Ahmad, 1937: 6). Without a 'consciousness of their political and economic rights', the liberal voice of anti-colonialism argued, these 'backward people ... (were) helpless before the physical prowess of their foreign rulers' (ibid.: 7) According to this line of reasoning, this denial of political and economic rights stemmed from the 'authoritative and autocratic' administration of tribal areas by 'a few government officials,' little to no literacy or local self-government among the governed populations, and the lack of 'any vital contact between the tribes and the civilized areas'. (Chandra, 2013: 151)

Significantly, there seems to be a sharp difference in the approach to tribal administration and policy to be laid down in the Constitution of India being then drafted by the Constituent Assembly between leaders like Sardar Vallabhbhai Patel and Jaipal Singh, a prominent Oxford educated tribal leader from Chhota Nagpur, and Nehru and Ambedkar. Patel probably was the first, then, to question the concept of 'tribe' in the Indian context. He expressed his discomfort with the notion of tribe in the course of discussion on the Report of Fundamental Rights Sub-Committee in the Constituent Assembly, thus:

> Now, with regard to the word 'tribes', my own feeling is that it is not an appropriate word. The expression 'protection of tribal areas', similarly, is not a happy one. This expression will convey the meaning that we are now concerned with the protection of certain areas. That is, if some external trouble is expected or if some encroachment is going to be made there, the protection of 'tribal areas', will carry a different meaning ... (how prophetic in the context of the 1962 war with China). What is the meaning of tribes. What is it that the word means, and is it so? It means something and it is there because, for two hundred years, attempts have been made by foreign rulers to keep them in groups apart with their customs and other things in order that the foreigners' rule may be smooth. The rulers did not want that there should be any change ... . All the laws that have been giving them protection are there. But have they protected them? (Saksena, 1981: 49)

Jaipal Singh, while commenting on the resolution regarding aims and objectives of the Constitution including safeguards for tribal areas, criticized these provisions as follows:

> What my people require, Sir, is not adequate safeguards .... We do not ask for any special protection. We *want to be treated like every other Indian* .... I take you all at your word that now we are going to start a new chapter, a new chapter of Independent India where there is *equality of opportunity*. Where no one would be neglected. *We are all equal.*

These views were far removed from what Nehru and Ambedkar believed to be the correct approach in this context. The Sub-Committee report on the proposed Scheduled Areas, chaired by Thakkar, agreed with Nehru and Ambedkar on the need to extend the protectionist provisions of the Government of India Act, 1935, to the new postcolonial constitution (Thakkar, 1947). The 'people of the excluded areas', it explained along the lines of the Simon Commission, had 'no experience of local self-governing institutions of the modern or statutory type and are of course not represented in the legislature' (ibid.: 4). The sub-committee report on tribal areas in Assam, too, regurgitated an old colonial trope (Chandra, 2013: 154–55).

The recommendations of the Thakkar Sub-Committee were adopted almost in totality and incorporated in the Indian Constitution which lays down in its Fifth Schedule, the provisions for the President to recognize certain areas as Scheduled Areas, and their administration. Similarly, the recommendations of the Sub-Committee, headed by Gopinath Bardolai, in respect of the North-East Frontier Tribal Areas (Partially Excluded Areas in 1935) were adopted to create Tribal Areas and their governance as per the Sixth Schedule. It contained provisions for setting up of Autonomous Districts and Regional Councils. Other special provisions relating to Scheduled Tribes that concretizes the older language of protection were also adopted as a part of the Constitution. The question that arises several decades after the adoption of this Constitution are: Why did it 'continue with a dysfunctional system' if the primitivist mix of protection and improvements had not worked earlier? Why was it expected to work in future? (Chandra, 2013: 155). Another related question is as to why in spite of these protectionist safeguards and recognition of areas as Scheduled Areas and Tribal Areas, along with the various provisions related to their administration, there is a widespread dissatisfaction in both the Scheduled and non-Scheduled Areas inhabited by the Scheduled Tribes as also some of the former Tribal Areas, now full-fledged states.

Haimendorf's study of tribal India (1982/1985) in which he portrays vividly the condition of the tribals in Andhra Pradesh and Arunachal Pradesh has been aptly subtitled, 'The Struggle for Survival' for the tribes. He is critical of the manner in which the special provisions for the protection and development of Scheduled Tribes are being implemented even to the detriment of tribals specially in areas where tribals are in a majority in their areas such as in Andhra Pradesh. For instance, the process of democratic decentralization or Panchayati Raj which was 'intended to take the place of the more paternalistic form of government characteristics of the days of British rule' has 'certainly boosted the tribal's self-confidence and has also brought them some tangible advantages' in states like Arunachal Pradesh and Nagaland where tribals are 'an overwhelming majority'; but in other areas such as Andhra Pradesh 'decentralization has had far from desirable results' (1982: 320). Elsewhere, Haimendorf, describing an outstanding tribal leader in Arunachal, appreciates how he 'evinced a breadth of vision and a refreshing realism which I have not often encountered among Indian politicians' (ibid.: 310). Concluding, Haimendorf holds out:

> The manner of the integration of the tribals into the wider Indian society will ultimately be determined by political decisions, and these will be made on the basis of moral evaluations. It thus seems that unless the intellectually leading sections of the Indian population develop a spirit of cultural tolerance and an

> appreciation for tribal values, even the most elaborate schemes for the economic improvement of tribal populations are likely to prove abortive (ibid.: 322).

The position on the ground is that there are armed struggles and movements going on for decades? The situation has been exacerbated in a large number of districts in central India, specially Bastar and adjoining districts of Chhatisgarh and Chhota Nagpur and other tribal areas in Jharkhand with the Maoist struggle and its sustained violence.

Women's Place in Tribal Rehabilitation

It is mentionable that Majumdar has emphasized in his approach to what he calls 'Tribal Rehabilitation' or 'Economic Rehabilitation', the place of the tribal women. He is appreciative of the general appearance and capabilities of the Ho women (Majumdar, 1937: 12–13) and how they have been participating in industrial and mining labour along with the men folk, specially in areas nearer to their villages for example in Noa-Mundi (ibid.: 185). Even earlier in his 1925 paper relating to the movement for social reforms among the Ho, he had rather critically mentioned the move to restrict women's participation in economic activities like visiting the tribal *hatts* or participation in dancing. Moreover, while discussing the practice of *gonong* (bride price) and various forms of marriage among the Ho, he had constantly portrayed how the Ho households come to have a large number of spinsters or young unmarried women who are something of a wasted human resource.

Perceptively, when discussing the 'Changing Canvas of Tribal Life', (1944/1958: 406–07) he brings up the plight of this section of women as follows:

> Every village has a contingent of able-bodied intelligent and hardworking women who cannot expect to settle down for want of suitable proposals or the incompetence of the young men to provide the necessary *gonong* or means to maintain life. These girls fade away without doing good to society, their time is ill-spent and where they find a shelter they drudge to keep it. The education of these girls, their training in the profession and vocations, will help the tribe to raise its standard of living; at the same time they can be put to gainful occupations which will contribute to the country's prosperity. There are several professions in India where women are needed, but to which they are not attracted. Nursing is a neglected profession in India. The entrants are not of quality, nor are the conditions of service so good as to attract women. The free and unfettered social life the tribal women lead in their villages, the hard work they are capable of doing and the unemployment in the tribal areas, are colossal waste of India's man-power. During the last War a considerable number of tribal women, generally from the Christian community in the Ranchi District of Bihar, were recruited to the W.A.C.I. and they filled many important technical and non-technical posts and acquitted themselves with credit. Tribal women trained in such vocations can adjust themselves to any situation more freely than their sisters from middle class families, and moreover they are a healthy lot. Today they spend their time in wasteful journeys from end to end of the tribal country, and even a 20-mile trek to a weekly market with an *anna* worth of Sag or leafy vegetables is wistfully looked forward to. In one weekly

> market in Chaibassa we estimated the total value of commodities, mostly produce of their kitchen gardens, at ₹ 11, at the prevailing market rate, and the sellers, mostly women, numbered 84. Similarly, the buyers who usually buy a little salt or a *pice* worth of tobacco leaf, or an *anna* worth of kerosene oil, number thousands, and the total purchases of a village ten miles away from the market amounted to ₹ 3.50 with the number of purchases as high as sixty. The crowd in a market is not composed only of buyers and sellers, the sightseers always outnumber the latter and their only interest is in gossip or drink at the booths, though rice-beer forms even today their main fare. Every woman in Kolhan spends half of her waking hours in work, which involves walking miles away and back, and if there is an urban centre in the neighbourhood, or a railway station, she will undertake a journey of several miles, morning and evening, to sell an *anna's* worth of vegetables or a seer of rice, coming back with a packet of salt or other small needs of the family. This is a colossal waste of man-hours and energy which can be avoided by proper planning and cooperative efforts. (ibid.: 406–07)

In this context, he has also discussed the desirability of recruiting suitable and educated tribal personnel from both the sexes to the post of Thana officers which in his opinion provides for a positive and healthy role in the new administrative set-up being introduced in Kolhan.

As Majumdar's ethnography spanned the polyandrous community in Jaunsar-Bawar, Tharus in the tarai areas of UP, denotified communities in UP and the Ho and Gond in Chhota Nagpur and central India respectively, he has come out with a rich analytical portrayal of the varied roles of tribal women far beyond the usual status discussion in the monographs of his times. In the polyandrous society he has particularly emphasized the contrasting positions of a married woman as *ranti* and *dhyanti* and how it is pivotal in enabling the women to relieve themselves of the acute stress of being a wife in fraternal polyandry. Among the Tharu, he has perceptively commented upon the women enjoying a better status and even discriminating against their husband because of the oral tradition that they were originally from ruling families. In the Ho context, he has also referred to the treatment of certain women specially widowed and older ones suspected of being witches. He has, thus, raised this problematic issue of the area which is still a rather widespread gender related crime there.

Rehabilitation of the Criminal Tribes, Now Denotified Tribes

Discussing the issues connected with the re-habilitation of the ex-Criminal Tribes and weaning them away from crime, Majumdar emphasized that whole tribes could not totally be criminals and only a few families or a gang may be prone to commit offences. Therefore, mere legislative action against the community as embodied in the Criminal Tribes Act was no remedy. The need was for an approach attuned to individual criminals of these tribes.

Then, the need is to remedy their economic conditions. In this context the occupational patterns of the tribes which largely emphasize criminal activities have to be attended to. Unproductive social and ceremonial expenses should be eliminated through propaganda and education. An organized distribution of industries may help them transfer their attention from crime to a settled life and healthy economic pursuits. Majumdar is critical of the administrative approach of setting up resettlement colonies where work and wages hardly match and thus they are exploited. Introduction of agriculture as an occupation would be difficult unless it is organized through cooperatives.

Majumdar observed that the children of the Criminal Tribes whom he examined were found to be highly intelligent. Therefore, there is a need to put them in healthier surroundings away from the influence of their parents and tribal elders. The establishment of boarding schools for them was one alternative. Another alternative, he suggested, was to select particular families and transfer them to cities or industrial centres where the parents can be profitably employed and children looked after in the special schools run for them. Such families should be carefully selected. All this would need competently organized re-habilitation and re-location, and this should be a central subject in order to avoid difficulties in finances and jurisdiction (as one tribe may be scattered over several States)

Majumdar had as early as 1930s noticed the state of Criminal Tribes as a collectivity, and quite a large one at that, particularly in Uttar Pradesh and other provinces of northern India. His focus was on their condition then and there and he discussed it without going diachronically into the factors, colonial or pre-colonial which had brought about their problems and criminality. Appreciably, the very first Volume of *The Eastern Anthropologists* in 1947 carries not only his article but several others on these communities and also a brief resume of the recommendations of the enquiry committee appointed by the government of Uttar Pradesh in the matter. Thus, his approach was humanistic and developmental without much thought for any dialogical and historical appraisal which seems to have been the line of study by some recent students. He was concerned more with the policies and programmes including the necessary legal provisions which would, in his view, pave the way for a better future specially for the younger generations among them and the non-criminal sections. In fact, in *Races and Cultures* (4th edition, 1961), his concern reflects something of an extreme viewpoint:

> Under the present arrangement, the children of criminal tribes grow up under parental care and take to crime more easily than they would otherwise. Some of the children of the criminal tribes whom we have examined were found to be highly intelligent, active and alert. It is a pity that this promise of manhood finds no expression in later life. Many of the children and students from criminal tribes whom we have talked to in Kanpur, Gorakhpur, Lucknow and other places, have expressed dissatisfaction with their parental supervision and have readily responded to the suggestion of a transfer of allegiance and also of place. It is necessary that these children should be segregated from their parents, but in healthier surroundings .... The children can be segregated, if necessary, by an Act of the legislature applicable to the tribes known to be 'criminal'. (221: 1961: 384)

And these suggestions are followed by an ethnographic note on the tribal and gang organization of these ex-criminal tribes to help one 'to evaluate the strength and weakness of the ex-criminal tribes'.

A brief note on the later day developments after the repeal of the law may not be out of place. A focussed planning for the ex-criminal tribes or denotified communities as they came to be called after the repeal of the Criminal Tribes Act has not been achieved even after 65 years of the repeal. In fact, the identities of this collectivity which needed a different kind of an approach for their healthy development has come under a segmental process of sectoral planning as some of these communities are listed under different categories as Scheduled Castes, some others as Scheduled Tribes and a bulk under other Backward Classes and Nomadic Tribes. This scenario, in a way allows some of them to avail of more positive discrimination than others. But, those in the categories of Scheduled Castes and Scheduled Tribes have to compete for it with others in these categories who are far more advanced economically and in education. Saksena observed that 'development has left out quite a number of castes in a comparative state of neglect. Generally, these castes are either small caste groups .... Or groups with an stigma of criminality' (2004: 481). Analysing the situation in UP, he observes (1977: 39–54) that extremely low literacy and deprivation levels prevailed among some of the 19 earlier notified Criminal Tribes and now listed as Scheduled Castes in the state. Even the special component plan for Scheduled Castes had not produced the desired result for them. Bokil, referred to earlier, has also observed similarly in respect of Maharashtra. On an all India level the National Commission for Denotified, Nomadic and Semi-Nomadic Tribes had submitted its report in June 2008 and it has still not been published. Gandhi points out:

> As a result, many of the needs of these communities are not fulfilled. For example, the budget allocated for the education, health nutrition, employment opportunities, hostel facilities, separate allocations are not made for the basic needs of these communities. (2013: 141)

Earlier, Gandhi and Lalitha had studied a process of social transformation in Stuartpuram settlement which has been achieving very encouraging results as a result of a concerted programme undertaken by social activists and their non-government organization with substantial backing from the Government of Andhra Pradesh (2009: 88–133). This documentation brings out how a systematic and integrated plan based on field survey to identify criminal elements and the problems can succeed if it is positively and well supported by the government which undertook the initial steps of freeing the settlements from the control of Salvation Army and settling lands and housing with the individual families.

Apart from such action for rehabilitation, the need was for creating an informed interest in the people who have been more sinned against than sinning. And, Majumdar did exactly this by publishing articles sometimes in the 1940s on two such tribes in the *Hindi Vishwa Bharti* (217–18: N.D.), a pioneering encyclopedic publication in Hindi. He cautioned against undertaking mere ameliorative measures, and piecemeal legislation. These people were in need of concerted action backed by experts and finances to carry it into effect.

6

Village Studies

Himalayan Polyandry – Tribe-Caste, Village-Region

Himalayan Polyandry – Structure, Functioning and Culture Change: A Field Study of Jaunsar-Bawar (1962) is an elaborate study of Jaunsar-Bawar area in Deharadun district (now in Uttarakhand state). The area has certain distinctive features, namely polyandrous family and society, a religious cult (Bhatt, 2010) and a Scheduled Tribe status for all the residents of this geographical area, designated as 'Jaunsari' in the Constitutional Order. However, the society has 'a multi-structure with only a few stereotyped castes divided into three groups with well defined traditional status' along with intensive discriminatory practices against the lowest castes.

The study has at its core a detailed ethnography of three villages selected on the basis of certain criteria, to present 'a representative character with regard to the culture of the region'[1]. Thus, the three village studies encapsulated here project the region – Jaunsar-Bawar. The fieldwork for this study was carried out by a large team for almost three years, under Majumdar's directions and frequent visits to its 'field centres'. It is the culmination of an interesting interaction:

> It was in 1937 that I got interested in the Khasas of Jaunsar-Bawar. In an informal discussion, my teacher, Professor Bronislaw Malinowski, discussed polyandry in the Himalayas, and referred to Jaunsar-Bawar. Although I had joined the Lucknow University in 1928, I did not know of the existence of polyandrous people in the Deharadun district, and felt ashamed of my ignorance. I promised Professor Malinowski that I would visit these people and plan a major field assignment there. This I did in the autumn of 1937. (220: 1962: viii)

He not only followed it up with a comprehensive study, *Himalayan Polyandry*, but also inspired and supervised one of his PhD scholars to work on the people in another part of the polyandrous area, Trans-Giri region of Sirmaur district, in Himachal Pradesh (Parmar, 1975). Y.S. Parmar became the first Chief

Minister of Himachal Pradesh when this state came into existence after the reorganization of the states in 1956.

Political History

Jaunsar-Bawar is culturally a part of a larger tract, sharing its characteristic features such as polyandry, a rather skeletal caste system with heavy overtones of discrimination, and the religious cult of Mahasu *devta*. Bhatt (2010: 47) describes this larger region as *Mahasu desh* which stands as a buffer between the western and the central Himalayas, a religio-cultural entity, lying in the districts of Deharadun, Tehari and Uttar Kashi in Uttarakhand and Shimla and Sirmaur also known as Nahan in Himachal Pradesh. In fact, Jaunsar-Bawar is an important part of this larger region because of its colonial and legal history. It can also be regarded as a 'geographic enclave that is relatively isolated from outsiders but whose people are quite conscious of outsiders' and where 'regional self-identification is usually strongest' (Mandalbaum, 1972: 360). Jaunsar-Bawar was annexed by the British in early 19th century after the Gorakha War. The other areas in the larger region, however, continued to be parts of princely states like Shimla, Sirmaur and Tehari. The colonial administration after taking over Jaunsar organized the administrative and legal system for the area as per their understanding and observations of the local practices. The traditional political system of the area, divided into Khats headed by Sayanas and a group of Khats headed by Sadar Sayana was retained. They imposed revenue collection through Sayanas with the last settlement having been made in 1884 and continuing till 1949–51. In consultation with Sayanas, they also codified the prevailing customs as reported to them into a *Dastur-ul-Amal* which standardized local conventions and practices with regard to land tenure and revenue, inter-village and inter-khat relations and the duties and privileges of the Sayanas. This codification also 'froze', in a way, the disabilities in landownership and other civil rights imposed against the lower castes, including certain discriminatory penal provisions for any crimes they commit against the higher castes. Thus, in a way, the local caste organization continued in this 'isolated geographical region' almost without any changes in the system which gradually came about elsewhere.

Under the Scheduled District Act of 1874, this area was also declared a Scheduled District along with many other areas all over the British India, such as Coorg, Southern Mirzapur, etc. This meant that the laws enacted by the colonial government for British India were made applicable to these areas selectively and with suitable amendments when necessary. However, none of the few castes, upper, middle and lower, in this area were ever recognized under any of the categories of the different Government of India Acts, such as 'backward tribes' as per 13th Scheduled to the Government of India (Provincial Legislative Assemblies) Order 1936, though 'Jaunsar-Bawar paragana of the Deharadun district' was declared a Partially Excluded area under the relevant Order of 1936 under the Government of India Act, 1935. The lower castes in this area such as Bajgi and Dom along with the Silpkar in the adjoining hill areas were given the status of Scheduled Castes under the Government of India (Scheduled Caste)

Order 1936. This status of the castes inhabiting Jaunsar-Bawar remained unchanged till 1967 when the first Presidential Order declaring five Scheduled Tribes in Uttar Pradesh under the Indian Constitution came into effect and included 'Jaunsari', in other words all the residents of the area, as Scheduled Tribes. However, with the coming into force of the Indian Constitution Jaunsar-Bawar ceased to be a Partially Excluded Area, along with Southern Mirzapur in UP because the Constitution did not recognize any areas of UP as Scheduled Areas (the term it used for the erstwhile Partially Excluded Areas)

Region and Civilization

The region, as described earlier, comparatively does not show many pronounced linkages with Hindu and Indian civilizational complex. This is mainly the result of its geographical isolation and difficult access as well as the development of a strong regional socio-religious tradition – local tradition. As Majumdar points out:

> Very little is known about the history of this region and of the local people, but the legends and archaeological evidence may well point to an ancient date. The local Brahmans and Rajputs claim the earliest origin. They associate themselves with the Pandavas of the Mahabharata fame whose monuments are supposed to exist at Lakhamandal, a village on the eastern border of Jaunsar-Bawar. It is from the Pandavas that they trace the origin of their prevalent polyandrous system of marriage. There have also been recently excavated, at the temple site of Lakhamandal, a good collection of stone sculptures dating back to eighth century A.D. On the other hand, there was found in the last century on the right bank of the Jamuna near Kalsi, in Lower Jaunsar, an inscription on a huge boulder containing the edicts of Ashoka, which shows that by the end of the third century B.C. this part of the country was no longer an uninhabited jungle. (220: 1962: 3–4)

Oral 'traditions and available documentary accounts, however, do not go further than a couple of centuries'.

A multi-caste structure here includes only a few stereotyped castes with several structural features of its own:

> As a matter of tradition, the village community here is dominated, both socially and economically, by the Brahmans and the Rajputs. There is practically no differentiation in status between the two, but they form two different castes despite occasional inter-marriages between them. In the case of inter-marriages, the children belong to the caste of their fathers. It is rather difficult to assess the inter-relations and relative positions between these castes and the Brahmans and Rajputs of the other regions of India. (ibid.: 23)

Moreover, the intermediate caste groups, artisans also show a lesser degree of hierarchal rigidity as marriages occur between Badi (carpenter) and Sonar (goldsmith) caste groups.

The religious complex in Jaunsar-Bawar is largely centred around Mahasu *devta*. However, Mahasu temples also enshrine Hindu deities like Bishnu and Kali. Bhatt has analysed these civilizational linkages recently, and comments:

> The cultic phenomenon of Mahasu is a local-regional phenomenon. It carries the identity of a *lok*. But, on the other hand, as evident in the symbols and rituals of Mahasu's puja-system, the system of *yajans* organized on the occasions of consecration of Chalda's temple at Thadiyar and Shanti Path (earlier known as Khursau Puja at Hanol) and Mahasu's identities as Narain, Raghunath, Thakur and Mahashiv, Mahasu phenomenon is also linked to the traditions of Shastrachar. Through this linkage of Lok-Shastra, hinging on the well-established world-view of unity in diversity, Mahasu phenomenon gets linked to a wider cultural-philosophical space of religio-cultural accretions and accommodation; and, that is the framework of Hindu (Indian) civilization. (2010: 393)

Elsewhere (220: 1962: 291–92) Majumdar has also mentioned that the 'indigenous system of education and training had a caste and economic basis' except in the case of 'Kashmiri Vidya' a native school of magico-religious practice aimed at training in the 'art of foretelling the future as well as of discovering and exorcising evil spirits? It is a monopoly of the Brahmans' by whom it was imported from Kashmir. A link with the *Mahabharat* is also there. A sacred wooden tablet inscribed with the alphabets of Kashmiri Vidya exists in Guthar village, near Lakhamandal and it is kept on a platform in the temple along with some weapons which are believed to have been used by the Pandava brothers, who had lived in this region for some time.

Referring to the integrated structure in the region, which in a way helps in maintaining a structural equilibrium, Bhatt has observed:

> Earlier, *Mahasu's* divination was functionally oriented to the ideology of maintaining the solidarity of the structure of family, hierarchy of caste roles, intra- and the inter-village relations and extension of faith in the tutelary charisma to those who suffered from body and mental ailments and calamities caused by physical forces of nature, epidemics and individual and communal problems caused by factors beyond human imagination and understanding. Now *Mahasu's* divination is sought for business prospects and for ways and means to economic prosperity and political success. (2010: 402)

In the context of dominance by one section of the population, the Rajput and Brahman, over the rest a potential factor may also be the ethno-cultural affiliation of different sections Majumdar concisely mentions this:

> As regards racial affiliation, the high castes show general resemblance to their equals in the plains, with the characteristics popularly known as 'Aryan' features. They claim to have immigrated from Kashmir or the north-west in ancient times, though some immigrant families from the neighbouring districts or states can also be found. The lower castes, especially the Bajgis and Koltas, have been regarded as aboriginals or belonging to an earlier wave of immigrants. They often have the features which may be regarded as derived from the Proto-Australoid strain, though mixed features are not uncommon. At any rate, there exists little certainly about their origin, or of the origins of other intermediate castes in this region. Socially as well as culturally, the affiliation

> and association of Jaunsar-Bawar and its people with Sirmur have been referred to; the plains people in the Dun and the Garhwalis in Tehri-Garhwal have also been their close neighbours. (220: 1962: 24)

Structural Features of Jaunsar-Bawar Society

We may now turn to briefly present the basic structural features of the society through the portrayal of the three selected villages.

Hierarchal status, social, economic and political dominance of Brahman and Rajput over the rest and a long history of more or less unchanging continuity in these relationships are characteristics of Jaunsar-Bawar. This structural pattern reflects itself *ab initio*, in the village settlement, its population composition and oral settlement history of villages. Thus:

> The caste-wise distribution of houses is one of the most striking and important features of the village settlement in Jaunsar-Bawar. Owing to the functional inter-dependence of all castes, the high castes, that is the Brahmans and the Rajputs, have to remain in the same village as the low-caste Koltas, as also with a few other artisan castes. The Brahmans and Rajputs are the traditional owners of land and masters of the village. They occupy the main part of the village, which is usually a level ground at an airy and high altitude. The Koltas, however, are given miserable shelters, which are built in one or more clusters, situated much lower down the rocky slope, or at the outskirts of an equal altitude, as for example in Thana, away from the main settlement. The intermediate castes, including the Badi, Sunar, Lohar, Bajgi, Nath and others, which usually form only a few families in each village, may take their residence here and there within the main cluster of huts of the high castes. (ibid.: 34–35)

Bhatt (2010) has also elaborately commented on the 'social structural setting' of what he calls *Mahasu desh*. He points out to the 'ideological conditioning ingrained in the traditional feudalistic social structure which the British supported and the local elite (the Rajput and Brahman) guarded zealously'. 'All the castes of the area were blended into Jaunsari (Scheduled) Tribe, contrary to the recommendations of the Kolta Enquiry Committee (1960) and the Joint Select Committee of Parliament set-up to consider the bill for revising the lists of Scheduled Castes and Scheduled Tribes, headed by a former Commissioner for Scheduled Castes and Scheduled Tribes, because of powerful lobbying by the political elite'. 'Soon the futility of the term Jaunsari tribe became apparent', as the Rajput and Brahman could usurp a major share of benefit' (Bhatt, 2010: 100–01). In Bhatt's opinion, 'the alien notion of 'tribe', is a recent superimposition on this age old indigenous ideological perspective on social structure' making 'caste and 'tribe' become inter-changeable terms obscuring the social reality as it is and as it has been in the ethnographic and historical accounts of Majumdar (1943, 1963), Saksena (1962), Parmar (1975), and others' (Bhatt, 2010: 75). However, Majumdar's views quoted in detail by Bhatt after these remarks clearly describes the caste structure of the area, having 'relative status is well defined and manifested in the rules of endogamy, commensality, social intercourse and distance, rules of pollution and purity and different styles of various castes'. Bhatt, however, adds that 'in this criteria, *karm* (occupational role which is existentially basic to caste in the agriculture-based traditional social economy), does not receive the emphasis it needs though in his further analysis Majumdar accounts for it' (ibid.: 77).

Further, Majumdar has used the term 'tribe' for the collectivity of people in Jaunsar-Bawar in his earlier publication, *The Fortunes of Primitive Tribes* (1943). But, *Himalayan Polyandry* (1962 and its reprint 1963) does not use the term 'tribe' in respect of the residents of this area who have been ethnographically dealt with either in terms of castes– higher intermediary and lower– or 'people' of Jaunsar-Bawar. The term 'tribe' has, however, been used in this later work only in the quotes from the earlier colonial authors. In fact, Saksena's *Social Economy of a Polyandrous People* (1954 and revised edition 1962) also does not use the term 'tribe' though the term 'jaunsari' is used for the people of Jaunsar-Bawar and the term 'tribe' too appears only in the quotes therein from Indological sources like *Vishnu Puran* and colonial accounts. Saksena also emphasizes that the institution of polyandry has been widespread not only in the larger region of northern Himalayas but also in other countries (1952: 22–25). This later categorization of Jaunsaris appears to be because of Majumdar's better appreciation of the issues underlying the refusal of the government to enlist it as a 'scheduled tribe' in 1950–51. The in-depth study conducted in the three villages for study selectively, reveals aspects of the Jaunsari's strong links with Kashmir and adjoining areas of Himachal Pradesh, and the area being a part of the very large tract practising polyandry as also the customary laws of Garhwal (the larger region) having common features with some of the Jaunsari traditional laws. And Berreman (1963: 65) has described Majumdar's study as that of 'the Indo-Aryan speaking Hindus of Jaunsar-Bawar, a small region of the lower Himalayas in the north-west corner of Uttar Pradesh'. It is, thus, implied that the Koltas are hardly a part of this valuable and 'hitherto invaluable ethnographic' account on only the Jaunsaris. He described Jaunsar-Bawar as a part of the western *pahari* culture area having widespread incidence of fraternal polyandry. It may be added that Grierson's linguistic survey also categorizes 'Jaunsari' as a dialect of the western *pahari* group of dialects spoken by people in different areas neighbouring Shimla (1959: 336).

In the social structure of Jaunsar-Bawar as a part of *Mahasu desh*, the village as special entity is important according to Bhatt (2010: 73). It emerges as a 'vertical unity of many strands'. It is not a 'forlorn and isolated community' but a part of the traditional network of another village organization. A better numerical presence of certain castes also makes some villages being referred to as Brahman, Rajput, Kolta, and Bajgi villages. Each village has its identity which is defined in various ways.

Needless to add that Jaunsar-Bawar shares this pattern of village settlement with multi-caste villages all over India. All the three villages share this feature. The three villages had multi-caste demographic composition in December 1957, in conformity with above analysis, as below:

1. *Lohari:* Rajput 65.9 per cent; Nath 2.7 per cent, Bajgi 1.9 per cent; and Kolta 29.5 per cent.
2. *Baila:* Rajput 59.2 per cent; Brahman 2.3 per cent; Badi and Sonar 12.9 per cent; Bajgi 9.5 per cent and Kolta 16.1 per cent.
3. *Lakhamandal:* Brahman 60.9 per cent; Rajput 3.0 per cent; Nath and Badi 6.4 per cent; Bajgi 0.5 per cent; Kolta 26.2 per cent; and migrants (Sindhi Rajput and Gurukha) 3 per cent.

The total population ranged from about 200–390. Oral history of settlements as recalled reported that the earliest settlers, for instance in Lohari, the Rajeu Rajputs now forming three clans (*aal*), came from Jubbal state (220: 1962: 40–41) with a Kolta ('their Kolta'). Similarly, the Baila Rajputs came from Sirmur and spread out to six villages in Jaunsar-Bawar. There is a village also called Baila in Sirmur and they all regard themselves as *kins*. This village also has a history of Rajput-Brahman marriage as Brahmans were earlier living at this site but later left it and the present village was founded by Rajputs. Afterwards, several Brahman families who settled there coming from Sirmur had to leave Baila as the village deity got displeased and asked them to leave the village. There are five Rajput lineages (*aal*) in Baila. The Koltas also came from Sirmur, having three *aals*. Lakhamandal, a Brahman village, because of its location on the periphery of Jaunsar-Bawar with easier communication with Tehri Garhwal, traces 'most of the present residents' both Brahmans and Koltas to the ancestors who emigrated from Garhwal (220: 1962: 40–49). Thus, Rajputs/Brahmans constitute the largest chunk of village populations and often the villages are known as 'Brahman or Rajput villages', followed by Koltas while the intermediate castes 'vary greatly in strength', in certain cases 'their presence may even be nominal in a village.'

> In short the village population in Jaunsar-Bawar is, as a rule, composed of a few of the stereotyped castes, stratified on both economic and socio-religious grounds. These castes are functionally interdependent as well as supplementary to one another but the strength of each of them in the population may vary from village to village. (ibid.: 54)

Political Structure of Jaunsar-Bawar

Traditionally, Jaunsar-Bawar has a well established and powerful organization focused on the system of *khumri* and *sayana*, both having a territorial multi-tier structure. Territorially, the traditional political system was based on *khat* (a group of villages) and village. Subsequently, in some *khats* a similar territorial sub-unit, *khag* with their own *sayanas* has come up.

Sayanachari

There are *sayanas* of the village and the *khat*. Previously the *khat sayanas* (*sadar sayanas*) had a superior group (for the entire Jaunsar-Bawar) called *chauntras* which was abolished by the colonial rulers.

Structure of Sayanadari

Now, there are *gaon sayanas* and *khat sayanas* (*sadar sayanas*), and a newly developing and transitional tier of *khag sayanas*, *khag* being a sub-division of the *khat*. The extent of multiple *sadar sayanas* in *khats* is reflected in the fact that nowadays there are 67 *sadar sayanas* among 39 *khats*. In some villages there are more than one *gaon sayana* belonging to different *aals* instead of the *gaon sayana* coming from the traditionally dominant *aal*. The details of *gaon sayanas* in the study villages show that in the cases of multiple *gaon sayanas* in a big village, they come from comparatively more important *aals*. The settlement histories of villages also indicate that village *sayanaships* is historically an extension of lineage *sayanaship*.

Functions of Sayanas

Sayana system carries significant autonomy in the area. *Khumri*, the village council is presided over by him and he is the final authority in intra village matters. He owes allegiance to *khat/khag sayanas*. Similarly, the *khat sayana* holds the key position in the traditional local government of Jaunsar-Bawar (ibid.: 142). *Dastur-ul-amal*, the codified customary law specifies some of the duties of sayanas of various levels like keeping zamindars (owners– cultivators) contented, collect government revenues according to custom and deal with inter village and inter *khat* matters. The *sayanas* have a leading role in the exercise of judicial functions in their *khumri*, as laid down in the *Dastur-ul-amal* of 1849.

Institution of Khumri

Khumri is like the panchayats of the rural areas. It continues, in spite of the statutory elected bodies as the most important and effective means of settling the affairs of the village community. The *khumri* in Jaunsar-Bawar have been formed on the basis of territory, castes and kinship, as *aal* is closely connected with system of *sayanas*. Caste *khumri* based on *aal* and *bhera* among higher castes generally overshadows the caste *khumris* of other castes in the village.

Territorial Khumris of Different Levels

These levels are: (a) village or intra-village, (b) inter-village, (c) *khat* or intra-*khat*, (d) inter-*khat*, and (e) the rare by held all Jaunsar-Bawar khumn. Among these, village-level *khumri* is most important. It has the heads of all families. Only in some inter-village disputes the *khumri* at that level takes place.

Functions of the Khumri

It functions both as a judicial body to decide disputes and as an administrative organ to manage all kinds of public matters in their area. The sample cases documented in the study indicate how *khumris* decide cases of theft, suspected witchcraft, division of family property and also inter-village disputes which may relate to common issues like drawing water from irrigation channels and management of rituals and festivals.

Socio-Economic Structure

In Jaunsar, the social and economic structure of the community is built around the family which is in turn conditioned by a 'tenacious and far more complete system of polyandry', the traditional landownership system, *aal* or *thok* (as it is called in some areas) which is a lineage system, and the kind of caste system in existence.

The Family System

The family is patri-local, patri-lineal, patronymic and with patriarchal authority. It takes the form of a joint family as it is a union of all male members of all living generations in the patrlineal line, along with wives and unmarried sisters and daughters. This polyandrous family in Jaunsar-Bawar also differs in the fact that even married women members frequently return and stay there for months and, further, the nuclear family is not as stable because the wife may go to their parental village for long periods and divorce is frequent. Thus, significantly, the family assumes a unilateral character and forms a unit of the lineage. Since all brothers marry together and have one or more wives in common, the family system is not only polyandrous but a 'combination of fraternal polyandry and polygyny'. Traditionally, the eldest brother is the representative of the family and controller of all the brothers in matters of marriage and conjugal life, as he marries the wife or wives. Thus, the brothers form an inseparable unit as 'fraternal husbands in the name of the elder brother'. The wives join the union individually, one after another. 'This form of marriage may, therefore, better be known as polygynandrous and this union is a polygynandrous family unit.' The eldest brother is known as *sayana* (this term is also used for village headman or *Khat* headman). He manages the family and represents it in the village meetings (*khumri*). The position comes automatically with seniority. The system has helped in consolidating the family unity as well as a cordial cooperation. The variety of adjustments by way of number of wives is seen to support this contention.

Majumdar observes that there is a geo-economic cause for such a complicated polygynandrous joint family in Jaunsar. Their type of agriculture-cum-pastoral economy needs a large number of hands being one of the bases in which limited means and resources may be marshaled to cope with the environment. This is also supported by the fact that this type of family is particularly found among landowner while its incidence among other castes is much lower. As already mentioned, landownership in this area historically had been restricted to Rajput and Brahman. Post-Independence government intervention has, however, now allowed the ownership of *nautor* lands (newly cultivated areas) and allotment of government lands to others.

Lately changes and modifications in the idea and practice of family have taken place. The factors bring cultural influence of outsiders as well as opening of the area. The degree of change, however, varies from place to place but the system as a whole 'does not seem to be dying, nor it is to be terminated so long as the local environment remains' (220: 1962: 77).

Lineage in Jaunsari Social Structure

A lineage consists of all the descendants in one line of a particular person through a determinate number of generations. A patriarchal or agnatic lineage consists of all the descendants through males of a single male ancestor (R.A.I., 1960: 88–89). Their kinship structure, according to the Jaunsari tradition has no *gotra* or clan, unlike the Hindus of the plains. However, there is the *kin* group known as the *aal* which is found invariably among the dominating caste group in the village. But, in Jaunsar, the generations which form an *aal* are not easily determinable. The members of an *aal* are believed to be real descendants of a common forefather who was an early settler in the village.

Member families of the *aal* usually count through common pedigree through the *bhera* which is a sub-division of the *aal* consisting of one or more families established on the division of an earlier family. In this way, they can trace their consanguinal relationship to the correct generation. Thus, *aal* is a lineage and *bhera* is a sub-lineage while the family is its basic unit. In addition, the *aal* also commands an extended membership through a local custom of 'fictitious kinship' tie under the name of *daichara* which means 'brotherhood' relationship, generally at the village level or extending to some adjoining villages from the same caste, Rajput or Brahman. Thus, among the Rajputs and Brahmans, the lineage has been elaborately worked out traditionally as a result of adjustment to the local environment. 'This system, in terms of *bhera* (sub-lineage), *aal* (lineage) and *daichara* (allied lineages) provides the foundations on which the villages were built up in the remote past. Jaunsari tradition has no *gotra* or *clan* among any caste. *Aal*, especially among the dominating caste groups, is universally found. The lineage system among Khasas is a segmented structure starting from the family and ending at the village or another village(s) level where too some *aal* members may be living. It usually enrolls all members of families of the dominating caste in the village and often a few allied villages. 'A fictitious kinship tie (*daichara*) or brotherhood relationship also makes the expansion of *aal* possible. *Daichara* union is a matter of both social and supernatural sanction (sought from Mahasu). *Daichara* is a local group including the whole of a caste group in the village and at the same time a kin group which forms an exogamous unit. The lineage system thus falls into six segments, namely, inter-village, village, linear-group, lineage, sub-lineage and family (220: 1962: 83).

The lineage system in other castes is quite fluid, as lineage depends on the size of the community and the duration of their stay in the village and also the socio-economic status of the caste. Founding a village and ownership of land is the root of lineage formation and this rests only with the Rajput and Brahman.

Functional Analysis of Aal

The main functions of the lineage system are focused on the *aal*, a well organized and stable unit with rules governing leadership, membership as well as rights and duties among the group members. Since *bhera* is not a stable group, the position of *bhera sayana* is not very well defined. *Bhera* is by and large a more intimate kin group than an *aal*. It is a direct extension of a joint family with members united by actual blood relationship, and living in the same part of the village, generally.

Members of an *aal* regard themselves as belonging to a big family (*kutumb*), observing strict exogamy and incest taboo. They are obliged to help one another on all crisis and social and ritual occasions like marriage, festivals like Bissu and Magh Mela and notably the annual festivals of making fermented cakes used for country liquor as a team. Disputes and enmity between family groups or individuals that grow to *aal* level assumes the form of *chhinga* or *barjan* which is ritual observance of the dispute initiated even by ancestor's vows before Mahasu. *Barjan* prohibits the *aal* members from eating from each others hand and keeping away from one another, even for generations, ending only by another ritual performance at the Mahasu temple.

Aal is also a local group in the village community. It has *bhera* as its basis and its ancestral site (*bera*) as the territorial centre and extends in the form of a *daichara* becoming as much a kin group as a local group of the village. The position of the *aal* as a local group becomes functional because a village community is usually dominated by the caste to which the *aal* of the original settlers belong. They have thus an authoritative voice in village affairs 'whereas other castes are only their sub-ordinate and followers' (ibid.: 95). The Koltas are, however, members of the village *khumri*. Historically, *aal* and its functional role is the culmination of settlements of various castes and *aals* in the villages. Obviously, therefore the dominant *aal* or *aals* have a determinant role in village affairs like C.D.P. proposals or use of water channels, etc.

The kinship system, its terminology in different categories and the reciprocity of relationships as well as the closeness among agnates which as a web is centred around the polygynandrous marriages and family has been elaborately dealt with by Majumdar in order to highlight the balance of the system. The distance or avoidance practised in personal encounters keep the system in balance and eliminates or smoothens conflicts. *Daichara* relations which are another specific feature of Jaunsari society are kept close to the joint family and the *aal* through the extension of similar kinship terms to its members. Non-related caste-men are also addressed with suitable *soga* relationship terms according to generation. As there is a plurality of males as fathers and females as mothers in a polygynandrous family, there are two special ways of differentiating the same category of kin in the family – occupational prefixes such as '*bakra baba*' for the parent taking care of goats for males and territorial, relating to women's natal village, in case of females. In the Jaunsari family structure, the dichotomous roles of a married woman – as a daughter-in-law in her husband's house and as a daughter in her home – also has a singular behavioural pattern. After marriage, a woman, *dhyanti*, in her father's house is allowed a lot of personal liberty and free life in the family as well as in her sexual alliances, while in her husband's house as a *ryanti* she has to observe decorum and sobriety expected from her. Majumdar comments that this sharp distinction between the two roles which also allows a *dhyanti* to stay in her father's house for long periods, functionally, relieves the strain, the women undergoes in a polygynandrous family with her being treated as 'no better than chattel which can be sold and purchased'. In other words, a wife here has a much greater responsibility as she has to cater to the needs and satisfaction of all husbands despite her possible liking or disliking (ibid.: 124). The relations between husbands and wives are 'never sacred nor so intimate or permanent as they are in the plains' (220: 1962: 125).

Traditional Inequalities, Behavioural Strains and Conflicts

The structural features of the Jaunsari society carry some high points of tensions and conflicts in the society. The most important of these is the sharp hierarchal system with the focus of power, economic, social and political, being traditionally and firmly with the Rajput and Brahman in almost the entire gamut of relationships. Then, the other such arena is the relationships between plural husbands and wives in a polygynandrous family with over arching authority of the eldest brother and also the subordinated position of women. Majumdar, however, points out that there are mechanisms built into the system to keep these strains and conflicts under control and thereby ensure a functional equilibrium. For example, the respect for the senior which is shown 'in the junior's general attitudes of obedience ... with sober and reserved behaviour in the presence of elders'; affection and love generally shown by the elders towards the juniors, and cooperation and equality among the family members. He observes:

> Although the family is commanded by the family *Sayana* as a patriarch, all members of the family are treated on an equal footing. They live together, work together and share their pleasures. All men and women get their share of work assigned by the *Sayana* and *Sayani*, according to their capacity. The Sayana and *Sayani* always look into both the common the individual interests in all fairness. Thus a spirit of cooperation prevails amongst all members and makes the family run smoothly. (ibid.: 131)

Similarly, conjugal relationship in the polygynandrous family means:

> The polygynandrous union has been established in the Khasa family due to the need of cooperative spirit and mutual consideration among all the husbands and wives. There is an economic basis for the husbands to control the wives, who are bought by bride-price. However, a dutiful wife is treated with respect, especially if she is the senior wife who is the *Sayani* or mistress of the house. All wives are entitled to all material needs as well as affection and love from all of their husbands, and a divorce may be sought only when they are aggrieved. The conjugal relationship, especially among the younger generation, is somewhat loose and never sacred as it is in the plains, due to the frequent occurrence of divorce and the conventional extra-marital licence enjoyed by both the sexes (ibid.: 132).

Gender discrimination is pronounced and on marriage the women's position again deteriorates due to payment of a bride-price for her and no inheritance rights. But, in these cases also, there is a double standard of behaviour:

> A woman has a choice between two standards of sexual conduct according to the situations she is in: as a *ryanti* at her husband's place or as a *dhyanti* in her father's house or *mait*. At her husband's place, she is decent and hardworking, in conformity with the traditional code of conduct of a wife in the house. At her *mait*, however, she is entitled to all liberty and free life. Neither is she required to work for the household, nor is she obliged to obey her parents' order or direction. And, what is worse, she is allowed to, and generally does, indulge in affairs with village youths.
>
> The villagers give three reasons for this licence to the dhyantis. Firstly, as child marriage is prevalent, the parents of the girl do not pay much attention to educate her, nor check her conduct, thinking that she would sooner or later be a member of some other household. Secondly, after her marriage, which is performed at a very early age and sometime in the infancy of the girl, she is no more a member of her father's family and therefore it is only her husband who can exercise control over her. Lastly, when the daughter returns to the village of her parents, knowing that she had to face and endure constant hardships at her in-laws, allows her a good deal of relaxation and freedom to move in the village and enjoy herself. (ibid.: 132–133)

Inequalities in inter-caste relations were firmly rooted in the strong bias of the customary law. The facets of discrimination were denial of landownership; denial of participation to Koltas and Bajgis in the *Khumris* of different levels specially the village level *Khumri* which has a pivotal role in the day-to-day economic relations; a large number of family members being in a state of bondage or serfdom emanating from indebtedness due to the poverty of the subaltern groups; exclusive control of the Rajput and Brahman over all celebrations of festivals, fairs; denial of access to inner parts of the temples and other civil rights through the dictates of village and inter-village *Khumris*, and so on. Any conflictual situations, which were perhaps, infrequent were also suppressed through the use of economic power, power to socially boycott and ex-communicate and giving religious sanctions to such decisions or denying even the favours granted through government decisions through the 'voice' of Mahasu *deovta* which came through his *baki* (mediums) who were Rajputs or Brahmans (220: 1962: 158; Bhatt, 2010). The upper castes even control the Kolta women who are often sent out to places like Delhi, Meerut, etc. for prostitution by upper castes middlemen, and the income thus obtained is partly used in settling family debts (JLBSIA, 1975; Hasnain, 2012: xvi).

The inter-family and intra-family cooperation and ordering of relationships, and the stability of structured hierarchal relationship among the castes as described above brings forth 'the unity aspect of relationships in the village' (Jodhka, 2000). Jodhka analyses how the village studies of Srinivas and Dube stress this 'unity' even though there is ample 'diversity' of village life in different parts of India. He further goes on to present the other viewpoint that of Majumdar:

> However not everyone emphasized the unity of the village the way Srinivas and Dube or earlier Wiser did. Some of the anthropologists explicitly contested

the unity thesis while others qualified their arguments by recognizing the conflicts within the village and the ties that villagers had with the outside world. For instance, Paul Hiebert in his study of a south Indian village, although arguing that the caste system provided a source of stability to the village, also underlined the fact that 'deep seated cleavages underlie the apparent unity of the village and fragmented it into numerous social groups' (Hiebert, 1971: 13). Similarly, Majumdar had pointed out that the assumption about village being an 'integrated whole, a way of living, thinking and feeling has its limitations in the Indian conditions'. Kinship ties integrated the village 'at different levels with the total social system of the country' (Majumdar, 1958: 325). However the more important fact that divided the village was its settlement pattern. (Jodhka, 2000: 12).

Here, Majumdar's views are confined to what he had said in his Gohana study. In the Jaunsar-Bawar study which came later he analyses further the inequalities and exploitative relationships in the three villages which show the pattern for the entire 'region of a few hundred villages'. Like Majumdar, Beteille too recognizes that there were spheres of life where the village exhibited the semblance of unity (Jodhka, 2000: 30); and also 'provided a radical critique of the unity-reciprocity thesis ... stressing on the coercive aspects of caste relations (ibid.: 14).

A closer reading of Majumdar's *Himalayan Polyandry* would, however, show that this 'cleavage', exploitation, serfdom and what one may call the 'structural devices in the socio-economic system of inter-caste relationships' between Rajput/Brahmans on the one hand and Kolta/Bajgis on the other hand were not projected with an emic view. Hasnain (1982/2012: xx) laments the paucity of any material on the Kolta, except for a pamphlet by Saksena (1960) and some pages in DNM's books (1960, 1962). Hasnain's study carries a moving description of the traditions or structured relationships with significant details. For example, describing the festivals, he (2012: 81) observes:

> Magh festival (Pahari Diwali), Besso fair, Jagra, Lanai, Panchom, Diwali, etc. are some of the important fairs and festivals in which the entire population, irrespective of their caste or economic status, participate, though in different ways. The degree and levels of participation of different castes may be viewed from two stand points, viz., that of Rajputs-Brahmans on the one hand and Kolta and other Harijans on the other. Although on some occasions Kolta and people of other castes do dance together and share some moments of joy and merry-making, yet there are many other occasions when participation is distinctly based on discriminatory grounds.

And, further:

> A highly derogatory act, violating every principle of human dignity, is performed on the third day of the festival; Koltas dressed as goat and sheep (by covering themselves with the skin of these animals) are yoked and are made to dance to the tune of noisy musical instruments obeying the command of a Rajput ... followed by a dance in which they are shown as dogs and cows acting on the instructions of the owner. The latter role is always played by a Rajput.

> Next day:
>
> The heavily decorated elephant of solid wood (and of course quite heavy) is lifted alternately by four Kolta over their shoulders and the senior Sayana or an elderly Rajput landlord sits over it with bare sword, while the Kolta carriers of the elephant and its rider dance to a slow rhythm. This dance usually goes on until every Kolta of the village has lifted the elephant at least once .... The above mentioned 'participation' of the Kolta portrays only some of the customs and practices in the entire gamut of socio-ritual realm of the society.

Bhatt (2010: 103–04) also describes these celebrations in similar details and says:

> It is significant that Koltas participation in this ceremony (elephant dance) is compulsory. Each adult male Kolta is required to lift the wooden elephant at least once during the ceremony ... indicate almost ritualized subordinate, serflike, menial and servile status of the Kolta in the local social structure. It finds expression in the social organization of Mahasu cult and the cults of other devtas ...'

Impact of CD Programme and Cultural Change

The impact of the project varies greatly from item to item, place to place and time to time. Earlier there were difficulties but an improvement in the situation has taken place. The appraisal of CDP in Jaunsar-Bawar emphasizes the following aspects:

(a) Identifying basic incompatibilities between the traditional culture pattern and the programmes which entail knowledge about their culture and resources, as well as the local needs in the context of the area and cultural life.

(b) Evaluating the level of success and the nature and extent of resistance, largely cultural, in order to find out an alternative. Further, analysis of CDP mechanism and working methods in its relationship with villagers and other departments indicating possible adjustment for improvement.

(c) The extraordinary type of cultural environment needs a very selective application. The terrain also has to be taken into account in order to make an impact for the better.

(d) It is obvious that adequate knowledge and understanding of the people and their culture is necessary in this area. The Jaunsaris have a hostile or skeptical attitude towards all outsiders. It was noticed that VLWs from the area were favoured. About outsiders, their experience is that they try to take all kinds of advantage.

(e) The people have a traditional attitude of fearful respect and submission towards government and its officials. They conceive government as an authority which wants money and have bitterness against restrictions imposed on the use of forests. Moreover, regular visits by government officers which could have changed the attitude were wanting.

(f) Caste differences and discrimination have a great role as the higher castes watch with envy and antagonism, the extra facilities allowed to the lower castes. However, the lower castes too are unable to take advantage because they do not have land or cattle needed for taking benefit of the schemes.

(g) The traditional leadership of Sayana, Aal, Khumri, etc. and the internal factionalism do not allow any role for women and the lower castes. These equations have to be understood for introducing CDP.

(h) Other factors which impede the progress of CDP are illiteracy, conservatism and superstition. For instance some programmes may be believed to be not acceptable to gods. However, as the villagers are pragmatic, only programmes which are suitable for their financial and environmental conditions have to be better pursued in the beginning.

Villager's Response

The harsh conditions have created extraordinary group cooperation among the people and they have to work hard for their subsistence. The participation of some more enlightened leaders was seen to create favourable response from the people especially the schemes connected with their agriculture and livestock. However, the long procedural delays in the cooperative society, for example discouraged participation. Similarly, *sharamdan* was not acceptable because people were busy or poor. Sometimes the programme suffered because the CDP staff failed to explain it and thereby convince the people. Certain conditions attached to the schemes which prevented the benefits for Koltas, etc. also needed amendments. The elections to Panchayats also sometimes initiated factionalism or antagonism and thereby retarded the progress of CDP. An instance as detailed is that of water supply to Nada village which remained incomplete for years.

Effect of Measures and the Felt Needs

Though the CDP records show progress, some of the programmes had only temporary effects or the impact was uneven. For example potato produce grew with fertilizers and pesticides in the lower Jaunsar area because of availability of water. In other words, this experience should have been made use of by providing irrigation before introduction of fertilizers and pesticides. Identification of felt needs is important but it has to be found out in detail for different villages, areas, and communities. Only some of the felt needs can be of general application. Obviously, therefore, the schemes should allow selective adjustment of the detailed items to be introduced in different areas. Landless, labourers, artisans, etc. need especially prepared programmes. Some felt needs like medical facilities, water management, etc. requiring larger investments have also to be adequately extended. The villagers generally felt that the CDP staff did not involve itself adequately in their urge for development.

CDP Mechanism and Working Method

In this section an appraisal of the posting of staff, its structure, etc. has been commented upon. Frequent transfers and long periods of vacancies adversely affect the programme and discourage the involvement of the people. Similar is the case with inadequate training and unsuitability. The technical staff needs to remain in constant touch with the beneficiaries so as to guide their progress. However, difficult communications in the area often discourage it. It has been noted that the construction of roads in the areas where it progressed, improved the situation. The attitude of the staff especially the field level staff (VLW) is of great importance but some of the staff was singularly lacking in this regard. To conclude:

> It is essential for the C.D.P. Authority as well as the C.D.P. staff to reconsider many of the important issues on which there was much discord between the government and the villagers. A case in point is the Panchayat, which should be reformed in certain respects to suit the local set-up. So also many local factors and villagers' opinions should be considered in regard to other issues. It is only when the villagers find their proper position and their own role of importance in the programme or the organization that they will take active part in it. It need not be emphasized that the final aim of the C.D. Project should be to lead the villagers to not only economic prosperity but also to social stability with self-confidence and self-restraint, which is essential for all groups of people who desire to work for a common good for the nation.
>
> The CDP staff, therefore, should not only work for the successful implementation of all the programmes on hand, but also help the villagers in preparing a background for themselves, to handle all the establishment and programmes in the next stage, which will come in due course. (220: 1962: 380–381).

A similar view has also been expressed in the context of a south Indian village on leadership of groups by the PEO, Planning Commission (1955: 142–43).

Discussion

Perhaps, Majumdar's restricted 'field view' of the three villages in the area was caused by his functional approach though he has, in a limited way, discussed changes in the community as a result of CD Programme and the introduction of statutory panchayats through the UP Panchayat Act, 1947, enforced in December 1953. He does, however, portend how this law may bring some change:

> This distribution of seats among different castes may not mean any positive proof of a comparative status of all castes, as the lower castes have yet very little courage and ability to speak before their high-caste counterparts in the Panchayat meetings. Nevertheless, it furnished a legal stand for the under-privileged group to demand a better living in the village. As regards the village dynamics, or the balance of power between different groups of villagers, it is as yet a monopoly of the privileged high caste people (220: 1962: 168).

Late Sunil Misra was a part of Majumdar's Jaunsar-Bawar team and subsequently did his PhD work in the area. A personal communication in 2014 provided certain instances of the change in the collective behaviour of Koltas as a result of a right to vote and the Community Development Programme. During the general elections of 1957, Gulab Singh, son of Sardar Singh, an influential

Rajput leader of Tuni areas was a candidate for the UP Assembly. He was opposed by Surat Singh, another Rajput leader and a candidate of Congress Party. Sardar Singh convened a *khat* Panchayat of the entire Jaunsar-Bawar and persuaded the Rajput *sayanas* to take a *lota-pani* oath in support of his son. The Kolta who were opposing Gulab Singh also held their panchayat and declared their concerted support for Surat Singh. However, Gulab Singh won the election and subsequently joined the Congress Party and also became a member of the UP Cabinet in the late 1960s and 1970s. Similarly, in a village near Lakhamandal, the Community Development Programme planned a water supply scheme for which pipes and other necessary equipment had to be carried to a higher point which was the source of water supply. It was presumed that the Kolta would provide the voluntary labour to carry the material. However, the Koltas enmasse refused to do this and their plea was that since they would not be allowed access to piped water, they would not contribute their labour. The stalemate was resolved when the higher castes promised that they would be allowed access to the water supply; though for ensuring the water for Koltas, two pipe lines were laid from the water tank, thus, providing a separate tap for the Kolta, thus, containing a discriminatory practice.

This limited coverage of the 'other' viewpoint can also be attributed to the members of the research team being identified as 'high caste' persons (most of them were that). As acknowledged by Srinivas about himself (1976: 197–98) and Beteille (1975: 104), they also were housed in the upper caste part of the villages which prevented their 'viewing hierarchy from the bottom up.' (Mencher, 1975: 117–128)

Hasnain's study of 1980s does briefly report the change as a result of the legal and administrative interventions of the government as follows:

> The last thirty years witnessed some changes in the life of Koltas especially since 1980s – after the promulgation of the Abolition Act (The Bonded Labour Systems Abolition Act, 1976). These changes are more visible in the villages located on the periphery of the roads. With the construction of more roads and pathways new markets have emerged increasing employment avenues and new avenues of livelihood. Wages have also increased. There is now increased movement and migration towards Himachal Pradesh in several villages in Jaunsar area. Not only new schools have been opened but the rate of enrollment in schools has increased appreciably .... True, the aspirational level of the Kolta has moved a little upward yet the means to achieve the goals have not increased proportionately (1982/2012: xiv–xv).

Functionalism has been variously commented upon for being conservative, evidencing a static bias and focusing on social order in its empirical or analytical narrative; generally stressing the equilibrium in the institutions and the interrelationships of individuals in a society. Even though Majumdar has almost from the beginning of his writings on Jaunsar-Bawar described the low status, and other disabilities of the Koltas including a denial of their entitlement to land ownership, he has hardly documented or highlighted the high degree of economic exploitation, bondage, sexual exploitation and the humiliating customs and practices intended to perpetuate this exploitative relationship. In his class room, Majumdar simply used to describe the Koltas as, 'hewers' of wood and 'drawers' of water in the Jaunsari society. The recent currents of resentment and the nascent movement of unity of the Koltas, if any, were hardly ever documented– the exception being the two instances of the Koltas and other artisan castes resisting the facilities for drinking water and irrigation not being extended to their areas and the effort of the Khasa to monopolize them (220: 1962: 324–25). It can be said that Majumdar was too much under Malinowski's influence and his study of Jaunsar-Bawar had the deficiency of functionalism frequently not addressing the 'issue of change, and when change is analysed, attention is on evolutionary rather than revolutionary forces or does not take account of social change especially radical change' (Turner and Maryanski, 1979: 116).

Mair (1957: 231–32) has opined that Malinowski was concerned with 'the problems of the imposition of the change by external authority'. Moreover, she comments that 'the interpretation of social institutions, at whatever level of development, as systems in which universally necessary ends are attained by the cooperation of organized groups' and the 'weakness' of such an interpretation is that it 'does not account for all social phenomena'. And, Misra provided instances of such a non 'accounting' as discussed earlier.

Berreman (1963: 65) has rightly described the ethnographic account as 'variously unduly evaluative and even ethnocentric, explorative, exaggerated and at times contradictory. Giving one or two examples of the ethnocentric nature of certain words used in the account and a striking contradiction about the caste affiliation of the *Baki* who have been stated to belong to Nath and the Bajgi, 'lower caste' on page 64, and as, 'always from the Rajput or Brahman caste', on page 262. The book does say on page 262 that 'Baki is always from the Rajput or Brahman castes, never from the Bajgi or Koltas', the description on page 64 says that, 'magicians or diviners', known as Baki are 'generally recruited from among the lower castes, from the Nath and the Bajgi. But, they are not necessarily hereditary professionals nor do they form an exclusive social group'.

Peter Prince of Greece and Denmark (ref. 1963: 166), who was a fellow student of Majumdar at Malinowski's seminars, finds the descriptions of the different roles of *dhyanti* and *ryanti* of the same woman, the main contribution to the knowledge of polyandrous people, in this ethnography. While he finds the details of the three studied villages, and the history of the region in part one as 'very thorough and well-done', he feels the analysis of polyandrous unit insufficient and also Majumdar's attributing polyandry to geo-economic causes without elucidating or explorating these factors, 'sweeping'. It, however, appears to this author that Peter's comments are somewhat inadequate because the structural features of the family unit as well as lineage unit (*aal*) are adequately descriptive and analytical in the ethnography.

Note

1. The Joint Committee of the Parliament constituted to consider the Scheduled Castes and Scheduled Tribes Orders (Amendment) Bill, 1967, while examining the Presidential order of declaring five Scheduled Tribes in Uttar Pradesh – the Constitution (Scheduled Tribes) (Uttar Pradesh) Order 1967 – recommended that 16 communities in Jaunsar-Bawar pargana in Deharadun district, Rawain pargana in Uttar Kashi district and Jaunpur pargana in Tehri-Garhwal district should be recognized as Scheduled Tribes in place of 'Jaunsari' in the Presidential Order. These communities, all artisan groups and groups with a low status like Dom, Bajgi, etc., are what Majumdar regards as 'aboriginals' in the area. Sharma (1976: 2) too has observed that 'Jaunsari is not a caste or 'tribe' but is a generic name for all those who are original inhabitants of Jaunsar-Bawar Pargana … . The above polyandrous region can be treated as a unit for development …'. However, the Bill as passed later did not incorporate this recommendation and 'Jaunsari' continued as such to be a Scheduled Tribe.

7

Village Studies

Gohana Kalan Near Lucknow

In the last quarter of the 18th century, the colonial administration of the East India Company began consolidating their administrative system over Bengal. Therefore, the knowledge of the internal political and socio-economic structure of India became a necessity for proceeding in this direction. The caste and the village were the earliest two configurations on the Indian scene which appeared to be important, in the colonial view, to understand the conditions of the Indian society.

Cohn (1987: 149–50) tracing historicity of the study of Indian society and culture mentions that William Tennant, a military chaplain, in a work published in 1804, had included careful observations of cultural practices in upper India. Tennant had applied the techniques which were typical of the earliest generation of anthropologists, i.e. observation and interviews with key native informants and knowledgeable Europeans. He described in detail a particular village 36 miles from Banaras. Another example of careful description of rural areas came two years later from H.T. Colebrooke, a Sanskrit scholar. This work combined both secondary material and his own observations about Bengal. Interestingly, Colebrooke observed that in rural India 'every profession, with few exceptions is open to every description of persons'. He was sure that, 'the caste system and the religious system were in no sense any bar to further development'. Cohn (ibid.: 166) writes that one can go back to the 18th century and trace chronologically a changing view of Indian society relating to two major institutions – caste and village. The history of the study of the Indian village in an effective fashion began with the intensive survey work connected with the British attempt to collect land revenue in the late 18th century. The view about the village in India which was articulated in the colonial literature of late 18th century was that India was a land of 'self-sufficient' 'little village republics' imbued with an ethos of intensive ties to the village and within the village; and an overall stagnancy as they had existed in this state from the days of Manu. Metcalfe described them in this manner in 1810, while Maine in the later half of the 19th century described the village as a very stable unit of Indian society based on 'patriarchal households'. Since the focus of Maine's study was land tenure systems, he also offered a typology of Indian villages depending on the 'nature of holdings'. Similarly, Baden-Powell describing the Indian village community at the close of the 19th century identified two types of villages– the joint and the ryotwary– and traced their roots to the Aryan and Dravidian social forms. Marx too, accepting these basic assumptions, lamented this stagnant state of an oriental social system and held the colonial rule responsible for it. Moreover, its economic system combining agriculture with manufacturing had also contributed to 'restraining the human mind within the smallest possible compass' thereby in a passive and unresisting state.

R.C. Dutt's, *Economic History of India* (1902) seems to have been one of the principal sources used by the 20th century scholars, publicists and politicians for the continuance of the myth of the Indian village community, which also became central to the Indian nationalist view of their past (Cohn, 1987: 159; Jodhka, 2012: 44–66).

Dumont has distinguished three connected but successive meanings of the expression 'village community' which seem to predominate in the three successive historical phases. In the first phase, a political society primarily, in the second phase a body of co-owners of the soil, while in the third phase it becomes to Indians the emblem of traditional economy and polity, 'a watch word of Indian patriotism'. Caste is underplayed throughout as 'community', in the prevalent ideology of the period is an equalitarian group (Madan, 2002: 31).

The specific characteristics of the Indian village in this colonial reporting or discourse were its autonomous existence even when empires and rulers tumbled around it; its self-sufficiency in the economic systems of production and consumption; homogeneity and smoothness in mutual relationships; and a collective consciousness about the village as an entity. Thus, the immutability or resistance to change by the village communities offered a kind of theoretical base or rationalization for the colonial administration which claimed to stand for measures to bring about change and modernity. As Edward Said (1979) has pointed out, the orientalist project 'generated authoritative and essentialising statements about the East and was characterized by a mutually supporting relationship between power and knowledge'.

Thus, the Indian village together with its panchayat system and a system of economic production based on traditional caste occupations presented a scenario of absence of free market, lack of competition and such other characteristics which were more or less a contrast to the attributes of a modern society, the West, and, therefore, an 'other'. This structure was supposed to be uniform all over the sub-continent, thereby ignoring the vast diversities and differences in different regions. In fact, this kind of an imagination of the Indian rural society went on to form the basis of the nationalist notion and a part of the ideology of the freedom movement, as pointed out by Srinivas, Dumont, Jodhka and others. It also formed the basis of some of Gandhi's vision and approach to what India should be once it attains freedom from colonial rule. It has been called the ideology of the village Swaraj (Jodhka, 2012: 46). 'Rural reconstruction' was therefore adopted as a policy goal after Independence and certain measures like the abolition of zamindari and statutory tenurial rights were the steps which had been initiated on the eve of Independence.

Village Studies After Independence

This focus on the village assumed a momentum, as a result of zamindari abolition and other connected legislation, and initiation of plans for a multi-faceted programme for 'rural reconstruction'. In this context, the 'young' (Jodhka, 1998) discipline of social anthropology took up studies of Indian villages during 1950s and 1960s in a big way. As Majumdar (168: 1955: v) points out, anthropologists and sociologists with their experience of micro-cosmic field studies had much to contribute. For anthropology, it was 'a natural extension of his interest in tribal studies, for the emphasis that he placed on the total approach and micro-cosmic studies puts him easily in an advantageous position with regard to rural assignments' (176: 1956: 95).

It was this congruence of several factors which provided a big impetus to village studies specially by social anthropologists from the very beginning of 1950s. The launching of national Five Year Plans included an extensive programme for the villages in its community development programme through block-based projects in October 1952; pilot work for this programme in collaboration with Americans; the academic trend of holistic cultural studies in little communities initiated by Robert Redfield and the interest of that school in Indian researches; and the resultant need of the administration for comprehensive baseline data and evaluation for which anthropology had methodologically equipped itself through its role during World War II in providing knowledge which could be applied. As Majumdar comments:

> ... The anthropologist's genuine field of studies is the Gemeinschaft; and in the context of the current modern process evaporation of tribal societies due to assimilation and/or extinction, he is compelled to turn his attention to the rural community .... (1956: 95–96)

Jodhka (1998) reporting on this trend, however, comments that:

> The western powers also had a great deal of political interest in the paths of development being pursued by different developing countries in the Third World. Much of this concern emanated from their anxiety about the possibilities of these countries choosing a socialistic pattern of development and their consequent tilt towards the then existing 'Soviet block'.

In fact, by the late 1940s several American universities had started taking keen interest in the study of cultures and civilization of India. In the Cornell University, M.E. Opler (1950) along with his collaborator Rudra Dutt Singh had interested himself in the Indian village and its hierarchal and inter-caste relationships. In 1952–53, Majumdar was a Visiting Professor in Far Eastern Studies in the Cornell University at his invitation and they planned a collaborative project between the Cornell University and Lucknow University. This collaborative endeavour was initiated towards the end of 1953 for an intensive three-year study of the community development projects in several selected sites of Uttar Pradesh. This was an effort to add guidance on the methodology of evaluation. The project was financed by the Ford Foundation and set up the University of Lucknow with Opler as its Director and Majumdar as its Co-Director. Its research goals or primary objectives of research were to analyse the process of cultural change; identify significant elements in the village culture which enhance or retard such changes; to determine which of these elements can and should be observed systematically in other community project areas; to develop and validate simple, easily applied criteria and methods for studying these significant cultural factors; to analyse the process by which changes from other origins become integrated into and are encompassed by the changing culture; and to identify the inter-relationship between initial and attendant subsequent changes. This study was to have inter-disciplinary teams of social scientists. The initial area for research was to be one of the newly set up community development blocks. Hence, the village Rankhandi in the Deoband pilot project, Saharanpur district, was selected, where it had been initiated from August 1953. Here S.C. Dube and others studied the impact of the C.D. programmes while several other scholars, including Hitchcock, Pauline Colenda and this author studied the other aspects including ethnography, inter-caste relations and panchayats. Another team which included Cohn studied Senapur a village in eastern UP Gohana Kalan, a village near Lucknow, which was not ... a community project area, was selected as a control village. Further, a village in Duddhi, Mirzapur district, was taken up as 'an area substantially dissimilar from the others under observation'. Earlier, Programme Evaluation Organization was also set up as a part of the Planning Commission simultaneously with the Community Development Programme for the evaluation of this action programme, its administration and impact.

Even though this project was, unfortunately, wound up mid-stream after about two years due to differences between the two directors, the studies including those taken up by Majumdar were continued with funds from the Research Programme Committee, Planning Commission, and the Ford Foundation and fructified in various publications. Thus, Majumdar entered the scene of village studies in early 1950s with his usual vigour and within a period of about five years (1954–58) he presented studies of a village near Lucknow, another village on the 'fringe' of UP (in Hindi), two edited volumes of what he called profiles of village life, and several papers evaluating the community development programme. Moreover, *Himalayan Polyandry* (1962) also comprised a study of structure functioning and culture change in three selected villages of Jaunsar-Bawar.

Broadly speaking, till the beginning of 1950s, the writings about the rural scene in India were of a generalized nature or over arching myths like 'little republics' and cameos drawn on the models of the western rural sociology, particularly American. Anthropological studies were then confined more or less to 'other cultures' viz., tribal India. However, anthropologists got interested in the study of peasantry at about this time which heralded village studies utilizing the methodology evolved by anthropologists. Robert Redfield provided the lead by adapting the approach to 'culture contact', 'social change' and 'transformation'- of the 'folk' into 'peasant community' through his conceptual development of a 'little community'. Atal (2004: 33) observes that anthropologists working among Indian tribes, though familiar with the fact of cultural contact and change, 'largely followed the tradition of ethnographic and wrote monographs in the idiom of an eternal ethnographic present'. The development of Redfield's theory and methodology contributed to extend their attention to rural studies 'at this critical phase' (ibid.: 34). The setting up of Community Development Programme and instruments of planning for change provided the forceful push for rural studies. The other considerations, which motivated anthropological village studies, were the fact that India was overwhelmingly rural with comparatively better facilities for research as compared to tribal areas and a wider potential of its applicability, as also the suitability of research techniques developed by them to typical Indian villages (ibid.: 32–33).

Mid-1950s, thus, came to be the period when the study of Indian village communities was being carried out by a number of scholars including several British and American scholars and Indians. Short accounts of the studied villages appeared in *The Economic Weekly* in early 1950s, and then in 1955 came some of the most important initial publications. These included edited volumes by MacKim Marriot, M.N. Srinivas and Majumdar and the first full-length account of a village near Hyderabad in Telangana region by Dube. Thereafter, in the late 1950s and 1960s, there came a regular flow of publications of village studies by social anthropologists and sociologists from different parts of the country. Almost, all the studies were holistic, based on intensive fieldwork carried out by the authors alone or with a team of investigators for a year or more and with the methodology and approach outlined above. However, some of the problem-oriented studies involved shorter fieldwork duration either with more or less the same methodology or often combined with survey method. The University of Chicago focused its attention on an exploration of 'various ways to the scientific and scholarly understanding of civilization' and in that direction found studies of Indian villages significant in order to 'see a civilization in *vivo*– within the context of family, neighbours, work, ceremonies and other circumstances that make up the round of life of a people (Marriott, 1955: vii). Redfield's conceptual model provided the anthropological studies distinctive modifications in the study of social structure, social change and the intimate connection of the working of social units with one another through social networks of various kinds. Singer's approach furthermore connected such studies to understanding the civilizational aspects in the Indian context as well as in respect of other South Asian civilizations (Singer and Cohn, 1996).

Majumdar's Approach

It may, however, be mentioned here that Majumdar was the foremost anthropologist who had been extensively studying and commenting on processes and results of social change in the tribal context, as well as the interface between the tribal society and the Hindu castes. He had, in fact, already postulated the process of there being a process of transformation and a tribe-caste continuum in India. Mukherjee aptly comments on Majumdar's contribution on this entire process:

> D.N. Majumdar, a product of Calcutta and later a student of Malinowski, was engrossed by the 'how' question, but not on the basis of a superficial rendering of the structural– functional approach. This is attested by his 'village study' (*Caste and Communication in an Indian Village*) and 'urban study' (*Social Contours of an Industrial City: Social Survey of Kanpur, 1954–56)* ... . Majumdar dealt with 'culturology' to begin with, and the problems of urbanization, communication, and the role of Indian sociologists in later years. (1979: 68–69)

Majumdar, in his address to the Conference on Anthropology and Sociology, under the joint auspices of Madras University, M.S. University of Baroda and the Chicago University, held on 5–6 November 1955, iterated his wide ranging views on the problems and prospects of rural analysis (176: 1955–56: 92–103). Among the issues he made out were: first, that the research assignments in our country were not, to say the least, problem-oriented and how indefinite and aimless our research projects had been; secondly, this situation needed more of cooperation and coordination between individuals and research bodies and better distribution of research funds; and it also needed far better communication between research workers and those needing it as they were in a position to use the results.

Touching upon the strength of anthropological approach of a total or holistic study, Majumdar remarked that often the micro-cosmic studies of rural life failed to do justice to the total structure that we aimed to observe. Giving certain examples of such a shortcoming, he pointedly commented:

> The functional approach made pretentious claims to study linkages, mutualities and reciprocal responses within a given milieu, but no functionalist has studied a tribe or a community with a complete coverage of the network of interrelationships. It is not possible, however penetrating our tools are. We must refrain from making a fetish of microcosmic or total approach, for no rural community is a closed unit today or was so before. A historical perspective is necessary to understand linkages and rural relationships, for the village has been built up or settled by people and has not preceded settlement by the people. (ibid.: 96)

Thus, in a way, Majumdar emphasizes the need to explore and document, in-depth, the links and relationships which the community either on the whole or through its constituent castes or certain individuals maintains with certain urban areas, villages or collectivities beyond its own village. This data would, in more than one ways, contribute not only to the totality of the 'little community' studied but also correlate its important institutions to the outer world and also explore the likely communication networks as carriers of change by way of development, awareness and education. Thereby, this input would expand the applied utility of such studies of village communities, empirically projecting their not being 'isolates' or 'little republics' in Metcalf's phrase. He has also pointedly commented on the deficiency of a historical element in the structural-functional approach underlying the anthropological village studies in respect of Indian village, and with his brief mention of the Gohana Kalan's oral historical traditions unfolded the links between 'little communities' and the Indian civilization. He further commented that anthropological studies of tribal communities, also of villages, had been generally of a qualitative kind and need inputs of quantification which are important in respect of demography and other baseline data which have great significance in the context of rural problems. Quantified benchmark data was essential for studying change and transition in culture which had become the major interest of the anthropologists or sociologists so that they can participate 'for planning for progress and rehabilitation'. He stressed:

> We need therefore to investigate the nature and characteristics of social change in different communities and social strata, to assist reconstruction. Innovation always produces resistance and yet innovation is the basic postulate for change. If it is inconsistent with the cultural assumptions of the people, it will produce violent resistance. If it is against the basic attitudes and values of the people, innovation may not have any chance of acceptance. Planned reconstruction of objectives must be stated in clear and unambiguous terms so that there is some chance of observing the reaction of individuals and groups for whom it is meant. It (programme) must be flexible enough to accommodate changes in response to the needs and responses of the people. (ibid.: 100)

Majumdar also expressed the view:

> Almost all users of research, in this case, the administration and the welfare organizations, think 'that research will be critical of their methods or policy (and therefore) it has become customary to dub social research as 'academic'. This may be an unconscious compliment to research, but the communication between the researcher and the users of research becomes 'narrower and difficult to pass knowledge'. In order to make the practitioner aware of the possibilities of research, our approach and findings must be competent. (ibid.: 100–101)

In this connection, Majumdar was also very critical of producing quick results through rural analysis. Commenting on the methodology of rural analysis he emphasized proper formulation of hypothesis for researches, creation of better baseline data to add to the quality of research specially in the context of suggesting definite and specific establishment of priorities for taking steps towards social amelioration. The research techniques emphasized by him in this regard were direct participation-observation, structured interviews and case studies rather than the questionnaire method. He cautioned particularly against the use of close-end questions as they were not comprehensible to the mostly illiterate subjects. Some other aspects in methodology which were vital for good research according to him were:

All the possible avenues need to be explored to check and countercheck the information collected. When collecting data regarding land holdings, village history, vital statistics, efforts must be made, where possible, to compare the information with available official records. In a qualitative study, the responsibility of the investigator increases with the complexity of rural problems and the size of the microcosm. Rapport is essential and is a long drawn affair. Adequate time schedule is a control for accuracy. Equipment of the field investigator both in theory and application and his knowledge of the language or the dialect spoken by his subjects must be underlined if we want objectivity in our approach. Personal good-will, trust and confidence create mutual esteem and understanding, while monetary inducements hamper smooth relationship between the investigator and the respondents. (ibid.: 102–103)

In conclusion, he labels some of his comments as being 'unduly provocative', and lays stress on the quality of investigations, his constant concern:

I would any day prefer to work alone, if I have the slightest doubt about the competence of my investigator or informant. What I shall sacrifice in time, I shall gain in accuracy. This is true both for base line studies as well as for the study of cultural change. (ibid.: 103)

Majumdar's firm belief that social anthropology and sociology can play a significant role in what he called 'rural reconstruction' and 'development' was voiced repeatedly. His address as the General President of the second All India Sociological Conference (December 1956) is devoted largely to this thought, with 'the almost breathless title' (Madan, 2013: 233). 'What the Sociologists can do …. What they must do …. How they can do … and, How they should do it …'. He says:

The community development programme has been launched for re-building the rural India which indeed is the real India. In so far as a large population of India lives in villages, the whole outcome of developmental planning here depends in a way upon the success or failure of the vast, revolutionary programme of rural reconstruction. Aimed at bringing about a transformation in the outlook of the people, so as to make them desire progress and feel needs, and welcome new knowledge by which to achieve it, inculcating in them a spirit of self-reliance and habits of cooperation, this programme involves vital stakes ….

Change in any socio-cultural system implies a correlated resistance, whose nature depends upon the given culture pattern and the type of change. It is, therefore, idle to think of effecting any successful change without a reliable knowledge of the varying effects and resistances of a given change in its relation to different culture patterns …. (178: 1956: 4)

In ultimate analysis the utility and productiveness of the community development programme will be judged by lasting and permanent changes it succeeds in bringing about in rural India ….

For any change in the social attitudes of the backward, rural and tribal groups, it is necessary to start with a change in their cultural environment: that is to

> say, technical improvement at the material productive level, and rather than any piecemeal attempt at converting, reforming or educating individual. Approach through the individual *foci* is atomistic and in so far as a traditional tribal or rural society is a web of institutional relations, this approach is not likely to yield any lasting results in the shape of community development .... (ibid.: 5)

> Community planning, like all other planning, is a question of priorities, in whose selection knowledge of the cultural matrix of the community is very important. (ibid.: 7)

Here, Majumdar's stand differed from the position taken by Srinivas (1960: 13) and later on by Beteille (Jodhka, 1998) who saw the relevance of studying the village only for a scientific understanding of Indian society. A number of Western and Indian scholars, Epstein, Lewis and Dube for example, were actively participating in honing the developmental process.

In this very context, Majumdar also perceived clearly how anthropologists and sociologists complement and in a way correct the role of economists. He argued:

> Indeed, the work of the economists is greatly valued; but about the social matrix of the villages, they appear to have merely scratched the surface .... There is a complete lack of first-hand studies of our rural life and the cultural setting that provides the stage for rural action. We, therefore, think merely in terms of the economic approach, of raising the levels of living, of reorganizing the employment structure, cottage industries, seasonal labour and Co-operative societies. Not that these are not important, or that we have not spotted the right maladies, but the approach to rural life has not been a total one ... Anthropologists particularly have been interested are macrocosmic studies, unlike the economists whose interests are macrocosmic, so that the net-work of exchanges, social and cultural, that determine rural life, its attitudes and fulfillment, can be viewed in the context of the cultural matrix and of social ecology. This approach enables us to understand the basic structural patterns, and integrative factors of rural economy which certainly cannot be ignored in any ambitious scheme of planning or action therapy. (168: 1955: iii–iv)

Majumdar felt that for achieving the goals of economic and social development, anthropology which had long been involved in advising the colonial regimes in India, Africa and elsewhere and which has resulted into a specialized branch, called Applied Anthropology, could vitalize sociology which had not grown because of being subordinated to economics. He also stressed a need for more 'fundamental research' in this area.

General Features of 'Village' as Projected by Majumdar

Majumdar's enthusiastic participation in village studies during 1950s is, as discussed earlier, distinguished by contributing full-fledged village studies in no less than three different socio-cultural and geographical regions of UP and the variety of composition, and other features of the five villages covered therein.

Majumdar's indefatigable devotion to fieldwork and graphic ethnography and his testing of some of his conceptions about communities (village in this case), social change in the context of interaction of differently graded cultures and how anthropology could be applied to facilitate development is reflected in these studies. These were conducted during a period of about five years (1953–57) by field teams trained by Majumdar, and published by the Asia Publishing House. However, only *Caste and Communication in an Indian Village* (1958) could be published during his lifetime. *Chhor* and *Himalayan Polyandry* came out posthumously though Majumdar had completed his introductory essays to these two publications in early 1960s shortly before his sudden demise.

Caste and Communication 'was welcomed by reviewers as an innovative study' (Madan, 2013: 231). This work has, rightly, been quoted widely in comparative studies of the Indian village in several contextual discussions by Mandelbaum, Raheja, Vandana Madan and Chauhan, among others. The other two studies no less rich, however, seem to have suffered something of 'an academic erasure' or misremembrance. The reasons which can be assigned for such a situation are that *Chhor* was published only in Hindi and *Himalayan Polyandry* was seen as a tribal study and not village study, which is only partly true as the study presents in its two main parts the ethnography of the three selected villages in the area and then the impact of the C.D. Programme taken up there. In one of his papers he calls, Jadi, the village described as a 'little community'. In this backdrop, we can now turn to elucidate how Majumdar saw the villages, in different regions of the state, and, broadly, how he conceptualized the village community, its internal and external boundaries, traditional and emergent institutions, inter-caste relations and power equations, the scenario of change, and the way he analysed it.

Majumdar has in his village studies followed a steady field view or field approach, describing ethnographic details and then trying to focus on the distinctive features of the studied communities. As a part of this manner of presentation, he has taken recourse to the use of certain concepts developed and used by contemporary social anthropologists, both Indian and Western. However, conceptual analysis orientation – structural-functional, little community, continuum sanskritization, dominant caste and so on – when applied into his perceptive ethnography, obviously, has often proved inadequate, and then he argues either about the inadequacy of these concepts and/or makes an attempt to develop some new concepts.

In this context, Sharma, one of his distinguished students, in the context of his own problem oriented village study makes some elucidating observations:

> I think the problem of defining concepts in sociology and social anthropology arises because when one goes to the field with a certain concept and observes some phenomenon which is related to the concept in some ways but is different in many other ways, he either stretches or narrows the concept to focus on the phenomenon he has observed. Some times one ventures to suggest a new concept which can signify the uniqueness of the phenomenon one has observed. (Sharma n.d., 184)

A similar approach of Majumdar becomes apparent when we look at the way he uses Redfield's conceptual frame of a 'Little Community' as applicable to Gohana, its way of life, internal and external links and boundaries and so on. Redfield's 'Little Community' should have, 'first, the quality of distinctiveness: where the community begins and where it ends is apparent' (Redfield, 1955: 4). Gohana is seen in Majumdar's study as distinctive because the village as such has been defined in the government records and the residents of the village are universally conscious of it. However, critically, village institutions like caste, economy, some traditional panchayats like that of Nai, Ahir, Dhobi (188: 1958: 95–99) and the ramifications of these institutions together with the value-systems do not reflect distinctiveness.

The second quality of the little community is that 'it is small, so small that either it itself is the unit of personal observation or else, being somewhat larger and yet homogenous, it provides in some part of it a unit fully representative of the whole. And, in this respect Majumdar observes:

> The study of a village as a whole, as an integrated way of living, thinking, feeling or as a constellation of parts, such as material culture, occupation, technology, kinship system, all leading to a proper understanding of the little community, has its limitations particularly in Indian conditions. An Indian village has a past, it has a value system, it is a sentimental system, all moored in the rich experiences of the past. At the same time, it is not limited by the four corners of the village. The kinship ties that exist in the village do not exhaust themselves in the village itself, but embrace people of distant and near villages; and crises, social and political, find the villagers in each others' lap, and a wide network of relations transcending the limits of the village bind together villages, and families, even distantly situated, so that an attempt to isolate a village would be impracticable. (ibid.: 325)

Ethnographic details, right from the historical links of Gohana with a group of 52 villages which came under the rule of a Chauhan Thakur from district Mainpuri during Mughal rule spell out its integration *at various level* with outside world.

Thirdly, the community is homogenous. 'Activities and states of mind are much alike for *all* persons in corresponding sex and age positions and the carrier of one generation repeats ... is equivalent to "slow changing"' (Redfield, 1955: 4). In Gohana, homogeneity is differential as caste and its exterior linkages have a contributing role. However, the attribute of being 'slow changing' is patent but often differs in degrees in respect of values, institutions and social organization but not at all slow in respect of material culture.

The fourth defining quality is that the community is 'self-sufficient and provides for all or most of the activities and needs of the people in it'. Redfield himself points out that 'a club, a clique, even a family is segmental contrasted with the integral little community. Gohana, as can be the case with any other Indian village, 'is not a stable unit', according to Majumdar. Service castes not residing in the village come to serve the village *Jajmans* from elsewhere. Migrants seek employment outside and vice-versa and village exogamy and other social practices connected with exogamous marriages contribute to defining or redefining dependence on the outside world.

Redfield has also subsumed this aspect in his methodology, by referring to, 'a community within communities' (1955: 113–131). He observes:

> There is, then, even in societies without the added dimension of gentry, town, or city, a kind of community much wider than the little community. We may study more closely than has yet been done these far-flung networks of social relations. They have their structure too. And where the small community does form a part of a national state, the rural networks include not only town or manor, but also the relations of village to village ... .
>
> Those who have recently been studying rural India tell us that in parts of that country the village is plainly an insufficient unity of study; it is no isolate but rather a focus for understanding wide and complex communities. One village may have traditional relationships through marriage and caste with scores of or even with several hundred other villages. There the village is a unit in some senses; in others the unit is the rural network or lattice. As work proceeds, we shall come to study these, and perhaps to distinguish types of rural lattices. In western Guatemala the rural lattices are composed chiefly of relationships of primitive commerce, with travel to attend festivals or to visit shrines constituting a secondary basis of connection among settlements. In India the castes and exogamous marriages make for rural networks based on more personal, intimate, and hereditary kinds of connections.

In the light of the above conceptual position of Redfield, we have to see how Majumdar viewed the Indian village.

Majumdar viewed the village in India as 'the pulse of India' can be felt in the villages in spite of the fact that the villages did not offer 'one social pattern; there are great variations in climate, topography and in population and, therefore the Indian village as we often speak of it is a misnomer' (188: 1958: 1) and emphasis most necessarily be on regional patterns. However, he asserts:

> The village can be seen either as a unit of territorial organization, in social or political alignment, as a symbiotic grouping of castes, high and low, or as a cultural background, of familial relationship, all of which have developed corporate living and factional jealousies. (ibid.: 3)

Mentioning the two contrasting views about the village being 'a matrix of colossal disharmony and factional intrigues', he says that both the stereotypes are 'partially true, particularly when we see the village at a distance, or for a short period' (ibid.: 3).

The last chapter of *Caste and Communication in an Indian Village* is entitled 'Village: A Concept, A Way of Life'. Elucidating this label, he says:

> A village is a way of life, because the people still live more or less as they did before–in spite of contact and communication. We can not ignore this way of life, if we want to level it up. It is through intimate knowledge of our rural life that we can discover the ethos and aspirations of our rural life. (ibid.: 328)

Then, the village is not merely a way of life, it is also a concept– it is a constellation of values and so long as our value system does not change, or changes slowly and not abruptly, the village will retain its identity, and so it has done till today. The continuity that one finds in other parts between rural and urban living– a 'continuum', as a noted anthropologist has described it– does not necessarily exist between villages and towns in India (ibid.: 329). In other words, he after initially elaborating the 'defining qualities' (Redfield) of a little community and finding them useful for defining Indian village adequately, points out the differences along with similarities and thus, empirically, brings out the realities; and in this process never forgets to highlight the changing elements in the communities' organization and potentialities for structural change.

The Gohana study has been presented through 13 chapters describing the village background, its social contours, inter-caste relations, group formation, panchayat and leadership, economy, patterns of family, life cycle rituals, religion, communication, recreation and the village as a concept; 'the way of life' as lived in Gohana, its communication and links with outside and its constellation of values, all of which contribute to its identity may now be highlighted in so far as some of the significant aspects are concerned.

Social Organization

> The social organization of Gohana is a complex cultural framework built round the traditional Hindu social system represented by the caste organization. Though the primary unit of the village society is the family, unitary or joint, caste division determines and decides all social relations. (188: 1958: 19)

The 15 castes in Gohana are difficult to classify according to the traditional *varna* system as there is a growing discrepancy between theory and practice. Caste ranking represented by inter-dining, acceptance of food and water, seating arrangement and manner of greetings cumulatively indicate the hierarchy. Often this position is also contestable as the castes, specially at the intermediate and lower levels are always struggling to place themselves higher than some others. Moreover, when we look at the power equations and structure in the village, the position may differ from the above mentioned set of parameters.

Thakurs and Brahmans who occupy the top rung constitute 23 per cent of the village population (21.5% and 1.5%, respectively). The Brahmans are regarded as highest in the hierarchy and 'even Thakur regard the Brahman as superior to them in status and recognize this in the seating arrangements' and greetings ... (ibid.: 20). They are engaged in priestly duties and also agriculture. In practising the accepted modes of cooperation in the village, based on reciprocity, Brahmans may 'take help from members of any caste without having to return it'. But:

> In practice, however, all respect and consideration shown to a Brahman is conditional upon the latter leading a strictly religious life, according to the scriptures, adhering to the prescribed norms. That a deviation from these may deprive a member of the highest caste of his sanctioned status is clearly

indicated in Gohana, where, because of their personal vices, the Brahman are beginning to lose ground. (ibid.: 21)

Thakur can be described as the dominant caste of Gohana as numerically they are 21.5 per cent (next only to Chamar who are 23.5%), own more than 41 per cent of the land holdings and, historically, for the last 250 years they had been the zamindars of Gohana as well as many villages surrounding it.

In the intermediate rung, there are nine castes, with Ahir (9.4%) followed by Kurmi (0.24%), comparatively higher than Gaderia (2%) and then Lohar (1.6%) and Barahi (2.5%), followed by a group of artisan castes – Kumhar (5.8%), Nai (3.1%), Kathik (0.5%) and Kalwar (2.1%) in that order.

In the lower category are Pasi (18.5%) and Dhobi (5.8%), followed by Chamar (23.5%) and Bhaksor, the lowest (1%).

Economy of the village is largely agricultural and no less than 14 of the castes depend on land either wholly or in part, Bhaksor being the only group which sustains itself exclusively on its traditional occupations. The artisan and service castes in most cases depend upon the traditional occupations but most of them also have lands of their own or cultivate someone else's land on *batai* or *pot* basis. The four village shops are run by Kalwars, Kathik and Thakur.

Thus, in a way, Gohana was in 1955 still, and in spite of its being so close to Lucknow, a representative kind of traditional village in so far as its economic structure and inter-caste relations were concerned. The changes, however, which had been taking place at a faster pace during the last one to two decades, have been graphically portrayed. Since the Chauhan Thakurs were till the abolition of zamindari in 1951 the village landlords and land owners, enjoying both prestige and power. Inter-caste relations in the village and the changes therein have been brought out through socio-grams focusing on the life cycle rituals in Chauhan Thakur families. These socio-grams clearly indicate the services and supplies provided by service and artisan castes and the gifts in cash and kind, traditionally reciprocal, given to them as also the changes which were observed during a period of nearly two decades. Ten castes, in all, figure in this documentation of reciprocal ties. This has been complimented with the relationships among other castes vis-à-vis the Thakur as well, in matters of food participation wherein the change during about 25 years has been depicted through two socio-grams. The broad trends reflected through the socio-grams and their accompanying accounts are:

- At the birth of a Thakur child, the Brahman prepares the horoscope and decides auspicious dates for connected ceremonies like *chhathi and Baraha.* Mainly, the Nai and Nain have a lot of duties in this connection including services at the time of the feasts. Bhaksorin helps at the time of delivery; Pasi carries the news of a birth to the community and also supplies leaf plates. The Luhar provides a knife, a *kada* (iron bangle) and a *kajrauta* (an iron case for keeping lamp black) and the Dhobi washes the clothes of the mother and the child. The Kumhar has no specific role and they attend only the feasts. Kurmi attends the feasts but takes only *pakka food* while the Ahir do not attend child birth ceremonies at all. The 'rewards' for all the services are mostly in the shape of grain, the quantity varying from caste to caste depending upon the nature of their work. There is a difference in the quantity of grain provided to them if the child is a girl, generally it is half in her case. Seven castes in all feature on this occasion.

- At the *mundan* ceremony, the Brahman decides the auspicious day, Nai shaves the hair while the Brahman does the *pooja* and also applies *loi* to the child's shaven head. The Luhar brings *akhat* (grain) while the Kumhar supply earthen articles that are needed. The Nai and Nain also serve at the time of feasts while the Pasi carries invitations and supplies leaf plates. The Dhobi and Chamar have no specific duties, but they get some *neg or inam*. The Bhaksor play their musical instruments and get food and *neg*. It is seen that in the *mundan* ceremony rewards are in the form of grain, cash, as well as clothes (in the case of Kumhar). Kurmi and Ahir, however, attend the feasts and partake in *pakka* food, if invited.
- The next important occasion documented is marriage. Here the Brahman has many duties relating to the different ceremonies. He also performs the marriage ritual. Barahi supplies a *pata* for seating and stand for the oil lamp while the Luhar brings a *kankan* and an arrow. The *kankan* has to be tied round the groom's wrist. For a girl's marriage he brings six iron rings and a *kankan* for the bride. The Kumhar supplies the required earthen pots while the Nai and Nain have to work almost constantly doing various duties including helping the bride in her bath, apply *mahawar,* help at the marriage ceremonies and also serve at the time of feasts. The Pasi also along with Nai join the *baraat* and works as watchman and for general help. The Pasi also remains in attendance more or less like the Nai. Dhobi and Dhobin too have certain assigned roles and the latter performs the ceremonies of putting *sindoor* in the bride's hair. The Bhaksor have to supply several items for different ceremonies. These are different kinds of baskets. Other castes, viz., Ahir, and Kurmi attend *dwarchar* (reception of *barat*) in case of a girl's marriage or join the *baraat,* if invited, and take *pakka food* in the feasts. Chamar may also join the *baraat* if invited. Such invitees usually give a *beohar* of one or two rupees. The details of what is given as rewards to different castes which serve on this occasion indicate that these are both in cash and kind. In some cases clothes are also given.
- At the death of a Thakur, again, the Brahman has many duties. He goes with the dead body for specific ceremonies and then for other ceremonies on the 13th day. He also performs the *annual shraadh* every year during the fortnight fixed for ancestor worship and performs the *barsi* ceremony one year after the death. Nai also accompanies the dead body and shaves the hair of the eldest son of the deceased; he also has duties on the occasion of *barsi.* What is given to the Brahman or a Mahabrahman are a number of articles which are believed to provide comfortable living to the soul of the deceased. The Nai also gets a share of these articles. Dhobi usually does not go in the funeral and comes only to give *mitti*. The other castes like Kurmi, Luhar, Bhaksor and Chamar have no functional role. Some of them may join others at the time of funeral or for the *barsi* feast depending on the quality of their relationship with the Thakur family.

- Apart from the life cycle rituals described above another occasion when inter-caste relations come into ceremonial play is *Katha recital.* The Brahman is asked to perform the *pooja* and recite *Katha* at the Thakur's place. He is paid in cash for this and also takes *prasaad.* Thakurs also invite Ahir, Kurmi, Luhar or the other castes for *Katha*. Reciprocally, the Thakur also attend *katha* in the houses of these castes. Kumhar supplies earthen pots and lamp while Pasi provides the leaf plates in which *prasaad* is given. Generally, their services are rewarded in kind. In so far as Chamar houses are concerned, the Brahman does not go there for *katha.* For them the *katha* is done under a *neem* tree which is believed to be the abode of Goddess Durga. Often, Thakurs accept the *prasaad* here as it is prepared by a Brahman. Bhaksor also come to the *katha* for *prasaad*.
- A discussion on commensal or 'food participation' by different castes with the Thakur has been documented in detail through two socio-grams, temporally, 25 years ago and now. These figures indicate that during the last 25 years a noticeable change has occurred in this regard. The Thakurs are now accepting *pakka food* from several more castes such as Kalwar, Kathik and Kumhar. Similarly, more castes are now accepting both *kachcha and pakka food,* from the Thakur, whereas previously they were accepting only *pakka food,* for instance Kurmi. The hierarchy of seating arrangement at the time of any feast has also been discussed. However, the relations of Thakurs with members of lower castes like Chamar, Bhaksor and Dhobi have not changed at all.
- The position of Chamars has been discussed in detail and shows that they are 'forced to lead a life of humiliation and degradation'. They could also not dare to use the main village streets if carrying hides. The Chamar, however, provide service to the Thakur and the latter use their position to meddle in the day-to-day affairs of the Chamars, thus turning their helpless position to their advantage. The Thakurs, it seems, particularly exploit their position of power over the Chamars when there are any disputes connected with illicit sexual relations among them or when they become indebted to the Thakurs due to their poverty. Certain other oppressive situations have also been detailed. There is, however, some resistance now growing among the Chamars. The Chamars now refuse to do *begar* for anyone. Another facet of this attitude is that the Chamar, because of their numerical strength and growing unity, are trying to foist themselves on other low status castes like the Dhobi and Bhaksor.
- The caste ethnography also notices the general tendency among the lower castes to adopt the ways of the higher castes for speeding up the 'social capillarity'. For instance, the Pasi in 1939 made a move to cleanse their food and drink habits, adopt education for children and start wearing *janeu* (sacred thread). This move began in the neighbourhood and also included a move not to accept *kachcha* food from any caste except the Brahman. This infuriated the Thakur, and in Gohana they decided to boycott the Pasi and also persuaded other castes to do so. There was a long-drawn tussle and the Thakur ultimately won by the end of the year. The Pasi had to give up their *Janeu*.

- Hierarchical distinctions among castes have also been observed when the children mix together. By and large, the children mix freely but there are nuances of behaviour and the higher castes, like the Thakur and Brahman, do not encourage free mixing. In the school, however, children of all castes sit together on the same benches. It is also seen that the children of the higher castes may abuse the lower caste children who do not dare to retaliate.
- There has been caste discrimination or restrictions on low caste people in the matter of dress. However, with the abolition of *zamindari,* these restrictions generally imposed by the Thakur on the Chamar and Dhobi but not extended to Pasi and Nai, are generally not being observed. The restrictions in the past were about putting on gold and silver ornaments, caps, shoes, and shirts and using umbrellas.

And, the specific and elaborate documentation of the exchange of gifts and services or artisan's products in this study has been used as a base for the 'transactions' approach to *jajmani* and inter-caste relations.

Inter-Caste Relations, Groupism and Leadership, Panchayats – Traditional and Statutory

Elsewhere, the changing patterns of inter-caste relationships during the last 20–25 years have been discussed with reference to commensal relationships, acceptance of food and water, and celebration of festivals? In these changes, the abolition of zamindari and the setting up of statutory gram panchayats have been a major factor. Trends like assertion for equality among lower castes and a resistance to obey unquestioningly the dominance of Thakurs are now visible. However, the fact remains that an opinion still persists that the caste system 'is God-ordained and as such no man has power to destroy it. Even among the lower castes who have been and still are harassed and ill treated, the opinion is that their economic conditions should be better but the caste system should not be done away with .... Most of the villagers are not in favour of interference in this respect by the government. They feel it, has no right to meddle in the affairs of god' (188: 1958: 81). Further, group formations are 'still on the basis of kinship. Tendencies towards division, however, have started, as also instances of support though still secondary, on the basis of interest'. Moreover, 'Nor are the groups so intensive as they used to be'. These trends reflect that structural changes in the village have been set in motion but they have yet to come about in an effective manner (ibid.: 92).

A similar situation is also to a certain extent seen in the emerging patterns of the working of panchayats, both caste panchayats and the statutory panchayats set-up in 1952, and the matrix of leadership. Before the creation of the *gram sabha*, the Thakur and a few other influential villagers played a vital role in settling disputes and effecting compromises. Now, the position is that cases are presented before the *gram sabha* as also some are brought before the village leaders. Moreover, there is still a lack of clarity in the comprehension of the villagers in the role of *gram sabha* which is a civic body, basically, and the *adalat* panchayat, set up for a larger group of villages, which is a judicial body. The cases which were settled or pending before these– traditional leaders' panchayat, *gram sabha* and *adalat* panchayat – indicate that the traditional leadership still commands confidence and successfully brings out peaceful settlements. Interestingly, Gohana has been comparatively free from serious criminal cases, may be, due to a legend that a *sati* had blessed the village that it would be peaceful. However, the over all situation also shows that the processes of communication connected with the objectives and details of forward looking legislative and government decisions need to be studied and developed. This aspect of communication has not been analysed even though the study claims to deal with communication. It seems that this is mainly due to the fact that communication channels as described and discussed in the chapter thereon needed to be telescoped with the data presented under inter-caste relations, panchayats, etc.

Communication and its Ramifications

Significantly, communication features in the title of the study, and the opening remarks in this chapter indicate that in spite of Gohana being only 8 miles from Lucknow, it is 'still a secluded place' and to many of its residents, 'Gohana is almost their whole world'.

Mechanics and channels of communication of ideas from the outside or mainly urban world as described are:

- A few people who visit the village officially communicate to the villagers a great deal of information on varied subjects. For example, *lekhpal* or *patwari* acquaints them with the decisions of the government and its laws mainly relating to land, taxation, etc. Tax collector from the tahsil office, postman and teachers in the village school are the other channels. The villagers gather around these people in their curiosity to know about such matters. Occasionally, visits by the medical personnel, and the former zamindar who is a professor in the Medical College of Lucknow are some other such sources. Certain cases of disputes documented earlier in the narration indicate how the latter acts as an advisor and a link in networking for some people.
- Some villagers also go to Lucknow daily or frequently for selling their products like milk, melons, etc. and bring information. Similarly, the villagers who go occasionally for fairs, religious gatherings or festivals as also the students who go for study in the Higher Secondary School are often the sources for dissemination of information.
- Glimpses of the world outside or even abroad have come to the village through two or three of its residents who were enlisted soldiers in the world war and also a foreign scholar who stayed in the village for a few months. Most of the important religious centres are known to the villagers only through a description of their importance and rituals. The Satya Narayan Katha or other religious discourses too are such sources. But, 'villagers enjoy stories but the moral of it fails to arrest their attention'.

- The primary school at Gohana established by the villagers' own efforts in 1942 and subsequently recognized by the District Board has two teachers who also teach the children 'cleanliness, tidiness, honesty and punctuality' have the effect of inculcating good behaviour. However, the attitude of the villagers particularly the higher castes is not receptive for education. In fact, the Thakur and Brahman have an attitude that education would lead to their children becoming 'degenerated city youths', while in the case of lower castes it would 'improve their status, and consequently (they) would claim equality with the higher castes'. Noticeably, gambling, smoking and petty stealing are commonly prevalent vices among the youth and children. The lower castes, however, favour education because they realize that it would help them to shake off the aggressive tendencies of the Thakurs'.
- By and large, though, there is curiosity for knowledge about the happenings in the areas of closer proximity, there is a critical attitude that these bring awareness which has baneful influences like losing faith in god, adopting city ways of wasting money and such other evils. Thus, 'to a villager, gaining knowledge means also loosing one's character; some villagers would rather be ignorant' (188: 1958: 207).
- The general elections and the visits of outsiders like party workers in that connection have had the effect of increasing social awareness and consciousness of political rights. They are in the process of realizing the importance of elections and their power to choose. This has, in turn made them more conscious and vocal about the performance of the government and the effect of certain measures like zamindari abolition or the special status for the untouchable castes on the equations of power and inter-caste relations in the village which they regard as sacrosanct even now. However, this awareness and expressions of demands and feelings also 'augurs well for the future of Indian democracy'. A commonly expressed demand for a radio in the village shows that there is now a feeling that they should have more knowledge and, 'knowledge dispels ignorance'.

These observations about the political situations in a village in proximity to the state capital of Uttar Pradesh make for an interesting comparison with Bailey's study (1970) of politics and social change in Orissa up to 1959. Focusing on Bisipara, an interior village, and Mohanpur, a village near Cuttack, it seems that Mohanpur was politically better oriented, aware and active in political matters as observed till the end of 1950s than Gohana Kalan as seen in the middle of the decade.

Summing up, Majumdar tried to make his first village study as comprehensive as possible. Almost all the three aspects of the community, beginning from its historical context to the latest democratic general elections and exploring the areas where change was needed as also the process through which the perceived changes had been coming about. It was intended as a baseline study for the introduction of C.D. Programme and other planned changes and its rich ethnography presents such data. Mayer reviewing it quite appropriately comments:

> Written to provide us with an ethnographical survey of an Indian village near Lucknow, as a basis for the evaluation of rural problems and social change in India. It is addressed not only to anthropologists, but also to a wide audience of administrators and development workers .... A wealth of material is contained in these accounts. Inter-caste cooperation is described in great detail, for instance, as are the changing attitudes of village caste groups to one another .... A book of this kind by its wide coverage invites readers to ask for more in their areas of particular interest (1960: 96).

As regards 'caste and communications' aspects of this study, it finds a mention as 'pioneering study of communication' done by any South Asian anthropologist. The graphic presentation of caste distances and how these have undergone changes during the last decades are one of its most 'fascinating aspect' (Agrawal, 2009: 423). Thus, it also facilitates an understanding of inter-caste relations and social distances maintained by them specially for the agents of planned change. Such village studies have been appreciated as 'significant contribution to communication anthropology' and the development of communication research. Even though it may not have directly touched upon the study of communication as it has now developed, the value of the book lies in its ethnography even though it may not be having some aspects as much graphic or quantitatively enriched as some later studies. But one can add that such 'richer' studies are often problem-oriented too, which *Castes and Communication* is not.

Mukherjee finds that Majumdar, 'later student of Malinowki was engrossed by the 'how' question but not on the basis of a superficial rendering of the structural-functional approach', which is 'attested by his village study' (*Caste and Communication)* and Urban Study (Kanpur). Majumdar dealt with 'culturology' to begin with, and the problem of urbanization, communication, and the role of Indian sociologists in later years' (1979: 68–69).

Atal (2004: 48–49) has commented on the waning interest of anthropologists and sociologists in village studies and made a strong plea for rejuvenating interest in village studies. He has advanced the view that the need for it is underlined by the fact that there still are several regions in the country from where not a single village has been professionally studied. Furthermore, cross sub-regional studies of villages have also to be tackled adequately. In this context, the importance of restudies of the villages, studied in 1950s, is also very important because such studies 'would provide a diachronic frame and help assess change that has taken place during the inter-regnum'. To this one can add the urgent needs for the study of the impact of some wide ranging statutory and programmatic measures, viz., democratic decentralization and Panchayati Raj, various labour laws, programmes for rural employment guarantee, decentralization of financial provisions to the block and panchayat levels, and so on. In this context, one has to appreciatively mention studies like Lieten and Srivastava (1999) radiating such works to the 'sub-regional' and 'fringe areas', in different states.

8

Village Studies

Tribe-Caste Village

Majumdar's village studies, which were all carried out by teams of investigators span over more than half a decade. Beginning from 1954, the field data for the studies was collected for a period of up to two years and the actual publications came in 1958 *(Caste and Communication in an Indian Village)* followed, posthumously, by *Himalayan Polyandry* in 1962 and *Chhor Ka Ek Gaon*[1] (in Hindi) also in 1962 though the publisher had ante-dated the book as published in 1960. As Majumdar desired that this book should be published in Hindi first and, later in English, the original English version had to be translated. This work was finished only by April 1960, but, after Majumdar's sudden death the publisher, it seems, delayed its publication till around February–March 1962 (Tripathi, 1962: *dha-da*). The original English manuscript had been lost and therefore no English edition could be published later.

The areas in which the studied villages were situated and their cultural background and composition also varied vastly. Gohana Kalan was a village which had started undergoing a process of rururbanization being situated within about 10 to 12 km from the then municipal limits of Lucknow. The three villages of Jaunsar-Bawar in *Himalayan Polyandry* were 'tribal' villages situationally covering the entire area and one (Lakhamandal) touching the adjoining caste villages of Garhwal. The village of *Chhor* was in real terms a tribe-caste village with a mixed population, situated in a geographical area far removed from the heart of UP, and touching the predominantly tribal districts in Bihar (now Jharkhand) and Madhya Pradesh (now Chhattisgarh). The district is situated on the south-eastern border of this large state.

Obviously, the ethnic composition and cultural scenario of these five villages (three in Jaunsar-Bawar; Gohana Kalan near Lucknow; and Dhanaura near Duddhi, the Tehsil headquarter in Mirzapur district (now Sonbhadra district) presented a wide gamut of culture contact situations seen in a state like UP. Taking a synoptic view, Gohana Kalan had a conglomeration of 15 castes with different positions in the hierarchy; while Dhanaura had 12 castes (about

75%) and five tribal groups (with about 25% population). In the three villages of Jaunsar-Bawar, the ethnic composition of Lohari and Baila was of the Rajput/Brahmans and Kolta, and Bajgi while Lakhamandal had these three groups and also some migrant population from Garhwal.

As pointed out by Madan (2013; 1983) Majumdar in his ethnographic studies dealt with contact of cultures, and the manner in which they change through such contacts of the cultures at unequal levels, and, then, a comparative evaluation of the health and development of such cultures. The range of village studies by him seems to be presenting such situations of contact of cultures with varied conglomerations. The first village study relates itself to the changing scenario of a rural population through the impact of urban contacts. In Dhanaura (Duddhi), it is the coming together of the indigenous tribal culture and the Hindu castes while in Jaunsar-Bawar, as well, the two ethnic groups, the upper (Brahman/Rajput) zamindars and the lower (Bajgi, Koltas) also present a cultural situation of the interaction between the indigenous lower caste conglomeration and the cultural imposition of the higher caste groups who had, perhaps, conquered them. May be, Majumdar had some plans to deal with these different situations of culture contact synoptically and theoretically after the ethnographic accounts had been published, which were, however, completed only just before he passed away. While the village studies were progressing, Majumdar published two edited volumes profiling aspects of village life from different authors in *Rural Profiles* I and II (1955 and 1960) and also a number of papers presenting a descriptive analysis of different institutions and impact of development in the villages under his study.

If we trace the holistic village studies in India on a map it emerges that most of the studies were made in Uttar Pradesh, Karnataka, Tamil Nadu, Andhra Pradesh, Kerala, West Bengal and central India. The villages were chosen on the basis of their being multi-caste villages. Except for Bailey's studies in Orissa, these village studies hardly included any full fledged tribe-caste configurations.[2] Majumdar appears to be the only scholar who undertook studies of a caste village, tribal villages and a tribe-caste village, the latter being *Chhor*. Thus *Chhor* emerges as a very important dimension of the holistic village studies of the mid-20th century, taken up by anthropologists. However, as Saksena (2006) has pointed out this village study has been completely ignored by all the authors reviewing and commenting upon village studies in India.

The reasons for this fate befalling the book appear to be that it was in Hindi and it was published posthumously. Since original works and that too of *Chhor's* level are even now hardly ever published in Hindi, it has escaped the attention of the social sciences academics. Even the University of Sussex's bulky epitomical publication, *Village Studies Data Analysis and Bibliography Volume 1: India* 1950–1975 (Lambert, 1976) does not cover it though it does include several studies in Hindi. *Chhor's* publisher, Asia, too perhaps failed in promoting it, may be due to their own problems.

Chauhan (2009), listing the villages studied in different parts of Uttar Pradesh, fails to mention the village Dhanaura and calls it Duddhi. He has in the text (ibid.: 46) mentioned it as the study of 'a fringe village where the tribals and other groups comprised a mixed tribe village situation'. But Chauhan does not take into account the theoretical and conceptual issues from *Chhor* while discussing this theme through other village studies. Vandana Madan (2002) and Madan even later (2013) do not take any note of this study.

II

Broadly speaking *Chhor* is a rich ethnographic account of this mixed village as well as an evaluation of the impact of Community Development Programme undertaken in the Duddhi block since early 1950s. Thus, it is a study of the village life documenting the cultures of the tribes and old migrant Hindu castes in this area, acculturation, symbiotic living and social dynamics of village life as also the changes envisaged and actually achieved by the planned development programmes. Its title *Chhor* is synonymous with 'fringe', and the term 'fringe' connotes clearly certain features, viz., its geographical location on the fartherest 'border' of the state and therefore a marginalized administrative reach, ethnic composition of the population not only in the village but also in most parts of the district with mixed tribal and caste population, the latter being generally old migrants from the adjoining districts of Uttar Pradesh, Bihar, and Madhya Pradesh, difficult communications such as no railway line, absence of vital bridges on rivers and streams, poor agricultural conditions due to the hilly terrain and lack of irrigation and almost no avenues of employment other than agriculture even a decade after independence. Of course, trading in the local produce and agricultural produce was also negligible and, according to a member of the field team stationed there, in mid-1950s, the tribal and other poorer sections were almost ignorant of the monetary values of their goods. The term 'fringe' has been used since long in social sciences but in a different context. It has been described 'as a transition zone between the urban and rural land uses'; 'combination of farm and no-farm occupations' in an area; and, thus, the urban fringe is 'relative to the expanding metropolitan city' and a village in the 'fringe' today may be engulfed by the developing metropolis tomorrow. The villages 'coming under this particular category of the 'fringe' exhibit certain common features' (Rao, 1991: 392).

Among Indian village studies, there are hardly any which cover such a multifaceted dimension. But, Bailey's *Caste and the Economic Frontier* (1957) does share these features. His Bisipara has been described as, a 'village in the remote hills of Western Orissa', located in a region which has been and still is a 'frontier in several senses of that word' (ibid.: 7). It is 'inhabited by an aboriginal people called Konds' ... 'and by Oriyas, who are Hindus' who began to 'push up from the plains about 300 years ago', and the 'region still shows many of the characteristics of a settlers' frontier'. Thus Bailey uses the term 'frontier' and the 'advance of frontiers' in economics and administration in this in-depth study of landownership, trade and business, impact of government policies and tribe-caste relations in this mixed village. His focus is on economic and political structure of the village. Majumdar's *Chhor*, on the other hand, is more of a holistic village study observing the dynamics of the relevant cultural facets of the tribes and castes and thus documenting the cultural changes brought about by a process of a peaceful kind of interface and what he calls 'trans-culturation' and thus creating, more or less, a continua. Thereby, the parameters and characteristics of a 'chhor culture' as a concept for the cultural study of this region have been presented by him (see characteristics 5–8 below).

The significant features of a 'fringe' village (222: 1960: *Jha, Ta*) roughly rendered in English could be:

1. The presence of a number of castes as well as tribes creates a situation where there are no stabilized relationships among them– as if there was no equilibrium – the different castes assuming importance at different times. Therefore, no caste can achieve dominance because combinations of other castes frustrate such attempts. Majumdar has used the picturesque expression, 'Andalucian blue' to describe this configuration.
2. The living standards of different castes and tribes do not show much difference.
3. In a fringe village, a continuous and not easily perceptible kind of a trans-culturation is facilitated. Not only the tribal communities adopt cultural traits from their advanced caste neighbours, the vice-versa also happens, specially in case of rituals, festivals, etc.
4. While in other villages, which are not fringe villages, wealth, social status, etc. greatly contribute to village politics and factions, here the government's patronage provides the lead, in a way, and its controls are far more effective.
5. In the villages, migrations bring about a new value system because the migrants have to orient themselves to the value system and aspirations of the original inhabitants (the tribals), and this makes the caste norms elastic, leading to a symbiotic pattern of living.
6. A significant feature of tribe-caste relations in fringe villages is that the migrant caste population initially gives a lot of respect and precedence to the leading tribal families and leaders but in the course of time the migrant caste groups set about exploiting the tribals, grab their lands and erode their status and influence.
7. Here, comparatively, more of tolerance is seen in social behaviour, rituals, religious beliefs, etc. This awareness and tolerance brings about some intensity and width of participation on social occasions.
8. Even though tribals adopt some of the customs and rituals of the migrant caste population, acculturation does not lead to a loss of tribal identity. The tribals are able to retain their cultural configuration because there are no dominant castes to impose their own caste norms on the tribals. The continuance of tribal structures, tribal practices, rituals and kinship terminology, etc., in the fringe villages is indicative of this situation.

In the preface itself, a note on another village, Beluga, in the area goes on to testify how these features are reflected in the inter tribe-caste relations in that village. Here, Majumdar using the term *'chhor-culture'* spells out a few more dimensions thereof (1960: *dha*) to provide a brief anchorage; Beluga has 57 families (34 tribal-Majhwar and Kharwar). The pattern of acceptance of food and water here by the tribal communities and caste communities from one another is seen to be particularly different from the pattern in the interior villages. Here the various castes share food almost liberally from each other except from Lohara; and water is accepted by all the tribes and castes from each other. Rice cooked in a metallic vessel is not treated as a *kachcha* food, which is accepted restrictively, but clean (not *ashudha*) and it can be accepted by all those castes accepting water from each other. Similarly, *roti* which is regarded as *kachcha* food elsewhere is regarded as *pakka* here and it is accepted by all the castes from one another except from Lohara.

III

The ethnography of the village has been presented broadly into three themes. First, the social and economic organization, inter-caste relations, kinship and family, life cycle rituals and religious beliefs and practices; historical account of migrants and the exploitation of tribal people at their hands, leadership and panchayats and village factions is the second aspect; and planned change, evaluation of Community Development Programme and reformist movements among the people is the third theme.

How far the ethnography documents reflect the characteristics attributed to the 'chhor culture' would show the quality of Majumdar's perceptive ethnography and his derivation of the concept of 'chhor culture' there-from.

Out of the 12 castes, two higher castes Brahman and Thakur/Chhatriya have a presence of around 10 per cent each, while Kalwar, an intermediary caste and Chamar have populations around ± 20 per cent; the tribal groups (five in number) with Majhi or Gond at 14 per cent, followed by Bhuiyan, Chero and Panika at about ± 3 per cent, form a total of 23 per cent of the village population.

The history of the village has been traced from its first survey by the British in 1874. The village had been founded by the father of Nanku Majhi, who was the zamindar then. As Nanku could not produce any document in support of his position, he was made the *supurdar* since the administration decided to establish a government zamindari in this area. At that time, almost the entire land was being cultivated by the tribals and the only non-tribals were government employees of the Duddhi Tehsil and government estate. Thus, the 'advance of administrative frontier' (Bailey, 1957) initiated the coming of non-tribals into the village. Nanku Majhi as *supurdar* and as a village leader had emerged as an outstanding village head in his lifetime till the end of the 19th century. He has been described as an impartial, sagacious and unchallenged leader (222: 1960: 61). The history of different factions in the village as it emerged after Nanku Majhi's death has been traced during the tenures of three *supurdars* who succeeded him, followed by the period after the abolition of the government zamindari in 1952. The next *supurdar* was a Brahman and then came a Majhi from Nanku's family followed by a Thakur. The narration of factionalism is woven around the changes in the *supurdar*. The supports and oppositions to the actions of the three *supurdars* as described in some details reflect, to an extent, how there occurred intra-caste and inter-tribal splits as also the role of different castes having substantial numbers. Thus, a near equilibrium-less situation and shifting roles and supports of different castes-tribes and intra-caste factions among Brahmans and Thakurs is reflected through this narrative. The last *supurdar*, who not only carried the more important factions with him but also had better leadership qualities, was elected as the gram-pradhan and the pradhan of the Nyaya Panchayat when these statutory institutions having areas of some other villages as well, were set up in 1950s. This discussion concludes with two observations, namely, intense caste consciousness of the residents of Dhanaura and each tribal group also assuming more and more the behaviour pattern of castes and flaunting a Hindu identity specially after the influence and spread of the Rajmohini Devi movement during the first half of the 1950s. The movement initiated by Devi was reformist and stressed adoption of vegetarianism, giving up alcohol and other drinks and practising a simpler and ritual free kind of a lifestyle with religious practices devoted to worshipping Hindu gods and holding gatherings for singing of *bhajan*, etc. This gave an impetus to the process of detribalization and acculturation, even furthering the process of syncretization or mixing of popular Hindu traditions (little traditions) with the magical and other ritualistic features of the tribes.

In a way, this characteristic of the 'chhor culture' which indicates the near absence of dominant leadership in the village community, what Majumdar describes as 'a near equilibrium-less situations and shifting roles and supports of different castes tribes' was perceived in a later study on extensive displacement and indifferent rehabilitation scenario in this area about 40 years after Majumdar's study. Then, Saksena and Sen (1999: 232–33) observed:

> Broadly speaking, leadership in the tribal areas predominantly inhabited by one or two tribal communities is found to be generally strong and well organized and buttressed with the traditional leadership conventions and its supportive institutions such as youth dormitories. Singh (1982) in his study of tribal movements found that tribal unrest assumes an organized character only among the large, homogenous land owning tribal communities who have a relatively strong economic base. In a multi-ethnic community, characterized by economic interdependence among different groups, a movement, particularly the one connected with economic issues takes a different course of development. But in an area inhabited by a large number of tribal groups mixed with a substantial proportion or emigrant non-tribal population leadership in the sphere of economy and secular interests of the community is found to be segmentalised, diffused and oft-changing. Here, the growth of any cohesive leadership is also hampered by a lack of education and awareness, especially among the tribal groups, and clash of tribe caste interests. No effective movements supporting or agitating for any common cause can grow out of such a matrix. Such a vacuum in leadership is often filled up by the entry of social or political workers or other functionaries coming from outside, often linked with some regional or national movements usually aiming at economic and social reforms. Some recent examples are the Naxalite cadres in Andhra

Pradesh (Adhikary and Bhattacharya, 1982) and in M.P., Sarvodaya workers in the Narmada Bachao Andolan, and Chipko elements in the Tehri agitation (Uttarakhand).

The second characteristic of little difference being perceived in the living standards of different castes and tribes is reflected roughly by the ethnographic details relating to housing, ownership of livestock, household utensils and other material culture. Similar is the case with dress and ornaments except that the women of well-off families wear some gold and silver. Exceptionally, a mention has been made of two or three Sahu (Baniya) families, who have gained wealth during a decade or so mainly through exploitative money lending and usurping land from tribals and Chamar families through certain processes which circumvent the law.

The process of 'continuous and not easily perceptible kind of a trans-culturation' which is the third characteristic, is documented in the ethnography relating to a large range of institutional and ritual practices. The impact left by the Devi movement in this regard has already been referred to. In the economic field specially agriculture, the role of the village Baiga who comes from the Chero tribe is seen universally (222: 1960: 20–21), adoption of lac collection by lower Hindu castes for subsidiary income, artisan work of Agharias for the entire village community, and Panika for clothes at least on traditional occasions are some of the trans-acculturative features. Aspects of inter-caste relations (222: 1960: 78–ff) such as the services from the Brahman *pandit* provided to at least one tribal group (Kharwar) at life cycle rituals and to more tribal groups for agricultural operations, mutual acceptance of water and *pakka* food between Thakur, Chero, Panika and Kharwar, and a similar relationship of all tribal groups with certain intermediary and lower castes have been observed. Further, relaxation and trans-culturation in this regard are reflected in the kinship terms (ibid.: 118–19). Rituals connected with marriage specially among Majhi and Chero also document some acculturative practices.

The fourth feature of fringe culture – government patronage and role in the formation of leadership in fringe culture instead of wealth and social status – is perceptible in the two chapters on Panchayats, factionalism and leadership patterns. When the 'frontier of administration' moved to Dhanaura, Nanku Majhi who was appointed the *supurdar* by the colonial administration emerged as an undisputed village leader with influence over the community's social, economic and religious life. Subsequently also factions grew with changing loyalties and leadership around the successive *supurdars*. After the abolition of government zamindari, the ex-*supurdar* could also assume the position of pradhan in the two statutory panchayat institutions– gram panchayat and adalati panchayat. Subsequent changes in reservation of seats and the position of pradhan under panchayati law and the influence of government policies and functionaries continue to be a prime determinant in this area. Bailey also discerns and comments on the role of the government in Bisipara which too is a mixed village of higher castes, tribes and lower castes where the 'administration frontier' has been advancing during the last 100 years: 'Under pressure of economic change, the political functions of castes are beginning to be taken over, as one might expect, by the ultimate political authority, the Government of India' (Bailey, 1957: 275).

The fifth characteristic of the chhor culture, namely, that the migrants (generally higher caste groups) coming into the villages founded by tribes orient themselves to the value system of the tribes and make caste norms elastic, leading to a symbiotic living, as discussed earlier has been amply illustrated through aspects of economic, religious and ritual practices. The cult which has developed around Nanku Majhi's *chabutara* and the celebrations of Hindu festivals like Holi and the inter-caste tribe pattern of playing Holi (222: 1960: 159–62) is further indicative of the scenario. The celebration of Karma, a tribal festival, (ibid.: 152) provides syncretic details of its celebration. The Mahadani *deosthan* which is the abode of the village goddess has a multiple significance and sacredness in the beliefs of both the castes and the tribes (ibid.: 165–66).

Characteristics numbered seven and eight are also mirrored in these ethnographic accounts. And so is the case with characteristic seven.

IV

As *Chhor* is a study of change and also the impact of Community Development Programme introduced in the area, the concluding part of the book portrays it in three chapters: the first one is on planned change, the second one is on reform movements and the third chapter contains a general evaluation of the work done under the Community Development Programme. Duddhi was one of the National Extension Service Block taken up in October 1953, covering 90 villages and a population of 35,000. The inhabitants of the entire area were mostly tribals with low literacy and poverty, poor agriculturists or agricultural labourers. The migrants who came for trade and business initially had achieved a better economic and educational level. Dhanaura was one of the 12 VLW centres. Duddhi then was a town with about 3000 people while Dhanaura had a population of around 850.

Evaluative comments on some of the important schemes comprising the CD Programme indicate their strengths and flaws. Shramdan, voluntary labour contribution, was to be taken up for various works of public benefit. Initially, it was a success but subsequently it lost its appeal totally because of its being seen as a revival of the old practice of *begar* by the poorer people, specially Chamar and tribals, and opposition to certain works by the traditional leaders or works chosen for some personal benefits. In this context, the building of good roads connecting various *tolas* was opposed by the Kalwars who thought that it would facilitate robberies and dacoities, by the tribals under an apprehension that it would disturb the peace and aloofness of the village, and Chamars alone supporting it because they thought good roads would enable them to reach home safely in the night even when in a drunken state. All this, when the village had a history of constructing a road in 1947–48 through organized collective labour. The construction of community centre or *panchayat ghar* became a target of factionalism and the scheme was shifted to another village. Some irrigation works were opposed because they had been planned to benefit one or two influential leaders. Certain other programmes like adult education, Mangal Dal, Bhajan Mandalies, and a Gram Laxmi Centre for training women and girls in household skills, had all started well and created enthusiasm among the villagers. However, these schemes had to be discontinued by the Block authorities because of budgetary constraints. Similarly, the training-cum-production centres set up for carpentry, tinsmithy, sewing and silk industry, all ended without providing livelihood to trainees because of various shortcomings. The cooperative society had a partial success though it was not able to adequately respond to the needs of the poorer sections. Agricultural extension and horticulture achieved some success because people adopted improved practices according to their own wisdom, resources and empirical needs. In horticulture, the Block was not able to meet the demand for saplings when the demand caught up later. A part of the animal husbandry programme like artificial insemination became popular after sometime but the delivery of services was not seen to be timely or adequate. In public health and medicine, care of expectant mothers and child birth became popular because of the missionary background of the midwife posted there. However, again, the training of local *dais*, a much needed element, could not keep up with the needs. Among prevalent diseases, programme for control of yaws, particularly common among tribals, was catching up. But, the inability of the Block to manage supply of potable and safe drinking water became a hurdle in controlling some of the most common diseases.

The chapter on reform movements describes in detail the promising beginnings and then fizzling out of the Rajmohini Devi movement, specially among the Gonds in the area, and the work of Irish priests based in a Christian mission in Duddhi. During famine conditions around 1951, Rajmohini Devi, a Gond woman of Sarguja claimed to have received some mystical message to work among her people. Therefore, she changed her family's lifestyle, adopting vegetarianism, giving up of intoxicants, regular worship and *bhajan* and adoption of virtues like truth and vice-free habits. She started holding prayer meetings and camps, touring extensively and thus gained a very large following including some prominent tribal leaders who, perhaps, thought that they would gain popularity and may benefit financially too as a result of being a part of the movement. Subsequently, Rajmohini also adopted certain practices which seem to have brought her close to the Congress party and thus assumed political hues. However, within a period of half a decade or so, her influence declined for various reasons including the acts of her followers who tried to make money, and the absence of any concrete programmes or measures which would ameliorate the condition of the tribal people. In contrast, the Irish mission set up in Duddhi had garnered popular appeal because of it providing medical services through an efficient and trained midwife and educating people. The substance of priest's speeches in *hats*, and fairs also had an element of appeal for the marginalized people in pleading for equality and showing them ways to improve their lot.

The general evaluation of Community Development Programme brings up certain basic issues which contributed to its achieving only a limited success and often becoming unpopular. First, its functionaries created a climate of high expectations among people which they could not sustain because of the manner of their own working and the processes and procedures of government. Another factor was the frequent absence of functionaries from their duty or the continuance of vacant post for substantial periods, and transfers after short tenures. Similarly, some of the programmes which became popular could not be sustained because of either budgetary constraints or transfer of popular and active personnel. Corruption and diversion of materials received for various programmes was another cause of widespread complaints, and all this was compounded by the delays in processing of applications for benefits. Ignorance of most of the C.D. personnel about the felt needs of villagers and their priorities and the cultural conditions of the area was also acutely felt by the people. A few suggestions have been made, in conclusion, to remedy the deficiencies, and proper orientation of the personnel is held out as an important part of such an effort. In conclusion, Majumdar observes that in spite of many shortcomings, the programme has created an awareness for a better life among the long-neglected common people. They have now begun to understand their problems and also their political rights.

V

The 'chhor culture' thus, presents a critical analysis and reference point in the communities living together, expressing a high level of inclusiveness and universalisation. Disputes between the villagers are not taken to courts or police but settled in the village itself, and the extent of social distance seen between tribes and castes and even among the castes in the interior villages is much less here. All the communities share the natural resources amicably. In the process, all of them also get to be vocal which is absent in non-fringe villages where certain castes and tribes, if any, are voiceless, more or less. Thus, in Majumdar's opinion the fringe villages and 'fringe culture' offer some kind of a solution to the 'meaningless caste-based complexities' in community life seen elsewhere and thereby presents a model for 'rural rehabilitation'. Majumdar also expresses his usual optimism, saying that the concept of 'fringe village' and 'fringe culture' outlined here would provide a base-line for facilitating evaluation of potentialities for cultural changes embodied in the very basics of our rural cultures; and thus creating a more receptive climate even for planned change (222: 1960: rna).

The description of the first characteristic of a tribe-caste village studied on the 'fringe' refers to a lack of stabilized relationship among castes and tribes, thereby a system lacking in equilibrium. Kuper (1973: 191) comments that a social system 'lacking in equilibrium' presents 'a problem to the functionalist, whose basic premise was that the system he was studying was well integrated and in-equilibrium. Gluckman had recognized the dynamism of social system but had posited the existence of periods of comparative calm and equilibrium of forces which could be studied in more or less conventional terms' (quoted in Kuper, 1973: 191); while Leach rejected this and advanced the view that, 'all societies maintain only a precarious balance at any time, and are really in a constant state of flux and potential change. The norms which exist are neither stable nor inflexible' (ibid.: 191). Majumdar's ethnography of the situation in *Chhor* seems to be holding out a view as a functionalist nearer to Leach in that in the 'chhor culture' the factions keep inter-caste tribe relations of the social system in a state of flux and potential change. But, the views of Gluckman and Leach are based on the African or Highland Burmese social systems which, it appears, are more prone to rapid and even violent changes as compared to rather imperceptible and smooth kind of loss of equilibrium and its resumption, characteristic of the Indian scenario.

VI

As Epstein states, 'most of the studies (village studies) so far available have been conducted by social anthropologists ... examining the complete interconnection of the different economic, political and social variables, which jointly make up the village social system ... and a *good* village study rests on its qualitative exposition of social processes' (1977: 127). She emphasizes the importance of restudies as comparisons over time and in a historical perspective particularly if the focus is on socio-economic development; and expounds the view:

> Yet rural research has now reached the stage, particularly in India but possibly elsewhere as well, when it becomes wasteful to encourage inquiries in yet unresearched fields. I suggest that it is now more efficient, illuminating and instructive to re-survey and re-study rural areas for which earlier findings are available than to continue extending into virgin territories. (ibid.: 128)

Chauhan (2009) however documents his revisits to five villages in Uttar Pradesh which have been studied by teams of researchers either simultaneously or in sequential studies. Through these visits he has tried to make brief comments on change and other aspects of rural life as documented in the studies, through discussions with the old informants of the earlier researchers and his own observations. Epstein's mention of some principal aspects of restudies also include identification and contact with earlier informants, consultation of unpublished field notes and other materials and need for a focused research. In the case of socio-economic surveys of villages, as well, the value of re-studies was realized and the Registrar General of India planned such re-studies of three villages each in the States where research and surveys were conducted as part of the Census of 1961 (Roy-Burman, 1977: 52–53).

In the case of *chhor ka gaon*, Dhanaura, two revisits were made by this author. The earlier, one, with Chandra Sen (who supervised DNM's team for *Chhor*), was in mid-1990s in connection with a study of displacement and rehabilitation of the people due to the Kanhar dam, and then a short field trip to the village was undertaken by him in February 2013. It was just a reconnaissance and an attempt was made during this short visit to identify how the village had changed during the last about 60 years, after it was studied by Majumdar. Mainly, broad trends of changes in the village and their agents, and variants in the impact on the caste and tribal communities and the institutions documented in *Chhor* were observed. Here, we will first give a general descriptive note on what was observed in the village, and thereafter to attempt a general analytical discussion of the change. The thorough ethnography of the community as it was in mid-1950s not only provided the benchmark, it also appeared to have touches of prescience.

The town of Duddhi has grown perhaps eight to 10 times in this period of 56–57 years. It now gives the look of a flourishing town with a population of around 30,000. By and large, the entire district of Sonbhadra has been industrialized, in patches, with large establishments based on the rich and varied natural resources of the district. However, it presents a picture of contrast– on the one hand the people are backward agriculturists depending largely on unirrigated land and supplementing their incomes from forest and wage labour and on the other hand there are large areas humming with a variety of heavy projects and ancillary industrial units (Saksena and Sen, 1999). There is large scale coal mining, cement production, thermal power projects, aluminium products, and dams and reservoirs for irrigation in their respective areas and also hydel power production. The setting up of these large projects has caused vastly improved communications by road and rail in the district. Duddhi itself is now a railway station on the Chopan-Garhwa Railway line which connects Sonbhadra to the adjoining districts of Garhwa and Palamu in Jharkhand. However, there are no large industrial units in the vicinity of Duddhi town or village Dhanaura.

The expansion of Duddhi town and the location of its railway station on the side where Dhanaura is situated has closely linked the village to Duddhi. In fact, the village boundaries lie just across to the east of *pakka* road by the side of the Duddhi Railway Station. A number of institutions of Duddhi are now located within the boundaries of Dhanaura. For example, an ITI which was opened in Duddhi some three decades back was shifted to Dhanaura with a substantial campus and buildings of its own. Similarly, the Mandi Parishad centre for the marketing of agricultural products in the area is now situated here. Kanhar Irrigation Project was launched in 1978 to build an earthen dam (3.24 kms long and 39.90 metres high) on Kanhar river with a canal system. The progress of the project was, however, interrupted but recently its expeditious construction has been ordered by the government. A colony for the officers and staff of this project, which had been built earlier, is now once again coming to life.

This project is likely to displace about 2000 families in several villages. This situation can also provide some fresh ground for naxalites to stir up violence. There were reports that the naxal leaders of this area who have connections with the widespread radical movement in the adjoining districts of Bihar, Jharkhand and Chhattisgarh, who were dormant for quite some time, may activate themselves. The district has, therefore, been in receipt of special grants from the central government for countering the naxal movement.

The expansion of Duddhi has been a result of increasing government activities and its becoming a trade/business centre for the adjoining rural areas. The prosperity and incomes brought about by the location of various factories at navigable distance from Duddhi, the setting up of a number of private educational institutions, the shifting of tahsil level courts and offices (S.D.M., Munsif, etc.) and the activation of the decentralized Panchayati Raj System after the 74th amendment to the Constitution in 1992 with a substantial devolution of financial resources to the panchayat level, buttressed by the vast expansion of central and state schemes for development, poverty alleviation, etc. and the forces of privatization and linkages to larger markets have contributed to Duddhi's growth, of course with a suburbanization effect on Dhanaura.

VII

The Village

A brief description of the present scenario of the village is now contextually called for. The *chhor ka gaon*, Dhanaura is now a much larger village. The gram panchayat of Dhanaura, as of now, includes two revenue villages, namely Dhanaura along with its *tolas* and Japla and its *tolas*. This panchayat now has more than 4000 voters, i.e., adults above 18 years of age, and therefore its population should be about 6000–7000 with Dhanaura itself having a population of around 4500 to 5000. The number of *tolas* has also doubled, perhaps informally, with areas having concentrations of certain castes/tribes being identified as their *tolas* such as, Baniya *tola*, Harijan *tola*, Brahman *tola* and Baiga *tola*. The composition of the population now is of five tribal communities with a predominance of Majhi or Gond followed by Chero or Baiga, Panika and Bhuiyan. As regards castes, two out of the 12 castes documented earlier (1955), Kahar (6 families) and Kumhar (7 families) are no more residing in the village. There has been a considerable increase in the migrants from within the district with a few from adjoining states. A substantial number of migrants belong to the Chamar caste and they had come from the Singrauli side, south of Duddhi, in early 1960s after displacement due to the construction of Rihand dam. The other migrant community is that of Muslims who also came to the village about 40 years back. The Chamar migrants from the south are still identified by some difference in their dialect.

The lay-out of the village has not changed, broadly. However, the concentration of certain communities in different *tolas* has made parts of the village congested though, by and large, the houses remain in the vicinity of the agricultural fields, as was the tribal pattern earlier, specially in the case of tribal communities but not so much in the case of higher castes like Thakur, Brahman, and Kalwar. There are hardly any *kachcha* houses to be seen now. A dense forest mentioned earlier about 3 km from the main village en route to Piparahi *tola*, has now largely turned into a scrub jungle with its rocky formation exposed. Similarly, the number of Khair (catechu) trees (from which *kattha* is made) and also the *mahuva* trees has also come down. The cultivated land in Piparahi *tola* which has substantial tribal residents has red and sandy soil and therefore much less fertile than the cultivated land in the main village and its other nearby tolas, owned by higher castes.

What strikes a visitor to the main village are the *pakka* roads within it and also to its *tolas?* These roads have been built during the last about five years. Since Dhanaura is the headquarter of the panchayat, there is a panchayat building in the village with the panchayat secretary running the office (see section IV – C.D. Programme).

VIII

Leadership and Factions

A general discussion regarding leadership in the village brought out the fact that the election of pradhan of Dhanaura panchayat and members is now an arena of participation by all the different sections of the village. As the law lays down that the post of pradhan, in a rotation, will be reserved for general candidates, women, and scheduled castes/scheduled tribes/OBC, any entrenched and vested interest in the post by any particular community or faction has become difficult. The Thakur family of the old pradhan, V.S., which was influential, has perhaps suffered a decline. In the present term, the pradhan is an OBC belonging to Kalwar community which is now, as in the past, an influential caste. In the previous term the post was reserved for women and a simple house-maker from a prominent Brahman family was the pradhan. Probably, the Brahmans and Kalwar still move together while the support of other communities specially the tribes and the Chamar is absolutely essential for their winning an election. Hence, it seems that the loyalties and support of these sections which would constitute almost 40 per cent of the village voters changes under different circumstances. Wealth, it seems has also come to be of much more importance in these elections. The present pradhan, S.K., is a rich businessman. He has the sole agency, for the Duddhi rural areas, for the products of Hindustan Lever Limited, Britannia and Parle. His godown and main centre for distribution is in Duddhi and he has a turnover, annually, of more than ₹ 20 crore. He also owns substantial lands in the main village, but lives with his extended family in two modestly built *pakka* houses. He owns several vehicles, tractors and motorbikes and so do a few others in the village. Presently, it appears that the Kalwars, Majhi and other tribal communities and Brahmans have eclipsed the Thakur, Baniya/Agrahari leaders.

Village Economy

Though no exact figures could be obtained (because the panchayat secretary was on leave), it was gathered that now as a result of zamindari abolition, land reforms and some redistribution and allotment of lands, the number of landless people has been reduced. However, the later migrants from the Singrauli side and some of the Muslim families are landless and those allotted land under land reform measures have got only small pieces of poor, unirrigated lands. They sustain themselves on a variety of activities – working for others as agricultural labourers, working under the rural employment scheme and working with contractors around Duddhi. Another source of earning some income for such families was collecting firewood from the adjoining forest areas for sale at

Duddhi and collecting stone boulders from the rocky lands around the village and selling it after breaking it. Thus, employment avenues and work opportunities are, probably, manifold now. A Chamar family which had shifted after displacement from Singrauli had no land and yet their living seemed to be moderately good and they were sending three children to a private primary school at Duddhi paying a monthly fees of ₹ 150 each.

Agricultural land which is cultivated in this revenue village was reported to be around 1000 hectares. However, the lands beyond those surrounding the main village were not very fertile and also lacked irrigation. Irrigation is mainly done from wells and also the *Bandhis*. The Lakara dam built in the first decade of the 20th century over the river Lakara had made it possible for certain areas on the eastern side of the village to be irrigated and therefore produce good varieties of rice. However, the water body for the dam has now been considerably reduced and the irrigated area from it is now much less. There is a move to improve the reservoir and resume more irrigated area. The main crops now are wheat and rice in the areas with better soil and irrigation, and maize, oilseeds and pulses elsewhere. The production of other coarse grains has been almost given up.

Awareness among the tribal communities specially Majhi, and Chamar among scheduled castes, has considerably increased with education and more opportunities for government employment due to reservation. It was gathered that the village now has from among these communities at least two PCS officers, several policemen and about a dozen other persons in different posts. Two such families have even left the village and settled at Allahabad (It is mentionable that even in the last decade of the 20th century the literacy rates among most of the scheduled caste/tribes in the district were less than 10 per cent and they lacked mobility and urban contacts). All this has no doubt created social capital for the village, specially for the marginalized communities, and provided them with network access to government agencies. Obviously Dhanaura has come out as a progressive village.

Educational institutions in the village now include a co-educational high school and secondary level schools for boys and girls, as also an ITI. Moreover, some students also go to the institutions in Duddhi specially private primary schools and technical institutions, which are said to be better in the quality of instructions than the government schools at Dhanaura and to the government degree college. The higher castes and OBC were reported to have several engineers, lawyers, etc.

The shifting of the government ITI from Duddhi to Dhanaura has had its own impact. It has meant that a number of educated people from outside and holding good positions are now working in this village, though most of them keep their families at Duddhi or elsewhere. The head of this institution informed us that the seats in the ITI were now fully filled up and the reserved seats also generally went to the scheduled castes/scheduled tribe candidates from this area. The trades in the syllabus here include fashion technology and dress making, apart from the usual vocational trainings like electricians, fitters, etc.

Moreover, this institution has been recently entrusted with a programme for skill-upgradation of the artisans in the area under the special programme to counter the naxalite movement.

IX

Religion, Beliefs and Festivals

Significantly, the first place to which this author was taken to for a visit was the *Chabutara* of Nanhe Majhi, founder of this village and its first *supurdar* after the British took over in the 19th century. The *Chabutara* now has a large area around it enclosed with a *pakka* compound wall and gate. The residents of the village and even those from other parts of the district make offerings on the *Chabutara* and believe that their wishes will be fulfilled. Every third year, on a day in the month of *Sravana* decided by the Baiga, who is a Chero, large crowds gather here. The Baiga performs sacrifices of a goat and cocks and makes other offerings. The people who come to this place are from all the communities including higher castes. The boundary wall has been built with contributions from a number of prominent and well-to-do villagers.

After the rituals at Nanhe Majhi *Chabutara*, the people chase all the evil spirits in the village by moving in a procession and making offerings at various places. This ritual ends at a *peepal* tree in the village which is a part of a small sacred grove devoted to *Mahadani*, also known as *Dinwar.* Sacrifices and offerings are also made here as *Mahadani* controls all the evil spirits. The Baiga leads the rituals here too and also performs a *havan*. Thus, the practices described in *Chhor* (222: 1960: 164–65) have not only continued but also gained, perhaps, some more following and momentum. The Chero Baiga is also a reputed '*jhar-phunk wala*', consulted by the villagers in times of any crisis. In daily life, he is a mason working mostly at Duddhi. He is one of the old informants' sons.

As regards religious worship, Shiv *pooja* is very common here. The village has three Shiv temples with large *chabutaras* built around them for the devotees coming there on festivals. These platforms were renovated and expanded in the past two decades or so. I was told that the tribals also worship Shiv.

We can now turn to see whether this 2013 scenario, in Duddhi and Dhanaura still reflects the 'fringe' characteristics, as per Majumdar's concept, and to what extent.

X

Chhor Culture: Revisited

The first trait of '*chhor* culture' indicates the absence of a permanent power-clientele relationship among different castes and tribes as different communities assume importance at different times. A limited critical analysis of these relationships as seen in the case of Panchayati Raj, agricultural labour, and similar relationship of contacts and communication confirm the presence and continuance and even reinforcement of this characteristic. Characteristic no. 6 highlighted the changing pattern of relationships between migrant castes and original tribal resident, where the initial importance/respect given to the tribes and/or their leaders changes in the course of time to an exploitative link. Today, this characteristic is not much in evidence because of the election strategies and the impact of widespread outside links and other factors on the subaltern, which have partly offset the influence of accumulation of wealth with traders as well. Moreover, the progress of tribes and scheduled castes in government jobs has had its own role in the equations of relationships. It cannot be said that exploitation has been eliminated but a good deal of freedom from it has been brought about by various factors like availability of wage employment elsewhere, and creation of new leadership and social capital among the marginalized. Even the later migrant Chamars in the village prefer to get wage employment with contractors, in *tendu patta* collection and sale, and the rural employment scheme. This kind of change is seen elsewhere also (Lieten and Srivastava, 1999; Cohn, 1987: 299). Cohn has, in the context of the Noniyas and Chamars of Madhopur, concluded that after a generation the power in the village would be in the hands of small farmers.

The second characteristic that living standards of different castes and tribes do not have much difference is only partly-true now. The linkage of the village with the town along with a general rise in the incomes of the different tribes and castes has made its impact. Today, there are hardly any *kachcha* houses to be seen and the wider contacts with the town have changed the scenario. That the ITI in the Duddhi runs courses in fashion technology and dress making is significant. The dress and ornaments in vogue earlier were not to be seen anywhere. Several aspects of this cultural pattern of the *Chhor* area had contributed to the lack of a leadership needed for any movement for the land rights of those people which were eroded by the abolition of the government zamindari and the subsequent transfer of lands *en bloc* to the Forest Department by the government after 1950 and also any agitation for effective rehabilitation of families displaced (Saksena and Sen, 1999: 235–245).

Characteristic three which emphasizes a gradual and silent kind of a trans-acculturation has assumed a wider and greater visibility as seen in the cult of Nanhe Majhi and various other practices including the worship of Shiva and other Hindu gods by the entire village.

Characteristic four points out to a comparative absence of contribution of wealth, social status, etc. to village politics and an upper hand for government patronage. The general observation, now, is that the panchayat politics has considerably diminished the role of social status but wealth is important. Government policies and their agencies now have more of a hand through Panchayati Raj, reservations and the accretion of social capital through various networks. Bailey's study also underlines such a view.

The fifth characteristic of migrants orienting themselves to the prevailing value system, leading to a symbiotic pattern of living, was more relevant earlier. The process of trans-acculturation between tribals and old migrants, it appears, has reached somewhere about a saturation point, bringing about greater homogenization in certain areas of their culture. In so far as the later migrants, with one or two generations of residence in the village are concerned the process must be going on, though they are still identified as being a separate entity mainly due to their '*boli*' of the South (dialect).

The seventh characteristic of more tolerance and social participation between tribals and others continues to be of salience. Though the process of change due to the impact of links with town, industries, flow of cash, etc. has been going on probably the dynamics thereof varies among different communities which can only be observed through participant observation and detailed study. During the brief revisit, however, it was observed that both the tribal and caste people in the village now have a better interaction with the outside world due to their mobility, facilitated by the railway link, roads, location of an irrigation project and an I.T.I. with its substantial staff, industrial activities in some centres which are not far off as also the employment and other programmes operated by the block panchayat with its offices in Duddhi town.

As regards the eighth characteristic of the tribals retaining their cultural configuration in spite of adopting certain customs and rituals from the old migrant castes population (Hindu), the observation would now be that the tribal identity and configuration has been underwritten by government policies. But at the same time, the mainstream culture is also having its continued impact. Generally, the people state that there is now not much of a difference between tribes and castes and some of the practices connected with life cycle and rituals may also have changed. The Rajmohini Devi reform movement and her teachings (222: 1960: 248–52) with a substantial following in this area in the 1950s had also created a climate favourable for the acceptance of the Hindu pantheon and practices, in other words an acculturative wave. The footprints of the process of development may also have eroded the configuration, at least peripherally.

XI

In conclusion, it would be *germane* to examine as to how far the concept of 'chhor culture' can be seen to have a methodological and empirical validity and utility across time and space. Any in-depth analysis of this issue would require further intensive re-study and research of secondary data. The importance of re-studies has been highlighted by a number of scholars; Atal; Chauhan; Epstein; Marriott; Shah among others. However the most patent question that arises in this context is how far certain other districts on the southern border of Uttar Pradesh, viz. Banda, Mahoba, Lalitpur and Shankargarh area of Allahabad district, and also in Madhya Pradesh which have tribal populations, share some or all the features of the '*chhor-culture*'. From his limited knowledge, this author can say that most of these other areas do not share many characteristics; and a cursory observation to explain this would be that most of these areas had been under personal zamindaris or the rule of princely states. This resulted into the domination by the migrants caste people both economically and culturally and much more acute loss of tribal identity and influence. For instance in the Shankargarh area the Kol were generally reduced to the position of just landless labourers often under debt bondage. The conditions in Duddhi and other parts of Sonbhadra differed basically due to these being in a government zamindari with some kind of an 'indirect rule' under the system of governance of the Partially-Excluded Areas under the Government of India Act, 1935, till the provisions contained in the Constitution of India (1950) were enforced. The Presidential Orders under the latter did not provide for a Scheduled Area in Uttar Pradesh or even the status of scheduled tribes to the communities living in Sonbhadra, Mirzapur and other contiguous districts. The consequences of this measure, heavily loaded against the tribes of this area, have particularly contributed to their losing land rights, benefits from positive discrimination and other policies of the government (Hasan, 1998; Saksena, 1998; Saksena and Sen, 1999).

The trends of change observed in Dhanaura further raise several sociological, political and economic issues connected with the rural scene in this region, as also in a larger Indian context. One is the pattern of changes in the power equations, factions and caste relations brought about by the Panchayati Raj with its increasing devolution of financial and civic role. As Arora (2013) has pointed out even in north-eastern India with its ethnic situation, the strong rooting of what she calls, '*procedural democracy*' and active participation in elections has yielded significant gains; then, how far the emerging identities and salience of certain government defined categories of castes or classes like scheduled castes, scheduled tribes, OBC have contributed to the different possibilities for opportunities and roles for them (Lieten and Srivastava, 1999).

If we go by Ghurye's classification of villages, Dhanaura is now in a process of changing into a *gram raja* or super village from a *grama* (in a detached region or hilly sector) and undergoing 'rururbanisation'. This change according to him implies physical, social and economic structural features. Physically, its location now adjoins the growing municipal area of Duddhi in a region with large patches of industrial activity; on the social side, there is the onset of formal and role-specific institutions, both educational and socio-political or the new orientation of old institutions; and in the economic field it is becoming part of an expanding economic 'frontier' (Bailey, 1957). However, this 'rururbanisation' or the process of 'suburbation', as Atal (2004) calls it, is now the continuous process of inclusion of villages within the expanding boundaries of municipal bodies. This is having its own impact and we need to understand the reality of both continuity and change in analysing this trend. Shah (2005) stresses the value of earlier studies here which would not only serve as benchmarks for change but also provide insights and understanding into the present, as well as offer general concepts for analysis. And this is very much the case with *Chhor* with its specific cultural feature. Atal's (2004: 48–49) observations in this context, already referred to earlier, stress the relevance and acute need for such 'area' and sub-regional studies.

When the villages are not spatially located in the range of suburbation, the much more intensive links now being forged through various institutions, primarily Panchayati Raj and processes like globalization, privatization and the resultant alterations in the management of the rural natural resources also have to be delineated. Presently, such studies are being undertaken but, by and large, only in crisis-ridden situations.

By the1960s, studies of village in India had gradually assumed a 'much more differentiated pattern' from a purely structural, functional approach for the study of 'little community'. Anthropologists and other social scientists, either individually or in teams have been developing a more sophisticated methodology of survey, case study and psychological tools for their problem oriented studies. There have been studies of communication links, voting behaviour, leadership, health practices and family planning and of the real motives in economic transactions. The pace of the process of 'urbanization' and 'modernization' has opened up further dimensions for studies in change and its agents and factors. Study of what have come to be called the 'metropolitan fringe' or 'frontiers' of trade and other economic relations, social effects of immigrations or 'parochial' or 'folk elements' in the urban culture of fast growing cities and the pattern of their habitations with ethnic conglomeration, and so on, are now the growing concern for sociological studies, of course using a variety in methodology and tools. The earliest studies finding mention with regard to some of these aspects are Bailey's (1957; 1960) focusing on the advancing 'frontiers' of trade and administration in the region of Kondmal, and linkages between castes, tribes and farther comparative political relationships and situation of the tribe-caste village of Bisipara and Mohanpura – a village close to an urban centre (1963). As Rao points out (1991: 392) the 'economic consequences of an expanding metropolis for the villages within its orbit are different from those that result from, say, an extension of the trader's frontier' (Bailey, 1957) ... or the introduction of 'canal irrigation', studied by Epstein (1962). Majumdar's study of Gohana Kalan 'a village near Lucknow' also finds a mention in this context as it 'notes that the village economy is influenced by the urban market, although in an indirect way' (Rao, Bhat and Kadekar, 1991: 368)

Notes

1. As no English version of the book is available in manuscript or print, all quotes from *Chhor Ka Ek Gaon* are translations from the Hindi text by this author.
2. Dube (1972: 195–99) has also described 'A Deccan Village', Dewara, which is 'a mixed village' in the predominantly tribal district of Adilabad in Telangana. It is a 'fringe' village in the sense the term has been used by Majumdar as it is situated 'on the northern fringe' of the Deccan plateau far from Hyderabad, almost on the outer boundary of the state where culture areas of Telangana and Marathwada meet the Gond areas. It has a population of a little more than 1000 with about 40 per cent being from three tribes and a range of Telugu speaking and Marathi speaking Hindu castes as also Muslims. Dube has briefly described the social structure of the village but no full-fledged village study has been conducted thereof. The village is seen as 'a distinct structural entity like the kin group, caste and tribe. All these entities control the conduct of the individual' (ibid.: 215). It is also part of a wider structure of 16 villages. And, the kind of social symbiosis obtaining in the village has led to a *distinct type of inter-group adjustment.* The tribal group maintains its distinctive socio-ritual pattern; but has accepted

> traditional arrangements of co-operative labour in the economic and ritual fields. (ibid.: 213)

Moreover, the artisan/service castes feature prominently in their socio-economic, religious rites and ceremony and 'are integrated on the basis of specialized village convention' in their cultural system. The culture groups or blocks participate in each other's distinctive ceremonies and seers and magicians from the Kolam tribe are summoned by the tribes, the Hindus and the Muslims alike. Significantly, none of the Hindus regard the Rajgonds (or any other tribe) who sacrifice cows and eat beef, as depressed or untouchable. Leadership in village affairs is largely with the Rajgonds. The brief details in this paper, thus, reflect some of the main characteristics of a 'fringe culture' but this can not, however, be examined in detail.

9

Urban Studies

Cultural Role of Cities

In the preface to Sabarwal (1978), Madan states that 'in recent years, there has been a welcome growth of interest among sociologist and social anthropologist in the study of Urban India ... .' However this interest in urbanization, industrialization and the cultural changes linked with these trends can be traced to several decades earlier.

Patrick Geddes (1854– 1932) who founded the Department of Sociology at Bombay University in 1919 was a geographer and town planner. He had been lecturing on civics and urban planning earlier at the Canning College, Lucknow (which was the base of the University of Lucknow) and the University of Calcutta. And, interestingly, Radha Kamal Mukerjee, the founder of the Economics and Sociology Department of Lucknow (where Majumdar came initially as a lecturer in Primitive Economics) found Geddes' ideas inspiring. There is, otherwise, little evidence of the impact of Geddes' approaches on sociology ...' (Munshi, 2007: 174).

Vidyarthi (1978: II) presents a comprehensive survey of urban and industrial studies in India. Tracing a 'constructive phase', he points out that urban studies by researchers from different branches of social sciences like economics, geography, sociology and social anthropology, were initiated in the country after 1951. The initiative has largely been attributed to the Research Programme Committee's (RPC), Planning Commission decision in July 1952 to sponsor 'field investigation and analytical enquiry for effective planning and suggesting solutions' (ibid.: 79), two problems connected with urbanization and urban development. Under this initiative, the RPC had, in 1954 and thereafter, sponsored studies of the cities of Agra, Allahabad, Aligarh, Amritsar, Baroda, Bhopal, Bombay, Calcutta, Chandigarh, Cuttack, Delhi, Gorakhpur, Hyderabad-Sikandarabad, Hubli, Jaipur, Jamshedpur, Kanpur, Lucknow, Madras, Poona, Ranchi, Surat and Vishakhapatnam. It appears from D' Souza (1974: 116–117) that till 1974, out of these 23 socio-economic surveys, reports had been published of 16 cities: Agra, Baroda, Bhopal, Bombay, Calcutta, Chennai,

Delhi, Gorakhpur, Hyderabad-Sikandarabad, Hubli, Jaipur, Jamshedpur, Kanpur, Lucknow, Madras and Ranchi. Bulsara was invited by the RPC to prepare a memorandum on 'problems of planned urban development' after analysing the data and integrating the conclusions from nine of these reports, viz., Baroda, Hubli, Hyderabad-Sikandarabad, Jamshedpur, Kanpur, Pune, Gorakhpur, Lucknow and Surat. Further, he could also use other 'published or non-published material available on the economic and social aspects of urban development and to bring out the main issues relevant to the problem of planned development in the country' (Bulsara, 1964: i).

In his memorandum, Bulsara has subsumed the subjects covered in these studies under the following headings (D' Souza, 1974: 116–17)

(i) Population with various demographic aspects
(ii) Language or mother tongue and religion of householders
(iii) Literacy
(iv) Internal migration
(v) Occupation and industry
(vi) Earnings and Income
(vii) Employment and unemployment Housing conditions
(viii) Social life

Two other impetus for such studies came from the UNESCO sponsored comparative studies of urbanization in South Asia and from the Chicago School of Social Anthropology to study the cultural roles of the cities and their contribution to the development of India's civilization in terms of the various dimensions including traditional and industrial urban centres.

Tracing urban studies by sociologists and social anthropologists, Vidyarthi (1978: II) portrays that initially such studies by sociologists and social anthropologists were focusing on specific problems seen as a result of urbanization and urbanism in different cities. The RPC programme, had involved sociologists and social anthropologists like Radhakamal Mukerjee, D.N. Majumdar and others in urban 'socio-economic surveys'. However, the parameters of these surveys were set out by the RPC which meant that despite Majumdar's obvious interest in the study of socio-cultural implications of industrialization, he had to delimit his reports in order to tow the line of studies as set out by RPC.

Anthropological Approach to Urban Studies and Majumdar

Ralph L. Beals (1951: 1–10) has rather concisely yet comprehensively commented on the state of such studies vis-a-vis sociology and social anthropology. He aims to 're-examine our discipline and its relations with the field of social science'. Broadly, he has pointed out that anthropology despite its 'asserted broadness of our interest' has not been hospitable as compared to sociology, to such studies. He attributes this to the sociologist's developing interest in the expanding cities of USA largely through immigrations and the resultant problems, while anthropologists were, 'rescuing the remnants of rapidly vanishing cultures' in North America. Beals' analytical discussion brings him to emphasize how the anthropological approach developed through 'acculturation' approach can contribute to the study of urbanism and urbanization and also an applied approach to its problems. The discussion concludes with a few seminal suggestions to develop an anthropological approach to urban and industrialization studies and thereby expanding it as its branch.

Significantly, the important paper on 'acculturation', presented by Beals in the Wenner-Gren Foundation International Symposium on Anthropology at New York in 1953, makes no reference to the potentialities of an anthropological approach to urban studies. Notably, none of the theme papers (Kroeber, 1953) too which discuss methodology, research and application of anthropology in different fields, touch upon urban problems and their studies. However, Majumdar, participating in the session, 'anthropology as a field of study', in the Symposium, was the only participant who emphasized how 'anthropological knowledge must be applied to the creation of wider scope and opportunity'. Mentioning some such areas receiving the attention of anthropologists in India, Majumdar states:

> The first anthropological study of the pattern of Indian city life has been undertaken in Lucknow, financed by the municipal board of Lucknow, and sociologists, psychologists, and statisticians are working with anthropologists on this project. The need for such collaboration has been fully recognized in India (Tax, 1953: 345).

Social Survey of Lucknow

The social survey of Kanpur (1954–56) by D.N. Majumdar has figured prominently among the urban studies conducted by sociologists and social anthropologists. Curiously enough, before the Kanpur study nothing could be found in various bibliographies (Sarana, 1960; Madan and Sarana, 1962) relating to urban social anthropology. It appeared as if Majumdar had undertaken the survey of Kanpur simply at the instance of the RPC. As his above statement of 1953 meant that there was an earlier work on the socio-economic conditions of Lucknow, a search for this study, definitely a first in urban studies, by a social anthropologist, 'holistic' or issue-related, yielded a substantive work, viz., *Social Survey of Lucknow: A Preliminary Report* (138A: 1951), published by the EFCS. A copy of it had to be hunted out. It carries no date but its introductory note by Majumdar in the capacity of the Organizing Secretary for the Survey, states:

> At the instance of the Municipal Board, Lucknow the Ethnographic and Folk Culture Society, undertook the task of conducting a social survey of Lucknow City in March 1951. The work was entrusted to five sub committees, viz., (1) Economic Investigation, (2) Education, (3) Medical, (4) Women's, and (5) Socio-Cultural. A random sample of the city population was taken .... Co-operation of the students was sought in the collection of data and they acted as part-time investigator ....

The report, or rather a compilation of five reports, running into more than 125 pages presents quite a comprehensive profile of the urban areas of Lucknow in 1951. The committees for this survey included a number of distinguished university teachers, including the faculty of medicine and social workers of the city. The economic investigation committee was headed by D.P. Mukerjee and had other prominent economists. Similarly, the other committees had a varied composition – education committee was headed by an educationist, medical committee was headed by a doctor from the King George Medical College and the women's committee was headed by a social worker. The socio cultural committee was headed by Majumdar with D.P. Mukerjee and two other sociologists as members. This study is thematically and empirically better focused on 'the cultural and social contours' of Lucknow than any of the other surveys conducted by sociologists and social anthropologists under the R.P.C. programme.

Basically, it is a descriptive report with its field data based on a survey of 802 families from the eight wards of the municipal area of Lucknow. The 1951 Census data as presented here indicates that Lucknow was a cosmopolitan city with at least a handful of people from different countries and Indian states living there, speaking no less than 38 languages with more than half with Hindi as their mother tongue and almost one-fourth reporting their mother tongue as Urdu. Other sizeable linguistic groups were Punjabi, Bengali and Sindhi. The city did not have a significant migratory population as 505 (out of 802) families had been living in the city for more than 50 years. Occupational distribution indicated that 'production other than cultivation, commerce and other services' (a 1951 Census category) provided economic sustenance to almost 98 per cent population. It portrays Lucknow at the turn of the second half of the 20th century as a city largely dependent on horse-drawn carriages and cycle rickshaws and cycles; and the cinema and radio and also coffee and tea houses and restaurants as the prime means of entertainment.

In the field of education the city appears as an important centre of the state. This part of the report presents some interesting findings on the kind of teachers that the students liked and the kind of books read by students at different levels of education. The type of films showing here is indicative of the people's interests. Coaching centres and such other later aspects of educational system were absent. Some other highlights based on field survey included sports and teacher-pupils relations.

The medical committee provides a picture of institutional care available in 1951, the most common diseases treated and also some details of how old prejudices and superstitions relating to diseases and care were still seen among certain sections. It also contains a review of the housing conditions, housing problems, slums and health habits. It mentions that family planning or planned parenthood work had just been initiated in the city and merely a section of the sample women were being exposed to the programme. There are also details of the city sanitation, slum clearance work and traditional systems of medicine.

The report prepared by the women's committee deserves mention as a very vital part of the report. It contains a rich and multifaceted coverage of not only the condition of women, specially middle class and lower middle class, in the city, but also their attitudes and views on a variety of issues. The findings are based on a 78-question schedule which formed the basis for interviewing no less than 735 women. The sample also included single women, widows and deviants like prostitutes. The report rightly describes this attempt as 'a canvas of great magnitude' (138A: 1951: 2), as the questions asked could be subsumed under the following major categories:

(i) women in the family with special regard to the nature of marriage, the role of other women members, domestic duties, child bearing and rearing and some enquiries bearing on domestic friction, family mores, decision-making and the like.

(ii) women in the world of work with reference to the extent of work outside the home, economic and social implications of such work as well as the prevalent attitudes towards work.

(iii) women and the law which includes property rights, legal issues connected with marriage, separation, divorce, adoption and so on.

(iv) women and politics comprising their use of the franchise, interest in politics, and political behaviour in general with some reference to their role in the panchayat.

(v) women and education which deals with the peripheral and very general questions of the extent of education, the areas of specialization and evaluation of the education thus received.

(vi) women and leisure, ranging from gossip and titivation to more organized activity.

The data also covers age at marriage, *gauna* that follows, forms and nature of marriage, marriage expenses, *mehar,* dowry and bride price and women's attitude towards marriage. The next theme was the pattern of family friction and authority in the family and, what the report describes as 'the eternal grind of birth and death repeated pregnancy, miscarriages and abortions, the problems connected with the rearing up of children and health.' As regards birth control, the reality was that 'contraception have not penetrated very far'. The attitude of women towards sterility, single women, widows and women at work was also covered. The few women working outside the households were found to be engaged in a variety of occupations. It was also seen that only widows, single women and women from Scheduled Castes or lower income brackets were found to be working while others were 'apathetic or timid towards taking to jobs'. The problems of prostitutes have also been highlighted. The study highlights the dependence of women and the fact that divorce, property right and other legal questions had not entered the scheme of things so far as the women were concerned. However, the influences of modernity were not entirely absent as reflected in their expectations and way of living. The survey also investigated the position of women with regard to education, sex education, health, etc.

The report on the condition of women in Lucknow highlights the focused attention that Majumdar attempted to give to what are known today as 'gender issues', in the urban context of Lucknow. In fact, this report covers more than one-fourth space of the survey report.

The last part of the survey report comprises the report of the Socio-Cultural Committee which was headed by Majumdar. It throws up some very significant aspects of the life of Lucknow people. First, no less than 63 per cent of the sample families had been living in Lucknow for more than half a century and only about 17 per cent had come to Lucknow during the last five to 15 years. This position presumably meant that residents of Lucknow shared a cultural life of their own which had some history. And, obviously in order to look closely into the specific features or traits of the culture of these people, and the effect of culture contact on different communities a focused enquiry was conducted in respect of the sample families. Therefore:

> We sorted out from amongst our sample two types of families: (1) Those living for more than 50 years and/or having their ancestral home in Lucknow (these represent the oldest type), and (2) those living since birth or for more than 30 years and/or having their *own* home in Lucknow, and they comprise 142 and 117 families respectively. However, in the first group are included 63 families (mostly Muslim) selected ad hoc on grounds of their peculiar characteristics (as representing the pure Lucknow type) ... .[1]

The ethnographic notes in the socio-cultural report on the two groups cover their dress and food habits, religious beliefs, rituals, interpersonal and inter-communal relations, and deviance by way of prostitution and other such sections which were a part of the culture of the city. The committee also tried to find out as to why Lucknow had been immune to communal disturbances. Most of the people said it was due to a spirit of fellow feeling and brotherhood among the inhabitance of Lucknow and specifically it was ascribed to: (1) the influence of common language, common dress and common social habits of Lucknow people, (2) Lucknow's peculiar culture, and (3) efficiency of the UP Government. A lesser percentage thought it was due to lack of industrial development and presence of medieval atmosphere in the town. Thus, an attempt was made to document the cultural patterns of the people of Lucknow as the city had some cultural flavour of its own. D.P. Mukerji used to often describe Lucknow as an 'island of culture', in his class, which concisely described the complexion of Lucknow urbanism, with hardly any influence over the adjoining rural or semi-urban areas.

The methodology of this urban study undertaken in 1951 shows that careful framing of questionnaire, their revision on the basis of preliminary enquiries and the presence of young students both males and females can be mentioned as salient aspects of this work. The analysis of data with percentages, incomes and religion-wise analysis and other details is also notably well done. And, mentionably an empirical investigation of some salient 'gender issues' as they are called today.

Subsequent Work

After the Lucknow survey of 1951, Majumdar's next work with an urban anthropological theme was *Educated Unemployment Among the University Students: A Pilot Inquiry*, authored by Majumdar and S.K. Anand (179: 1956). It was also published by the Massachusetts Institute of Technology, Centre for International

Studies, Cambridge, Massachusetts. The survey was carried out among those students of Lucknow University who had received their master's degree during the five years (1949–53). The universe of enquiry consisted of 2513 students in 24 subjects – males 2218 and females 285. Out of this a sample of 36 per cent (903 students) selected on the basis of stratified random sample were investigated. The survey was conducted through a mailed questionnaire. Out of the sample (903), it was responded to by about 40 per cent, which was about 14 per cent of the universe of enquiry. The findings of the survey are summarized below. The MIT took up this publication as it was highlighting the emerging problems like unemployment among the educated. Pinpointing the urge for social responsibility in this study, Majumdar wrote:

> Unemployment is a curse, a tragedy, a challenge to society. In a welfare state, the social loss resulting therefrom is an intolerable enervation of society's vital lifeblood .... Without a guarantee of the right to work, democracy is devoid of its essential economic nucleus. Hence there is a clear shift of stress today from a vague concept of democracy to that of a planned social order the essential core of which is full utilization of human resources (179:1956: 1).

During this period the social survey of Kanpur was also being conducted by a team headed by Majumdar, and the three main persons conducting this study were Majumdar as Director; N.S. Reddy as Deputy Director; and S. Bahadur, Statistical Officer. The other members of the team included two Supervisors and nine Investigators. It was reported in *The EA* (1955: 1: 3) that 'the field survey (in Kanpur) is complete and the data were being processed for the report which was however, published in 1960 by the Asia Publishing House as *Social Contours of An Industrial City-Social Survey of Kanpur 1954–56*. A reprint thereof was also published in 1975 in the USA by Green Wood Press Westport, Connecticut.

Among the urban surveys sponsored by the RPC during the 1950s, Majumdar's study of Kanpur survey has been favourably noted by Ramkrishna Mukherjee (1979) thus:

> And 'urban study' (354); the latter also earning the credit of perhaps being the first comprehensive survey of a town in India on a sociological (instead of a purely economic) base. Majumdar dealt with 'culturology' to begin with, and the problems of urbanization, communication, and the role of Indian sociologists in later years ... fall into the category of emphasizing the 'how' question in a thorough going manner ... (ibid.: 68–69).

Retrospectively, however, one can comment that the Kanpur survey could not present the rich socio-cultural data which had been collected by the team. As Vidyarthi (1978 Vol. II: 92) specifically points out:

> Despite the author's obvious interest in the study of socio-cultural implications of industrialization and in spite of administering the sociology oriented questionnaire to nearly 2000 people, he had to delimit his report in order to tow the line of similar studies concluded by the R.P.C. of the National Planning Commission.

Briefly presented this data is contained in the last about 10 pages of the Kanpur survey under the heading, 'The Cultural Content of Urbanization'. The relevant part of the questionnaire 'socio-cultural background' had, however, included 32 questions covering various aspects like religious beliefs, rituals, marriage and family, dress, interpersonal and inter-communal relation, etc. very much on the lines earlier followed by Majumdar in his Lucknow study.

Contents of the Kanpur Survey

Vidyarthi (ibid.: 92) comments that the study of Kanpur ... was undertaken with a view to assessing:

> 'The complex conditions of urban life in an Industrial Metropolis.' In the light of his field inquiries as a social anthropologist, Majumdar promises 'to make a departure from the routine type of socio-economic survey that have been carried out in different parts of India' and 'to initiate a major probe into factory life with all its sociological conditions shape labour, and the success or failure of industrialization would depend upon the recognition such sociological contents.

The overall aim of the survey (200: 1960) was to assess the complex conditions of urban life in an industrial metropolis. The city had a population of 7.05 lakh in its Municipal and Cantonment areas and it may be noted that much of the area included in the municipal limits was, in fact, not urban 'but suburban'. For the coverage of the universe for survey, the localities on the outskirts which displayed a considerable extent of economic integration with the city, were selected and the far flung settlements were excluded. Thus, a population of 5.55 lakh was covered in the universe and a two stage stratified sample was adopted on the basis of the *mohallas*, *chacks*, etc., listed in the Municipality register, formed the universe. The sample was about 5000 households. The bases of statistical formulations of sampling and factorization have been presented in detail.

The study is divided up into three sections – general, covering history of the city and its growth; brief discussions of the present day civic problems and situation relating to industrial employment and unemployment, etc.; the second is divided into six chapters, viz. sex, age education, and caste; migration; levels of living; housing and neighbourhood facilities; occupations; and industry; and unemployment; and section three on family planning enquiry with eight chapters, viz., introduction; child birth indices; maternity pattern; indices of mortality and survival after birth and survival of male and female children; abortion, still births and twins; planned parenthood; patterns of family size; and knowledge and practice of contraception. The study concludes with an additional note on the cultural content of urbanization as mentioned earlier. The entire statistical data, a map of Kanpur showing areas of study along with some photographs and the schedules used for survey go as appendices.

Section 1

Kanpur was an important part of the RPC study because it was then the second largest industrial centre of northern India after Calcutta. The First World War has brought about a rapid expansion with natural growth, rise in the number of mill workers and the problems of congestion and slums. In 1919, the city got its Improvement Trust. After depression, the growth of the city again caught up from the early 1930s. The Trust also initiated schemes for constructing the residential buildings *ahatas* and colonies for the industrial workers. The study observes that 'present problems' of the city are the result of the hectic growth of population during the Second World War. This also led to haphazard expansion during the decades of 1940s and 1950s, having a very large number of slum areas with nearly 500 *ahatas* or tenement houses with large populations. The congestion was seen mostly in the central part of the city with widespread insanitation and 25 per cent of the cities population having no access to central water supply, the limited capacity of sewer system for a population of about 2 lakh only was another cause of unhygienic conditions. The medical and public health facilities too were quite inadequate in the city and so was the case with the public transport bus system. Added to this was the insufficiency of the roads which measure only about 150 miles in length leading to congestion of traffic and its interrelated problems. The influx of 'refugees' after Independence further compounded the problem of congestion and encroachments. The city is also a centre for marketing of certain types of raw material like leather, machine parts, cotton and oil seeds. It is also a centre for wholesale in textiles.

With a labour force of about 69,000, Kanpur had 273 registered factories out of a total of 1341 in the state (1953). During that year, the number of women industrial workers was less than 1 per cent of the total adult employment in industry. It is also notable that the employment of women has been declining from 1942 onwards. The decline has been attributed to paucity of residential accommodation, maternity benefits and some social causes like *purdah* and joint family living in the rural areas from where the labour migrates. The women can be easily left behind in the joint households. Juvenile labour was almost absent in the factories.

The general trade depression has caused a number of retrenchments and lay offs causing substantial unemployment in the industries in Kanpur. Taking recourse to rejection figures in the employment exchange, the report analyses the occupational and educational distribution of the unemployed. The employment exchange has also sponsored a scheme providing regular guidance to educated and uneducated persons. The difficulties encountered by this kind of service have also been discussed. It suffers from lack of cooperation from the mills which resort to not notifying their vacancies, heavy rejection of sponsored candidates, etc.

Section 2

The survey: This section contains the main findings of different aspects of the survey. It is divided into chapters on the demographic and educational levels, religion, caste and income profiling of the population, their migratory status, economic levels, housing and facilities including civic facilities, occupational structure and its economic dimensions, and a detailed analysis of the unemployment situation.

Kanpur acquired a place on the map only after the advent of the British. The foundation for the modern industrial development was laid in 1860 when the Kanpur Cotton Committee was formed. This association brought into being the Elgin Mills in the following year. Since then the history of Kanpur was one of growth of trade and industry. The industrial output reached its climax in 1945 when 116,252 workers were employed. When the survey was conducted, there were 273 factories employing 68,832 workers.

Main Results of the Survey

Of the populations covered by the survey, 37.47 per cent are children under 14 years of age. The males aged above 14 years constitute 34.96 per cent and their female counterparts 27.31 per cent. Among the recent immigrants, who came to the city between 1951 and 1955, there are only 60.9 women aged over 14 years for 100 men of the same age group. Taking into consideration the population of those aged 6 years and above, it is found that 34.20 per cent are illiterate and another 33.03 per cent have had primary schooling only. Only 8.95 per cent have received college or technical education. Seventy per cent of the heads of households have reported themselves to be immigrants, i.e. those who came to the city in the pursuit of a vocation. Taking only those who came to settle in the city after 1940, they constitute 38.11 per cent of the total. Of all the immigrants, 76.13 per cent have come from rural areas, 21.81 per cent from other townships and 2.05 per cent from other countries (mostly from Pakistan); 45.68 per cent of the migrants have come from the same or the neighbouring districts. The proportion of migrants from other states of India has steadily increased from 7.81 per cent in the pre-1940 period to 19.57 per cent in the years between 1951 and 1955. About 23 per cent of the immigrants have come to the city on the strength of having some friends or relatives to find them some means of livelihood and 18.44 per cent have found their way to the city under an inner compulsion of searching for a job or in the vague hope of finding some source of subsistence. In the case of 17.82 per cent, lack of sufficient landholdings in their former homes has been the main reason for the city-ward migration. While 58.43 per cent of the migrants visit their former homes once a year or more frequently, only 14.63 per cent have never visited their places again after settling down in the city. As many as 75.58 per cent of the migrants do not remit any money to their family in the native place. This suggests that their economy is not really able to support them as well as the family. Only 31.47 per cent send less than ₹ 20 per month; 8.1 per cent between ₹ 20 and ₹ 50; 1.67 per cent between ₹ 50 and ₹ 100; and 0.53 per cent over ₹ 100.

Family Size and Levels of Living

A family has on an average 4.36 persons. Its size varies from migrants to non-migrants. An average family has 5.41 persons among the non-migrants, 5.03 persons among the pre-1940 migrants and 3.75 persons among the post-1940 migrants. The per capita income is found to be ₹ 30 per month; 56.94 per cent of the populations having a per capita income of less than ₹ 30 per month. Taking all those who have a per capita income of less than ₹ 40 a month, they constitute 71.78 per cent of the people living in the city.

Housing and Civic Amenities

A quarter of the city's population resides in localities recognized as slum areas. While 18 per cent of the residents live in their own houses, the rest live in rented quarters. It is an indication of the standard of life in the city that 30.04 per cent of the families pay less than ₹ 5 per month as house rent. Only 30 per cent of the households live in buildings with *pakka* walls and *pakka* roofs. Only 32.16 per cent of the families have electric lighting; 35.12 per cent of the households have no taps either in their own flats or in common with the co-tenants. Over 64 per cent of the residential units have no regular drains and 52.47 per cent have no enclosed open spaces around. The congestion in the city can be gauged by the fact that 61.91 per cent of the households have only one living room each and 70 per cent of the households cannot claim to be reasonably proximate to any parks.

Occupation and Industry

Only 2.59 per cent of the city's earners are in executive, managerial and technical posts while 8.81 per cent are working as typists, stenographers and scribes. People engaged in trade and commerce constitute 20.64 per cent of the city's earners. Petty traders together with hawkers constitute 13.43 per cent, while traders with a considerable business turnover constitute 6.57 per cent. Manual workers account for 30.02 per cent of the total earners of whom 17.41 per cent are skilled workers (other than artisans), and the rest are unskilled workers. The factories, on the whole, provide manual work for 22.25 per cent of the earners, which is itself a measure of the industrial complexion of the city. The shoemakers, tanners and cobblers together constitute 1.83 per cent of the city's working population. This figure includes only those who are working at the level of artisans and is exclusive of workers in the leather factories. Textiles constitute the major industry, providing work for 26.92 per cent of the earners. Next is the food stuff industry absorbing 14.97 per cent of the earners. The leather industry accounts for 6.94 per cent of the employment and the metal industry for 6.91 per cent. Over 62 per cent of the total earners are employees. Only 7.33 per cent come under the category of employers and 20.14 per cent are own-account workers (or self-employers) and 6.24 per cent are family workers.

Unemployment

The unemployed constitute 6.32 per cent of those who are aged above 15 years and who are able-bodied and are anxiously looking for job. Among the unemployed, 53.93 per cent are below 25 years and 19.88 per cent are above 40 years. Over 16.32 per cent of the unemployed are illiterate; 34.77 per cent had primary education; 32.55 per cent had secondary education; and 12.25 per cent had college and technical education. More than 35 per cent of the unemployed are seeking white collar jobs of the lower grade, i.e. typists, clerks, sales assistants, etc.; 17.61 per cent are seeking skilled manual work; 11.20 per cent want to establish their own business; 4.5 per cent seek work in the mills; 2.45 per cent are looking for unskilled manual work; and 0.7 per cent stated their object as any suitable job. The last group, however, consists of some educated people also and hence their response cannot be interpreted as meaning that they are all prepared to take up any non-manual work. Relating the job sought with the job previously held, it works out that 32.21 per cent of the unemployed are seeking the same type of job as they held earlier. If the freshers who constitute 37.42 per cent of the unemployed, are excluded, it turns out that 51.72 per cent of those who have held any job before are seeking the same type of job again. As regards length of unemployment, 13.56 per cent are without a job for over 3 years and 24.91 per cent are without a job from one to three years. Of those unemployed who have had secondary education, 40 per cent are without a job for more than a year. Significantly, of the unemployed with college education, 60 per cent are without a job for more than a year, and this underlines the problem of educated unemployment in the city.

Section 3: Family Planning Enquiry

A new schedule for collection of fertility and family planning data was administered to married women in about one-third of sample households. In all, 1525 married women of different age groups were interviewed.[2] The mid-stream introduction of this survey also meant that this part of the survey had to be confined only to areas where population was predominantly of the lower groups. This was:

> perhaps a virtue – as most of the subjects investigated belong to the lower stratum of society which exhibits in the most pronounced form the evils of unchecked multiplication (200: 1960: 151).

This section is divided up into eight chapters, viz., child indices, maternity pattern, indices of mortality and survival, births and survival of male and female children, planned parenthood, mother's view of family size, and knowledge and practice of contraception. The study compared attitudes of the women according to different religious groups, income groups and educational levels of age groups. In the case of Hindu women child birth and maternity pattern has also been studied in terms of age of the women at *gauna*. Briefly, the findings which show noticeable demographic trends are:

1. A child birth index of 6.66 for women of completed maternity experience. It compares fairly well with the figure of 6.73 given for the central plains of U.P. (Sample Census of Births and Deaths, 1953–54). But the birth indices of women of many other age groups in the Kanpur sample are higher.
2. The child birth indices for women aged over 45 years in the four income groups are, respectively, 7.04, 5.88, 6.7, and 7.0. There is further indication that this pattern of differential fertility is not one which applies to the present generation of women alone, but is likely to manifest itself in the coming generations too.
3. Proportion of female child births per 100 male children among the four income groups were 87.7, 79.7, 85.8 and 91.8, respectively.

4. The study indicated that Muslims had shown greater fertility than the Hindus. The birth index among Muslim women was 7.6 as compared to 6.5 among Hindus, and the proportion of female child births among Muslims was much higher than among the Hindus.
5. The data also revealed high rate of child mortality which according to demographers sets in motion a trend of high fertility. There was no disparity in the mortality rates of male and female children.
6. Contrary to the common belief that the women of lower classes have an attitude of resignation towards the number of children, it was found that a large number of them (50%) had a 'glimmering desire to limit the size of their families. Further the existing knowledge of contraceptive techniques was found to be extremely poor with only seven per cent having an awareness of the means to prevent conception.
7. Birth indices in different age groups show that the number of children borne peaks at 25–29 years of age, and the age at which *gauna* had taken place had a definite bearing on fertility. The birth index of Muslim women in the highest income group of over ₹ 200 showed a jump of 7.7 as compared to 5.04 among the Hindus.
8. The mortality rate of children was high at 392 per 1000. It was lowest among the children of mothers of the youngest age groups and increased gradually with the mother's age. Differences among Hindus and Muslims were that Muslim women had lower child mortality rate then those of Hindus among all income and age groups. Mentionably, the lowest income groups among Muslim had a mortality rate of 3.5 as compared to 4.6 among the Hindus.
9. It was also seen that deaths occurring during the first year of life are about thrice the number of mortality cases taking place between the end of the first year and the end of the third year.
10. As the total of male children born is higher than female children, obviously the birth and survival indices for male children are higher. In the case of survival of male and female children, there was little variance among different income groups and between the two religious groups.
11. The study also goes into the incidence of still births, twins and their sex.
12. The chapter on planned parenthood included the attitude of the women to sterility, attitude to restricting the number of births and spacing of births. In their attitude to sterility, a majority of Hindu women considered it as a misfortune and only 35.2 per cent had showed an unorthodox attitude of equanimity. Among the other religious groups, the two kinds of attitudes were roughly 50 per cent each. There was no noticeable difference in different income groups in this regard, but the attitudes to sterility varied according to different groups from illiterate to well educated. As regards the women's attitude towards restricting the number of births, out of the total sample of 1525, 49.8 per cent wanted to restrict the number of children while 33.2 per cent did not, and nearly 17 per cent were

indifferent. Significantly, Muslim women had a much higher percentage of those desirous of restricting the number of children and also of women indifferent to this question, as compared to Hindu women.

13. Regarding knowledge and practice of contraception, the study presented a rather dismal picture. Contrary to the positive desire to restrict the number of children by nearly half of the respondents, over 90 per cent of them did not have any knowledge of the methods to do so.

The Cultural Content of Urbanization

This last section of the Kanpur study is a short essay on urbanization as seen in a growing city like Kanpur. It may also be mentioned that Majumdar wanted to present an in-depth study of the cultural content and its various changing aspects as reflected in a sociological analysis of the additional data which had been collected in the course of the survey. This part of the questionnaire, inter alia, sought information relating to marriage, preference and qualities expected in the marriage partners by men as well as women, and problems of dowry and age difference between spouses. Further, it also had surveyed migrants' links with their kinsmen and also the kind of interpersonal relations of the informants. Questions were also asked relating to religious practices, festivals and attitude to other religions, diet, dress and changes therein, amusement and recreation, participation in games and various other aspects of their social life. The work on this additional part perhaps stopped on his sudden demise. The study in the RPC format too was published posthumously. The report says that 'we are presenting some data on social life of Kanpur in the hope that this might canalize future research in family and urban living' (200: 1960: 211).

The statistical data presented on the cultural aspects, first covers distribution of cases of one or more marriage, time gap between the first and subsequent marriages, difference of ages at the time of marriage, difference of age between spouses at the time of marriages and the attitude of men to women in so far as other aspects of socio-economic life was concerned. The findings were that nearly 75 per cent males had married only once while about five per cent had married more than thrice. The gap between age of husband and wife was more than even 10 years in the case of about 7 per cent of the marriages. The age at which women were generally married indicated that more than 53 per cent were married at the age of 15 years or even less and nearly 10 per cent of them were married to widowers, implying a considerable difference in ages.

As regards attitude to women taking up work, nearly 30 per cent agreed that women should earn while the rest wanted the women to look after the households. The respondents who preferred their women to work came mostly from lower income groups but also from among the middle class especially in the cases where women were educated. The preferred jobs were for teaching even as tutors. Significantly, as many as 72 per cent men were in favour of elementary education only for the women and did not like the idea of giving higher education to them. Nearly 48 per cent of the respondents were in favour of dowry and wanted to perpetuate the practice. In addition there were about 17 per cent persons who were indifferent and were likely to accept a dowry when offered. Noticeably the positive attitude towards dowry went up with advancement of age of respondents.

The report comments on the conditions in certain areas of Kanpur which badly lacked sanitation and other facilities and were highly congested. Yet, many respondents were inclined to settle permanently in Kanpur. Backdrop for this attitude was that the villages had also lost the cohesive force they previously had and factionalism and family intrigues were on the increase. The enquiry revealed that the economic forces which were responsible for the rapid urbanization of Kanpur, could not maintain a steady flow of working population to Kanpur. Migration to Kanpur had to be seen in the context of the rural scene, which today had assumed a complexion very much different from what it used to be. Those who could not adjust themselves at first to the new setting which appeared to have nothing material to offer in the long run except the inconveniences of city life like congestion and unhealthy surroundings, and an insecure life for most appeared to have changed their values and oriented themselves to urban living. New migrants came with new values. The lower castes from the villages found that they could escape from the stigma of untouchability; while the upper castes from the villages had lost much of their importance in religious and other institutional fields. It was also true that Kanpur could not change the face of the nearby villages, even advancement in regard to various fields of activity; except that the educated persons of the villages were the foci of new urban values. These people had very little to offer to the villagers. Thus, the study highlights a significant cultural feature that the educated from the villages migrate, in spite of difficulties, due to the pull factors of the cities. Thereby, on the one hand the villages lost their educated people who could have been agents for a change for the better, while the cities also hardly obtained incremental advantages of healthy urbanism, as such people form a 'floating population' with the life of the migrants divided up between their villages and the city.

It has been commented that most of the cities of Uttar Pradesh including Kanpur and Lucknow largely retained the 'aura of medievalism' and they were seen to be only experimenting with many facets of modernism. The cities also had a floating population particularly in case of men who migrated without families and generally faced acute problem of residential accommodation. This was the greatest single factor that maintained and perpetuated a floating population with its linked evils of crime, delinquency, prostitution, slum life and alcoholism. Of the respondents, 65 per cent did say that drinking was not bad, and it was noticed that most of them were trying to procure it in spite of the prohibition (200: 1960: 219).

The report ends with an exhortation and emphasis on the role for the sociologists:

> ... Our towns and cities are growing, our vigilance must not wane, sociologists must line up for social research and help the administration in its assigned task of building an urban population, socially aware and mentally conditioned for city life. (ibid.: 219)

Concluding Discussion

Beals (1951: 6) had emphasized that essentially, the coming of migrants in large numbers to an urban area, relates to 'acculturation' problem and, therefore, the 'cultural distances separating each group from contemporary urban culture' have to be observed. Moreover, his hypothesis is that 'rural urban acculturation and cross cultural acculturation differ only in degree and do not represent substantially different process of change' (ibid.: 7). He, however, adds that certain specific 'features as urbanization, heterogeneity and stratification' have also to be focused in ancient cities of India and China. In certain areas of Latin America, the immediate effect has not been urbanization of the country but the depopulation of the country in favour of the city.

Beals' analytical discussion on cultural role of cities concludes that the anthropological approach developed through studies in 'acculturation' can contribute to the study of 'urbanism and urbanization' leading also to an applied approach to the consequential problems. Majumdar with 'acculturation' studies as his forte had, in passing, stressed this aspect in the Wenner-Gren Foundation Symposium in 1953 mentioning his social survey of Lucknow in 1951. He certainly targeted to achieve such an objective, partially or wholly through a study of Kanpur which was the foremost industrial city of UP when he initiated its study in 1954. He clearly states his objective:[3]

> Find out the extent and content of urbanization. The sociological factors in the urban setting ... both integrate and disintegrate social life. A major probe into factory life with all its sociological concomitants ... and the success or failure of industrialization would depend upon the recognition of such sociological contents. Our interest was more on the cultural side than on the impact or demographic (200: 1960: x).

Yet, the contents of this report had a trend setting effect in urban anthropological studies mainly because it provides rich 'statistical data on social life, family, caste clustering, and social life of the migrants as well as the impact of Kanpur on neighbouring villages', but 'Kanpur could not change the face of the villages even adjacent to it in regard to various fields of activity' except that it provided opportunities for migration and employment to the educated persons from rural areas and the lower castes as a escape from the stigma of untouchability' (Vidyarthi, 1978: Vol. II: 93–94).

Majumdar has called Kanpur 'an industrial city' but he does not on analysis, find the conditions there as of industrialization. This condition of the city as being not really urbanized and thereby not having any urban impact can be accounted for thus:

(i) Kanpur or any other town in Uttar Pradesh has not developed a 'fringe of urbanization as has been possible in Bombay, Calcutta ... .' The reason is that the labour here does not come from the neighbouring villages alone but from the eastern districts and even from outside the state. Just, a depopulation of the country in favour of the city, to use Beal's words.

(ii) Absence of a fringe is partly due to the dichotomy that exists between urban and rural living, practices and attitudes, very much a traditional condition.[4]

(iii) The factories have built slums in the city but they have not considered the desirability of settling the labour.

(iv) The apathy to and neglect of labour, in our country, are rooted in our caste structure which is a hierarchical system. This reminds one of Beal's suggestion.

(v) The socio-economic studies of urban areas have not so far examined the sociological factors in the urban setting which 'have both integrating and disintegrating effects'.

He throws up the possibilities of answering these questions through a 'major probe into factory life with all its sociological concomitants, for the social background and antecedent social conditions shape labour, and the success or failure of industrialization would depend upon the recognition of such sociological contents' (1960: x); thus, emphasizing the 'how' question in a thorough going manner (Mukherjee, 1979: 69). But the published work is, noticeably, without such an analysis.

It appears that this aspect of the effect of industrialization and the anthropological study of the cultural role of expanding cities in rural or tribal heartland were grounded in Majumdar's ethnographic study of the Ho labour in the mines and factories of Chota-Nagpur. His earlier field studies as presented in *Transition* (60: 1937) and *Affairs* (131: 1950) had enabled him to offer some pragmatic observations and suggestions of an applied nature in this regard. Significantly, two of his distinguished students, Vidyarthi and Ganguli, pursued these objectives later. Vidyarthi in his study of Ranchi and the adjoining areas of Chhota-Nagpur (1970) carries this agenda further. Ganguli, one of his postgraduate students in 1956–58, had in his study (1958) of the growth of Jamshedpur had in his master's dissertation also made observations relating to the pan-tribalistic impact and other related issues of urbanism. The UNESCO study of the problems of urbanization relating to the growth of steel towns in India, studying the problems of urbanization goes into these questions of rural-urban and tribal-urban continua much deeper (Vidyarthi, 1978 II: 102–3).

Bose's, *Social Survey of Calcutta* (1968), has dealt with the issues of integration of urban life and industrialization in a more focused manner with a human-geographer's approach. In this study, besides making general observations on the distribution of linguistic and religious groups and their occupational specializations in the 80 wards of Calcutta, and a survey of voluntary associations, considerable data were collected on the basis of the study of their family histories of a number of old influential families in different wards. Bose had also summed up his findings in an article in the *Scientific American*, 'Calcutta, a Premature Metropolis' (1965), thus:

> that the diverse ethnic groups in the population of the city have come to bear the same relation to one another as do the castes in India as a whole ... .

> Actually, the superstructure that coheres the caste under the old order seem to be reestablishing itself in a new form. Calcutta today is far from being a melting[5] pot on the model of cities in the US ... .

Thus, Bose has through his intensive socio-cultural and linguistic data lent support to what Majumdar had observed almost a decade earlier in the Kanpur survey.

Going through the Kanpur study, it strikes one that it presents a very wide range of statistical data presented through analytical and comparative tables (more than 190 in number) as the preceding commentary on its contents would also convey. Basically, the statistical data belongs to two groups – one that (section one) covers the social aspects, viz., sex, age, education and caste, composition of migrant population, and its causes as well as the resultant conditions after the shift. This also comprises the position of income, housing and infrastructural and service facilities in the city. The data on occupation and unemployment are quite revealing in their thoroughness as the levels of unemployment has been related to education, pervious occupation, duration unemployment and nature of jobs sought by the unemployed. In section three, the data on family planning enquiry presents some demographically critical data as it goes into child bearing patterns, mortality and survival of children, aspects of age, income, religion, age at marriage and all the related factors in fertility. The question of planned parenthood and family planning have also been examined in the backdrop of social and psychological attitudes and correlated with education, age and family circumstances like the role of other family members, etc., along with the mechanics of avoiding contraception. It may be mentioned here that, Majumdar had represented India, Pakistan, and Ceylon in the World Population Conference at Rome in mid-1954. This conference was the first international conference on population under the auspices of the United Nations. At the Conference, inter alia, demographic patterns including the various factors in fertility and efforts at family planning were discussed, mentionably the higher fertility experience of India and Japan. The Conference had taken note of the lack and limitations of demographic data from the developing countries which brought about a 'sub-division of its meetings broadly into East and West' (B.B., P.R. Caud FAAM, 1955: 188). The interaction which Majumdar had had with international experts in demography, perhaps, further influenced his designing the statistical format for this study with his statistician.

A review of this study appreciatively mentions the tables 'with accompanying analysis, treat education, religion, caste, income, industry and occupation ... family planning. Depth of the work is reflected for example by the presentation of data on the unemployed ... also reveals many interesting local answers to some of the questions frequently asked about the Indian city' (Ellefson, 1961: 559).

Thus, it can be said that at a time when there was not much anthropological work done on urban India, Majumdar could generate interest and studied industrial city of Kanpur as well as capital city of Lucknow.

Notes

1. They were not included in our sample (though for the purpose of investigation they have been included in general survey, otherwise based on strictly random principle). This unduly inflates the percentage of Muslims in the first category and may be expected to have some distorting effect on our conclusions. In view of the fact that such families represent the decadent feudal and semi-feudal nobility, an enquiry into their methods of living, and beliefs and manners is not without interest of its own. In drawing out conclusions, community-wise, on the basis of percentages, however, such families have been excluded. (ibid.: 8)
2. For this study, the investigators were all women with masters degree in sociology, some of them married. This made rapport easy and the respondents discarded reticence and became vocal.
3. However, the uniform approach called for by the RPC and the short time available for preparing the report constrained from emphasizing the socio-cultural study in spite of having collected the data therefor. Obviously, this data could not be utilized as the report submitted to the RPC itself was published posthumously.
4. It may be mentioned here that a similar cultural state or way of the life was discerned in Majumdar's study of Gohana Kalan a village very close to Lucknow in spite of its links of communication. See the relevant chapter.
5. Because there are not enough jobs to go around, every one clings as closely as possible to the occupations with which his ethnic group is identified and relies for economic support on those who speak his language, or his coreligionists, or members of his own caste and or fellow immigrants from the village or district from which he has come. By a backwash, reliance on earlier modes of group identification reinforces and perpetuates differences between ethnic groups.

10

Applied Anthropology

In natural sciences the distinction between pure and applied aspects of study is immediately obvious. Moreover, experiments and controlled observations make their results repetitive and subject to checks. Anthropology like other social sciences presents a rather different picture. Here, the material for study is not amenable to any controlled experimentation and predictability. As Hogbin observes:

> The term 'applied anthropology', it is true, has been current for at least a generation, and anthropologists, in this context sometimes referred to as 'social engineers', have at different times advised on native administration, factory management, and propaganda for broadcasting to foreign nations. But they have never been able to achieve any specific end or promise any specific device. (Hogbin, 1957: 245)

Another question of this issue is the value orientation of the objectives or goals set to be achieved through any application of anthropological knowledge relative to a people. It also assumes prime importance because all efforts for the application of anthropological research arose initially in the context of colonial administration. Historically, anthropologists too had little to offer to the administrator or the people till the theoretical underpinnings of the discipline lay in evolutionary and diffusionist theories which in a way also supported the approach initiated by the missionaries and, by and large, followed by the administrators in their criticism of 'native institutions' and the need felt by them in bringing about changes according to the values of the West and Christianity.

In this scenario Malinowski, in 1922, published a paper on 'Ethnology and the Study of Society' (1922) which the general public must have found revolutionary. He put forward a theory of culture as an integrated whole and stressed that if any part was tampered with, a general collapse might follow. No institution, he declared, should be condemned merely because it differs from our own. An attempt should be made to explain it, to investigate its function and find out what biological needs it fulfils. This meant, in effect, 'going a long way towards justify it.' (ibid.: 248)

What followed was Malinowski's critical appraisal of colonial policies relating to the change and abolition by law and through administrative measures certain institutions among the African people and thus indirectly a concern with the application of anthropology in Africa. A corollary of this approach was the need and value of training the administrative officials of the day about 'cultural integration and the interrelationship of the institutions'. However, Malinowski never could:

> Work out a satisfactory theory of social change. Cultures, in the words of Bartlett (1943: 12), have hard and soft parts which respectively resist and yield to change. Armed with a thorough knowledge of the community concerned, anthropologists can say which is which; but they still lack any comprehensive hypothesis applicable to all cases. Under the influence of outside contact certain old customs and beliefs have everywhere vanished without leaving a trace, others have persisted despite efforts to suppress them, and still others have been transformed. (Hogbin, 250)

Application of Anthropology and Study of Social Change

Madan (2013: 32) reviewing Majumdar's earliest cultural anthropological contribution notices that his earliest papers (he mentions the three published in 1923) were a study of culture traits. But, soon thereafter 'we find him writing about social change, particularly in situations of cultural contact' which become 'Majumdar's lifelong concern'. And, in this regard, Majumdar anticipated Malinowski by arguing that there are cultures which are weak and cultures which are dominating and when coming in contact with each other, the former either perish or survive by adopting and adapting features from the dominating culture, often that of conquerors. It can be added here that in this process of analysis, Majumdar developed the strength of his confidence in the application of anthropology by arguing that an anthropologist with his thorough knowledge of the cultures in contact and the likely outcome thereof can delineate a path for a smooth change, beneficial to both the cultures and avoiding confrontation. Thus, Majumdar in a way reflected the close relationship between anthropological interest in cultural contact and the application of anthropology to administration. Of course, the approach was contextualized in terms of the colonial administration of his time. Quoting Majumdar's writings of 1936 onwards, Madan concludes that 'Majumdar's formulation of the nature of the dynamics of culture change', came about after mid-1930s.

Beals (1953: 622), writing on 'Application for Anthropology Today' traces the interest in the study of contact phenomena and practical application of anthropology suggests:

> Interest in contact phenomena in Great Britain and elsewhere may have had a similar origin, although it would appear that functionalism was the major reaction in Great Britain to the study of memory cultures. Rather I would tentatively suggest that the origin of interest in culture contact in Great Britain

> stemmed from two sources, namely, the increasing urgency of practical applications of anthropology in colonial areas and in part as a reaction against certain limitations inherent in the more formal functionalist systems ... . Studies of culture contact offered the opportunity of applying the best of the functionalist approaches, as within a dynamic framework of change. (Beals, 1953: 622)

As Beals has pointed out in British anthropology, the cultural contact situations were depicted as those of social change 'while the American anthropologists had started using the term 'application' to refer to the transfer of cultural elements through contact between groups, as early as 1880' (Keesing, 1953: 12). The Indian subcontinent more or less since time immemorial had been a scenario full of contact situations. Keesing (ibid.: 19) notes in his review of the decade 1910 to 1919 that 'a noteworthy group of studies relate to India, some by Indian scholars'. Reviewing Keesing's 'Chronological Bibliography' for the earliest Indian works, one finds River's *The Todas* (1906); and in 1909, 'An Essay of Constructive History of the Oraon and Mundas' (F.A. Grignard); and 'Evaluation of Religion' (H. Gulliford). However, from 1911 onwards, one can find S.M. Mitra's 'Analysis of Indian Unrest' and S.N. Singh's 'Indians Untouchables' and subsequently essays on themes like 'Aborigines Changing into Chandala Castes through Hinduisation and conversion of Santal to Hinduism', 'Dravidian Gods in Modern Hinduism' and 'Hinduisation of Aboriginals' and S.C. Roy's 'A New Religious Movement among the Oraon' (1921).

In this backdrop, we find Majumdar writing on the basis of his field trips as a postgraduate student on 'Cry of Social Reforms among the Aborigines' (9A: 1925: 285–290). This paper published in the *Modern Review* discusses his observations among the Ho. This paper is noteworthy particularly because it covers the following aspects:

- The influence of social culture has reached the most secluded nook of our land that is the aboriginal people who supply us a clue to the evolution of primitive society.
- Their culture more or less stagnant and traceable to the very early period of their existence has received the light of culture to some extent ... or fast lighting the candle of civilization (The language reflects the evolutionary approach of the time).
- The change is 'with the help of Christian missionaries'.
- The aboriginals 'although, they are surrounded by cultured people on all sides have preserved much of their habits and customs.
- Anthropologists should lose no time in collecting all materials about these primitive people as in a decade to come, all that was primitive in them would perish adding only a blank page to the diary of the curious.
- Christian missionaries have built churches and schools 'spread amongst them and light candle of culture'.
- Missionaries have awakened consciousness among the people to rid themselves of peculiar customs that seemed disgraceful for example, *thumkurias* among Oraon.

- Majumdar quotes Roy about several Oraon institutions, customs, etc. appearing to be resultants of a mixture of their own ideas with those of Mundas and 'Hindu ideas are, to some extent and Christian example is, to a smaller extent exercising disintegrating influence'.
- Speaking of the Ho, Majumdar mentions their religious beliefs, etc. and, then, the problem in marriage of girls due to high bride-price and how it was at the root of tolerance for sexual license.

Here, Majumdar interprets the efforts of the educated Ho to eradicate such practices 'to save their society from wreck and ruin'. Then, Majumdar describes the background of the resolutions for reforms passed in several meetings in Kolhan and the ethnographic background for these changes. In this context, Majumdar also mentions infringements of certain customary taboos among the Ho, like commensal relationship with low Hindu castes, keeping of women of low social position as mistresses by Ho men who were not able to marry, avoiding any contacts with low castes people who eat beef and so on. He mentions that 'the practice of *duma* and *sisun* that is use of drums and loud music for dances were 'looked down upon by the cultured neighbours as very low and degrading'. The resolutions mentioned are quite extensive and include giving up of late night dances, high bride-price, taking away women forcibly for marriage, young women visiting *hats* for labour work, delivery of firewood by Ho at the residence of Dikkus and several others.

Significantly, Majumdar also in a very nascent way anticipates a role for application of anthropology and also 'reporting and analysing a reformatory movement' among the Ho as early as mid-1920s, when he observes:

> It seems apparent that the aborigines have determined to purge themselves of whatever is old or antique with them. The time has changed, their outlook has also widened. Education, cultural contact have changed their angle of vision and they must be encouraged to cleanse the Augean stables. But, one thing must not be neglected. The state of affairs in Kolhan surely demands a sympathetic consideration from all who have an interest in the socially regeneration of India, but this regeneration should be worked out with great caution. Everything, old or antique, is not bad, there must be something sound in the old tribal life, otherwise it could not have stood the test of centuries. (9A: 1925: 289)

In conclusion, Majumdar also outlines the state of Ho economy. How the Ho were satisfied with what they extracted from the forests and primitive agriculture as well as some cash income earned through *lac* production. He pointedly adds the manner in which the Hindu neighbours exploit and extract the cash income of the Ho because they do not know the value of money. This attitude is also reflected by the decision of a 'high government officer' asking the heads of schools in Singbhum not to grant free studentships to Ho boys because the Ho 'are getting richer day by day'. Thus, it seems that even at the stage of finishing his student career, Majumdar was reporting quite perceptively on various issues connected with both social change, agents of change, need for a selective path for change employing the application of anthropological knowledge analytically, and even observing a social movement among the tribe he had taken up for intensive study.

In a paper entitled, 'Race and Adaptability' (30: 1929), we find some further development of Majumdar's thoughts on the study of culture contact, change and visualization of a role for practical anthropology. This paper was written about a year after he had joined the University of Lucknow as a lecturer in Primitive Economics, and he had initiated a study of the tribal people in Mirzapur district of southern UP, the Korwa to begin with. Viewing the conditions among the Korwa in the backdrop of the large tribal populations of India, he observes that the tribe which was 'such an active and powerful tribe' are at present 'a dying tribe with little or no ambition in life living in stressful circumstances for food and due to exploitation'. Analysing their demography, he finds decimation, like the Birhor. Looking for the factors causing this situation, he argues:

> If the rapid disappearance of the primitive tribes is one of the inevitable results of the progress of civilization and if it is due to the change from the free and unfettered life of the jungle tribes to a so-called ordered existence or a life of degraded serfs– which have been more or less responsible for a complete change in their mental outlook, it is all the more essential that the factors of this civilization should be analyzed and some sort of protection should be provided for, in order to enable them to hold their own against the onslaught of foreign ideas. (ibid.: 150–151)

In support of his argument, he goes on to analyse the factors of 'mal-adaptation' which are many, particularly denial of access to forest and their being restricted to rocky and unproductive land which makes them poor agriculturist, scarcity of water, new diseases, as a result of contact and exploitation. Under these conditions, they can either face extinction or absorption into population possessing a stronger vitality. And here, he compares cultures in contact situations according to their strong or weak or equal vitality or equal social status and how the results of contact vary with different combinations in vitalities of cultures thrown into contact. In this context, he also comments that the populations which come to possess a racial mixture through miscegenation gain in both 'vitality and status' through a comparison with Polias or Rajbansis of northern India and also the 'racial intermixture between the Indo-Aryans and the Dravidians'. He expresses his anxiety as follows:

> Instances are not rare when a sort of protective administration of the tribal territories has led to favourables growth of the tribal stock. We plead for the same treatment to the Korwas and other primitive tribes of India. Crime against trees should be prevented but that should not lead to a crime against man for certainly man deserves greater attention than trees. (ibid.: 156)

Historically, it may be added, that the area 'south of Kaimur range' in Mirzapur district of UP was one of the areas under protective provisions under the Government of India Act 1919. Though Majumdar had written about the tribes of that area, specially the Korwa, in a number of papers and also in more details in *Fortunes* (1944) and *Chhor* (1960) when this administrative system had ended, he has never examined in detail or commented on the system of governance and operation of different laws in the area. This, in a way, leaves his application of anthropological knowledge to the known conditions there half way.

Subsequently, in 1936 (no. 56), Majumdar provides a more focused perspective on what he intends as a protective frame for tribal rehabilitation. Here, he contextualizes the contact situation in terms of the impact created by administrative officers, missionaries, traders and vendors going into tribal areas, establishments for exploiting mineral resources, expansion of transport and communication, and restrictions on shifting cultivation and other facilities in the forests as also the influence of caste system and Hindu religious tradition. This leads to a critical examination of certain aspects of the administrative system in these areas as well as some of the laws which are unsuitable. The system of education introduced by the missionaries and also by the government, has certain unsuitable features. Moreover, the new diseases resulting from contacts are beyond the indigenous pharmacopoeia and other traditional ways of healing but the extension of modern medical facilities is too insignificant to cope with the situation. The demographic trends among some of the tribes have also been examined. Economic exploitation of tribals and the inadequacy of laws and governance has also been highlighted, broadly. As discussed elsewhere, Majumdar questions the desirability of exclusion of certain areas under the 1935 Act and argues for setting apart funds, in accordance with the tribal population, from the provincial revenues 'for the development of the tribal areas and for welfare work among them', under careful supervision for protection as an imperative. He observes that the primitive tribes of India represent a vigorous and sturdy stock that needs a forward policy of economic uplift and not a policy of isolation.

His field experience by this time also leads him to conclude that the impact of Christian missions' work in the field of education and economic and medical services too had not been entirely beneficial. It had created a chasm or fission in the tribal society as also the coming up of a class which was trying to lead a more luxurious life than they could afford. In this context, he pleads for some 'organized mission work among the tribal people by the Hindus'. This comes more as a plea to offset or balance the 'splendidly organized' educational and benevolent institutions of the Catholic missions which also receives support from the colonial government.

After a large number of papers on the Ho, Majumdar's doctoral work on this tribe was published in 1937. Its title *A Tribe in Transition – A Study in Culture Pattern,* spells out its focus on change and the problems connected with this 'transition'. It is regarded as the first problem-oriented ethnographic study of Indian tribe. And, apart from his emphasis on the functionalist's approach, he also made an attempt to show how the patterns of Ho culture had been undergoing this 'transition'. A further and more detailed study on the Ho came much later after more fieldwork in 1950, entitled *The Affairs of a Tribe – A Study in Tribal Dynamics.* In this decade (1930 to 1939), Keesing (1954: 38) mentions:

> Group of anthropological studies worth selecting out consists of works by anthropologists employed by governments overseas, mainly with an applied emphasis. Notable examples are the New Guinea studies of Williams (30–49, 33–42, 33–41, etc.), Chinnery (32–10), Todd (35–59), and Groves (36–17, etc.); also studies by Mills (31–32) and Hutton (38–41) in India, Noone in Malaya (36–67), and Brown and Hutt (35–9) and a number of others in Africa (see under 'functionalism' above).

Majumdar had been mentioned earlier in this bibliographical review.

In *Transition*, Majumdar holds that primitive culture is dynamic and changing, and stresses the need to understand *how* these changes occur, *who* are responsible for introducing them, and *what* are the chances of survival of these introduced traits (60: 1937: x). Thus, in this study he also tries to focus on the ways which 'are still helping to hold their own against heavy odds' (ibid.: 195) and finds 'a large number of more or less important elements in their culture', viz., the compact area they live in with maintenance of traditional system of land tenure in the government estate. In addition the conservative elements among the Ho along with the newly emerging upper class in Kolhan which also acts as buffer and model for the changing youth. Further, there is the social distance between the Ho and the Dikus, which has engendered a sense of rivalry and jealousy (ibid.: 195). All these are the factors contributing to a 'peaceful social progress', as noticed among the Ho.

In the subsequent study, he identifies the problems which the Ho have gradually come to face and how the administration through indirect role has created a clash of traditional and new government nominated leadership and other difficulties connected with industrialization, exploitation and so on. He finds that Ho are very much sensitive to be 'regarded as silent spectators or ignored apathetically by their alien neighbours'. There is resentment among the people against tribal officers, the closed mentality developing in Kolhan, introduction of a *thana* system without any thought on how the tribals would react to it and the disintegrative impact of industrialization. Then, he comes out with a few suggestions for a more acceptable and smooth approach to bring about change. In his introduction, he writes about the base of a culture which he finds to be the resultant of the interaction of four crucial variables which arranged in the order of importance, were Man, Areas, or Resources and Cooperation (MARC). The Area is terrestrial, Resources is made up of animal and plants, soil, environment so to say, Man is organism with basic needs and through Cooperation produces human culture and derived needs arise. MARC as an interdependent functional unit provides the base of a culture and it is an *elastic* concept to a point. He puts the relationship of these factors to Base and the resultant K as,

B = K = f MARC.

In his discussion he analyses how changes in C, and also R which includes technology as variables, can bring about desirable adjustments or maladjustments in B. The implied approach here is that adjustments in these variables if they are based on intensive studies can smoothen the path of change. As discussed elsewhere, he had also indicated that these factors could be measured and thereby adjusted or readjusted, using statistical methods.

Thus, Majumdar advocated an approach to the tribal problems which as observed by Madan (2013: 34):

> Was based on a concept of creative or generative adaptation: he was against wholesale cultural invasion from the outside, but feared that, unless helped, weaker peoples would fail to withstand external pressures. For him Verrier Elwin's crusade in favour of leaving the tribes alone (see, for example Elwin, 1943) and G.S. Ghurye's counter-campaign to treat them as indistinguishable from backward Hindus (see Ghurye, 1943) represented a Rousseauan romanticism on the one hand, and a political posture on the other, rather than the fruits of objective scientific inquiry.

Madan rightly comments in this context that:

> Majumdar did not elaborate the strategy that he may have considered adequate for the purpose and it is rather curious that he should have considered it merely a matter of information about and understanding of tribal cultures. (2013: 34)

Vidyarthi reviewing the course of 'applied anthropology in India' (1978 II) points out that Majumdar attempted a 'more or less systematic and analytical publication about tribal populations' and in the special number of *The Eastern Anthropologist* in 1949 on Tribal Welfare included a number of papers 'on the importance of applied anthropology'. It for the first time described the various approaches to tribal problems and views of anthropologists and social workers on the general and specific aspects, and most of the important anthropologists (except for Dr Elwin and Dr B.S. Guha) made a re-evaluation of anthropological position and came out with the theory of 'planned acculturation', inter alia, calling for:

> The need of the social workers was recognized, but anthropological training for welfare work was emphasized. Some of the following features of 'scientific planning', were given special emphasis:
>
> (i) Study of individual tribes and tribal groups and their basic problems, needs and necessities.
>
> (ii) Careful planning on the basis of specific problems and needs of individual tribes and areas.
>
> (iii) Adequate specialized training for social workers in tribal areas and general and practical training for administrative officers and other workers engaged in tribal areas.
>
> (iv) Active participation of the tribal elders in the planning and execution of schemes (Vidyarthi, 1968: 126–27).

The papers also indicated aspects of tribal problems in some of the tribes that deserved immediate attention, viz., public health and sanitation; economic welfare, land and labour problems including administrative reforms; tribal education; socio-economic reforms; problems of tribal integration with larger society (ibid.: 126).

A smaller group of anthropologists showed its indifference to all these developments and remained satisfied with the academic interpretation of anthropology. Another group of anthropologists employed by the government in the museums and survey works just pressed for the expansion of their departments and they were satisfied with what little the government did for them (ibid.: 126–27).

The decade of 1940s provided Majumdar the opportunity to associate himself with the 1941 Census operations in the United Provinces. He not only conducted an intensive anthropometric and blood group survey of a large number of persons from different castes and tribes but also collected detailed ethnographic data on the criminal tribes, the Tharu, the polyandrous people of Jaunsar-Bawar and other tribes, specially Korwas in Mirzapur district. The ethnography is contained in the *Fortunes of Primitive Tribes* while his findings of the racial composition of the people are broadly given in *Races and Cultures of India*. The detailed findings are contained in the full work co-authored with P.C. Mahalonobis and C.R. Rao with a foreword by the Census Commissioner (117: 1949).

The ethnographic note on the Korwa (90: 1944) further documents the various aspects of maladjustments of this small tribe already raised in his earlier papers. He had detailed cases depicting Korwas' 'loss of interest in even living', taking the death of a son with great equanimity or indifference, lack of compliance with the decisions of panchayats for no reason, loss of faith in the religious practices and medical practices of their Chero and most importantly some sort of a retarded development of personality encouraging lack of social solidarity and a passivity. In comparison Majumdar describes how the Tharu have adapted in their culture a changing response to their material needs, positive reactions to reformation and education and even a better physical condition achieved through marriage in a larger circle. These comparisons employ what can possibly be achieved among the Korwa also if a careful thought-out plan is taken up with suitable measures in expanding their economic base, and medical and educational programmes. These case studies, so to say, are indicative of the manner in which each such small tribe in peril should be dealt with. One is also reminded of Sol Tax's Fox project and how it could achieve results when anthropologists became planners and also the agents of action.

The Tharu ethnography, apart from highlighting the facets which has already been discussed elsewhere explicates how they have adapted a careful process of selective adoption of traits and customs from neighbouring cultures, the way in which their culture has been built up in response to their material needs and highlights the high status or dominant position of the Tharu women. Their physical features present a mixing and their blood grouping a likely resistance to malaria. The ethnographic notes on the Khasa or polyandrous people of Jaunsar-Bawar and on the criminal tribes of Uttar Pradesh have been discussed elsewhere.

The extensive anthropometric and serological data regarding Uttar Pradesh (91: 1944: 70–71) makes an attempt to figure out the racial status of the castes and tribes of the state. The people are largely homogenous in ethnic traits and although cultural difference exists and even dialects vary, the cultural pattern shows an integrated pattern. The data points out to a gradual lowering of racial status from the Brahmins to the aboriginal tribes and the order of social precedence to a degree corresponds to racial purity or hybridization. The survey, however, showed:

> The classification of the castes in Uttar Pradesh cannot be absolute and that racial types may not be determined with the existing technique. The switch-on to genetic study of the social groups is necessary both in the interest of anthropometry and of the qualitative improvement of racial type. (ibid.: 71)

Significantly, the criminal tribes of Uttar Pradesh numbering nearly two million, show a lot of inbreeding and interbreeding and thus eliminate any possibility of what was earlier regarded as inheritance of criminal tendencies. The ethnographic data, however, clearly documents how a culture of crime has been continued.

Application of Anthropology and Rural Development

C.D. Programme was launched in India on 2 October 1952 and the planning through Five Year Plans was initiated in 1953. Majumdar's conviction that anthropology could offer 'useful knowledge and usable advice to the policy maker, the administrator and the social worker' was based on his earlier work, primarily in the tribal areas. Therefore, his response to these developments was 'positive and dramatic' in Madan's words. He took up this work as a challenge and busied himself in a number of rural studies which have been discussed elsewhere in this work. It may also be recalled that by this time the prevailing prejudices against anthropologists rather than anthropology as Majumdar has said were on the decline and anthropologists were associated with these efforts as evaluators and for data profiles along with economists and sociologists. His approach as pointedly described by Madan (2013: 39) was:

> As an anthropologist, he had always concerned himself with the 'here-and-now' of the peoples he had studied. It was precisely in this same spirit that he turned to the study of the problems of rural and urban development, and he did so with immense zest and confidence. Noting the long-lasting interest of economists in rural studies, but castigating them for a preoccupation with the perfection of techniques of quantitative analysis and a neglect of 'the cultural background' and 'the interrelation that exists between different sets of social phenomena', he too (like Mukerji) called for a holistic approach.

Starting from early 1954, Majumdar took up his village studies. A number of papers were published from 1955 onwards (170, 176, 181, 183, 196, 202) and the book on Gohana-kalan, in 1958. The publications on Jaunsar-Bawar and Dhanaura, however, came posthumously. In 1955, his address as the Sectional

President Anthropology to the first Indian Sociological Conference at Deharadun, and in 1956, his Presidential Address to the second Indian Conference, were also primarily devoted to the rural study and change, planned as well as internally generated. The later Address at Patna in a way is his testament as an anthropologist who had devoted most of his work to the study of culture change and application of anthropology; intended to help elimination of friction and bringing acceptance or germinating ideas for change in the human society. Madan (2013: 39) has very succinctly quoted Majumdar's enthusiasm for a better future and confidence in the capability of social science to contribute to its making. Expressed in Majumdar's own words, thus:

> If social relations at any stage of development hinder or hamper the historical productive relations, that is the relationship of man to nature, the only way to avoid catastrophic cultural blow-up is to modify the existing social relations. Here comes the real role of a sociologist, for in this sense his discipline represents an instrument of social policy. With his expert knowledge of social relationships, the sociologist can help predict, control and direct social change and speed up social progress. (178: 1956: 131)

Majumdar was obviously as confident of the usefulness of sociology as some of its European founding fathers. Accordingly, he pressed for an active association of sociologists and anthropologists with the planning process, training of personnel and evaluation.

In the 1950s, Majumdar had also responded to the planner's initiatives for documenting the problems and extending diagnostic suggestions in respect of our fast growing urban centres. At the invitation of the municipal corporation of Lucknow, he made his pioneering study of Lucknow (referred to in a discussion at the Symposium of the Wenner-Gren foundation) in 1915 and thereafter the industrial city of Kanpur as a part of a larger programme of the study of a number of cities initiated by the Planning Commission. His urban anthropology has been discussed elsewhere.

Application of Anthropology in Government: Majumdar's Perception

By and large, the entire discussion relating to Majumdar's writings on application of anthropology, touches the fields of administration of tribal populations, social reforms and social work, intra-tribal and inter-tribal relations, perception of tribals in industries and mining and the prevailing state of positive or negative reaction of the tribal people as also rural populations to their contacts with outsiders and the measures and programmes undertaken by the government. We find that Majumdar has examined all these aspects in the frame of social contact or cultural contacts and, then, described its outcome with its various shades of adjustments with implications of the usefulness of anthropological data and findings to eliminate problems and difficulties. The question would arise as to why Majumdar has not elaborated such implications to prescribe, say clinically, what measures by way of policies and programmes can be adapted by the government and non-governmental organization towards that end. Majumdar has summed up his perception of the Indian situation very pointedly while speaking in the Wenner-Gren seminar at New York. In a session on 'problems of application of anthropology in government', presided over by Margaret Mead, he observes that:

> I agree with Professor Nadel that the role of anthropologist involves the collection of data, broad surveys, and also giving advice to the administration and, if necessary, handling the materials. The anthropologists in India are in a difficult position with regard to the last. Anthropological knowledge is welcomed by the administration, but the Anthropologist is not. In this peculiar situation it is necessary for the anthropologist to diffuse knowledge rather than to do anything of a practical nature. However, in recent years his advice, if not his direct intervention, has been actively utilized. For example, two or three communities in the United Provinces, deprived of their salt-making economic base by mass production, turned to petty theft. Anthropologists hired by the government discovered that their demoralization really came of their having been lowered in caste from Rajput to untouchables by becoming salt-makers. When physical measurements showed them to be Rajputs and they were restored to census recognition as Rajputs, the problem eased.
>
> In India, biologists describe population trends and processes in terms of the logistic curve of population growth. Some groups are decreasing in size, some leveling off, and some increasing. The latter are the 'have nots,' and thus the problem is one not only for the anthropologist but also for the economist.
>
> It is difficult to study values in India now because India is in a state of flux and because, after long suppression, the diversity within Indian value systems must be allowed to crystallize … . (Sol Tax, 1953: 183)

Majumdar's Perception of Scope of Anthropology

In the Wenner-Gren foundation, symposium of 1953 anthropology was discussed as a 'field of study' particularly applied anthropology in government–in different countries and the United Nations. Majumdar reviewing the progress of anthropology in India spelt out its different division and their growth in India which needs to be quoted here, in extenso:

> … anthropology in India, and I shall simply indicate the trends and activities pertinent to this field. They will be treated under two broad heads– physical and cultural, as follow:
>
> … Since 1921[1], when anthropology was first introduced into the curriculum of Calcutta University, it has enjoyed state encouragement … . Indian anthropologists saw the need of orienting their studies to the requirements of day-to-day life, and anthropology slowly acquired an applied role.
>
> Since it is believed that anthropological knowledge must be applied to the creation of wider scope and opportunity for individuals and groups, certain anthropological problems are receiving priority. Some of the spheres of interest of cultural anthropology in India are studies of caste mobility; cultural

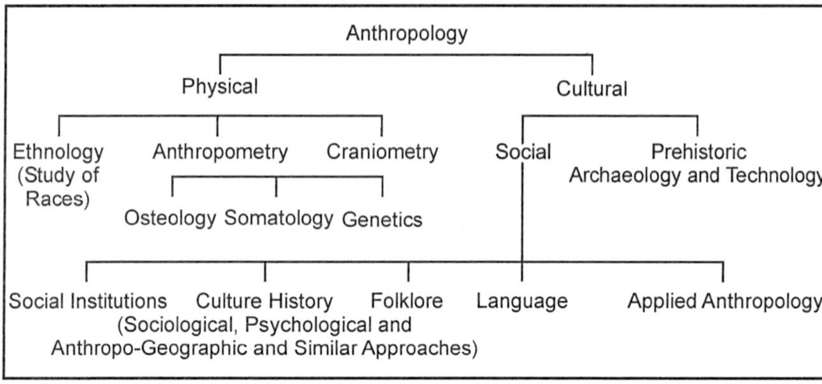

dynamics; transition in tribal life; the processes of acculturation, assimilation, and the rehabilitation of refugees; causes and consequences of the infamous Bengal famine; problems of contact and clash of cultures in the north-east borders of India; the nature and cure of labour unrest; conflict and social distance between castes and communities; studies of tension between social groups; and rural and community studies.

The first anthropological study of the pattern of Indian city life has been undertaken in Lucknow, financed by the municipal board of Lucknow, and sociologists, psychologists and statisticians are working with anthropologists on this project. The need for such collaboration has been fully recognized in India.

In our study of tribal transition, we are surprised to note the speed of the acculturative process in backward areas. Tribal labour migrants to plantations and liminal towns, to the steel and textile industries, and the degree of adjustment effected by these people to technology do not support Professor Northrop's illuminating conclusions ... (Sol Tax, 1953: 343–45).

Concluding Discussion

Majumdar's writings on the potentialities in applying anthropological knowledge to eliminate strife and confrontation in the multifarious contact situations in the country can be defined in their scope into two periods– the colonial period up to 1947 and post independence period, 1947 to 1960. Broadly, one can see that during the colonial period he had almost totally confined himself to tribal studies, the areas of which were Bihar, Central India and Uttar Pradesh. By and large, as discussed here, his approach is functional analyses of the organization and institution and also beliefs and attitudes under the impact of contact and how these are affecting the equilibrium or smooth functioning of these communities. He has also added his findings of changing patterns as a result of the contacts. In the context of such analyses he pleads for some changes contextually in the administrative setup highlighting the need for an indirect rule and at the same time eliminating the sudden changes in leadership pattern, working of industrial and mining centres in the areas, land systems and other protectionist's measures, etc. At places he presciently forecasts and warns about the likely discontent and contra-acculturative movements. In addition, he also pleads for a new pattern of financing the welfare and developmental activities in the excluded areas and for the tribals as well as a set of suggestions countering the Christian missionary activities with their undesirable effects, by other agencies particularly Hindu reformist organizations. His suggestions have far reaching implications in policy and pleas for a pro-activist role for non-governmental bodies. However, most of these analytical writings contain only broad suggestions and he has almost in no case attempted any detailed and precise prognosis and diagnostic needs in terms of an anthropological approach to the specific problems, even as a test format. Moreover, the analytical observations with their overtones for applicability remain largely within the parameters of the colonial policies and their definitive categories then.

In *Races and Cultures*, however, he has made some very significant observations on the ongoing colonial narrative. And it, noticeably, predicates the strong current of recent anthropological critique of the post-colonial view of the tribal problems and the nature of constitutional provisions laid out in 1950s. This has been discussed elsewhere in this work. His pointed comment is:

> Imperialism at the end of the nineteenth century, besides developing an individualistic-capitalistic economic structure of the Euro-American type[2], among other things may be credited with three other results. *A theory of 'racism'*, a social theory of diffusion which was parallel to and a justification of imperialism, and a shrewd emphasis on a more careful and accurate study of primitive races so that the imperialists, in the words of Geoffrey Gorer, 'could govern the subject races in their colonial possession without having to massacre them' (In other words the power of knowledge). The white man in the tropical countries wanted cheap labour, markets and slaves; in the temperate, he wanted space to settle. Both depended on the removal of friction and hostility and that was how the study of primitive people gained a functional status with governments charged with the administration of primitive and backward peoples. The theory of diffusion that all social improvements were derived from a single source (usually Egypt) was a great justification for the repetition of this process by a single conquering power, usually England or Germany. Recent studies of savage cultures; the attitude of the white man with regard to the 'native' who is still regarded as half animal; the study of social disintegration among the aboriginal population in India, in Melanesia and Australia, which shows that the 'native' cannot stand the strain of coping with sexual antagonism or family conflicts unprotected by the traditional customs or protective myths; or the study of dissolving social structures, and the effect of disorganization on individual psychology: all these have been taken as evidence of the competence of the imperialist powers as colonial rulers. (91: 1944: 37)

It appears that this profound analytical observation of his goes almost unnoticed as it is contained in the context of a discussion on racial prejudice, which is an oft recurrent theme in his writings. It should also be seen that he had made these observations in the year 1942 in the course of lectures he had delivered to the ICS probationers (the 'steel frame' of colonial governance) and minor princes or ruling chiefs of smaller princely states of the time.

Notes

1. The preceding part of his presentation was as follows:

   An account of Archeology is included in my paper for the Handbook of World Resources for Research and Education in Anthropology ... our finds of bones, fossil, or other have been few and systematic search in this direction has not yielded many dividends .... In 1931, the census department initiated a second racial survey, in which a new classification was adopted ... and interest aroused by this inquiry led to a rapid development of anthropometric research, resulting in completion of three more racial surveys during the last ten years ....

   In recent years, serological research has been much emphasized .... Twin studies, inheritance of diseases, and growth studies figure in anthropological programs, as well as investigations on the nutritional status of social groups ....

   The first significant impetus to cultural anthropology can be traced back to 1774, when Sir William Jones .... There followed a period of feverish activity on the part of administrative officers of the then Indian Civil Service to record the ethnography of the country, taking the form of several detailed volumes of ethnographic literature on customs of the tribes and castes of India.

   In 1912, the first monograph on an Indian tribe was published by the pioneer anthropologist of India, the late S.C. Roy, and was followed by several more monographs by him and his students and by the personnel of the Indian Civil Service. Many of these monographs are known for meticulous and objective evaluation of Indian tribal life.
2. Here he stresses, in a way what Mukerjee had analytically observed and emphasized in his institutional economics in the 1930s when Majumdar had joined Lucknow to teach 'primitive economics'.

11

Contributions to Other Branches of Anthropology

This chapter briefly presents Majumdar's writings and his analysis regarding Caste System and the changes in its forms and practice, and also his contribution to the study of demography specially tribal demography and folklore on which he had focused in the early stage of the activities of the Ethnographic and Folk Culture Society. It also includes a presentation on Majumdar's extensive work in physical anthropology and its significance.

Caste and its Changing Patterns

Caste has been the basis of Indian social structure. Hence, no social scientist writing about India can really go without discussing caste as an institution and in practice. Majumdar has, however, dealt with the caste system less frequently, as compared to his studies on tribes and, then, his focus is on the changing processes in this context. Later in mid-1950s, he took up village studies, observed the origin of caste dynamics of the system, and its ramifications in the villages he studied as also in his urban studies to some extent. The unfolding of Majumdar's views in this regard may now be examined from his writings.

Elsewhere, we have already seen how Majumdar started focusing on the process of change, its agents and their impact, right from 1925 when in his field trip to the Ho area as a student, he observed, 'the cry of social reforms amongst' them (9A: 1925). However, he, in the typical evolutionary-diffusionist perspective of his day, discerns the 'influence of social culture' and finds it undesirable because it was going to erase the patterns of a primitive culture which anthropologists must study. Discussing the resolutions adopted by the several Ho gatherings for social reforms, he traces most of these reforms to an impact of missionary culture and also what he describes as certain practices, 'looked down upon by the cultured neighbours as very low and degrading'.

These include dance and music, the institution of *dhumkuria*, tribal female labour in the bazaars, high bride-price, etc. But, the very next year 'an instance of the conversion of tribes into castes in Bengal' (16 and 17: 1926) attracts his attention and he documents the process through two papers on the Polias, Babupolias, Palias or Rajbansis presented in the Indian Science Congress. Here, and in a paper published later (23: 1926: 155–73), he discusses at length the manner in which this particular community has made efforts to change their status from a tribe to a Hindu caste in the Kshtriya *varna*. Calling the process, 'gradual and insensible the transformation of tribes into castes has been going on from very early times'. He goes on to discuss how 'the processes involved are many and, varied and interdependent to some extent. The four kinds of processes, suggested by Risley, by which the transformation is effected, are then described. Briefly, it would include some rich and influential members of a tribe 'manage to enroll themselves in one or more distinguished castes', usually Rajputs; a number of aborigines joining some Hindu religious sects; an entire tribe or a large section thereof enrolling themselves as Hindus under the 'style of a new caste ... with remote origins but readily distinguishable by its name'; and, a whole tribe or a section thereof becoming 'gradually converted to Hinduism without abandoning their tribal designation. He, however, suggests an additional fifth type of practice 'being commonly adopted in the outlying parts of Bengal and Assam' (ibid.: 156). Here in which 'an individual member' of a tribe 'adopts a surname and a *gotra* of a particular caste' thereby managing to enroll himself as a member of that particular caste and in due course intermarries with the members of that caste. He discusses these processes and how Brahman priests, mainly because of their poverty and greed, play a pivotal role in the progress of such a transformation which includes the use of the sacred thread and establishing the process of a new identity. Through comparative examples from Bengal, all these processes have been discussed in a concrete manner. Majumdar also observes that the 'complicated process involved in the transformation of tribes into castes' reflects how the tribals 'with a progressively wide outlook of better life and status show tribes 'a partially for Hinduism'.

As regard the case in point, Babupolias or Rajbansis, the data from Census of 1921 documented their presence in four districts of Bengal, two of which are now in Bangladesh. The Census of 1901 had also recorded that 'Koch, a well known tribe of north Bengal and also Assam were returned as Rajbansis'. The Rajbansis numbered more than 17 lakh in Bengal alone in 1921. In support of their claim they traced the caste name Polia through a Sanskrit word, 'pal tak', which means 'run-always'. The legend in this connection being that they were the Kshtriyas who fled from their original settlements to avoid the wrath of Parshuram, the Brahman *muni* who was the avowed enemy of the Kshtriya. Further, the move of precipitating the larger Polia community into Rajbansi-Polia and Babupolia and a resultant move on the part of the Rajbansi-polia to claim a higher status than the Babupolias, has also been documented. The entire community has taken to a common *gotra,* Kashyap, even though the Kshtriya gotras are ordinarily exogamous. Interestingly, the paper also refers to the community following certain Muslim practices like 'nika marriage', as a form of marriage, as also their beliefs having origins in a tribal nexus. Recently this movement among Rajbansis (1910–1937) has been studied as a caste movement by Basu (2003).

Hutton has quoted this case study by Majumdar in the context of his observation that, 'like caste *varna* is to some extent fluid ... . It is wider and vaguer (persons belonging to one *varna* in one locality may be otherwise classified in another) than caste like which it is a variable social unit'. Discussing his conclusion further, Hutton focuses on the example of Kshtriya *varna* as this *varna* is 'claimed by Brahmans to have been extirpated by Parshuram' and points out that if it was so, this *varna* 'has been replaced by manufactured Kshtriyas'. He further observed that 'Kshtriya rank is claimed by many whose title is one of function or of creation rather than inheritance' (Hutton, 1946, 1980: 67).

Thus, it can be said that the case study of the Polia documented by Majumdar at the earliest stage of his anthropological profession came to be regarded as the analysis of the well-recognized process of structural change occurring in India in the form of the efforts of certain tribes to transform themselves into castes, often linking it with claims of belonging to a high *varna* like Kshtriya. However, later on Majumdar in his various studies of cultural change among tribes also identified that in this process the tribes often landed into joining the status of the lower or exterior castes. The social categories (tribe-caste) were, however, colonial concepts crystallized through the census operations beginning in the late 19th century. During the post-colonial period specially after the Constitution enshrined a policy of affirmative discrimination for the tribes listed as 'Scheduled Tribes', widespread movements have been carried out by the tribes, which had in the past demanded and agitated to move into the rank of a Hindu caste, for inclusion in the list of Scheduled Tribes. Concretely, among this community itself, the Koch-polias of Assam succeeded in gaining the status of a Scheduled Tribe while in Bengal a widespread demand for creating a tribal homeland for the Rajbansis in the districts of Cooch-Behar and Jalpaiguri has also come up.

The recent overall position among the Scheduled Tribes in this regard is the conclusion reached by the Anthropological Survey of India through its People of India project:

> The tribes have generally remained outside the varna system. Therefore, only 11.8 per cent of them recognize their place in it. Another 31.6 per cent are only aware of the varna system. Among those who recognize their place in it nearly 8.3 per cent claim to be Kashatriya, 7.5 per cent Shudra and 0.9 per cent Brahman, (Gaddi Brahman, Pangwal Brahman, Kagati and some among the Jaunsari claim to be of the Brahman varna), the Pardhan tribe, claims to be Vaishya. When it comes to the self-perception of a tribal community in the regional hierarchy we find that 171 tribes, i.e. 26.9 per cent see themselves as being of a high status, while 298 tribes (46.9%) perceive themselves as being in the middle position. About 25.3 per cent, i.e. 161 tribes see themselves as being

of low status. Others see over 11.2 per cent of the tribes as high, 39.2 per cent as medium and 49.4 per cent as of low status (Singh, 1994: 7).

Majumdar in his numerous papers on the Ho and other tribes of Chhota-Nagpur has, while commenting on the contact situations with the Hindu castes, been critical of the exploitative practices of Hindu landlords and traders and vendors in the tribal areas. Then, in *Transition*, he focuses on the conditions of this tribe particularly mentioning the failure of the tribals to 'escape derision at the hands of non-tribals' and how it has contributed to developing an inferiority complex among them, and further how this is creating a feeling of contra-acculturation, warning about the serious consequences if it is allowed to grow (60: 1937: 'The Prospect'). In a subsequent paper (68: 1938) discussing the adverse impact of the Christian missions, Majumdar points out that the financial and material support extended by the missionaries is 'the primary attraction in conversion rather than any religious conviction. The converted tribals give rise to a divisive society. Here, Majumdar is clearly supportive of initiating a wide programme to counter their impact on the part of other agencies particularly the Hindu organizations. He elaborates this approach through an eight-point scheme which includes raising of funds, training of workers and creation of suitable institutions. In 1939, his Presidential Address to the section of anthropology in the Indian Science Congress, which has been discussed in detail elsewhere, documents the close relationship between the tribal groups and the Hindu castes mainly the functional castes providing various services to the agriculturists. They have been conditioned into a stable pattern of social and economic life. The rulers of the state and their Brahman priests have created these patterns through their respective roles in the celebration of a fortnight-long Dusserah festival.

Origin of Castes

The various aspects and views connected with the origins of caste system in India have been discussed by Majumdar in *Races and Cultures of India*. He observes that the complex nature of the caste structure is obvious from the fact that, 'yet a valid explanation of circumstances that might have contributed to the formation and development of the system has not emerged'. He goes on to examine the views of the various Indologists, sociologists and anthropologists briefly mentioning Apte, Senart, Mac-Iver and other western sociologists and, then, the views of Roy, Dutt and Ghurye. He also comments on the views of Rivers and Hutton among others. Examining these diverse views and combining them with the findings of his own anthropometric and somatometric researches and also the conditions seen by him in his field studies in contact situations, he broadly brings forth the following analyses:

1. Manu's belief that the *varna* system emerged from the person of Brahma is seen by him to have two parts. First, that of a mystical origin and the second one, partly historical and partly functional, explaining the working of the four-fold social division. Taking the divine origin 'as an allegorical

explanation of the functional division of society', the theory assumes practical significance'.

2. This association of the system functionally with occupations and a gradation implied into it is a part of the explanation for the origins of caste is important. But it is not solely responsible for it. As the few occupations followed in India traditionally cannot account for the large number of castes and sub-caste seen today.
3. In the above context, Majumdar stresses the racial significance of the caste system as recognized by Risley as the word 'varna' means colour as well as class, 'but the three high *varnas* were originally distinguished ... by the various shades of colours ... resulting from the intermixture between the immigrants an Indo-Aryan racial stock and the indigenes. This should also be seen in conjunction with Roy's view that the Hindu caste system was a result of the interaction between the Indo-Aryan *varna* system on the one hand and the tribal system of the pre-Dravidian and the occupational class system of the Dravidians'. Such a clash of cultures and contact of races brought about the crystallized social grouping of caste in India. Intermarriages and *anulom* marriages contributed immensely to the prolification of castes and sub-castes.
4. The elements of social distance, commensal taboos and so on can broadly be traced to Hutton's and Roy's view that there was a widespread belief in *mana*-like principles both in the tribal world and in the beliefs of the immigrants.
5. The hierarchical element in the system should be identified with Brahmanism or the 'three original *varnas*' which retained their positions and, thus, placing the priestly castes uppermost. However, these groups had also been able to retain their racial purity to a greater extent. This has been supported by Majumdar's own anthropometric survey in UP, Gujarat and Bengal.

Broadly, the scheme of clustering on the basis of D^2 statistic reveals various anthropometric and somatometric characteristics shared by the groups. The details of this clustering have been discussed elsewhere. By and large, Majumdar agrees with Hutton's views that a number of factors had contributed to the emergence and the development of the system (1946/1980: 190) briefly the factors highlighted by Majumdar include primitive ideas of power of contact in persons or food and mana, certain beliefs in magic, clash of cultures and races characterized by colour prejudice, conquest and domination. The development of classes among tribes and castes as a result of differences in economic assets had also become a contributing factor.

In *Matrix* (98: 1947) where Majumdar discusses the problems of Indian ethnology, he points out that one of the issues is how far 'can a knowledge of race elements in the population be of practical importance and how far the observed differences between the various endogamous social groups are biologically consequential?' (ibid.: 182). Discussing his surveys in UP, Gujarat and Bengal, in this context, he offers the following evidence:

> In U.P., among other things there exists some correlation between racial and social status while serological evidence supports that of anthropometry (ibid.: 183–84). In Gujarat, the evidence indicates some evidence of alignments of castes and social groups including Muslims (ibid.: 189). In this discussion he also highlights two important observations, namely, that even though the boundaries of provinces have not been demarked on the basis of culture or race, there exists an intimate race relationship between groups high and low in the same geographical area (ibid.: 198); and secondly, 'how physical anthropology must take the help of social anthropology, knowledge of the social history of the people, into account otherwise purely morphological study of racial types would be of doubtful gain' (ibid.: 197).

Majumdar dwelt so elaborately with the origins of caste system and also the truth of its racial bases mainly because then in the 1930s, and also the next decade, race related issues were important. In fact, these questions had been long debated and Majumdar 'considered his intervention in the debate of a decisive nature: his data were reliable ... and methods of analysis sophisticated, involving the use of refined statistical techniques' (Madan, 2013: 230). To this, one can add Majumdar's long-standing basic focus to the study of social change and his strong faith in the application of anthropological knowledge and analysis – as seen in his writings about Rajbansis and the emergence of castes at various levels from a tribal matrix under the impact of colonial policies and increasing contacts between a majority of tribes and the Hindu society.

In the next decade of 1950s, the village came up as a centre of interest when an extensive community development programme for rural development was taken up. With Majumdar's constant concern with change and also what Madan describes as his being 'very receptive to new ideas', Majumdar took up his chain of village studies, as already discussed in earlier chapters. Unlike Srinivas, Majumdar was keen on discovering and recommending an effective interventionist strategy for rural rehabilitation. Thus, we see in his presidential address as Sectional President (Anthropology) in the first Indian Sociological Conference (172: 1955) emphatically asserting, inter alia:

- Social sciences must adopt an interdisciplinary approach so that it can be applied to the social situations in the interest of change for the better.
- The methodology essential for achieving these ends should encompass study through records and direct observation and, of course, the well tried anthropological methods of establishing 'complete *rapport* with the people', participant observation and intensive studies by investigators having a knowledge of the language of the people under study. Only, then, 'the social research competence can be harnessed' to 'problems of rehabilitation and social reconstruction'.
- Elaborating the manner of study of structural groups in our villages, he makes out some salient points relating to the study of caste. Outlining, in this context, three periods of caste history – in the times of Manu, in the medieval period, and toady – he underlines the dynamic and changing aspects today of caste system which had become rigid and stereotyped in the medieval period. His view is:

> The caste structure has been fighting a war of survival, and is mobilizing forces which were dormant or unintegrated. Though the battles are being lost, the outcome of the war is too premature to predict. To the social functions of the caste are being tucked politicoeconomic function resulting in a caste awareness which may yield the 'forbidden fruit' (ibid.: 12).

However, no detailed connotation of this phrase and how it is growing are added. Arguing, thus, he emphasizes his observation on the village life.

- We have idolized our village life and emphasized its stability and changelessness as reflected in the earlier writings on Indian village. In order to make the village studies by social scientists more applicable and oriented to change he would like to provide a new orientation through a focus on dynamics of culture and acculturation and also the experience of the American social scientists in this field. Spelling out this approach, he offers suggestions for rural studies as area studies and also for tribal studies with a view to planning (172: 1955: 1–19).
- In this light, his first published village study (188: 1958) along with papers on some aspects contains an entire range of observations 'as an innovative study'. Firstly, it documents chronologically the change in inter-caste relations in Gohana-Kalan (170: 1955: 91–214). The period covered is about 20 years and almost the entire relationship, social, commensal, way of greetings and *jajmani* transactions have been covered. The analysis emphasizes the changes, and also attempts to identify the communication channel affecting the change. In this way, Majumdar portrays both structural and behavioural changes in the institution of castes. Further, in its concluding chapter, he redefines the concept of a village in India and how it differs from Redfield's concept of a 'little community'. In India a village has a value system and it sentiments moored in past. But not ... limited by the four corners of the village. Its kinship ties embrace people of distant and near villages as well and situations of crises, find the villagers together. Hence:

> ... an attempt to isolate a village would be impracticable. A village may be conceived – and I feel there is sense in doing so – so not as a self-contained unit, but as integrated at different levels with the total social system of the country. Just as there are different levels of cultural development, there are different levels of integration (188: 1958: 325).

Furthermore, he finds that these ties and links or the proximity of this village to an urban area (Lucknow) has not urbanized it, as it is not absolutely communicating village. In fact, there is reluctance of the village folk to urbanization, referred to rather derisively as *shahri*-ways. In this connection the pattern among different castes, particularly the most important castes of ex-zamindars, the Thakur, comes out in different shades. These patterns have also been linked with a chronological account of leadership, factionalism and endeavours of government policies aiming to egalitarian inter-caste relations and traditional discrimination against lower castes.

With reference to the concept of there being 'a dominant caste' in a village, Majumdar argues that the dominance of a particular caste in a village is determined not simply by numerical or land owning strength but also by its status 'in a group of neighbouring villages' as only, then, 'the numerical preponderance in a village can be cashed'.

Majumdar observes that the kind of attitudes and values that the village people have, indicates that a village is still 'the nucleus of the Indian sentiment system. Therefore, from an operational point of view in the effort to bring about changes, there is likely to be a resistance to change unless the manner, in which change is extended, incorporates safeguards for the maintenance of this sentimental system. Therefore:

> An orientation of the value system has to be worked out, side by side with sponsored changes and action programmes, for the latter may not always fit in with the system of values or the ties that bind the villagers to a common living and sharing of culture. (ibid.: 330)

It may be added that the observances and beliefs connected with hierarchy and restrictive social relations between different castes have been underlined as a part of this sentimental system of the villages

Demographic Studies

Majumdar's contribution to demographic analysis with reference to India has its roots in both the tribal demography, and population scenario and the problems connected therewith for the entire country. However, it is significant that his interest in tribal demography along with an attempt not only to identify the trends of tribal population as a whole but also the case of individual tribes came quite early in his writings. Writing on race and adaptability (30: 1929), Majumdar stresses the need for the study of factors which cause the decline of population and even extinction of certain tribes 'in the interest of science as well as for safeguarding minority interest'. Among the causative factors, he discusses it as a result of progress of civilization or mal-adaptation and also certain diseases, etc. Comparatively, he starts by mentioning statistics, particularly of barrenness and sex ratio, relating to the Ho and the Korwa of Palamau and Duddhi and also the Birhor. Concluding, he is of the view that the decline is caused by 'something wrong in the process of adaptability'. He continues to dwell upon this aspect of the tribal situation in the country while he makes a plea for their better treatment (56: 1936). Here he comments on the declining population of certain tribes as reflected in the Census figures between 1881 to 1931. The tribes identified are Toda, Asur, Korwa and Andmanese. In this context it can also be added that his stay in Cambridge could have contributed to a focus on this aspect as Rivers from Cambridge had studied the Andmanese.

Subsequently in 1939, he had also participated in the Second Population and Family Planning Conference, where he had presented his views on the conditions of the tribes. Thereafter, came Majumdar's active association with the decennial Census from the 1941 Census, as mentioned elsewhere. In this

Census, he was asked to prepare a report on the tribal people, apart from an anthropometric and serological survey of the UP. Moreover, various dimensions of vital statistics relating to the population of two urban areas – Lucknow (138A: 1951) and Kanpur (200: 1960) – too figure prominently among his works later. Majumdar was also a member of the International Union for the Scientific Study of Population and in this capacity he had participated in the World Population Conference 1954 held in Rome under the auspices of the UNO. In this conference he was representing India, Pakistan (including the present Bangladesh), Burma (now Mynamar) and Ceylon (now Sri Lanka).

The survey of the UP tribes and castes and the ethnographic notes on tribes and anthropometric and serological data contributed to his focusing further on the declining Korwa population and the contributing factor therefore with a comparative analysis with another UP tribe, the Tharu, who in Majumdar's opinion were thriving due to their adaptability to the contact situation (90: 1944).

The deliberations at The World Population Conference in Rome in 1954 have had a great impact on the demographic studies and the designs for population statistics and their analysis. Some of the important subjects discussed, included mortality trends, fertility trends and demographic aspects of economic and social development. The discussion relating to these trends were examined more thoroughly by subdividing its meetings broadly into East and West so as to highlight 'contrast between modern industrialized countries with their generally low fertility and mortality favourable resources and effective collection of demographic data, and the less developed countries with high fertility and mortality and limited data' (B.B, P.R.C. and F.A.A.M., 1955: 187: 88). Among countries of higher fertility the experience of India and Japan was of particular interest; and the ways in which India is not matched by a general ability to carry out the effective practice of birth control, as compared to Japan. For their urban studies, the R.P.C. later added a focus on fertility patterns and factors determining the adoption of contraceptive practices has to be seen in this context as well. Majumdar in his own study of Kanpur as already discussed elsewhere has intensively analysed these aspects of urban demography.

The paper, contributed by Majumdar for the Conference (166A: 1954: 155–172), deals with the interrelation of demographic and cultural factors. He highlights how there are differential fertility rates prevailing among the tribes and castes of India as two categories; and moreover there is seen a differential fertility among different castes and tribes individually, as well. Such differences prevail in spite of the fact that the 'various castes in a locality, or a region, are more or less integrated in a hierarchical social organization' (ibid.: 155). Therefore, India's population is not merely a statistical problem; it 'is neither a question essentially of finding food ... but it is largely social and cultural and must therefore be treated as such'. Institutional practices like marriage forms too have their influence on demographic trends and these practices are caste and tribe specific. Age at marriage, which is largely determined by mores of a caste/tribe has a significant bearing on the number of children born to a woman. These culturally related factors create conditions that even economically better off sections in the same caste show the same trends in sex ratio, fecundity, child mortality, etc. As regards tribes, even two sections among the same tribe, one more Hinduized than the other, have differential fertility. Similarly, tribes living in the excluded or partially excluded areas which generally continue to retain their own customary practices, laws, and institutions show differences in fertility as compared to those living outside such areas. He expresses the view that the fertility rate, strangely enough, is found correlated with the general pattern of ethnic differences. Majumdar, however, argues that if there is widespread ascent in 'prosperity', the fertility rates will go down, irrespective of the status of the group, caste or tribe, and upper-lower castes and Hinduized or primitive tribes. In this regard, the approach also has to take into account the criticality of certain smaller and primitive tribes showing a low rate of growth and even decimation. The contributions of their traditional knowledge of birth control practices including the indigenous practices of using certain roots, herbs, etc., for abortion and ritualistic periods of abstinence, etc. are also relevant.

Besides the above specific writings focusing on various aspects of demography, monographs on the Ho and the polyandrous people of Jaunsar-Bawar contain substantive discussions on tribal demography. Thus, we find that his writings have links with census, their basic source of demographic data as well as analysis and comments in the field of ethnography and also family planning. The findings of the data collected through the Kanpur survey finds mention, in detail, in the first ICSSR survey of research in sociology and social anthropology.

The Matrix of Indian Culture (98: 1947) had earlier included two lectures relating to demography – 'tribal demography' and 'problems of population'.

The first lecture deals broadly with the details of the vital statistics related to the tribal population of India and how these statistics are deficient. He emphasizes that no descriptive note on a primitive tribe or a monograph on them can be complete without reference to their size or population, its density and distribution and at least a simple analysis of their vital statistics. He argues that the 'size of the population of tribes determines its cultural stage' and comments that these aspects about individual tribes or the tribal population of the country as a whole had escaped the attention of anthropologists.

Mentioning generally the diverse population of India having every conceivable type of cultural development and degree of isolation from civilization, the tribes have a whole range of variations in their culture and in their fertility. However, the information relating to the demographic conditions among these tribes is far from satisfactory.

He observes that contact with civilization of the primitive races have produced social and moral depression and resulted in apathy to life. This kind of suffering has caused a lower fertility among them. He is critical of the failure on the part of the census to present a complete demographic picture of tribal India, primarily because the census department was being setup only for a limited period for the purpose of conducting and reporting on the census. Moreover, vital statistics also suffer from the lack of public interests verging on apathy. The problem is compounded by the vastness of the country and illiteracy, ignorance and superstitions of the masses. He quotes the Public Health Commissioner, Government of India, about the inaccuracy in registrations of births and deaths. Referring to certain estimates made in Baroda that registration of annual births were far from correct, by as high as 50 per cent, Majumdar argues that if that was the condition in an area with compact villages what would be the adequacy or authenticity about 'the size of primitive families'. Here also he had expressed his views about the value of the statistics collected for primitive tribes, traditional practices and herbs known to them to eliminate unwanted births, an annual search and killing of witches among certain tribes of Chhota Nagpur and the high homicidal rate among certain tribes. Other practices were delayed marriages caused by the high bride-price and recognized practices of abortion among both unmarried and married women. Further, a longer period of sustaining children on mother's milk and periods of celibacy as practised at the time of certain rituals also are factors that affect fertility. In this context, ethnographic examples have been cited from Assam, Orissa and Chota Nagpur. Various kinds of marriages prevalent among the tribes also find mention in this regard, as also infanticide due to multiple causes and internecine tribal feuds. Mention has also been made of V.D., Yaws and other serious diseases like Tuberculosis, the results of 'contacts with civilization' which have affected the populations.

Majumdar refers to two opposite views regarding 'the fecundity of primitive people' – one view is that primitive people have a high fecundity and the other one is that this rate goes up from primitives to advanced people. The latter view based on some biological evidence claims that there was a connection between lesser development of the reproductive organs and a lower degree of fecundity, which Majumdar questions. The other view is arrived upon by the supposed co-relation between high standards of living and low birthrate. Majumdar proceeds to examine this problem with reference to 'the data available, much of which have been collected by me and my students.' The conclusion and observations from this data are, briefly, as follows:

- Climatic differences affect the menarche as in tropical countries, girls are likely to menstruate earlier. Since India is a country having varied climate differences, varieties in this regard are likely. The data on 367 women from seven tribes (Ho, Munda, Saora, Kuki, Garo, Tharu and Chero) shows that 3.3 per cent had menarche below 10 years of age and 78.4 per cent had between 10 to 19 years, as compared to 92.0 per cent among girls on all-India basis arrived at by the age of consent committee. A significant fact was that among Mongoloid tribes the age of menarche was seen to be earlier.
- Considering age at marriage, the broad observation is that there was a longer gap among tribal women than among others between menarche and motherhood primarily because of late marriage and absence of child marriages. However, in certain tribes like the Korwa, incidence of sterility was high because of ill effects of contact and their barrenness did not entail any social stigma, contrary to the common attitudes among other tribes.

- Majumdar's analysis also goes into the incidence of abortions, which was quite difficult to collect in field inquiries. It could be gathered from 151 women from among the Ho, Korwa and Tharu tribes and the number of women who admitted to have had abortions was 42, while the rest either did not reply or they were unmarried girls. Some women also confided that they were not inclined to have children after the age of 30 years because of their larger participation in the domestic as well as economic pursuits of the family.
- The data on fertility – showing the number of children per completed family, where the last child was about 12 years of age among certain tribes indicate that the fertility of tribal women in India appeared to be higher than that of those outside India (comparisons made between American, Indians and tribes in other parts of the world). A probable reason, which Majumdar attributes, is that the 'influence of contacts has not been as disastrous in India as elsewhere.'
- Some comparisons have also been made on fertility data arrived at in the Census of Assam (1931). It is seen that fertility among the Hill tribes is higher than that of the advanced groups. Majumdar also points out that the ratio of males to females among the tribes is favourable to females, as compared to caste groups.
- Mortality rates in tribal society are higher both among children and adults. Investigations in certain areas have brought to light the phenomenal absence of aged people among the primitive tribes which points out to the fact that high fertility among tribals is offset by a high infant mortality. A comparison of vital index emerging from some data show that 'even the dying Korwas are replacing their deaths and have margin for increase', while the Ho and Tharus have a pretty high vital index.

To sum up, Majumdar says that if we do not want our data to speak more than what they can, the discomforts of tribal life though very real as most ethnographers will agree, have not so far engendered any great crisis, yet it is time that attention were paid to remedy the grievances of the primitive tribes. Most of the discomforts are remediable and it is probably true that many of these have been brought about in recent years, with the increase of contacts of the tribal people with the 'so-called civilization'. The future tribal policy must take the related demographic knowledge into account as otherwise even a protective system of administration may lead to their maladaptation, even their exit.

The second lecture connected with demography is on 'Problems of Population'. It begins with some general comments on the high rates of growth of population, particularly in Asian countries. In India, the disparity between the distributions of population is noticeable and it may be traced to physiographic factors. He goes on to describe how the climate and environment in a particular area determine its productivity by way of food and the resultant higher density of population. Briefly, he goes into the controversy of how fertility goes down with a general rise of standards of living and the other view that when density of population increases and avenues for economic cooperation expand there is a rapid growth of population, till it reaches an asymptotic level beyond which there is no apparent increase.

In the Indian context, the increase in population has been fast since 1931. Earlier, the census figure from 1881 onwards indicates an irregular increase. Every alternate decade recorded a heavy rise in population, followed by a slowing down in the next. The next issue discussed, a very significant feature of any demographic analysis, is the question of quality versus quantity in population and there is also the issue of political situation.

Since fertility has been negatively co-related with social status, this differential fertility causes great social concern. It has meant that any country having a large section of less integrated population finds them with least survival value. In India this situation has lead to the extinction of tribal communities in India. This differential rate is also seen as a result of caste hierarchy. Further, the sex ratio also differs from caste to caste and it is seen that the ratio of women to men among tribals and lower castes is better than the higher castes. Another factor which contributes to this state is a higher mortality of male children at different periods from conception to birth. Majumdar underlines the problem of a healthy and fit population in a country like India where the poorer sections are phenomenally prolific. Analysing the trend of migration historically, Majumdar points out that in the earlier days, migrations were caused by climatic changes and the flow of people was to the areas with better climate and geographical conditions. But today, it is the political and economic controls that regulate migration and hence people go to a place with better avenues. Here, Majumdar, in a prescient way, brings up the problem of heavy migrations from certain districts of eastern Bengal to at least three districts of Assam. The migrants were mostly Muslim peasants who had been attracted to Assam due to its fertile land yielding luxuriant crops of jute and rice. The prosperity that the migrant peasants enjoy also facilitates polygyny and a clear population growth results.

In this context, there is some discussion on practices connected with hypergamy and how it has introduced great complications in marriage and family life in Bengal. For instance, it also leads to female infanticide and the neglect of female children is historical. Kulinism, which has lad to many complications was an exotic institution placed on the soil of Bengal by a ruling king due to his regard for racial purity. In the case of Kulinism and its social and economic implications, Majumdar also discusses another socio-economic problem of Bengal, viz., that of Bhadralog and how the rise of this class of educated middle class has resulted in the neglect of education and other facilities and flow of economic resources to the agricultural communities in Bengal and the resultants backwardness. He also traces the problems connected with dowry to the rise of Bhadralog.

Majumdar complains that the quality of demographic conditions cannot be improved without collection of comprehensive data relative to people with favourable health conditions and emphasizes the need for 'biological education regarding the inheritance of mental and physical characters for the people at large'. The need for collection of data about various kinds of handicapped persons in the course of census or sample surveys has also been highlighted here. Thus, Majumdar in the course of these writings raises issues, gives warnings and expresses concern for different sections of tribes and castes and for the country as a whole. The colonial administration had constantly neglected these in their census operations as they had no process of planning, which cannot be undertaken in the absence of data.

Folklore Studies

Folklore forms an important area of anthropological and sociological studies. It includes different forms of verbal art such as folklores, myth, legend, folk songs, proverbs and riddles and folk art, crafts, customs, medicine, recipes, games, dance, mimicry, speech, etc. As a branch of study, folklore was till recently recognized as a part of Indology, in India. In fact, even the term 'folklore' was systematically used for the first time by W.J. Thomas, a British antiquarian, in 1846 as till then scholarly works on material of folklorist nature was being carried on under various labels such as popular literature (Vidyarthi I., 1976: 331).

As the Asiatic Society of Bengal was founded mainly to pursue studies and research in Indology, its journal established in 1774 became initially the medium for publications in this branch of knowledge, as well. But, *Indian Antiquary*, the Journal of the Anthropological Society of Bombay which started publication in 1886 gave maximum support to folklore. S.C. Mitra, the eminent folklorist started publishing on a variety of topics connected with folklore in *The Journal of the Asiatic Society of Bengal*, quarterly journal of the Mythic Society, *Journal of Bihar and Orissa Research Society* and also *Man in India* after its start in 1921. Mitra worked mainly in Chota Nagpur during a long period from 1890s to mid-1930s. It is notable that his documentation not only covers the different streams of folklore but also the entire geographical area from the tribal areas of Chota Nagpur to rural areas of Bengal, as well as the individual tribes in Chhota Nagpur, Orissa and Bengal.

Majumdar's interest in and study of the anthropological significance of folklore, particularly tribal folklore, had its source in the writings of Roy and also L.K. Anathakrishna Iyer. Dasgupta (2007: 140) mentions that Roy's objectives in establishing *Man in India* included the study of folklore. Advocating a common global endeavour among anthropologists towards the development of folklore studies and significance of anthropology, Roy stated:

> A systematic and classified collection and careful recording of different classes of Folklore material, district by district, taluque by taluque, and thana area by thana area or pargana area by pargana area as is being done for the country areas in England, and for other local areas in other parts of Europe and in America, is the first and most imperative task awaits students of Indian Folklore (Roy, 1933: 311).

Iyer's lectures on ethnography in the Calcutta University also referred to the importance of folklore and details of beliefs and customs collected through direct fieldwork. The comprehensive ethnographic studies being made in Assam and Bengal had already contributed richly to this kind of literature and the province-wise compilation on castes and tribes also included folklore, myths connected with religious beliefs, origins, etc., proverbs and other similar material. Roy's ethnography on the Munda (1912: 317–56) documents the folktales, riddles and proverbs as well as their songs. It also highlights how an ordinary Munda's instruction and the knowledge of his culture comes from this source. The time in the youth dormitory is spent in memorizing, and learning through, this oral material. The songs documented by Roy have been analysed for their contents and educative value in the everyday life and aesthetics of the Munda.

Majumdar's ethnography on the Ho through his various papers and the two books (60: 1937; 131: 1950) contains some significant material on folklore highlighting their functional place in Ho culture. He has discussed the games played by the children and their riddles. Further, he has also narrated the legends connected with the origins of the Ho *killis*. Among the Ho songs, he has highlighted how these reflect their values as seen in some notable patterns in Ho behaviour. Some of them are their hospitality (60: 1937: 81–82), pride in their own culture (96: 1946: x–xi), festivals (131: 1950: 216–17) and the need for keeping themselves aloof from the Dikus (60: 1937: 113–14). Recent additions to the folk-songs through the compositions of school teachers and students also underline nationalist sentiment (60: 1937: 18). He has also analysed the actual incantations that the tribal priests mumble in their ritualistic performance, in order to point out how these texts address, 'Dessauli, which represent the ex-supernatural power of their habitat ... villages ... .' (79: 1940: 72–73). *A Tribe in Transition* (1937) contains selective material on folklore. In the revised and enlarged version of this monograph, *The Affairs of A Tribe* (1950), the inclusion of such material was enhanced with an appendix on folktales and correlating certain values in the Ho culture to their traditional folksongs and folktales. It may be added that Roy's monograph on the Munda too had appendices on Munda legendary history and legends of origin.

The most significant step in Majumdar's contributions to the study of folklore was his plan to publish folk songs, tales, etc. from different regions of UP and adjoining MP and assuming the general editorship of this series of publications, entitled, *Folk Culture Series*. The first volume thereof entitled, *The Snow Balls of Garhwal* was published in 1946.

Earlier in 1945, Majumdar had founded the Ethnographic and Folk Culture Society at Lucknow. This cultural society born in obscurity later attracted attention and larger participation which facilitated the publication of the 'Folk Culture Series' and other similar publications. In 1947 he had also founded a quarterly journal, *The Eastern Anthropologist*, and the first few issues of this journal contain rich material on folk songs and other forms of folk literature from different regions of UP and, also the Bhil of Gujarat by T.B. Naik, one of his students. Naik subsequently contributed richly to the documentation of folk songs, etc. as Director of the Tribal Research Institute, Chhindwara (Madhya Pradesh). He also produced gramophone records on tribal music.

In an introductory essay, 'The malaise of culture', included in the first volume of the series, Majumdar comments that the 'study of ethnology and ethnography which includes folk culture as well has not yet received recognition ... and not filtered into the curricula of university courses in northern India'. Further, he highlights how folk songs, folk art, folk ways and mores represent the mechanism of cultural control and ensures submissions to the values and pattern of the society concerned. He has illustrated this with examples from the songs of Dube's collection from Chhatisgarh and his own from the Ho of Kolhan. Dube's *Field Songs of Chhatisgarh* (1947) came as the second volume in the series. In this volume, Majumdar's introductory essay, 'The United Provinces: A Cultural Mosaic', discusses five points which in his opinion are requisites of a field investigator going into a field to study folk culture. Here, Majumdar was offering guidelines on 'how to make amateur collecting, more effective' and difficulties encountered by the folklorists continually. Such issues were also raised by Thompson (1953: 579) at the Wenner-Gren Symposium in New York.

Vidyarthi (1978) has presented a comprehensive review of folklore researches in India. His survey almost exhaustively takes into account the writings on both tribal and rural folklore from different states and regions and also under the various themes of folklore. Vidyarthi has also taken into account, by and large, the efforts for compilations of folk songs, folktales, etc. in English as well as in Hindi and other regional languages. Later on some scholarly work with theoretical interpretation was done by Indra Deva, one of Majumdar's students and published in *The Eastern Anthropologist* and elsewhere (Deva, 1956; 1966: 350–64; 1978: 375–88; 1989). Broadly speaking, if we analyse his survey the observations that emerge in the perspective of Majumdar's contributions to this field are that in the north India, Majumdar initiated publications in this branch on a systematic scale in mid-1940s. With the founding of EFCS and *The Eastern Anthropologist* he brought into focus the rich folklore literature of the Himalayan areas as well. This work was done enthusiastically by several of his students from these areas. One of them took up his doctoral work[1] under Majumdar. The folk and tribal traditions from Eastern Uttar Pradesh, Bundelkhand and Kaimur Hills (Duddhi) also became the points of focus. He was able to inspire a number of his students and associates, the evidence of which we can seen in the publications sponsored by the Ethnographic and Folk Culture Society and contents of its journals.

The later 1930s perhaps saw the publications of folk songs in Hindi and other regional languages, mainly Hindi. Most of these were from Rajasthan where earlier work in this area had been done by William Todd in the 19th century. In the early 1940s, Verrier Elwin had started his work in the Maikal Hills and published his folktales of Mahakosal in 1954 to be followed by a long series of folklore collected from a number of tribes in Madhya Pradesh and Orissa. W.G. Acher also started his distinguished chain of publications in this branch of ethnography.

Physical Anthropology

Majumdar belonged to the first generation of trained anthropologists in India and hence the major part of his works were of a pioneering nature. He has been called a 'general anthropologist' and one can even say that he was a general anthropologist par excellence because his contributions to both of these major branches of anthropology were substantial and also multi-dimensional. Since, this work is mainly concerned with Majumdar's contributions to social or cultural anthropology, this chapter will deal only broadly with his physical anthropology. And, his work was considered to be quite significant in this branch by no less an authority than Penniman, as follows:

> An active centre for physical anthropology has arisen in India (see Majumdar), where notable work has been done in connexion with the census (Guha, 1935; Mahalonobis et al., 1949), and from where important contributions to anthropological statistical theory have come (Mahalonobis et al., 1949; Rao, 1948). A journal of vigour– *The Eastern Anthropologist*– is now appearing. (Penniman, 1935: 401).

Thus, 'general anthropology was not a mere slogan for Majumdar, it reflected his firm conviction' that a unified science of man was possible and racial factors obtained through anthropometry and somatometry could explicate socio-cultural situations. To quote Madan, in his writings in *Races and Cultures* (and also *Matrix*):

> We meet Majumdar the 'general' anthropologist, analyzing data about social reality in terms of an interactionist paradigm, as it were; put otherwise, he uses physical and cultural anthropological data to produce an integrated understanding of the social reality. The focus here has been broadened to include both tribes and castes; the data are anthropometric, serological, and cultural. The populations/communities investigated are castes and tribes of the then United Provinces and the Gujarat region of what was the Bombay province. (Madan, 2013: 230)

Majumdar himself strongly felt that defining precisely the racial background of cultural life and assessment of the respective roles of race and environment was essential and the study of physical factors was not simply meant for a chronological study of human origins. In India, racial studies, not adequately scientific though, had been used for perpetuating social incompetence or social distances and, therefore:

> In any case a simple presentation of certain aspects of the biological evidence could be usefully employed to discourage false caste claims in India, while the facts of human biology will certainly mitigate caste and communal antagonism as well as untouchability if this biological evidence is widely disseminated among the masses. (91: 1944: ix)

Majumdar initiated his researches during the period 'when only a few anthropologists existed in India'. By and large, during this period, descriptive aspects played a dominant role but Majumdar, according to R.D. Singh:

> As he proceeded, he incorporated into his interpretations the interplay of the biologic, the social and the evolutionary factors in operation. In general, two perspectives seem to emerge: one, that Majumdar's work was of a traditional

> style physical anthropology, and two, that within that traditional style there were some fundamental but powerful sparks of a very significant kind which seriously kindled the enthusiasm of his contemporary colleagues, his students, and even his rivals. In my assessment the two are codependent, where the former provides the basic foundation and the latter the emergence, the growth and new directions that bloomed into areas like human physical growth, medical, environmental adaptation, evolutionary, demographic epidemiology and the like. (Singh, 1999: 302)

As pointed out by Singh, Majumdar's contributions lay in several important physical anthropological researches of his times. We may, therefore, discuss briefly the most important such studies.

About 125 years ago, when physical anthropology made its debut in India, it started with anthropometric studies encouraged by the colonial rulers. Its main focus was directed towards the understanding of physical body variations in human populations. It intended to give metric expressions to the descriptive observations contained in various accounts relating to Indian populations. During his stay in Cambridge for his doctoral work, Majumdar also trained under G.M. Morant, one of the most prominent physical anthropologist of those times which updated him in the techniques of anthropometric and somatometric studies. Morant's significant contributions were in the field not only of measuring variations in human populations but also the evolutionary gradations of pre-historic skeletal remains. Moreover, he, along with a few others, had also contributed 'much to counter this (Fascist) abuse of anthropology'. He gave this 'contentious' issue in both its biological and ethnic aspects', the most serious examinations during late 1930s (Weiner, 378, 407). It is seen that Majumdar was greatly influenced by these studies of Morant. We find frequent references to this kind of pseudo scientific misuse of racial anthromorphology by the Fascist governments in his writings.

The study of the Kolerian tribes of Chhota Nagpur, particularly Ho which was initiated by Majumdar some time in 1923, had included anthropometric studies (4: 1924; 9AA, 15: 1925; 24: 1926). However, by the end of 1920s, we find Majumdar trying to examine the racial implication, if any, in environmental and cultural adaptability of a tribe (Korwa) and its likely demographic impact (30: 1929). Later in 1930s, Majumdar had engaged himself in the study of UP tribals, and ex-criminal tribes which had a large presence in this province. Two papers also explore the relationship between language and racial affinities of the Austric speaking tribes of India, on the basis of anthropometric data (70: 1938). In this very paper, he also raised the question of exactitude and accuracy in obtaining anthropometric measurements so as to ensure meaningful comparison and in this context touched two very thorny issues connected with details of techniques and samplings in B.S. Guha's anthropometric work for the 1931 Census, and his analysis of the racial composition of India to include a substratum of Negrito elements in the Indian population. He had also expanded his study of physical characters to the identification of blood groups (77: 1940; 83: 1941) and their distribution among different castes in the United Provinces.

But, his major breakthrough was made possible when M.W.M. Yeatts, Census Commissioner of India for 1941 Census invited him to conduct an anthropometric survey of UP, the importance of this offer was:

> Under the terms that he would provide detailed descriptions of the anthropometric techniques used in measuring the subjects; and he readily agreed to do so.
>
> The significance of this condition lay in the fact that most of the earlier researchers in India had neither given elaborate details of the techniques employed in their measurements nor had they provided the definitions of landmarks they used. Only casual remarks were made on the procedures. Problems were also seen in the method of collecting samples. Yeatts (Mahalonobis et al., 1949) wanted an unbiased sample and aimed at conclusions based on the theory of probability. To meet these objectives Majumdar collaborated with Mahalonobis. This collaboration was to expose his data and methodology to a thorough scrutiny by a person no less than Mahalonobis. He was so confident of his techniques and committed to the cause that he accepted a challenge which none of the previous Indian physical anthropologists had faced. He sincerely believed that anthropometric techniques are essentially not only a matter of training, i.e., a simple mechanical procedure, but that they requisite ability, understanding, application, experience and sound trained judgment, and its procedures demand full comprehension and long practice. (Singh, 1999: 303–04)

The UP survey was solely conducted by Majumdar with some assistance from his student volunteers and government officials. In order to subject the data to the statistical approach developed by Mahalonobis, Majumdar made a choice for definitive characters which could more easily be expressed in mathematical numbers so that there could be no room for subjective judgment. Moreover, while taking measurements, the people who assisted him, were also expected to ask for rechecking of the measurements. Furthermore, in spite of the availability of standard charts, he eliminated the use of data on skin colour, hair or eye colour because he felt that these characteristics could be misread because of the influence of the country's tropical climate, brilliant sunlight and a mass of people going bare bodied to variable extent. Singh (1999: 304) observes that such 'reservations were the first to be voiced and emphasized in this context, whereas some other contemporaries had only advocated for them un-reservedly' without realizing how the climate and socio-economic conditions of the area in which the survey was being conducted, affected these characteristics.

Thus, in his offer to collaborate with Mahalonobis in the UP survey, in pursuance of the terms set out by the Census Commissioner, Majumdar opted not only for an authentication and statistical scrutiny of his anthropometric data but also for a far more sophisticated technique of statistical analysis as compared to the Pearson's Co-efficient of Racial Likeness (CRL) in use for such analyses earlier which had now been found to have serious weaknesses[2]. The development of the D^2 – Statistic by Mahalonobis may be accounted to, inter alia, his curiosity on the race origin and race mixture. 'Mahalonobis' interest of group divergence was also influenced' by Brijendra Nath Seal's 'Address on Race

Origins', delivered in 1911 (Dasgupta, 1995: 486). Mahalonobis had, therefore, analysed the data on Anglo-Indians of Calcutta, collected by N. Annandale, and:

> This was the first time that data relating to a true biologically mixed population were studied by statistical methods. Mahalonobis was able to develop deeper insight and better grasp in statistical methods through the analysis of this set of data. (ibid.: 1995: 486)

Subsequently, Mahalonobis made an attempt to get more insight into the nature of caste similarities and dissimilarities in terms of broader social and geographical division of the inhabitants of Bengal and its neighbourhood by subjecting Risley's data of the 1891 Census in a long paper (1925). This was followed by Mahalonobis' analysis of Chinese data and Swedish data (Mahalonobis, 1928, 1930). And, 'at least, in 1936, he was able to formulate a distance measure incorporating the correlations between different characters' (Dasgupta, 1995: 495).

As regards the meticulous examination of any anthropometric data by Mahalonobis before analysing it, according to Dasgupta (1995: 490):

> Although Mahalonobis tried to devise suitable statistical methods in order to analyze some given sets of anthropometric data, he did not accept any such set of data without proper scrutiny of field records and possible measurement errors. He used these data only after appropriate corrections. In particular, he examined Risley's data quite rigorously and reconstructed the set (1933, 1934).

Interestingly, it appears from Dasgupta's comprehensive paper on the evolution of D^2 – Statistic of Mahalonobis that the latter never used B.S. Guha's anthropometric data collected during the 1931 Census for his analyses. The first phase of Mahalonobis' work on group divergence and generalized distance measure ended in 1936. He shifted his interest to the 'development and application of statistical methods in relation to various socio-economic issues in India'. However, as Dasgupta observes:

> Later in 1949, Mahalonobis participated in the programme for statistical study of anthropometric survey in the UP in collaboration with D.N. Majumdar and C.R. Rao. Their development and findings came out in Sankhya (1949). This set of anthropometric data was collected in the field survey by D.N. Majumdar in connection with the population census in India in 1941. Anthropometric measurements of about 12 characters for 2836 individuals belonging to 22 castes and tribes in U.P. (a province in India) had been collected.
>
> The generalized distance measure of Mahalonobis was extensively used in this paper ... .
>
> This paper, among other results, presents a clustering method and some methods for selection of characters.
>
> The analysis presented in the paper led to suggest three basic clusters–namely, the Brahmin group, the Artisan group and the Tribal groups, besides some other clusters in between the above basic clusters. (ibid.: 1995: 496)

Race Elements in Uttar Pradesh

The data collected from UP according to Majumdar, indicated:

> The order of social precedence of the principal castes and tribes of Uttar Pradesh begin with the Brahmins at the apex of the social pyramid, the tribal groups at the base, while the various other castes maintain a sliding scale of precedence through marked differences between them in racial features and in serological incidence. The scale which starts with the Brahmin reads as follows: the Brahmin, the Kshattriy-Rajput, the Khattri, the Vaish, the Kayastha, the Ahir, the Kurmi, the Kahar, the Teli, the Chamar, the criminal tribes like the Habura, Sansiya, the Karwal and the Bhantu, and tribal groups, the Oraon, the Chero and the Korwa. (Majumdar, 221: 1967: 67)
>
> On the basis of anthropometry and serology, the racial status of the castes and tribes can be figured out. We have in Uttar Pradesh (1) a long headed and largely fine-nosed type represented by the Brahmin, the Khattri and the Kshattriya, also in some ways, the upper and pedigree Muslims, (2) a long-headed flat-nosed type represented by the tribal elements in Mirzapur, but not the criminal tribes, and (3) an intermediate-headed type with medium to short nose, represented by the Tharu and other Mongoloid elements in Tarai. In the north of UP there is a slight immigrant strain of broad-headed, olive-complexioned people, whose immigration into the state can be dated with precision. The first type is probably Indo-Mediterranean, the second is proto-Australoid, the third is Mongoloid, and the fourth is of Alpine strain.
>
> In spite of what we have said, Uttar Pradesh is largely homogenous in ethnic traits, and although cultural differences exist, and even dialects vary from one part to the other, there can be no doubt that the ethnic frontiers have broken down, and the barriers of culture cannot be too stiff to prevent the people to integrate themselves into a pattern and a type.
>
> Both anthropometry and serology point to a gradual lowering of the racial status from the Brahmins to the aboriginal tribes and the order of social precedence may be said to correspond with the degree of racial purity or hybridization. If the Brahmins, for example, started with a diluted blood, they have succeeded in resisting further dilution more than the other castes, but if they had started with purity, they have maintained it more than the other castes. The Survey showed that the classification of the castes in Uttar Pradesh cannot be absolute and that racial types may not be determined with the existing technique. (ibid.: 71)

Use of Mahalonobis' D^2-Statistic

According to Singh (1999: 305) D^2 statistic indicated a clear pattern in physical appearance into three basic clusters called 'B' consisting of two Brahmin groups, 'A' of four artisan groups, and 'T' of eight tribal groups. Other groups occupied positions between these three main clusters. All put together they formed a main sequence. Four other groups consisting of Bhantus, Habaras, Doms, and Bhils stand out of the main sequence with their individual features. Majumdar went beyond this statistical representation and devised a three-dimensional model to elaborate the intergroup relations and distances. He included several characters in this model. It remained on display in his departmental museum-cum-lab, attracting attention of interested scholars for more than three decades after his demise. This has proved to be a unique display and reflects his genius of imagination. These results clearly indicate that there is no exclusiveness in any caste groups including the Muslim. They form a continuum with minor divergences based on the degree of intensity in following and maintaining the marriage patterns, thus restricting or directing the inflow and outflow of genetic components in various groups. Thus he gave a severe blow, based on scientific evidence, to the divine origin of caste myths and their diversity. Some tribal groups which stood apart from the rest, obviously represented their isolation from the mainstream and thus accentuated distinctive characteristics of their own, *vis-à-vis* others (Singh, 1999: 305).

As a result of the survey of UP and Majumdar's collaboration with Mahalonobis, the latter felt that a similar investigation in 'Bengal would throw some light on the various controversial issues relating to the ethnic composition (of Bengal)'. The survey was conducted in 1945 but its final report was published in 1960 after Majumdar's demise. Subsequently, the Gujarat Research Society invited Majumdar to undertake an anthropometric, health and serological survey of Maha Gujarat or Cultural Gujarat. The report of this survey could, however, be completed by early 1949.

Findings of Maha Gujarat Survey

This survey also included a study of health and nutrition of children and families in Maha Gujarat or Cultural Gujarat which included Kachh and other areas which subsequently came to form parts of the present Gujarat state. The anthropometric measurements for this survey were all taken by Majumdar himself as was the case with UP and Bengal, and the physical measurements covered the same standard characteristics. Its report was published in 1949 and A.R. Sen was its co-author with Majumdar while Kunwar Kishan co-authored the section on serological status (116: 1948–49; 118: 1949; 121: 1949). Its findings in brief are:

> To sum up, the 24 castes and groups can be broadly classified into five compact clusters with Bhil, Bhangi, Bhil and others, on one extreme of the ethnic scale with Parsi and Bhatia on the other. It is gratifying to note that the conclusions emanating from the study of reduced C.R.L. in the preceding pages support to a great extent the results obtained from the study of individual characters.
>
> In fact the above analysis has been useful in supplying some additional information regarding the composition of the various clusters and their relative distances from each other. For instance it has thrown additional light on the patterning of the castes and tribes, Kunbi Pattidar, Sunni Bora, Luhana, Memon, Khoja, Nagar Brahmin, Audich Brahmin, Oswal Jain, Rajput, The sub-clusters formed by the groups (Kunbi Pattidar, Sunni Bora, Luhana, Nagar Brahmin, Audich Brahmin) and (Memon, Khoja), which ultimately go to form

the main cluster– a point on which information was rather incomplete in our study of individual characters.

If we put the clusters in tiers, the Bhil, Bhangi, Bhil and others will form the bed, the Parsi, Bhadela, and Bhatia, the topmost tier, and in between the tiers will be found the rest of the clusters in ascending order, they being (Koli, Artisan, Misc. group I, Macchi-Kharwa), (Kunbi Pattidar, Sunni Bora, Luhana, Memon, Khoja, Nagar Brahmin, Audich Brahmin, Oswal Jain, Rajput), (Mher Wagher, Miana, Rabari). (132: 1950)

As regards the contribution of serological evidence, the report states:

In a way, the serological evidence does not run counter to that provided by anthropometry and even if we have not established correlation between blood groups and anthropometric characters, we have not found our analysis devoid of significance. The scope for further inquiry is amply indicated by our Survey, and we feel that in respect of inter-group and intra-group relationship, the racial and serological investigations have provided the anticipated results. It would be fruitful to study intra-group variations among the castes, high and low, for anthropometry has proved to be an efficient tool in determining race affiliation and distance and with the aid of serology may be expected to unfold further the tangle of race origins. A historical study of race origins would be possible when we have complete data on inter-group and intra-group race relations. (132: 1950)

However, some observations made by Majumdar in the introduction to the report are critical and reflect the liberal perceptive that Majumdar had in the context of cultural dimensions of his work in physical anthropology. He says:

In any case, Gujarat presents a homogeneous population or one tending towards it, and a realignment of the boundaries of Maha Gujarat is likely to help to integrate races and cultures into a people with a past and an enlightened future. On face transpires in the analysis of racial elements in India, and that is that the various cultural regions have assimilated different race elements in a way to obliterate distinctions based on superficial divergences in head form or in the shape of the nose, and what has been possible in a cultural area is equally indicative of the whole of this sub-continent, so that the future of Indian people is, not likely to be controlled by racial expansion but by integration of cultures which have been produced by different races working a common destiny. The untouchability in India and the backwardness of tribal cultures is a transitional phase, perpetuated in the interest of alien invaders or usurpers, and knowledge of race origins and of cultural parallisms will help rather than retard reconstruction and integration. (132: 1950)

The anthropometric data collected in respect of Gujarat, was subjected to both C.R.L. and D^2 – Statistic but the analysis made through the latter method, probably could not be published.

Findings of Bengal Survey

This survey covered 3681 individuals belonging to 67 social groups and 29 districts of undivided Bengal in 1945. The post-war conditions and the possibilities of a partition had created difficult and uncertain conditions specially in the Eastern parts of Bengal but Majumdar did complete his work in spite of the difficulties. Primarily the data was rural and it was elaborately scrutinized checked and verified at the Indian Statistical Institute.

> The analysis of the data demonstrated that regional differences existed within a social group, be it a caste, tribe or a religious group, e.g., the Muslim. This was an important contribution. A second important fact also emerged: that sometimes there was a closer resemblance in characters between different caste groups within a district than between the same caste members residing in different districts. Thus inter-caste similarity and intra-caste variations which had not been noticed and emphasized so far became very important for comparisons. In other words, it became imperative to consider geographic influences, if any, along with the nature of caste in terms of genetic make-up. In other words, terms frequently used like 'Brahmins of Bengal' or the 'Rajputs of Northern India' referred more to generic rather than specific characters. A further analysis of the data also pointed out that the total facial dimension was (and is) subject to increase in the third decade of life and therefore not a suitable dimension for comparative purposes. This dimension is primarily influenced by the growth patterns and their velocities including the teeth. A similar conclusion would emerge in later life when the teeth are reduced in dimensions because of attrition and final loss, but this would be on the negative side. Thus and emphasis on growth patterns and their influence in variations was brought to the fore. In other words the selection of traits for comparative purposes had to be revised.

Majumdar's efforts in the systematic collection of data under strict control and scrutiny, provided a further testing opportunity for Mahalonobis' Generalized Distance (D^2), and it proved to be a useful tool in a wide variety of fields. It also helped to evolve simpler tools to examine broad differences between groups of individuals belonging to widely separated geographical regions (Mahalonobis, in Majumdar and Rao, 1958: iv) (Singh, 1999: 307).

The Negrito in India Particularly its Tribal Population

Majumdar's critique of the anthropometric survey connected with the 1931 Census by Guha and how the Census Commissioner for 1941 Census insisted on authentication of the manner in which anthropometric data was collected by Majumdar has already been discussed. Moreover, the other significant disagreement which was the outcome of Guha's observations of racial affinities of the people of India (Census of India, 1931, Vol. 1, India Part iii-b, Ethnographic Notes). Guha had concluded that the earliest human inhabitants of the Indian peninsula of which any trace survives were Negritoes, an observation shared by Hutton (ibid.: 1946: 2–3). The findings were basically related to the peninsular tribal populations like Kadar, Veddid of Ceylon and Andmanis in Bay of Bengal. Traces of Negrito substratum were also attributed to mainland populations in Bengal and Gujarat and Bhils in Gujarat. This view of the Negrito being the earliest substratum in Indian population 'who must have been displayed or supplemented by the proto-Australoid', was strongly contested by Majumdar on the basis of his surveys in U.P., Gujarat and Bengal as also his analysis of the anthropometric data collected by others. Singh's observations about these views are rather forthright:

> Majumdar loved to accept challenges and got involved in them with enthusiasm and vigour. His critical approach and independent thinking put him straight into the middle of the controversies. His involvement into the critical evaluation of the negrito element as a substratum in the Indian population put him face to face with some of the contemporary physical anthropologies like B.S. Guha, S.S. Sarkar and eminent persons like J.H. Hutton and others who put forward or endorsed that view. He rallied forth the observations from earlier studies and refuted the basic concept, though accepted that here and there a few traits were visible in individuals in certain groups. He basically challenged the efficacy and the nature of data in utter disregard of the presence, the movements and admixture of groups in the ancient populations of the sub-continent. And this challenge he took single handed. In doing so, he did not accept the statistical results blindly, and emphatically remarked that 'the more we study human material on the evidence of osteometry, craniometry or somatometry, the more we are convinced of the need for caution in interpreting the data, while the statistical techniques or tools so far evolved to aid our analysis are not by any means sufficient to resolve our doubts' (Majumdar, 1961: 55). He maintained this view throughout his writings. (Singh, 1999: 308)

Majumdar's survey in Maha Gujarat clearly made him to conclude that the Negrito element could not be a substratum and it was only an admixture primarily in coastal areas where some small colonies of immigrant Abyssian and other African populations could be found.

Later research, it seems, has proved Majumdar to be right. Mukherjee (1996: 45) points out:

> Thus, the hypothesis of widespread Negrito racial affinities in the mainland of India is the weakest link in the chain of Guha's theory of racial history of the people.

Mukherjee has also found fault with certain other genetical arguments (ibid.: 66–67) of Guha and recapitulates Majumdar's contention about the details of the 1931 Census of anthropometric survey as below:

> Guha did not describe the techniques used for taking measurements except that a slight amount of pressure was applied in eight of the measurements. The Commissioner of the next Indian Census of 1941 realized this and insisted that D.N. Mazumdar should provide detailed descriptions of the procedures he would adopt. (Mukherjee, 1996: 55)

Hutton has also in the third edition (1961) of *Caste in India* included some additional information relating to the Kadar's:

> In line 2 of page 3 above I have substituted 'possibly' for the 'probably' of the first two editions .... At the same time it seems to me on purely general grounds

> that the Negrito is unlikely to have been absent the mainland of the Indian peninsula ... and he is visibly present in the Bay of Bengal ... if he was present in India he is likely to have left some traces in the existing population, for man is an incorrigible miscegenator. Of some such physical strain in the Naga Hills, with its many cultural links with Melanesia, I feel confident from personal observations. Since writing the above a team of five physical anthropologists of the University of Calcutta's Anthropological Department have made a detailed physical survey of the Kadar, and conclude that the feature which some anthropologists (including myself) had taken to indicate a Negrito strain are really due to a negro admixture. See *A physical Survey of the Kadar of Kerala*, by S.S. Sarkar, Gautamsankar Ray, M.R. Chakravartti, A.R. Banerjee, and Papia Bhattacharjee, Memoir No. 6 (1959) of the Anthropological Survey of the Government of India. (Hutton, 1961 third edition 3 note)

Majumdar's strong and repeated critique of Guha seems to have generated acrimony in their relations[3].

Human Growth Studies

The extensive anthropometric and somatometric surveys conducted by Majumdar and the group-focused statistical analysis inspired Majumdar to consider the cultural conditioners, apart from solely racial or physical factors, like diet, nutrition, etc. to the metabolism, health conditions and growth of children among different groups of Indian population. His considered observation was that:

> The health of a nation is not merely a nutritional problem, but it is also anthropological. The anatomical, physiological and pathological conditions of cultural groups come under the scope of anthropological studies, as intimate relations have been found to exist between racial and cultural influences, and problems of growth and hygiene. Racial and cultural influences determine in certain ways the form and function of the body and although individual differences may not be significant in the context of national health, the range of variations in form and function in individuals constituting a social group, is an important field of investigation and has to be pursued with meticulous care. Besides the problems of national health and eugenic programmes must be broadly based on such objective data. (143: 1951–52: 1)

Thus, from Majumdar's point of view a physical anthropological approach was necessary but such studies had never been made in India though in other countries such studies had been undertaken much earlier. He also noticed that a few studies of the status of children's health and nutrition had been undertaken by the pediatricians. Therefore, he took an initiative to secure financial help from the Government of Uttar Pradesh for the study of 'the problems of growth of children' from the anthropological point of view as one of his permanent programmes of research. The paper referred to above was a part of the outcome of this study.

Earlier he had concretized his interest in the research in this field by making a very limited study among 104 Ho school children (124: 1949) and health conditions among the castes and tribes of Gujarat as a part of his survey of cultural Gujarat. The latter study had appeared in co-authorship with S. Bahadur (123: 1949). In Gujarat, he had analysed the Basal Metabolic Rate (BMR) of different castes and tribes in order to assess their health conditions. Very briefly the findings were:

> On the basis of the classification of the social groups at various ages with respect to B.M.R. we find the Bhatia, the Bhadela and the Luhana come at the top, with Audich Brahmin, Nagar Brahmins, Oswal Jain, Rajput, Kudbi Pattidar occupying an intermediate status, while the Koli, artisans, Miscellaneous, Macchli-Kharwa, and Bhangi are at the bottom. (123: 1949: 120)

The study of Ho school children was not, however, conducted through single sampled measured ones and could not therefore indicate growth. However, his culturally significant conclusion was:

> All that we attempt here is to find out the nature of the growth curve among the Ho boys from a single sample measured once. It is interesting to note that there is a gradual increase in weight and stature in the early ages and this increase becomes quick and rapid as we move from the age of ten upward, as will be evident from Table III. The increase in weight must be proportional to increase of stature, as it should be, unless there is something impeding the process of growth as for example, when fat accumulates without any corresponding increase in stature or a boy gets taller and taller hence thinner and thinner with no simultaneous increase of flesh on the bones. The rapidity of growth after the 10 year age stage may be explained in view of the fact that a Ho child is normally well cared for and at this age, children particularly boys go along with their parents to fields and forests and help themselves with the produce of the forests, fruits and roots in abundance, and the game from the chase. (124: 1949: 202)

The Lucknow study was far more comprehensively oriented to growth. It was sampled randomly and covered children in various schools from different social groups studying in no less than five educational institutions. The main conclusions of the study were:

1. Though there is a constant increase in the body measurements even from the early childhood, the rate of increase remains considerably slow up to the age of 13 or 14 years.
2. After 14 years of age, there is a marked acceleration– the body measurements show a marked increase.
3. The rate seems to be most accelerated during the age period of 16 years to 18 years.
4. After 18 years the rate of physical development is up to slowed down and we find that the increase continues to some extent up to the age of 20, but, afterwards, the attained growth is maintained with no further increase.
5. The growth of certain parts of the body stops even at earlier stages.
6. The effect of heredity has also been reflected from the present analysis. The Shia students measured at Husainabad School, show marked superiority.

> They have a fair complexion, long and thick bones, fine nose, long face and tall stature. Their diet contains more of meat but less of milk and milk products, while the students of the Kurmi Pathshala, who came from low class manual labourer, have short stature and retarded physical growth. (143A: 1951–52: 16)

According to Singh (1999: 309):

> Two observations, among many, were of significance and in consonance with later observations on secular trends in growth spurt during the adolescent period reported by Satyanarayana with others (1980). These were: 1) that all parts of the body do not grow at the same rate and at the same time, and 2) that hereditary and dietary factors do affect stature, bone growth and some facial features (Majumdar and Bahadur, 1951). This again was a step ahead of his times. The height and weight studies fall in the routine category of researches, but cross-sectional studies on growth patterns of some body components was another field where the contributed and drew attention toward an important area for research. His overall contributions– the challenges thrown to him and interpretations offered by him– prompted further studies and attracted many interested and competent physical anthropologists to carry out further researches in this field.

The aims of this study was further recognized in mid-1950s by the Indian Council of Medical Research. The Council proposed an ambitious growth study programme on children, covering several studies under Majumdar's supervision. Majumdar associated P.C. Biswas, Professor and Head, Department of Anthropology, University of Delhi, with this study and functioned as its director till his demise in May 1960. Therefore, the completion of the study was long delayed and its report(s) were published much later.

Singh (1999: 310) is critical of one aspect of Majumdar's research efforts in this field:

> His choice of only traditionally favoured cranio-facial characters in all of his anthropometric studies including the growth studies, is beyond discernment. More so, when he was aware of the facts of growth processes and trends, and an addition of a few other measurements of body segments would not have made much dent on time and effort ... the science of anthropometry lost a wonderful opportunity to add some valuable data to its armory at a fraction of the cost involved.

Serology, Environment and Health

Weiner (1935: 376–77) describes the discovery of new blood group gene systems for analysis of racial affinity as having far reaching results in the existing reinterpretation of the conceptions and classifications of race. These discoveries could shed a new light on racial mixture and the conditions of isolated groups. Thus, there were possibilities of the pertinence and feasibility of investigations of bodily fitness, nutritional status and climatic adaptation in either a biotic or social context. Majumdar did not lag behind in this field and in the early 30s, initiated studies in blood group distribution in Indian castes and tribes. A mention has already been made how he conducted serological tests on a large scale during his surveys in UP, Gujarat, and Bengal. His data for these provinces runs into dozens of tribal and caste groups with a total sample of several thousands with each community represented by a sample of one to two hundred mark. In fact, his serological researches point in various directions. According to Singh (1999: 311):

(i) He did not accept the traditional views on caste origins and their static nature, and challenged it on the basis of scientific evidence.
(ii) He considered various population groups in India as a part of a continuum with highly overlapping traits and suggesting.
(iii) Group mobility, vertical and/or horizontal was a factor to be seriously considered and finally.
(iv) Genetic isolation through endogamy in various degrees in groups, producing various identifiable characters in different environmental settings and later being incorporated by others, needed to be taken into consideration as well. He suggested that adoption and variation were subject to various factors involved into the formation of population groups over a period of time.

Basing his comments on serological as well as other criteria like anthropometry and serological data, he firmly concluded that 'our knowledge of purity or mixture of various ethnic groups is not sufficient'. And, therefore, Singh observes:

> Although elsewhere he tried to give a definition to the terms caste and tribe, but while discussing the anthropometric and serological data from Bengal he openly admitted that 'We have no definite connotation of word caste, or tribe, at what point a tribe ceases to be a tribe, at what point an inbreeding group becomes outbreeding, or splits up into smaller endogamous units ...' (1958: 115). In other words he leans towards the idea that most population groups have porous boundaries, a fact which anthropological demographers have come to realize of late. (Singh, 1999: 311)

Significantly, he also observed and emphasized, in the course of this study of the distribution of A and B blood groups:

> A high B percentage existed among the social groups– castes and tribes– who are 'exposed to unhealthy and inhospitable regions or are habitual victims of malaria.' (1961: 97). It was obvious from the scrutiny of the data from U.P. collected in the 1940s. This emphasis focused attention towards a systematic study of the association between the blood group B, sicklemia and malaria in India. (Singh, 1999: 312)

Writing about blood groups of castes and tribes of Bengal (1960) he pointedly observes:

> During the past 20 years studies have been made of the distribution of the blood groups in practically all the races of the world. In India much work has

> been done and more is on the way. A correlation table of blood groups and somatometric traits, indicates great possibility. Studies have been made of the ethnic elements in various parts of India, and we have blood maps and distribution maps of the various anthropometric characters. This gives us hope for the future. If the racial basis of the social structure is not important or significant, the genetic status of ethnic communities, castes or social groups, will be important information in the context of our national health and control of diseases and cacogenics. (111: 1960)

Thus, Majumdar initiated some exploration into the cacogenics in respect of communities which could be a prey to certain specific diseases.

Rupkund Explorations

Elsewhere, Majumdar's two trips to the lake of Rupkund at a height of 18,000 ft in Garhwal has been described. This arduous climb was taken up by him when he was almost 55 years of age. During the second trip, he collected a large quantity of material. R.D. Singh, who was one of the six persons accompanying him, makes the following observations about the expedition:

> The Rupkund material is one of the largest series of skeletal material in India, and has rich potential for further research and interpretation in terms of historical, socio-cultural and palaeopathological perspectives. He very much realized its potential and wanted more time and opportunity to work further on it. However, pressed for time and resources he could visualize the difficulties and intended to release a report on the data, seriously anthropological in nature. Unfortunately a full report could not be published because of his sudden demise in 1960 .... In this last venture he did not hesitate to approach persons like J.B. Griffin, the then Director of the Museum of Anthropology, and M.R. Cane of the Radio Carbon Laboratory, Ann Arbor, Michigan, USA. In a way, with added experience he grew fond of collaboration and stated that it 'can be secured without a big dent to the vanity of the anthropologist' (1958: 93). His efforts to collaborate are indicative of a devotion to the cause of the science greater than any of his contemporary Indian physical anthropologists had shown on an individual basis (Singh, 1997). (Singh, 1999: 313–14)

Notes

1. Probably he did not complete it as he joined politics and was later a minister in UP (96: 1946: 20–87). He was also instrumental in involving Majumdar in the Rupkund investigations.
2. Much was once hoped from Pearson's 'Coefficient of Racial Likeness' as a statistical device for expressing, by reference to a number of characters considered together, the degree of affinity between different groups. Serious weaknesses in the coefficient have been pointed out both in its theory and its use (Fisher, 1936; Seltzer, 1937). Recently, in Mahalonobis's 'Generalized Distance Statistic', a greatly improved method for making such group comparisons has become available and has been applied in a number of studies (Mahalonobis, Majumdar, and Rao, 1949; Trevor, 1947) (Penniman, 1935: 397).

3. Incidentally, a very senior anthropologist who is no more, commented to me in a personal discussion about two years ago that the history of anthropology in India might have vastly changed, had Majumdar been selected as Professor and Head of the newly created Department of Anthropology in the Delhi University in 1948. But, Guha as an expert had his role in getting him rejected. Another retired faculty member and one of the earliest students of this department, subsequently in the course of a personal discussion made an addition. His perception was that at the time of this selection, Guha was interested in ensuring some place for himself in this department after his retirement from the Anthropological Survey of India. Therefore, he selected a person who had the reputation of being an easier and compliant personality as compared to Majumdar. However, this person also at the opportune stage ensured that Guha would not join the Department at Delhi University in any capacity.

Map Showing Areas of Majumdar's Research

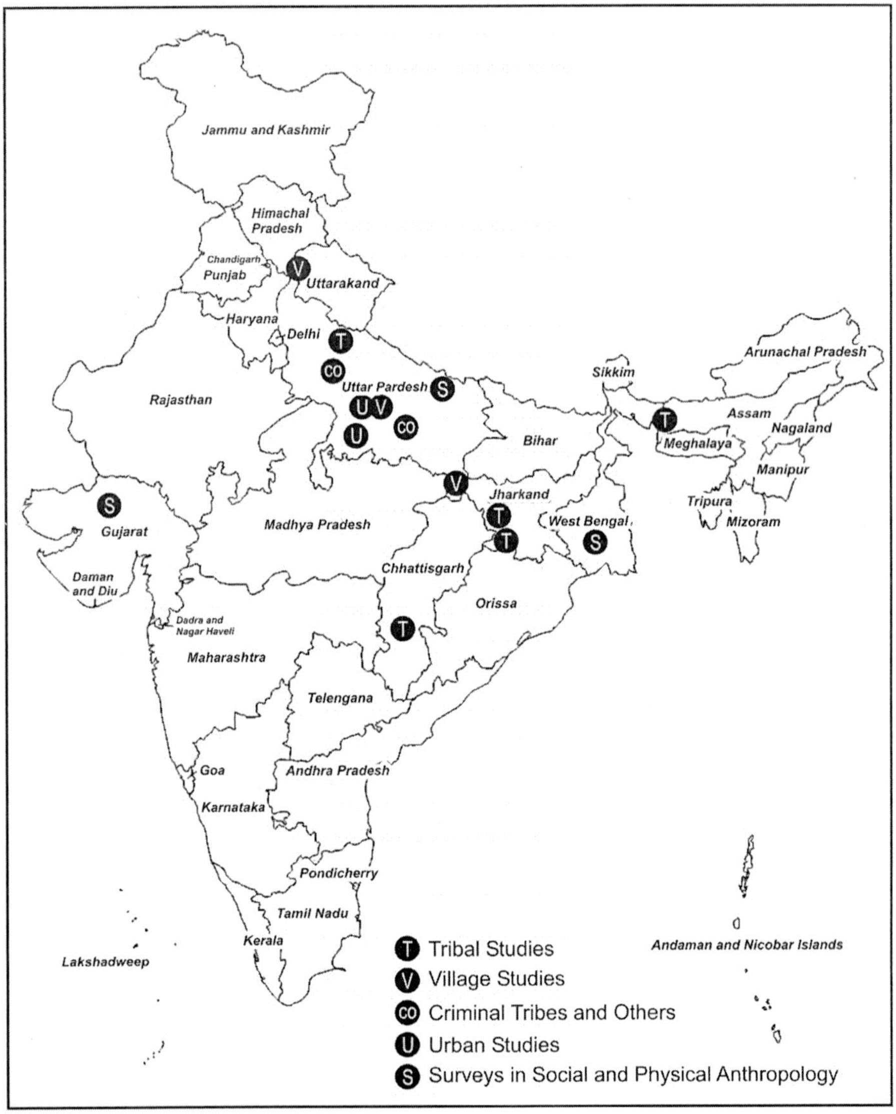

12

Majumdar's Academic Journey in the Perspective of Sociology of Knowledge

Contributors to the sociology of knowledge have almost universally emphasized and demonstrated how the developments and narratives of sociological studies are embedded in the social, economic and even physical environment of their times. These focii also, to a great extent, spell out the themes they investigate or analyse and also their theoretical and methodological approaches as human beings themselves cannot think and act in vacuum and the ordinary human beings cannot transcend these barriers imposed on human behaviour. But, often ideas for change and modifications are emanated by some outstanding individuals. This is true about the ideas in behavioural, ideological and academics as well. For instance, the emphasis on urban sociology, and widely based investigations and studies in the USA, and even the development of case study method and related statistical methods were responses to the problems of delinquency, crime, economic tensions and the resultant social environment created by the influx of migrants and their location in certain urban centres. Similarly, the development of French Sociological School had its matrices in the strife and civilian unrest rooted in the religious and political movements.

When we look at Indian Sociology, the earliest writings such as that of G.S. Ghurye, Radhakamal Mukerjee and D.P. Mukerji are an attempt to focus on providing sociological interpretation of the classical and historical past of India as reflected in the texts and scriptures and identifying the changes through empirical or earlier studies of situations obtaining in the society. Clinard who was associated with the Ford Foundation in India, and Elder (1965: 583) have in their paper offered a rather detailed viewpoint on the progress of sociology in India in the context of sociology of knowledge. They observe that 'prominent Indian sociologists have chosen to reject the western assumptions' in favour of classical, Indian assumptions. And, the authors base their observations on the thrust of the Presidential Addresses of Majumdar, Mukerji, Saksena and

Mukerjee to the All India Sociological Conferences in the 1950s, and how there is emphasis on the use of historical religious material to understand the present.

However, Clinard and Elder comment that Indian sociologists have chosen to reject the Western assessment was not true even much later. Dube (1977: 10), in his Presidential Address to the Indian Sociological Conference 1976, focuses on the 'implantation of Indian data of categories of analyses successfully employed elsewhere as the cause for confusion'. Singh (1973: 22) points out that 'historically, the building complex both of social anthropology and sociology in India are derived from the Western colonial interpretation of the Indian society which has contributed towards exaggerating the segmentary and pluralistic foci of the Indian Society at the cost of integrative ... '. The observation regarding colonial or western categories has been particularly emphasized for the category of 'tribe' in India detached from the larger civilization context'. Explicating its implications Singh (ibid.: 22–23) argues:

> Thus, colonialism historically conditioned the paradigms of the Indian social science by making its conceptual frame-work fragmentary and non-systemic. For instance, the tendency to conduct studies of tribes as distinct entities, unrelated to the structures of caste, of villages unrelated to urban centres, and of communities independent of the national society became more and more pronounced in Indian sociology. This dominated not only the academic field but deeply influenced also the tribal and other social policies of the government. By such conceptual and substantive fragmentation, Indian social science was further alienated from the dynamics of Indian society and deprived of the stimulus for an innovative élan.

In the background of sociology and anthropology, it may be observed that their origins 'go back to the days when British officials discovered that knowledge of Indian culture and social life was indispensable to the smooth functioning of government' (Srinivas and Panini, 1973). Efforts in this direction were initiated around 1770s. However, the first all India Census of 1871 was the formal new institution, 'for collecting vast quantity of information and the first Census of the 20th century, 1901 under Risley, established an ethnographic survey as a part of census. Earlier in 1787, the British Orientalist, Sir William Jones established The Asiatic Society of Bengal and 'one of the main activities of the Society was the publication of a journal devoted to antiquarian and anthropological interest' (ibid.: 1973). The foundation of teaching in both sociology and anthropology, including social anthropology, came about almost simultaneously in the universities of Bombay and Calcutta, creating the Department of Sociology and Civics and the Department of Anthropology and Ancient Indian History in 1919, respectively. Calcutta had a post-graduate course in Economics and Sociology as early as 1908, and Radhakamal Mukerjee who brought Majumdar to the University of Lucknow, Department of Economics and Sociology, was from its first batch (Madan, 2011: 120). Even in mid-1970s Dube (ibid.: 11) critically observes that:

> Consider the meaningless quarrel over the respective spheres and importance of sociology and social anthropology in India. Consider also the deliberate

severance of connection between sociology and social anthropology on the one hand and history and Indology on the other. How much more meaningful the notions of sanskritization and dominant caste would have been, had they had historically specificity and depth.

He further pleads for cleansing of thought ways and work ways of the colonial virus and further 'encouraging interdisciplinary dialogue and collaboration'.

The academic background and development and progress of Majumdar's academic work at Lucknow where he worked throughout his life has to be considered in the context that he joined at Lucknow in the newly founded Department of Economics and Sociology. The founder of this department, Radhakamal Mukerjee, had the wide vision of an interdisciplinary approach through the inclusion of a formally trained anthropologist teaching the 'primitive dimensions of institutional economics as also the Indian sociological panorama, thereby enriching a more comprehensive analyses. Majumdar was subsequently able to expand this small area of inclusion of social anthropology in the syllabi of economics to a full-fledged group of papers on offer to post-graduate students. However, his training at Calcutta and subsequently at Cambridge and London had also equipped him as a 'general anthropologist'.

Majumdar had gone to Cambridge in 1933 and he was admitted to the Degree of Doctor of Philosophy in the University in 1935. His thesis entitled, 'A Changing Austric Culture' was submitted in May 1935 in the Faculty of Archaeology and Anthropology in the University, under T.C. Hodson's guidance. His seven examiners included M.C. Burkitt who had been working in the field of pre-historic archaeology in India. In 1935, he was the only Indian to get this distinction (Cambridge, 1935: 267 and 809). In addition to his doctoral work in social anthropology, Majumdar also studied 'physical anthropology with Professor G.M. Morant, serology with Professor R. Ruggles Gates and worked in the Galton Laboratory, London' (Madan and Sarana, 1962: 11). 'Galton had founded the study of Eugenics and also experimental psychology and he and Karl Pearson applied statistical method to its study' (Penniman, 1952: 137–39). Thus, Galton had contributed to the development of modern sociology as well. Majumdar had also attended Malinowski's seminars at the London School of Economics along with several other students including Prince Peter of Greece (Peter, 1963: 166). He was highly impressed with what Malinowski propounded as his new theoretical approach in social anthropology– functionalism. Thereafter, Majumdar would always 'discuss Malinowski's contribution to social anthropology feelingly and regarded him as his teacher' (Sarana, 1961: 106). He 'dealt with culturology to begin with, and the problems of urbanization, communication and the role of Indian sociologists in later years'; and conducted his village study and can be given 'credit of perhaps being the first comprehensive survey of a town in India on a sociological (instead of a purely economic) base' (Mukherjee, 1979: 69). At the same time his physical anthropology could not find a place in the curriculum and he started pressing for a separate department of anthropology to enable him to include various other branches of anthropology as well which were not included in the courses of the Department of Economics and Sociology. And, his quest for expanding the knowledge in the field of a more comprehensive study of the racial and physical composition of the Indian society led him to taking up such studies in Uttar Pradesh and other states from 1929 onwards which created the basis of his integrated approach to the study of society and culture, taking racial, somatological and socio-cultural dimensions together in his analyses.

Regarding the basic sources of knowledge for Indian sociology being historical and classical, D.P. Mukerji's Presidential Address to the first sociological conference had emphatically asserted that high quality sociological research in India could not be conducted without a 'thorough grounding in her history and classical languages .... .' And without it social research in India 'will be a pale imitation of what others are doing'. Mukerji held out that sociology was principally the study of perditions'. Clinard and Elder have further reinforced their basic argument by presenting an analysis of articles appearing in the *Sociological Bulletin* (1952–63). It reveals that only 22 per cent of the articles were primarily empirical data based and another 13 per cent with secondary empirical data while the remaining 65 per cent were based on historical and other data with no empirical base. They have also pointed out that the emphasis on village studies by Indian sociologists was motivated by their view that rural India was the real India, a remark voiced by Majumdar in his Presidential Address to the second Indian Sociological Conference in Patna. This was subsequently reiterated by another president, R.N. Saksena, and in Majumdar's first village study (1958). And it was a fact with more than 80 per cent rural population in the country, then.

Through this discussion, three significant aspects of the pattern of accretion to knowledge in Indian social sciences, specially during almost a quarter century from the later 1940s can be discerned. First, this period shows acute consciousness and effort on the part of social scientists, mainly social anthropologists and sociologists to direct their empirical studies to provide basis for identifying and documenting the outstanding national problems. Second, during this period, both social anthropologists and sociologists irrespective of their departmental identities were contributing to exploring these national issues. Thirdly, this was the period when 'Indian scholarship had not distinguished between the two disciplines' (Patel, 2011: xiii), as reflected in the writings of Dube, Srinivas, Majumdar, Roy and Beteille. The researches in this direction were greatly facilitated through funds from Government of India, and some American universities and agencies. Moreover, the taking up of the Five Year Plans and community development also provided a great fillip and urgency to these developments in anthropology and sociology. In addition, prominent American scholars both sociologists and anthropologists began taking keen interest in researches in India and the responsiveness to some of these initiatives by the Indian social scientists, provided a big momentum to the post-colonial growth of sociological knowledge. As mentioned elsewhere, Majumdar was prominent in this regard and in collaboration with Opler of

Cornell University in USA took up a project of research in several rural areas of UP in early 1950s.

II

The trends in the academic works and thought of Majumdar from 1923 to 1960 can be attempted now by a close reading of his writings, his teachers' as well as his peers' works in social sciences, the manner in which he cultivated and oriented his students from 1928 onwards to the day of his sudden demise in 1960, and also the orientation and growth of the institutions he founded and the journals he established.

In this context, one has got to mention the observations which have been made about the work of the pioneers in social sciences particularly sociology and social anthropology, as contained in several recent edited volumes dealing with the history and contributions of the earlier sociologists and social anthropologists of India, individually and collectively. Editors Uberoi, Deshpande and Sundar (2007) lament that 'Indian sociologists and social anthropologists have only scant regard for the work of their predecessors'. They have observed that institutional memories are notoriously short, records and manuscript, etc. are hardly ever preserved and there is a lack of centralized archives for depositing such materials. Thus, 'altogether we just do not seem to have the interest in disciplinary history', though we are now catching up. These observations are perhaps more realistic in Majumdar's case, even though he made the singular achievement of having founded two institutions – Department of Anthropology at the University of Lucknow and the Ethnographic and Folk Culture Society, as well as the journal, *The Eastern Anthropologist* which is now completing almost 70 years of regular publication, a rare event for individually-founded academic journals. His sudden death also meant that his papers, correspondence, manuscripts, etc. were probably neither in a properly arranged collection nor were these preserved in the two institutions. Moreover, he was survived by only his wife and a teenaged daughter who decided to shift to the former's natal home in Calcutta, leaving all such materials including the collection of his books and copies of published papers, etc. with the Department of Anthropology, soon after his death. Another very recent instance of this trend can be reported from Ranchi where Roy's descendants sold his house, the base of *Man in India*, and probably disposed of his rich collection of tribal artifacts from the 19th century, books and journals including old volumes of the *Man in India*, as scrap.

Majumdar's Earliest Teachers

S.C. Roy and L.K. Ananthakrishna Iyer had both achieved prominence in anthropological studies in the second decade of the 20th century. Iyer had by then presided over the section on ethnography/ethnology of the Indian Science Congress in 1914 and 1916. Both of them were invited to join the faculty of the Calcutta University in 1920. Roy was 'a visiting lecturer ... for a few years from time to time: (Sarkar, 1991: 17). Iyer too 'join[ed] as a lecturer, a position that he held till 1932' (Danda and Chakrabarti, 1989: 2). Iyer and Roy were both 'leading the fieldwork team in 1923' from the Calcutta University which included Majumdar (see photograph on p. 264 reproduced from the *Man In India*, Vol. 71, No. 1, March 1991). Other members of the faculty were B.A. Gupte, R.P. Chanda, R.C. Chakladar, and P. Mitra, all were well known workers in the various fields of anthropological researches (102: 1947: 40). Mitra's work was on prehistoric India and Chakladar's and Chanda's was on race.

Apparently methodology in fieldwork, style of ethnography and choice of its subject material, as seen in their published works, and teaching, would have influenced their young students. Majumdar has repeatedly acknowledged Roy to be his mentor as he chose to pick up the Ho of Chhota Nagpur for his later work with active help from Roy. Some of the other subjects in which Majumdar got interested later, such as criminal tribes, were the ones which have featured in Iyer's ethnographic work in south India.

Iyer once again presided over the Anthropology Section of the Indian Science Congress in 1924 as it was christened in 1921, and published his Castes and Tribes of Cochin and Mysore. He gave lectures on ethnography at the Calcutta University (Iyer, 1925). K.S. Singh (1989: 10) commenting on L.K.A. Iyer's ethnography and its relevance, describes him as 'an ethnographer par excellence in survey tradition', and observes that he was 'more than an ethnographer'. He was deeply interested in 'macro historical processes of change'. Kalpana Ram (2010: 73–77) analyses how Iyer pursued his 'agency role in his assignments of ethnographic surveys' preferring first hand investigation over issuing of questionnaire to minor functionaries' (ibid.: 77), and contextualizing the people through his 'musicological style' of photography'.

Roy known for his encyclopedic work on Chhota Nagpur, was a prominent teacher in the Department of Ancient Indian History and Anthropology, University of Calcutta since 1920. He was also Majumdar's guide for his study of the Ho'. Sarkar (1991: 24) describes Roy as a teacher, thus:

> As a devoted teacher S.C. Roy was a living source of inspiration to many students in whom Roy felt the spirits of fruitful research. His approach to the students was out and out conditioned by affection and for them Roy spent much of his time, energy and money without bothering a little for his personal life. Nirmal Kumar Bose, S.S. Sarkar and D.N. Majumdar – the three stalwarts in the anthropological domain in India – received primary training in anthropology from Roy .... Despite his multifarious preoccupations Roy used to go through critically the works done by his students .... Roy not only accompanied Dr D.N. Majumdar personally to the Kolhan region to make him acquainted with the Ho tribe but also he provided Majumdar some of his own notes on the tribe that he collected with an intention to write a monograph on them.

Majumdar took up intensive fieldwork among the Ho after doing his post-graduation and he was also then a Premchand Roychand scholar which was a singular honour for any researcher in the Calcutta University. Of course, he remained in constant touch and guidance from Roy and therefore it would be essential to note some vital steps in the intellectual journey of Roy around this time. Dasgupta (2010) traces a shift in Roy's perspective after 1921 itself. Roy had realized the shortcomings of the early evolutionary theory of culture specially in the context of his tracking tribal migrations and the transmission of cultural elements from one people or area to another and the intermixture of races and cultures. This trend can be discerned from his second monograph on Oraon (1928) which revealed 'a scientific Roy, for him, fieldwork and participant observation as advocated by the functionalist school now became a fetish' (ibid.: 152). Moreover, his refined methodology for research as seen in his diary titled, 'ethnological notes', stressed some guiding principles for a researcher, viz., (i) he should equip himself with the theoretical study of the subject; (ii) have a clear idea of the nature of the problem for observation; (iii) prepare full and complete record of observations supported with photographs; (iv) make a full analysis of the data and; (v) significantly, omit all theoretical consideration in the report. It is also seen that by the time of revising the Oraon monograph, Roy had started questioning the colonial social category, 'tribe', as he felt that it 'was a static social category'. Dasgupta also finds an inkling of Roy's 'own religious leanings' and a 'cultural affinity born out of an Indian identity', in his writings at this point of time. It may also be mentioned that subsequently, by 1930s, Roy had shifted his focus from academic anthropology to 'activism' and 'expressed nationalist's views' as well while he was associated with the constitutional reforms before the Government of India Act of 1935. In the process, he also contributed significantly to the formation of an 'Adivasi identity' with a regional base as strengthened in the movement for Jharkhand (Upadhyay, 2011: 284). By this time, Roy's perception of anthropology also highlighted its useful application to 'certain crying problems of our national life': its likely potential for help in promoting mutual amity and bonds of unity between diverse people; devising and adopting suitable methods of acculturation and also adjustment of the 'jungle tribes to dominant higher cultures of their completely civilized neighbours' through such methods of acculturation.

III

Majumdar at the University of Lucknow

Mukerjee in his inaugural address in 1921, emphasized his views that 'sociology entered into his enunciation of the scope of Indian Economics through his emphasis on the 'region' as the appropriate unit of study. He conceived the region as a geographical, biological, economic, social and structural complex. This led to his emphasis on the study of ground reality from interdisciplinary and comparative perspectives' (Madan, 2011: 122). In keeping with this perspective of economics, Mukerjee decided to bring Majumdar in this department in 1928 – a decision which Madan described as 'interesting and even daring'. Majumdar was considered a promising researcher, and:

> To justify his appointment, Mukerjee convinced the vice chancellor that, in a country like India, the study of non-monetized economic transactions was

> imperative. Accordingly, Majumdar was appointed as lecturer in 'primitive economics', which embraced hunting and food gathering tribes, shifting cultivators, village artisans, craftsmen, and the like. To fulfill his full share of teaching responsibilities, Majumdar once told me, he had also been assigned a course of lecture on monetary economics. This made good sense within the recommended comparative perspective (ibid.: 135).

Thus, Lucknow became 'an influential centre' for teaching and research in sociology and social anthropology, probably the fourth in the country. Since Majumdar was a member of Mukerjee's department till 1950 when he was made Head of a separate Department of Anthropology, some salient aspects of the disciplinary environment in this department would be contextually relevant. Mukerjee's approach was underlined by a 'clear conception of the scope and method of an interdisciplinary social science embracing economics, sociology, political science and social philosophy' and this integrated approach had 'stimulated in him the desire and striving to envisage Man, Society and Civilization as wholes that defeat any compartmentalization'. Mukerjee' broad humanism was rooted in his readings of Western social thinkers such as Adam Smith, Comte, Marx, Mill and others. Importantly, 'nationalism provided the framework within which holism and humanism were established as the bedrock of Mukerjee's intellectual quest. Revitalization of village community and developing regional economics were an important part of Mukerjee's approach to a nationalist reconstruction of the country. Mukerjee has also emphasized the importance of historical and comparative methods in the study of regional and cultural differences; in tune with the understanding of those times, he called for a greater knowledge of race psychology and of diverse social schemes and standards of people as also the interplay of factors like climate and other regional differences. In the course of his lectures Mukerjee treated topics like economic behaviourism, the anthropological and institutional perspectives like that of caste, guilds, etc. on economic activity, need for humanization of economics and the relevance of biology, geography, ecology, sociology, psychology, psychoanalysis, ethics and even physics to economics. Quite significantly Mukerjee used the comparative method in the analysis of institutional economics to question the absolute and inviolable character of the prevalent economic theories in his *Principles of Comparative Economics* (1922). It was:

> Read widely and has long been recognized as a classic. It was this book that made Melville Herskovits, who shaped the discipline of economic anthropology, acknowledge Mukerjee as a pioneer in the field (Herskovits, 1952: 23). The economist-turned-anthropologist, Raymond Firth, noted Mukerjee's plea for a comparative approach involving Western and 'non-Western economic forms', but doubted that economists would be convinced (Firth, 1951: 126–27; Madan, 2011: 127).

During 1930s, Mukerjee brought his thinking and writing on the scope and significance of the economic science to a conclusion. Writing about the social science generally, he observed that the core problem was that of providing an adequate understanding of the relations between the individual and society and their reciprocal relations to the environment.

This somewhat long discussion on Mukerjee's intellectual contributions throws valuable light on what was the stream of thought, and taught in the Department and how Majumdar's knowledge of social anthropology and tribal cultures and institutions was to be relevant and subsequently developed, particularly in the context of UP.

IV

Taking the above disciplinary environment in the years immediately before and after his coming to the University of Lucknow, Department of Economics and Sociology into account, we may now try to demarcate the reflexive trends in his own writings, teaching, research and intellectual growth.

Broadly speaking, it would systematize our analysis if we identify three phases in this progressive journey. The first phase would generally be from 1923, when he published his first paper in the *Man in India* till the beginning of 1933 when he left for Cambridge. The second phase can be identified as starting from 1936 after his return from Cambridge to the department at Lucknow and till about 1946–47 when the country's political and social scenario was undergoing a change. It was the post-war period and the coming up of Partition and Independence. The third phase can be identified from 1947 onwards till his death. Independence brought a new environment for creative activity with the adoption of the Republican Constitution of India having some special provision for tribals and others like untouchables and lower castes which had been an important focus for Majumdar's work; followed by the process of all-round development through Five Year Plans and community development projects. Also frequent opportunities for interaction with American anthropologists as well as Commonwealth anthropologists and participation in international symposia and other fora. Majumdar's academic and intellectual progress can now be usefully seen in the frame of sociology of knowledge in the course of these three broad phases.

Going through Majumdar's bibliography of writings, one can say that right from his student days, he was a prolific writer and the contents of his writings reflect him as a 'general anthropologist' touching upon various branches like physical anthropology, social anthropology and some prehistory and linguistics. During 1923–27, before he came to Lucknow, he had published 30 papers of which 10 presentations in the Indian Science Congress were abstracts, The Ho ethnography and physical anthropology of the Ho are the themes mostly. Mentionable are two papers, one of 1925 relating to a movement among the Ho for social reforms in their institutions and practices caused primarily by the influence of missionaries and Hindu neighbours. The second one on the Rajbansis of north Bengal commenting on the process of a tribe's endeavour to be recognized as a Kshatriya caste thereby showing an early interest in the process of tribe-caste continuum. During 1928–33 while in Lucknow, before he went to Cambridge, Majumdar had published 29 papers. These include his first set of papers on the Korwa initiating his perspective on the factors adversely affecting a tribal culture and the community's 'loss of interest' in life and a decline in their numbers. Discussions regarding decline of population even threatening extinction among some tribal communities in Melanesia had led W.H.R. Rivers', 'promulgation of the theory that societies might lose the will to live if they were deprived of the institutions on which their interests were focused, in 1922' (Mair, 1957: 230). The other area in UP which interested Majumdar was the cis-Himalayan Rawain-Jaunpur. Among these publications there was also a focus on tribal institutions like religion, couvade, totemism and formation of clans and his standing interest, viz., clash and fusion of cultures. A paper on the economic background of social institutions in primitive society (36: 1930) stresses the significance of economic considerations motivating certain customs and institutions. For example, the youth dormitory having a significant role in the tribe's economy and so on. In other words, his emphasis was on a functional inter-relationship of institutions and a perspective for analysing economic relationships through the context of social institutions.

Briefly, the salience in his empirical approach, its methodology and conceptualization could be identified as:

- The importance of personal and intensive fieldwork among the communities or people studied and the use of their own dialect/language.
- Appreciation of historicity of the contact situation between the tribes and the Hindu population around them with its religion, caste and hierarchy patterns, and also the inter-tribal contacts and resultant change.
- The serious limitations or deficiencies that he perceived in the evolutionary approach, then followed in anthropology in understanding the cultural processes in India particularly the change both in the tribal and mainstream culture.
- The comparative strength in the functionalist approach put forth by Malinowski in his initial writings during 1920s which had been taken note of by Roy while Majumdar was working among the Ho.
- The significance of varied racial features of the Indian population, trends in racial admixture, and the interplay of race and culture through migrations, neighbourhood, etc.
- An acute appreciation of how the concept of 'tribe' being a static and well defined community, not being the ground reality in India due to migrations, racial inter-mixture and inter-tribal cultural cross currents. As also the impact of the contacts with Hindu castes and the colonial influence which was so patently implied in his use of the term 'transition', and also his constant attention to observing changes.
- Linking of anthropological findings to certain colonial policies, decisions and personnel to highlight the need for a better understanding of tribal culture, also, thereby, facilitating trans-culturation in its varied forms.
- Some of the very significant aspects where Majumdar differed from Roy's preferred method of anthropology were omitting all theoretical discussion

in the field reports and identifying elements of the contributions of the people studied and how much had been borrowed by them.

V

Majumdar at Cambridge

Majumdar went to the Cambridge University in 1933 for his doctoral work. Therefore, some recapitulation of the teaching of anthropology and its faculty in the Cambridge University from the point of view of sociology of knowledge should be germane to an understanding of his intellectual journey. Anthropological studies were inaugurated in Cambridge on 17 November 1904 by Sir Richard Temple, noted in his day as an administrator in India and as an Orientalist. In 1932, anthropology got its first chair, the William Wyse Professorship, and T.C. Hodson was appointed to it. Both Hodson and his successor, J.H. Hutton, were from the ICS and 'authorities on the ethnology of India' (Fortes, 1953: 3). Among others who had been in Cambridge were W.H.R. Rivers, Department of Psychology, known for his field work among the Toda. As mentioned earlier, Hodson was Majumdar's guide for PhD.

From the very beginning, a stress was laid by Temple on the importance of anthropology for those whose work 'lies in distant lands'[1]. This faith in the practical usefulness of anthropology that 'stemmed directly from the theory of the organic evolution' developed into the belief that the 'science of culture (anthropology) was essentially a reformers science'.[2]

As regards its courses, the University had a diploma in ethnology since 1908 and a Tripos in archeology and anthropology was instituted in 1919. Significantly, in 1920s, Indian probationers (ICS) were also attending these courses as a part of their training. By the turn of 1930s, the evolutionary theory had fallen to pieces and Malinowski's functionalist approach came to the fore. Fortes holds that the chief innovation for which functionalism stands was a contribution of the Cambridge School of Anthropology in the shape of Haddon's principle of the 'intensive study of limited areas'.[3] It meant making of social anthropology as an empirical discipline and as a branch of natural science. In Cambridge, there was also an emphasis on multiplying the frames of references for anthropological research. Its Tripos had been based on 'alliance between archaeology, social anthropology, and physical anthropology. Another focus of study in Cambridge had been to 'fight against obscurantism and the perversion of knowledge', its case in point being 'race discrimination which is an invention of western civilization', and this area of study 'had also been bequeathed to us by Haddon's generation'.[4]

Discussing the intellectual background in Cambridge in mid 1930s, one has to take note also of what Kuper (1973) comments. Broadly, he finds that Haddon's leadership actively contributed to making Cambridge an important centre for professional fieldwork. However, the trained workers had to rely upon interpreters and the fieldwork was not long enough in duration 'but more obviously there was a change of emphasis away from theoretical preoccupations and towards field research' responding to 'the calls of ethnography' (ibid.: 18). Cambridge, thus, in mid-1930s, 'was still slumbering in the pre-Malinowskian era'. And, Fortes 'took over a weak pre-functionalist department in Cambridge in 1950, and he set about its transformation' (ibid.: 158). 'Moreover the anthropology being taught at the time at Oxford, Cambridge, and University College London was largely mistaken and misguided– not only by modern standards, but by the standards of the day at the LSE and in America. It was full of diffusionist and evolutionist assumptions, and confused by doses of physical anthropology, still racialist in orientation, technology, and preposterous theories of religion' (ibid.: 129).[5]

The above picture of Cambridge and Haddon, and then Hodson as its heads, during the time Majumdar was there, help us in understanding a few significant initiatives which he took on his own, and which later contributed to the body of knowledge of anthropology in India created by him. First, he attended Malinowski's seminars at LSE and, thus, oriented himself in the then upcoming theoretical frame of functionalism and the kind of methodology and fieldwork which it recommended. Secondly, he also trained under Morant, Galton and Ruggles Gates to update himself in physical anthropometry, somatology and genetics; and also developed his interest in the study of cultures particularly the use of this concept in the ethnography of India, as he had also given lectures in the department at Cambridge on Indian culture. Thus, Majumdar's stay in the United Kingdom in the thirties was a focal point of his career in anthropology. He got himself acquainted with the latest development in both physical and cultural anthropology (Sarana, 1961: 106), and, critically, did not confine himself to the academic environment in Cambridge, then, solely.

Mukerji (1962: 8–9) briefly outlines these developments, thus:

> His scholarship is a fairly long story .... But he began to change his views a little: his interest became cultural as different from its being purely ethnological. When he went to Cambridge and London, in the mid-thirties, he came under the influence of Malinowski even though he was primarily influenced by the veteran Indian ethnographer, Sarat Chandra Roy. Later on still the influence of Kroeber on him was very clear. He also escaped from ethnography through his interest in blood groups, in statistical surveys, in demography and in the study of growth among children ... to estimate his contributions to 'culturology', there, essentially, he did not distinguish between the terms of content and function a la Malinowski and the formal integration of Ruth Benedict.

VI

Return from Cambridge and the Ensuing Years

Majumdar's progress after his return from Cambridge in 1935 is now being broadly explicated. During 1936–1947, his publications included papers, books and substantive works connected with his surveys starting with the UP survey in connections with the Census of 1941. This is also the period which Majumdar calls a period of critical approach in the progress of anthropology in India (102: 1947: 19). The publications on conditions of the tribal people in India receive a good deal of attention through both ethnographic notes on individual tribes and critical, action-oriented discussions. As also his enunciation of his analytical theory, if it can be called as such, in analysing the different situations of culture contact. Two papers (55–56: 1936) discuss the deterioration in the condition of tribes and, then, in the second paper there is a diagnostic presentation of the problems as a result of contact with caste and mainstream culture, colonial policies and missionary activities. This paper was written after the continuance of tribal areas being listed as Excluded and Partially Excluded Areas for administration under the Government of India Act 1935, he provides a way of creating financial and concomitant administrative infrastructure for ensuring positive measures to bring them expeditiously into the mainstream. This diagnostic and applied suggestion has been discussed in detail elsewhere. In 1937 (60: 1937) he published his doctoral thesis after some modifications as *A Tribe in Transition: A Study in Culture Pattern* which in methodology went beyond the functional approach and was acknowledged as a path breaking work on culture change. Thus, it marked 'a new departure in Indian ethnological literature' in the words of Hutton. Some critiques, however, find that the ethnographic description of the Ho institutions and social patterns are too brief. The issues raised therein and in his later work on Ho (131: 1950) have been discussed elsewhere. In the ensuing years, his ethnographic interest widened to certain other areas of UP like the *Tarai* area in which live Tharus and Bhoksas and Jaunpur Rawain and Jaunsar-Bawar in Garhwal which was a polyandrous region. A paper on modern trends in social anthropology (66: 1938: 162–76) concisely states Majumdar's analytical conclusions and views relating to evolutionary, diffusionists and functionalist's theories, their limitations in approach and how the concept of a pattern or *gestalt* can complement anthropological studies of culture. Further, this paper covers how anthropology as an applied science has been put to the use of administration and for the benefit of the tribes there and, then, how a clear anthropological delineation of contact situations in India can make anthropologists help administration and reduce frictions. He also goes on to discuss the changing demographic picture of certain tribes. In another incisive paper on the effects of Christianity among tribal people, Majumdar points out how the missionaries have helped the tribals to a certain extent but also given rise to some basic problems like conflicts between the convert Christians and non-converted sections. Here he also proposes an eight-point scheme for spelling out the manner in which the activities of the missionaries can be countered by the Hindu and other such organizations.

In 1938 came an important event in the history of anthropology in India when a joint session of the Indian Science Congress Association and the British Association was held at Calcutta on the occasion of the silver jubilee of the Indian Science Congress. After joint deliberation, plans for future anthropological research in India were drawn. The Indian Science Congress of 1939 was also a very significant stage in Majumdar's analytical journey. He presided over the anthropological section at Lahore and delivered his Presidential Address on the cultural contact situation in Bastar. This session was also a joint session of the Indian Statistical Conference and the anthropology section of the Indian Science Congress. Professor Mahalonobis had presided over the former and 'discussed the importance of statistical analysis of anthropometric data and suggested a more intimate liaison between stasticians and anthropologists ... (which) bore considerable fruit as shown by subsequent events' (102: 1947: 20). Subsequently, in 1940, he also followed up his views on Ho religion in a volume of festschrift for S.C. Roy edited by Mills, Majumdar and others and an elaborate ethnographic note on the cultural pattern of the polyandrous people of Jaunsar-Bawar.

In 1941, the Census Commissioner of India initiated a scheme of an anthropological and serological survey for the United Provinces which was carried out by Majumdar. This survey covered about 3000 people belonging to 21 castes and tribes. The ethnographic material was published in *Fortunes* while the anthropometric data was analysed in collaboration with Mahalonobis and C.R. Rao, fruitfully using the D^2 statistical test of Mahalonobis in its analysis. The results were published by the Indian Statistical Institute (117: 1949). Subsequently, Majumdar also undertook similar surveys in Gujarat (118: 1949) and parts of Bengal (221: 1961: 81–85). This period of Majumdar's extensive work in anthropometry, somatometry and blood groups led to his enunciation of a strong argument refuting any clear racial bases for caste origins and beliefs in the hierarchy of certain caste groups. He emphatically voiced the view that a simple presentation of certain aspects of the biological evidence could be usefully employed to discourage false caste claims and certainly mitigate caste and communal antagonism as well as untouchability. Demolition of the myth of race through scientific data and thereby improving the race relations had been a focus of the Cambridge department as discussed above. The rise of Nazism and Fascism leading to the Second World War in 1939 was the background for Majumdar's extensive researches and several later writings (101: 1947; 98: 1947) in this area, with the problems of Indian castes and tribal situation in mind.

The 1940s also brought an increase in his teaching load in the Department of Economics and Sociology. Now at the post-graduate level the sociology group or B group as it was known had two papers of which one was taught wholly by Majumdar and another one partly in the final, and one paper in the previous. This was in addition to the heavy time consuming work he had undertaken in the Census survey of UP and his writing ethnographic notes and compiling the data and participation in analysing the data generated by this survey. Besides, in 1945, he along with his students founded the Ethnographic and Folk Culture Society. A programme for publications under its aegis was drawn up and the first publication was on folklore entitled, *Snowballs of Garhwal*. He was also having close interaction with his students on the fieldtrips and a number of them had taken up different kinds of studies. His first PhD scholar, Kunwar Indrajit Singh prepared his thesis entitled, *Gondwana and the Gonds*. In 1947, he founded the Society's journal, *The Eastern Anthropologist*, and took up the heavy load of editing it. In addition he was also associated as one of the editors of the *Man in India*. Thus, the end of colonial rule shows him actively furthering study and research in anthropology in its various branches. In the year 1942, he was the first anthropologist to participate in the training of ICS Probationers and Chieftains of minor princely states, when he was invited to deliver a course of lectures on Indian anthropology at the ICS Training Centre, Deharadun. Thus, Majumdar joined, in India, the practice of training colonial administrators initiated long back by Cambridge. B.S. Guha gave lectures to the next batch of ICS Probationers (1943) and thereafter recruitment to the ICS was stopped.

This was also the period when a debate relating to the policy frame for the tribals in the country around Elwin's views had arisen. Majumdar as discussed elsewhere was critical of isolationism and pleaded for an informed and scientific anthropological approach which is seen in its details in his writings during 1940s, till Independence. This entire question has been discussed elsewhere and the views expressed by him in his writings and of course his teachings and lectures have been expatiated in the relevant chapters of this work. His faith in anthropology and adding to its body of knowledge and reach in its application to administration and for the betterment of tribal conditions made him utilize the forum of *The Eastern Anthropologist* through a special tribal number in 1949. It may, however, be commented that expression of the anthropologists' views also remained 'feeble and fell far short of consolidating autonomous and realistic tradition of Indian social science', to quote Y. Singh (1973) and supported by others. In fact, in the case of anthropologists, the wide publicity of Elwin's views had made the anthropologists suspects in eyes of the new nationalist regime which came to power in 1946.

Recognition for his work came in 1950 when he was given a personal professorship of anthropology in the Department of Economics and Sociology. This was soon followed by the creation of a separate department of anthropology of which he was appointed the head. And, he with his typical zeal went about planning the courses in the department and the selection of the faculty. Some of the courses of anthropology at the postgraduate level were common with sociology group at least for the first few years, a practice which certainly had advantages for the students specializing in social anthropology.

VII

In the light of what has been said earlier about Majumdar's work and academic journey, his sense of alienation from the Department of Economics and Sociology had by now become quite acute. Since he was producing substantial work in physical anthropology and regarded the contribution of this branch of anthropology as very valuable for its application in various fields, he was constantly feeling that the set of courses available in that Department were not doing full justice to anthropology as a full-fledged scientific discipline. By now, he had also separately established an anthropological laboratory in the University, and of course, the EFCS and these two now became the fora of his identity. Historically, even till 1940s anthropology was treated 'primarily as a general, all embracing discipline' (Firth, 1957: 6). And for Majumdar physical anthropology with its various aspects of significance for social anthropology in the field of the nature of cultures and personality as well as in the context of untenable claims of racial superiority and so on, were weighty issues. In fact, these had great relevance for analyzing contact situations with all their implications in the Indian context. And, therefore, Majumdar embarked upon his studies of racial composition including somatology till early 1950s. Subsequently, in quick responsiveness to national issues relating to health particularly in case of neglected groups like tribes and children he initiated studies on growth as well as genetics, as discussed elsewhere in this work. Of course, he always had a batch of students who were toiling along with him in advancing the cause of anthropology and participating in field work. He was not opposed to an interdisciplinary approach, but felt that anthropology should be given an upper hand because of the wide scope of its coverage in the study of 'Man'. This was a point he was always stressing in his classes in the combined department as personally communicated by C. Lakshmanna to this author, and this was done by Majumdar through a gesture of parting his hands wider when he mentioned anthropology as compared to sociology.[6]

Majumdar's Academic Work From 1947 to 1960

Before exploring how Majumdar progressed with his work, it would be useful to see how the work in Indian sociology and social anthropology has been seen in its constitutive parameters by some of the prominent people in the discipline. Danda tracing the historical growth of anthropological knowledge points out that its growth as a 'body of knowledge' had its origins in the earlier *Smritis, Manav Dharma Shashtra*, (literally the science of man) dating approximately to the 14th century BC which delineated 'a clear distinction between man as a self contained individual and man as a member of the society and the interplay of these two roles in different situational contexts' (Danda, 1995: 24–25). The other identity of anthropology as an 'academic discipline' originated only during colonial rule and, significantly, 'under normal circumstances, the two traditions merge together to develop a common stream. Due to certain specific inherent reason this was not to happen in India' (ibid.: 30).

Similar views have been expressed by Y. Singh (1973: 14–18) when he says that the fact that 'social science as a profession itself was a byproduct of the colonial impact', which gave a 'tilt to the social role and relevance of social sciences'. This caused social sciences to lag behind in responding to the challenges of major changes to the structure of Indian society often caused by the colonial policies and made its conceptual framework fragmentary. The well known examples of colonial social categories such as a tribe have been adduced. Singh further observes that even though some social scientists, mentionably D.P. Mukerji and G.S. Ghurye, rejected such an approach, and favoured the Indological sources, 'all these currents of social science during the freedom movement remain feeble and fell far short of consolidating an autonomous and realistic tradition of Indian social science'. Srinivas and Panini (1986: 34–35), however view the scenario rather differently.[7]

The paper by Culinard and Elder (1965) already referred to, however, observes that the Indian sociology and social anthropology needs 'a better dialogical relationship' with other countries; more emphasis on empirical foundations rather than teaching alone; and appreciating the importance of 'action-oriented research' which occasionally provides the basis for more important theoretical developments. And, therefore, they approvingly mention the collaborative research projects with American and European institutions and scholars, criticizing in the process, the action of six social scientists from Lucknow who complained that the American research projects in India had non-academic motives in concentrating on communication, etc. It may be mentioned that Majumdar in his Presidential Address to the anthropology section to the Indian Social Conference 1955 had bitterly criticized the manner in which such collaborative projects were being handled in their designs and implementation and failed to provide opportunities to Indian personnel for training in research methodology and preparation of reports[8]. Obviously some of Clinard and Elder's comments are biased. But, the fact remains that the Indian social scientists have to 'define and formulate our social research priorities entirely on the basis of our own problems of nation building and social change' (Singh, 1973: 27); and the areas of research should shift to structural issues and their dynamics as also a critically adaptive and indigenized methodology because 'to analyse these factors models cannot be borrowed from abroad, although awareness of other models may enrich the insight of the social scientists' (ibid.: 25). Further, Singh stresses the need for developing a genuine professional outlook among Indian social scientists. Such views had been expressed earlier by Dube (1977: 11–12) and Oommen in his plea for contextualizing sociology in India (1983: 130–31). In the latter's view, if sociology has to be relevant its practitioners should internalize the value package contained in the Indian Constitution specially because:

> The social engineering involved here– the selective retention of our tradition, informed borrowing from other cultures and the judicious mutation of the two– will have to be a process peculiar to India. The primary task of Indian sociologists today is to understand, analyze and facilitate this process. (ibid.: 131)

VIII

Post-Colonial, 1946–1947 to 1950

By 1946, when Majumdar delivered the Sri Mahadev Hari Wathodkar Memorial Foundation lectures in Nagpur University, the end of colonial rule in the country was in sight. Majumdar says that he accepted this invitation because 'he did not want to forego an offer which rarely comes to anthropologists in India' and he has dedicated his published version, *Matrix* (98: 1947) to his pupils of the MA final class in anthropology, 1947, whose 'love and loyalty I sincerely reciprocate'. This work has importance because it crystallizes and voices his convictions and objectives in his academic and intellectual journey. Some of these basic issues are:

- His methodological approach appreciative of the value of functionalism prefers a combination thereof with psychological and configurational approaches to find cultural ethos more perceptively.
- In the problems of the application of anthropological knowledge Majumdar stresses that administration of primitive and backward people is its most complex problem, made more complex by the contact situations, war in the North-East and such other factors. However, 'problems of administration of primitive and backward tribes were not being taken seriously in India' while 'the aim of administration should not merely be to reduce friction ... but to shape cultural life of the primitive and backward groups in such a way as to bring them in line with their more fortunate compatriots without destroying or degrading in the process'. And, their problem has been 'raised from the plain of anthropology to that of sociology, even of politics through which the confusion remains in the minds of the public regarding the system of administration to be setup in tribal areas (98: 1947: 62).
- Thus, he advances an anthropological approach, and then goes on to discuss a three-fold classification of tribes on the basis of their cultural conditions. Critically examining the system of indirect rule in Chhota Nagpur in its actual working and the interplay of other factors like missionary activity, he then highlights the incidents of confrontation. Thus, focusing on the urgent need to formulate a clear tribal policy, eliminating the deficiencies and setting out positive goals. Subsequently, he examines the various models of the process of 'acculturation' with an aim to guide it so that the various groups of people:

  > Sharing 'the same territory and forming parts of the same economic structure, can live, each its own life without fusion, having symbiotic or commensal relationship with one another, adopting desirable traits from one another and even acculturating on a generous scale, yet maintaining an identity of language and culture .... A sort of cultural federation, in which mutuality and reciprocity rather than submission and suppression would provide smooth working of the federal structure and adjustment of the various groups to one another without undue hardships or discomforts to the cooperating units .... What is needed is mutual respect and understanding, and where the dominant or ruling groups has shown such respect and understanding cultural adjustment has been smooth and easy. It is I think possible for the tribes to-day to feel more secure and take greater share in the cultural progress of the country provided the attitude forced on the caste people by the numerical preponderance of the tribes and backward groups is not merely used for political expediency but as a sincere gesture towards a broad cultural movement' (ibid.: 173–74).

Madan (2013: 34–35) commenting of this rather scientific and ethnographic knowledge-based approach to acculturation has perceptively pointed out:

> Again, no question about the desirability of the civilized ways of life were asked beyond their being regarded as open to synthesis indicating his (Majumdar's) clear preference for 'acculturation', but at the same time acknowledging the risk of reaction or 'contra-acculturation'.

Affairs (1950), in the old style of ethnography ... states his position on the problems of 'acculturation' and the notion of development of culture' (ibid.: 35). However, its last chapter entitled, 'The Prospect', also takes into account the policies being framed through special provisions in the new Constitution for the tribal people, of course in the backdrop of the debate of isolationism versus assimilation and its different approaches. The salient features of Majumdar's critical discussion here are that the problems of the tribals have to be viewed specifically for different groups: priority for tribals in the areas where disintegration of tribal life has been going on, for example, Chhota Nagpur, Assam and Orissa in order to assess with competence and sympathy, the issues of tribal adjustment; recognition of cultural levels of tribals for plans of rehabilitation which should not be drawn on 'a set formula as is being done'; careful planning for tribal areas, undergoing industrialization; and need for raising the skills among tribal labour. With these objectives he stresses, inter alia, the importance of economic measures, education, focus on development of tribal women, reforms and modification in criminal laws applicable to the tribals. It is followed by a warning that their problems may assume hydra-headed proportions if distress flourishes due to the administration's ignorance and lack of sympathy, and already the cup of tribal life is full of miseries'. It may be added that in a note of comments relating to the identification of the characteristics of 'tribe' (193: 1958: 1–4), he spells out a way to steer through the problem of identifying tribes correctly for scheduling under the Constitution. An issue which has really assumed 'hydra-headed proportions' due to its politicization and lack of sympathy on the part of administration, particularly in the light of the report of the first Backward Classes Commission[9].

Some other papers by Majumdar during this period are also mentionable. In two papers, reviewing anthropology during the war (99: 1947) and progress of anthropology-1911 to 1946 (102: 1947) he observes that even during the war years, Indian anthropologists made significant researches in ethnographic studies, anthropometry and racial biology and studies on ethnic affiliation and kinship terminology. Thereafter, during its 'critical period' starting 1938, it progressed from an attempt to reconstruct the history of culture to a realization of Indian needs and requirements for a critical appraisal on various aspects of tribal and folk life as well as racial basis of caste hierarchy and tribe-caste continuum. The contributions made by Aiyappan, Dube, Elwin, Grigson, Mills, Furer-Haimendorf, Karve, Srinivas and Majumdar himself find mention in the course of these narratives. Racial problems (101: 1947); the conditions of the criminal tribes and the urgency and manner of remedying their problem; and a few more (106: 1947; 127A: 1949) also focus on other national issues and policies. *Races and Cultures of India* which was first published in 1944 and its later editions incorporate Majumdar's views on the special provisions in the Indian Constitution sanguinely adding that they might prove to be an adequate frame-work for governance.

The Last Decade

The decade of 1950s was an extremely busy and rather overcrowded with the multifarious directions of Majumdar's work mainly in response to the country's development by providing the research support for this purpose. Moreover, he participated in important international fora also in connection with his demographic work and the prospects of anthropology in academics and application in governance. Most of these issues have been discussed in the relevant chapters in this work. However, it would be useful to briefly mention some of them.

- Contributing to the anthropology of urban development which was initiated by him with the publication of *Socio-Economic Survey of Lucknow* (138A: 1951) through the coordinated efforts of an interdisciplinary team. Then, the *Social Survey of Kanpur 1954–56*, which, inter alia, explored the process of urbanization through industrial expansion of city and its neighbouring rural areas.
- Studies of a village in the suburb of Lucknow exploring the cultural situation in the rural area, the communication channels within and out of it, and how far the urban culture was affecting it. Another village study was in an area which was described as a 'fringe' area of UP administratively, geographically and culturally with its mixed population of tribes and castes in its villages, and spelling out the characteristics of its 'fringe culture' with certain positive features of give and take. And, another structural and functional study of three villages in a remote polyandrous region.

  Thus, he contributed a very wide range of micro level rural studies exploring rural urban, tribe-caste and regional contexts as also the impact of directed change through community development programmes. Exploring the later aspects he published a number of papers focusing on the quality of programmes, reasons for their being rejected or accepted, quality of personnel and the manner of the governance of this vital programme for rural development.

- A study of educated unemployment highlighting the pitfalls in our education system and how it was likely to contribute to a much larger problem in providing employment.
- Taking up studies with potentials of application in physical anthropology, such as growth of children, medical anthropology, etc.
- With the aim of making his department a centre for applied anthropology and its usefulness for administration, he had tried to set up a diploma course in tribal welfare and administration for which the Government of India were likely to come forth with funds. However, the university administration under Mukerjee, the then Vice-Chancellor, reportedly, did not agree to the proposal from the central government.

X

In the foregoing discussion an attempt has been made to identify the bases or the heuristics of Majumdar's thinking and writings during nearly four decade of his 'doing anthropology', as one of the foremost professionals of the first generation. This analytical presentation also takes one through the paradigmatic changes which occurred in anthropology, specially social anthropology during this span as Majumdar was known for keeping himself abreast of the developments in the subject and the problems and issues in focus.

The very first anchorage for his thought, and of course writings, lay in his perception of social or cultural change as unwrapped through intensive field work with carefully crafted methodology. He was a 'born field worker, as it were', to use Madan's phrase, and 'Majumdar turned into a changed person when in the field', according to a member of one of his field teams in 1950s. Even while emphasizing the relationship between sociology and anthropology in his later years (1955), he expressed the view that data should flow from anthropology to sociology and theory from sociology to anthropology. His convictions about fieldwork and the need for making it as thorough as possible emanated right from his postgraduate training with Roy, and later it received a further edge at Cambridge (see Fortes, 1953), and on top of it his becoming a devotee to Malinowskian functionalism. But his perception of the dynamics of the Indian society, particularly the tribal context which was then the main area of anthropological studies, revealed the roots for his critique of functionalism. Along with it emerged his interest in the American approaches to the study of culture and its change and he has also been called both a functionalist, a function-structuralist and a culturologist. These concerns in his thought and approach were further explored in the Indian tribal context in the published form of his Cambridge thesis and its updated version in (1950) which was widely recognized as a pioneering study in social change. Here he also initiated anthropological interest under the impact of industrialization to which later on several students of his contributed richly.

Another theme that he almost continuously pursued was the question of race and culture. Again, his training in physical anthropology while in England in mid-1930s, the emphasis in the Cambridge academics on racial questions and also the then prevailing atmosphere – the rise of Nazism, the outcome of colonial policies and the effects of missionary work he had observed in India provided the empirical template.

The foci of Mukerjee's foundational sociology – interdisciplinary research, importance of traditional institutions and the related cultural factors, and contextualizing sociology and economics in the Indian culture and needs also provided an impetus to Majumdar's academic perspectives. One may even hurl a guess that Majumdar's approach formulized as MARC, in his second ethnography of the Ho, had links with Mukerjee's thesis on environmental determinism and social ecology.

In Lucknow he grew into a 'strong positivist more strongly grounded in empirical bases than the other two members of the Lucknow triumvirate with an infectious confidence in being able to provide scientific and practical suggestions for bringing about the desired changes – application of anthropology'. The sweep and strength of his conviction in this regard – that sociological knowledge can efficaciously provide the base for development and solution of economic and social problems – was almost utopian. This courage of conviction pushed Majumdar to vigorously involve himself in the national goals of development as

Man in India: Vol. 71: 1: 1991

S.C. Roy leading the fieldwork team from the Department of Anthropology, Calcutta University in 1923 (Photograph was taken in front of *Man in India* office, Ranchi). *Standing* (*L* to *R*) – Mr Venkatram; Kshitish Ghose; Taraknath Mukherjee; Ganendra K. Roy; Kalinarayan Bhattacharya and Biswapati Gupta. *Sitting* (*Middle row*) – Surendra K. Chakraborty; Ajit Gupta; Rai Bahadur Prof. Iyer; Rai Bhadur S.C. Roy; Jamini Dutt and Jiten Ghosh. *Sitting* (*Front row*) – Promode Gopal Roy; Dhirendra N. Majumdar and Nirmal Ch. Sarkar.

also the planning of state policies to bring about a democratic, egalitarian, plural and civilized regimen for post-colonial India. At the same time he realized that 'change is easiest to effect but most difficult to stabilize', in Robin William's words which he quotes (178: 1956: 9–10). His field observation had made him conscious of the difficulties due to the vast range of differences in the cultural patterns of the Indian people, particularly tribes. Therefore, we have to be prepared for an overall change in the context of a total dynamic cultural situation (ibid.: 10); obviously with well-honed strategies, policies and plans.

His utopia perhaps lay in Lord Raglan's words that 'we cannot become civilized unless we are all civilized' (96: 1946: xii) which he has quoted more than once in his writings. Broadly speaking he aimed to 'civilize' those claiming to be civilized into an inclusive and plural society and not 'savaging' them (Guha, 1999)[10]. And this he calls as an axiom of social life.

Notes

1. Here he was echoing what Haddon called a 'practical value', explicated thus:

   They often quoted examples of the price paid for ignorance and the gain reaped from knowledge of the customs and institutions of the people of India, Africa and Oceania; for the 'practical' meant for them what could be used for the benefit of the native peoples, and not solely for the advantage of the European rulers. (Fortes, 1953: 4).

2. As Fortes (1953: 7) explains:

   So it (evolution) emphasized the unity of all mankind. But it also brought out their differences and the obvious supremacy of European civilization; and this required a notion of grades of culture which, in the evolutionary context, meant a concept of progress.

3. Majumdar has narrated how Malinowski had viewed Haddon, thus:

   In 1935, I remember an incident that happened during my stay in London which goes to show that a functionalist is not necessarily a blind addict to his theory or even to methodology. The late Prof. Malinowski in his seminar at the London School of Economics, celebrated the eightieth birth day of the late Sir Alfred Haddon and welcomed the distinguished guest as the 'father of functional anthropology' which proved that the continuity of anthropological thought could not be ignored even if there were fundamental difference in approach to cultural problems. Prof. Haddon did not refute this 'accusation' but hoped that the functional approach would not be the last one, though its emergence probably was a historical necessity. Alexander Lesser in his article on 'Functionalism' (ibid.: 26–27).

4. Fortes emphasizes:

   There is not a shred of anthropological evidence to justify race discrimination. It is the duty of anthropology to proclaim this truth and to continue dispassionately to investigate the biological and social qualities of human groups without regard for race privilege. These, too, are tasks calling for the alliance of all branches of anthropology and archaeology; and this applies equally to the work of routing the less malign forms of obscurantism which thrive on ignorance of the incredible variety of human social, political and moral institutions (1953: 46).

5. Assessing the trends in the four centres of social anthropology in England (London School of Economies, University College London, Cambridge, and Oxford) Kuper observes that, 'social anthropology in the modern sense was firmly established only at the LSE'. In 1937, Oxford was taken over and the other two departments were 'captured only after the War'. Some of Kuper's comments come alive when the Mss of Majumdar's thesis in the Cambridge Library are compared with the book, *Transition*. In the manuscript, there is no long discussion of approach methodology– functional, gestalt and pattern with some discussion about Radcliffe-Brown, Malinowski, Benedict and Majumdar emphasizing that his approach was a synthesis. The manuscript also contains some anthropometric data and in both the versions there run undercurrents of a diffusionist approach. The two reviews of the book by Mair (1939: 28) and Powdermaker (1940: 794–95) point out that the theoretical bases for the ethnography as discussed in its 'Introduction' are not concretized in its contents.

6. Lakshmanna has also recapitulated that the teaching in the Department of Sociology centered 'around theory, traditions, modernization and interdisciplinary and multidisciplinary approach to the study of the problems and issues' and, thus, 'the interest and themes were varied and many' ... . Majumdar's basic interest was social and cultural anthropology, urban social tensions, problems of hill and tribal folks (2012: 5–6).

7. During the pre-Independence period of 1930s and also 1940s, sociology was 'not respectable, anthropology was suspect' in the nationalist's opinion as an

instrument of colonial policy and 'writing about such unpleasant things as caste division, child marriage ... '. But, a small band of scholars including Majumdar continued their work analyzing fundamental social institutions such as caste, untouchability, religion, etc., in spite of this unfriendly if not hostile environment. Moreover, while Indian scholars were influenced by their Western, mostly British, teachers and colleagues in various ways they cannot be accused of being imitative. Thanks to the empirical tradition and field work, the Indian situation did impinge itself upon them and force them to keep Indian society and culture all the time before them (Srinivas and Panini, 1986: 34–35).

8. In 1953, Majumdar was the Co-Director with Opler of the Cornell India Project, funded by the Ford Foundation for a period of three years, which was perhaps the largest such collaborative projects in social sciences, then. S.C. Dube's critical study on C.D. Programme, *India's Changing Villages*, was based on work in this project. However, Majumdar withdrew from this project midway when he felt that Opler was ignoring him while taking vital decisions and, also, a shadow was cast on it on the grounds raised by the six social scientists, a criticism which was also noted in the Indian Parliament. Also see Saksena (2010: 75–84). In November 2013, Danda, in a personal discussion with this author, said that Opler (under whom he had done his PhD in the 1960s) had pointedly mentioned to him that his relations with Majumdar had turned sour because 'some others' had created misunderstandings between them.

9. Majumdar states that:

   A tribe is a social group with territorial affiliation, endogamous, with no specialization of functions, ruled by tribal officers, hereditary or otherwise, united in language or dialect, recognizing social distance with other tribes or castes, without any social obloquy attaching to them, as it does in the caste structure, following tribal traditions, beliefs and customs, illiberal of naturalization of ideas from alien sources, above all conscious of a homogeneity of ethnic and territorial integration.

   Further, he argues that scheduling of tribe should not be based only on these criteria and 'if the economic condition and the degree of acculturation are such that they have already been leveled up', a tribe should not be scheduled, for example the tribes of Duddhi or Raj Gonds of Sarguja. Moreover, parts of a tribe can also be scheduled depending on levels of acculturation, for example different garden labour. Majumdar suggests that lists can go up after applying the test which are easily applicable.

   He also suggests the test to be applied in case of scheduling of caste:

   1. Extent of education
   2. Economic security
   3. Property
   4. Status in the caste hierarchy in the area they inhabit.

   This will rule out omnivorous classification of castes who are advanced.

10. See the discussion in chapter 5, earlier.

13

Summing Up and a Word

> In India ... each generation of sociologists seems too eager to start its work ... with little or no attention to the work done before. This amnesia about the work of their predecessors ... . (Andre Beteille, 1997: 98)

Majumdar has not fared much differently in this 'amnesia', and T.N. Madan's writings about him are exceptions that prove the rule. More than a decade back, he was delivering a lecture in the Ethnographic and Folk Culture Society. He had then observed that Majumdar's work needed a detailed study, and later advised me to attempt a comprehensive study on Majumdar. I had agreed to try my hand at it, as I had been a student of Majumdar for about five years and subsequently his junior colleague for a year and, thus, I had developed some personal ties with him. Even after leaving Lucknow for Delhi, Majumdar always during his frequent visits to Delhi in the last almost three years of his life kept in touch with me. I recall with some nostalgia the last visit of Majumdar to Delhi where he arrived from Calcutta, and stayed in my small flat for two days which provided me an occasion to know him better. Subsequently when I retired and settled down in Lucknow, I resumed a close association with the Ethnographic and Folk Culture Society and also with the Departments of Anthropology as well as Sociology in the University of Lucknow, taking up lectures in some courses and participating in the seminars, etc. Later the society resolved to appoint me as an editor of *The Eastern Anthropologist*, and this association continues.

This work was planned by me initially to study, in depth, the entire range of Majumdar's vast writings and to then, present his views and contributions for the benefit of the later generation of anthropologists and sociologists. Thus, to use Madan's phrase (2013: 365) it was an attempt to 'make audible' his 'lost word', and, additionally, my quest to explore and hear echoes, so to say, of his voice.

Madan who has also been my teacher in the final year of post-graduation even in his initial advice emphasized how ethnography and anthropology in its totality had undergone a sea change from the time when Majumdar was working and, thus, highlighted the difficulties in hearing the 'echo'. He, however, advised and steered me throughout for about three years of this work, and then his *Sociology at the University of Lucknow* was published in 2013 and it provided me an anchorage, as it were.

Majumdar's writings are voluminous as the readers can themselves perceive from his bibliography and so are the works of various academics of his times and a large number of his distinguished students that can contribute to profiling Majumdar. Since I had the privilege of knowing most of his prominent students and later day anthropologists and sociologists personally, I could gather a great deal of information not only through the reading of their writings but also through formal communications and informal discussions with them. But, I must caveat that this effort is far from exhaustive. The absence of any papers of Majumdar in the two institutions he founded and built up had its own handicaps, and I had to depend, mainly, on the available published materials, almost entirely out of print and even library circulation.

This project also aimed at rediscovering Majumdar in his various roles – as a person, as a teacher, as an institution builder, a pioneering anthropologist; and, broadly, assessing his writings in relevant fields with a view to discovering how his 'lost word' had revertibrated in the anthropology of his times. Further, it was also an attempt to delineate whether any of his views and suggestions are reflected prognostically in later day developmental programmes and government policies and approaches.

Broadly, Majumdar's work can be classified into tribal studies with focus on cultural contacts and change; village studies with emphasis on inter-caste and tribe-caste relations, social structure, etc., analysed from the angles of change, particularly the planned change and development. There is a constant stress and explication of the applied facet of anthropology in his studies; and his efforts to extend the reach of anthropology beyond academics, as a body of knowledge, to other sections including planners, administrators and students in general, to make them conscious of the plurality of the Indian society and its dynamics. One can add to this his making anthropology take roots in an area like UP with few tribals, right from the time of his coming here in late 1920s. And now anthropology is available as a subject of study at pre-graduation level in UP. Therefore, one can best describe Majumdar's relationship with anthropology in S.C. Dube's words that, his 'zest for anthropology was *infectious*. He lived anthropology, talked anthropology and, I suspect even dreamt anthropology' (1993: 30).

II

Before summing up the salient findings and recension of Majumdar's works, I would like to add a few words here about Majumdar and the India Coffee House, Hazaratganj, Lucknow. Actually in his remarks about the Coffee House in those decades and 1950s and D.P. Mukerji's person (2013: 372–73, 375–376 note 8 and 9), Madan has very rightly criticized Visvanathan's 'slightly derisive' description of Mukerji 'as ... a Coffee House intellectual ...' (2006: 244). The intellectuals of Lucknow in those days and the Coffee House can under no circumstances be 'derisively linked'. A number of senior faculty members, except Radhakamal Mukherjee, from the Arts, Art and Architecture, Law and Medical faculties of the University of Lucknow, as well as intellectuals from other walks of life, journalism, politics, etc. used to frequent the India Coffee House in the evening and Sunday mornings. Majumdar's visits there were regular. He used to go first to the Universal Book Store, the largest stockist of quality books as also the publisher of the books of the Ethnographic and Folk Culture Society and some of his own books. And then to Ram Advani, the book shop which always displayed the best collection of books in social sciences, before reaching C.H.. Before leaving Hazaratganj, Majumdar was particular about having a *pan* (betel leaf) from a Bengali's stall near Universal. He used to sit with prominent authors like Yashpal, editor Chalapathi Rao and often his academic guests, and some junior faculty members as well. Here, the discussions were not only about current events but also their own creative plans and progress. I remember being introduced to at least three distinguished anthropologists at Majumdar's table in the Coffee House. Madan has given this place of gathering a very suitable intellectual description as a 'public space', 'and a place of communicative action'[1].

III

Born in 1903, Majumdar had an outstanding academic carrier and grew into one of the most prominent professional anthropologists of the first generation of such scholars. He was one of the very few professionals who kept his research interests active in various fields of anthropology as a general anthropologist and contributed richly to both social and physical anthropology. His sound grounding as a field worker made his study of the Ho the earliest work focusing on culture change in Indian anthropology.

Teaching at Lucknow, he also picked up from the prevailing environment in the Department of Economics and Sociology, an interdisciplinary approach to which he contributed his own element of the sociological dimensions of physical anthropology. While in the Cambridge University for two years in mid-1930s he had strived to give himself the widest possible and latest orientation in both the main branches of anthropology including the latest in social anthropology, functionalism from Malinowski himself. His intensive and analytical observation of the Indian situation, however, contributed to his looking for a combination of theoretical frames and methodology for his ethnographic studies. This effort enabled him to 'deal with culturology' along with a 'not superficial rendering of the structural functional approach' in the words of Mukherjee (1979: 68). For instance, analysing the Indian tribal scene he had pointed out that there was also the ground reality of long inter-tribal contacts and the resultant impact, and here he was ahead of Malinowaski in bringing up this shortcoming in Malinowski's theoretical frame for the study of culture change, having its bases in the African scene, primarily; and widening his approach to ethnography. In his dealing with the 'social equilibrium' aspect also in functionalism, his methodology made a departure.

After his return from Cambridge Majumdar's participation in the Indian Science Congress intensified and during its session in Calcutta (1938) he actively participated in drawing up a plan for anthropological research in India along with British anthropologists. The next year he, as Sectional President of Anthropology addressed the Congress with his perceptive and thought provoking essay on acculturation which was the outcome of his fieldwork in Bastar. The plans for expanding anthropological researches, however, were constrained due to the World War. Yet according to Majumdar Indian anthropology continued to pursue its agenda rather well even in the years of war (102: 1947).

In 1940s his efforts at firmly establishing anthropology in the central and northern India culminated into his establishing an anthropology laboratory for a widespread anthropometric and ethnological survey under the 1941 Census operation of UP. This was followed by his establishing the Ethnographic and Folk Culture Society and its English journal, *The Eastern Anthropologist*. The EA came to have an international standing right from its initial years due to Majumdar and Furer-Haimendorf being its editors. Thus, in a way he turned into a 'one man radiation centre' for anthropology as he also started gathering a batch of students around him who were loyal, actually more to anthropology than to him. In 1950, he was given a personal professorship, a rare honour followed by the setting up of a separate Department of Anthropology. His department was described after his death as 'the most active department of anthropology in South Asia'. His contributions found international recognition in the early 1950s when he was one of the two anthropologists invited from Asia to the Wenner-Gren Symposium. The other invitee was from Japan. In fact his 'culturology' was better received by the American scholars than the British. Later he represented India, Pakistan, Burma and Ceylon in the UN sponsored World Conference on Population in Rome. The range of his interests which included demography and urbanization inspired him to contribute a social survey of Lucknow which can certainly be called the first study in urban anthropology in India, and thereafter came his survey of Kanpur. The two institutions because of the dynamic leadership of Majumdar both in academics, and his guidance to the students in having carriers in anthropology added vigour to Majumdar's agenda of radiating anthropology. Anthropology gained a wide base in public knowledge, providing exposure of young minds to our country's cultural variety through popular writings in Hindi. Also, there came presentation of stage shows and exhibitions, and multi-pronged research activity. Added to this was his keenness to advance anthropology not only as a branch of knowledge but also as an academic discipline through the medium of Hindi. Some of his outstanding students enthusiastically pursued these goals from their own departments, for instance Vidyarthi at Ranchi. His department at Lucknow was attracting students from far off states by this time.

IV

Summarily, the large number of writings by Majumdar on the tribal situation, on cultural contacts and their positive and negative impact provides the following impression:

- Historical conditions of contact have been continuously changing the tribal cultures in varying degrees, complexion and nature.
- Tribes have been transforming into castes, rarely higher castes and mostly into lower castes.

- Territorial concentration in certain areas by one or a few tribes is also varied though affinities in identity and culture can be discerned.
- The changes in political and social organization, institutions have been gradually occurring often undermining traditional institutions, authority and leadership and even creating classes in otherwise egalitarian communities.
- In some of the tribal communities there has always been a hierarchical and feudal system, the origins of which Majumdar has attempted to decode.
- A functional and configurational analysis of the cultures studied mostly shows equilibrium but it has been disturbed in varying degrees in certain tribes as a result of a variety of contacts– the neighbouring castes, missionaries, traders, government policies and its execution through personnel who are deficient in more than one ways.
- The situation as seen by Majumdar opens up ample scope for application of anthropological knowledge.
- In spite of many negative hues as revealed through his observations, Majumdar's remarks carry a strong positivism and hope though he has sounded critical notes of warning alarms in the form of growing contra-acculturative forces, changing attitudes and so on and again hopes that these forces would not be allowed to go out of hand.

Thus, in spite of the fact that he did not carry out any substantial tribal studies in the post-colonial period, his words carry a serious note of timely warning about the situation. Subsequently, in his presidential address to the Indian Sociological Conference in 1956 he emphasizes the need for a carefully drawn up tribal policy. However, the exercise of putting a national tribal policy in place is still going on and in the meantime extremist movements have gained momentum in extensive tribal areas. As regards the tribal programmes, the contents of his books on the Ho and other papers carry significant suggestions which appear to have assumed relevance in the strategy for tribal development later after 1970s. These relate to how the tribal programmes can be adequately financed, drawing out detailed development blue prints for the tribes which are more backward which is now a tenet for the Primitive Tribal Groups (PTG) development, and area development plans after demarcating small and manageable tribal areas. Another important set of conclusions from his studies relate to the manner in which the extension of industrialization and mining activities should be handled in the tribal areas. He had also suggested a set of criteria which would enable the authorities to properly identify the tribes and also castes deserving to be scheduled.

Majumdar's village studies were taken up in quick succession from 1954. His perspective in these studies was to convincingly demonstrate the utility of anthropological methodology developed in the study of tribes for the studies of villages as 'little communities'. The other perspectives were to suggest a blue print for the reconstruction and development of rural India which was actually the real India. In the process, he wanted to show how this approach was better than the approach of economists and how applied social sciences could help the national plans for community development. The ethnographic and functional analysis of the village communities, he studied, contribute in indicating the weaker aspects of various government policies and the implementation of the community development programmes. Keeping in view the variety of social life in the country, he studied one village near Lucknow and another village in the fartherest corner of UP having substantial tribal and caste populations and situated in an area where tribes and castes met, and thus a 'fringe'.

In the village first mentioned, he also emphasized the changing inter-caste relations, role and position of castes and factions in the power equations and the channels of communications which link villages not only to a group of villages around but also to a larger area. Thus, an Indian village had never been an isolate. His focus on communications and, then, also the process which maintained the patterns of village culture in this village near Lucknow is significant. In the second village mentioned here, he had identified some outstanding characteristics of tribe-caste relations and how these contributed towards creating an equilibrium in this 'fringe' culture and the factors that could change it, as well. The third project of village studies was located in three villages taken as samples for a structural functional study of a polyandrous area in Deharadun district. Here, again he documented the social structure of this area where the caste system was far from complex. In this area he explored how the traditional inter-caste relations, between Khas (Rajputs and Brahmans), a few artisan castes and a couple of untouchable castes determined the economic, social and power relations. And, then, how and to what extent the community development programme, the Panchayati Raj and general elections and the egalitarian and democratic policies of the government had been received by the different strata of the polyandrous society. Of course, there were suggestions of an applied nature flowing out of this extensive and long study of more than two years and his earlier writings about this area– Jaunsar-Bawar.

Majumdar's contribution to urban anthropology lies in a social survey of Lucknow. In this survey, he along with other senior faculty members of the University drew up a methodology which was interdisciplinary and the work was conducted by small committees of experts along with a group of students. It is mentionable that till then no Indian anthropologist had taken up any urban study. His next urban study was part of the Research Programmes Committee's plan to get 14 cities studied with focus on urban problems, the kind of urbanization which had been going on and also the demographic features of the studied settlements with special attention to the measures introduced for family planning. Majumdar perhaps took up Kanpur because he wanted to unravel socio-cultural aspects of the kind of urbanization going on as a result of industrialization, unique to Kanpur which was the only industrial centre in Uttar Pradesh. Therefore, he collected data in the course of this study about the city's socio-cultural patterns, besides wide ranging survey results relating to employment, skills, demographic patterns, etc.

Majumdar's address as General President of the Second All India Sociological Conference (1956) can be regarded as the last statement of his academics and its implications for national policies and their implementation and also his ideas on the kind of application it can have in national reconstruction. Majumdar, in his opening remarks, said that the Society's choice of him as General President was that of 'an anthropologist indicating the linkage and intimate relationship that India has been foraging at between the two disciplines (anthropology and sociology)'. Thus, he begins by stressing the 'kinship between sociology and social anthropology' and traces it through the work of various eminent sociologists and anthropologists. He observes that both anthropology and sociology aim 'at a general understanding of the structure and functioning of society at different levels', and how anthropologists have taken up the studies of complex society and civilization.

He opines that the community development programme and development planning taken up in India should be a common focus for studies in sociology and social anthropology. In this context, he points out how 'change in socio-cultural system implies a correlated resistance' which again depends upon the cultural patterns of the relevant socio-economic system. In fact, the success of community development programme will depend on the stability and permanence of the changes it succeeds in bringing about in rural areas. Similar objectives have to be kept in mind for tribal groups, as well. Therefore, he avers that the approach should be to direct the change at its bases in the institutional patterns of the targeted community and not to emphasize just on individuals. So the agents of change – the personnel – should focus on institutions like kinship and panchayats and cooperatives as their channels of communication and foundations of change. In this connection, inter-group relations have to be unravelled and taken into account. At the same time, the programme must priortise the community's needs properly, keeping in view its cultural matrix.

Discussing tribal scenario, he stresses the need for a carefully planned tribal policy and strategy. These must keep in focus the present conditions of 'contacts and more contacts intensified' by better means of communication, widespread rush of non-tribals to the areas of industrial and mining activities in the tribal areas and all the concomitant factors. In this context, he pointedly refers to the tribal upsurge in NEFA (now Arunachal Pradesh) and some other areas. It is notable that in this connection he specifies the strong desire of the 'people at all level for cultural development and far more freedom than they now possess. This must be taken fully into account. And, ignorance of the larger society about the tribals which not only alienates them but also contributes to their problems. The address ends with an optimistic note. It thus emphasizes Majumdar as an 'activist –interventionist', a role which he was assuming during his last years of life, as observed by Madan while including the presidential address as one of the readings from Majumdar (2013: 233).

When one thinks of his sudden demise while he was so busy imaging his further work, it opens up a whole vista – particularly in view of Vidyarthi's telling us that there were plans for him to head a premier research institute in Bihar, after his retirement from Lucknow.

Note

1. S.C. Dube was for about two years a lecturer in the Department of Political Science, Lucknow University and also a close associate of Majumdar in the activities of the Ethnographic and Folk Culture Society, and taking some classes in anthropology in the Department of Economics and Sociology thereby sharing Majumdar's burden. Dube referred to the Coffee House, thus:

   Beyond the academics, there was lively political interchange, meetings in the Coffee House with important public figures, representing a range of political persuasions, from Communists to Lohiaites to Congressmen, including the occasional presence of a charismatic parliamentarian, Feroze Gandhi. (Saurabh Dube, 2007: 457).

Bibliography of Professor D.N. Majumdar[1]

1. 1923. 'The custom of burning human effigies', *MII*, Vol. 3: 97–103.
2. 1923. 'Notes on kali-nautch in the district of Dacca', *MII*, Vol. 3: 202–16.
3. 1923. 'Customs and taboos observed by an East Bengal woman from pregnancy to childbirth', *MII*, Vol. 3: 232–42.
4. 1924. 'Physical characteristics of the Hos of Kolhan', *JPASB*, Vol. 20: 171–80; also *MII*, Vol. 5: 83–114.
5. 1924. 'Some of the characteristics of Kolarian songs', *JPASB*, Vol. 20: 181–92: also (Abstract), P. (Twelfth) ISC, p. 265.
6. 1924. 'The traditional origin of the Hos: together with a brief description of the chief Bongas (Gods) of the Hos', *JPASB*, Vol. 20: 193–98.
7. 1924. 'On the terminology of relationships of the Hos of Kolhan'. *JPASB*, Vol. 20: 199–204.
8. 1924. 'A few remarks on the Sema Naga kinship terms', *MII*, Vol. 4: 193–208.
9. 1925. 'The birth ceremonies of the Hos of Kolhan', *MII*, Vol. 5: 175–82.

9.A* 1925. 'Cry of social reforms amongst the aborigines', *MR*, March.

9.AA* 1925. 'Physical characteristics of the Hos of Kolhan', *MII*. Vol. 5: 83–114.

10. 1925. 'Some ethnographic notes on the Hos of Kolhan', *MII*, Vol. 5: 183–89.
11. 1925. 'Some out-door and sedentary games of the Hos of Kolhan', *MII*, Vol. 5: 190–98.
12. 1925. 'The Hargari and its origin', *MII*, Vol. 5: 199–204.
13. 1925. 'Religion of the Kols' (Abstract), P. (Twelfth) *ISC*, p. 263.
14. 1925. 'Significance of totemism' (Abstract), P. (Twelfth) *ISC*, p. 265.
15. 1925. 'The physical characteristics of the Kols' (Abstract), P. (Twelfth) *ISC*, p. 266.
16. 1926. 'The Polias, Babupolias, Palias or Rajbansis: An instance of the conversion of tribes into castes in Bengal', (Abstract), P. (Thirteenth), *ISC*, p. 326.

---

[1] In the text all references to Majumdar's works have been made thus: (Sl. No. in this list: year: page) for example his paper at one above will be referred to as (1: 1923: 97–103).

17. 1926. 'The kinship terms of the Polias, Babupolias and Rajbansis in north Bengal', (Abstract), P. (Thirteenth) *ISC*, p. 326.

18. 1926. 'A few types of dramatic and sedentary games of the Hos of Kolhan in Singhbhum' (Abstract), P. (thirteenth) *ISC*, p. 326.

19. 1926. 'Marriage customs of the Hos of Kolhan' (Abstract), P. (Thirteenth) *ISC*, p. 327.

20. 1926. 'Ho belief about disease, death and after' (Abstract), P. (Thirteenth) *ISC*, p. 327.

21. 1926. 'Ethnographic notes on the ideas about eclipses, excommunication, adoption, rain-making, hoarfrosts, and hail-stones, dreams, earthquakes, etc. of the Hos' (Abstract), P. (Thirteenth) *ISC*, p. 327.

22. 1926. 'Ho life in Ho riddles' (Abstract), P. (Thirteenth) *ISC*, p. 327.

23. 1926. 'Pseudo-Rajputs: The Polias, Palias, Babupolias or Rajbansis of north Bengal. An instance of the formation of tribes into castes', *MII*, Vol. 6: 155–73.

24. 1926. 'The bigonial breadths of some of the Hos of Kolhan', *JPASB*, Vol. 22: 347–49.

24.A 1926. 'Marriage and betrothal among the Hos of Kolhan', *JPASB*: 199–168.

25. 1927. 'A few types of Ho songs', *JPSAB*, Vol. 23: 27–36.

26. 1927. 'Death and connected ceremonies among the Hos of Kolhan', *JPASB*, Vol. 23: 37–44.

27. 1927. 'Some of the worship festivals of the Hos of Kolhan', *JPSAB*, Vol. 23: 277–85.

28. 1928. 'Some norms of Ho culture', (Abstract), P. (Fifteenth) *ISC*, p. 317.

29. 1928. 'The cult of the dead among the Hos', (Abstract), P. (Fifteenth) *ISC*, p. 318.

30. 1929. 'Race and adaptability', *JPASB*, Vol. 25: 149–56.

30.A 1929. 'On the Korwas of the United Provinces', *MII*, Vol. XXV.

31. 1929. 'Maternity and couvade in primitive society', *MII*, Vol. 9: 66–71.

32. 1929. 'The Korwas of the United Provinces', *MII*, Vol. 9: 237–50.

33. 1929. 'Sex and sex-control in primitive society', *MII*, Vol. 9: 251–66.

34. 1929. 'The cult of the dead amongst the Korwas', (Abstract), P. (Sixteenth), *ISC*, p. 318.

35. 1930. 'Social organization amongst the Korwas', *MII*, Vol. 10: 104–15.

36. 1930. 'The economic background of social institutions in primitive society', *MII*, Vol. 10: 150–66.

37. 1930. 'Totemism and origin of clans', *Journal of the American Oriental Society*, Vol. 50: 221–32; also (Abstract), P. (Seventeenth) *ISC*, p. 394.

38. 1930. 'The Korwas and their country', (Abstract), P. (Seventeenth) *ISC*, p. 395.

39. 1930. 'The cycle of life amongst the Korwas', (Abstract), P. (Seventeenth) *ISC*, p. 396.

40. 1931. 'The clash and fusion of cultures in perganah Dudhi, district Mirzapur, UP', *MII*, Vol. 11: 54–55.

41. 1931. 'The Daarlung Kukis of the Lushai Hills', *MII*, Vol. 11: 55–56.

42. 1931. 'The position of woman in Ho society', *MII*, Vol. 11: 56.

43. 1931. 'Sorcery and divination in primitive society', *MII*, Vol. 11: 56–57.

44. 1931. 'The economic life of the Hos', *MII*, Vol. 11: 56.

45. 1931. 'Economic background of social institutions' (Abstract), P. (Eighteenth) *ISC*, p. 414.

46. 1931. 'Economic life in primitive society', (Abstract) P. (Eighteenth) *ISC*, p. 414.

47. 1931. 'Economic life of the Korwas', (Abstract), P. (Eighteenth) *ISC*, p. 415.

48. 1931. 'Forms and functions of primitive religion', (Abstract), P. (Eighteenth) *ISC*, p. 415.

49. 1931. 'Marriage and marital life among the Rawaltas' (co-author S.D. Bahuguna), (Abstract), P. (Eighteenth) *ISC*, p. 415.

50. 1931. 'Religious life among the Rawaltas' (co-author: S.D. Bahuguna), (Abstract), P. (Eighteenth) *ISC*, p. 416.

51. 1931. 'Festivals among the Rawaltas', (co-author: S.D. Bahuguna), (Abstract), P. (Eighteenth) *ISC*, p. 416.

52. 1932. 'Marital problem: a new orientation', *MII*, Vol. 12: 161–74.

53. 1932. 'The cycle of life amongst the Korwas', *MII*, Vol. 12: 255–75.

54. 1933. 'Disease, death and divination in certain primitive societies in India', *MII*, Vol. 13: 115–49.

54.A* 1935. A Changing Austric Culture. Ph.D. Dissertation No. 708, May (Mss Consulted in the Manuscripts Reading Room, Cambridge University Library on 4 July 2005).

55. 1936. 'The decline of the primitive tribes in India', *The Journal of the United Provinces Historical Society*, April.

56. 1936. 'A plea for better treatment of the aboriginal population in India', *Calcutta Review*, October, 67–75.

57. 1936. 'Food and feeding among the Austric tribes', (Abstract), P. (Twenty third) *ISC*, p. 395.

58. 1936. 'The concept of disease in Austric culture', (Abstract), P. (Twenty-third) *ISC*, p. 396.

59. 1936. 'The spirit of Bongaism' (abstract), P. (Twenty-third) *ISC*, p. 397.

60. 1937. *A Tribe in Transition: A Study in Culture Pattern*, London: Longman, Green & Co., vii+xii+216, illustrations, Bibliography.

61. 1937. 'Comparative anthropometry of a group of Saoras of both sexes', *MII*, Vol. 17: 77: also (Abstract), P. (Twenty-fourth) ISC, p. 336.

62. 1937. 'Some aspects of the economic life of the Bhoksas and Tharus of Nainital Tarai', *Journal of the Anthropological Society of Bombay*, Jubilee Volume: 133–35.

63. 1937. 'The cultural pattern of the Tharus', (Abstract), P. (Twenty-fourth) *ISC*, p. 335.

64. 1937. 'The material culture of the Rawaltas of Rawain' (co-author: S.D. Bahuguna), (Abstract), P. (Twenty-fourth) *ISC*, p. 338.

65. 1938. 'Racial admixture in the United Provinces', *MII*, Vol. 18: 9–18.

66. 1938. 'Modern trends in social anthropology', *Calcutta Review*, February: 162–76.

67. 1938. 'The marriage and nishpat customs of the Rishis' (Abstract), *MII*, Vol. 18: 59.

68. 1938. 'The tribal population and Christianity', *Modern Review*, May.

69. 1938. 'Race and language in India', (Abstract), *Nature*, Vol. 141: 1019.

70. 1938. 'The relationships of the Austric speaking tribes of India, with special reference to the measurements of the Hos and Saoras', *Proceedings of the Indian Academy of Sciences*, Vol. 7: 1–21; also (Abstract), P. (Twenty-fifth) *ISC*, p. 1.

71. 1939. 'The Murias of Narayanpur, Bastar state' (co-author: Kr. Indrajit Singh), *MII*, Vol.19: 68.

72. 1939. 'Sex and marriage in the Doon district', *Calcutta Review*, March: 309–18.

73. 1939. *Tribal cultures and acculturation*, Presidential Address, Section of Anthropology and Archaeology, Twenty-sixth, Indian Science Congress, pp. 46; also in *MII*, Vol. 19: 99–173.

74. 1939. 'Primitive society and its discomforts', *Proceedings of Second Population and Family Conference*, 1939.

75. 1940. 'The culture pattern of a polyandrous society', *MII*, Vol. 20: 82–83.

76. 1940. 'The racial composition of the polyandrous people of Jaunsar Bawar in the Dehradun district, United Provinces', *Journal of the United Provinces Historical Society*, Vol. 13: 35–50.

77. 1940. 'Blood groups and their distribution in certain castes in the United Provinces', *Science and Culture*, Vol. 5: 519–22.

78. 1940. 'Preface' in *Essays in Anthropology Presented to Rai Bahadur Sarat Chandra Roy* (eds), J.P. mills, D.N. Majumdar, et al. Lucknow: Maxwell Co., V–VIII.

79. 1940. 'Bongaism' in *Essays in Anthropology presented to Rai Bahadur Sarat Chandra Roy* (eds), J.P. Mills, D.N. Majumdar, et al. Lucknow, Maxwell Co., pp. 60–79.

80. 1940. 'Some aspects of the life of the Khasas of the cis-Himalayan region', *JRASB*, Vol. 6: 1–44.

81. 1941. 'Racial affiliation of the Gonds of the Central Provinces', *JRSAB*, Vol. 7: 35–56.

82. 1941. 'Book notices of how to make a little speech by G.M. Allen', *MII*, Vol. 21: 255–56.

83. 1941–42. 'Blood groups of criminal tribes', *Science and Culture*, Vol. 7: 334–37.

84. 1942. 'The Tharus and their blood groups', *JRASB*, Vol. 8: 25–38.

85. 1942. 'Blood groups of criminal tribes', *MII*, Vol. 22: 65–66.

86. 1942. 'Blood groups of the Doms', *MII*, Vol. 22: 239–44.

87. 1942. 'Anthropometric measurements of the Bhils', *JGRS*, Vol. 4: 220–37.

88. 1924. 'The blood groups of the Doms', *Current Science*, Vol. 11: 153–54.

89. 1943. 'Blood groups of tribes and castes of the UP with special reference to the Korwas', *JRSAB*, Vol. 11: 81–94.

90. 1944. *Fortunes of Primitives Tribes*. Lucknow: Universal Publishers.

91. 1944. *Races and Cultures of India*, Allahabad: Kitabistan, p. 285, Bibliography.

92. 1944. 'Racial affiliation of the Bhils of Gujarat: of the Panch Mahal district and the Rajpipla state', *JGRS*, Vol. 6: 172–86.

93. 1944. Review of Verrier Elwin's Maria Murder and Suicide, *MII*, Vol. 24: 88–94.

94. 1944. 'What is Frazerism?' *MII*, Vol. 24: 269–70.

95. 1946. *Race Elements in Gujarat*, Bombay: Gujarat, Research Society.

96. 1946. 'The malaise of culture', in *Snowballs of Garhwal* (Folk Culture Series) edited by D.N. Majumdar, Lucknow: The Universal Publishers Limited, i–xiv.

97. 1946. 'Biometric analysis of anthropological measurements on castes and tribes of the United Provinces', (co-authors: P.C. Mahalanobis and C.R. Rao), P. (Thirty-third) *ISC*, p. 138.

98. 1947. *The Matrix of Indian Culture*, Lucknow: the Universal Publishers Ltd., pp. vii+242. Bibliography.

99. 1947. 'Anthropology during the war', *American Anthropologist*, Vol. 49: 159–64.

100. 1947. 'The United Provinces – A Cultural mosaic', in S.C. Dube's *Field Songs of Chhatisgarh*, Lucknow: the Universal Publishers Ltd., III–XVIII.

100.A* 1947. 'Some folktales of Kolhan (Singhbhum, Bihar)', in *Folk Songs of Chhatisgarh*, Lucknow: Ethnographic and Folk Culture Society.

101. 1947. 'Racial Problems in Asia.' New Delhi: Indian Council of World Affairs (paper submitted to the Asian Relations Conference).

102. 1947. *Progress of Anthropology in India (1911–46): A Brief Review*, Jointly published by the Indian Science Congress Association and the Council of Scientific and Industrial Research, p. 31.

103. 1947. 'Blood group distribution in the United Provinces', (co-author Kunwar Kishen), *The EA*. Vol. 1: No. 1: 8–15.[2]

104. 1947. 'Report on the serological survey of the United Provinces, 1941 Census', *The EA*. Vol. 1: No.1: 8–15.

105. 1947. 'Some folk Tales of Kolhan', in S.C. Dube's *Field Songs of Chhatisgarh*, Lucknow: The Universal Publishers Ltd., pp. 66–95.

106. 1947. 'The criminal tribes of northern India', *The EA*. Vol. 1: No. 2: 33–40.

107. 1947. Review of W.G. Archer's, The Vertical Man. *The EA*, Vol. 1: 66–69.

108. 1947. Review of W.V. Grigson's, The Challenge of Backwardness, *EA*, Vol. 1: 8–15.

108.A 1947. Review of The Gypsy Scholar by Shamrao Hivale, *The EA*, Vol. 1: No.2: 65–60.

109. 1948. 'Rh frequency in the people of Lucknow', *Heredity*, Vol. 2: 399–401.

110. 1948. 'Blood groups in the Gujarat Population', (co-author; K. Kishen), *JGRS*, Vol. 10: 161 ff.

111. 1948. Review of Verrier Elwin's, The Muria and Their Ghotul, *The EA*, Vol. 1: No. 3: 42–47.

112. 1948. Review of Marriage Magazine, *The EA*, Vol. 1: 47–48.

113. 1948. Review of Furer-Haimendorf's, The Reddis of the Bison Hills', *The EA*, Vol. 1: 48–49.

114. 1948. Review of Swami Akhilananda's, Hindu Psychology, *The EA*, Vol. 1: 49–50.

115. 1948. Review of Mrs I. Karve's, Anthropometric Measurements of the Marathas, *The EA*, Vol. 1: 50–51.

116. 1948–49. 'Serological status of castes and tribes of cultural Gujarat', (co-author: Kunwar Kishen), *The EA*, Vol. 2: 92–97.

117. 1949. 'Anthropometric survey of the United Provinces: A Statistical Study', (Co-authors: P.C. Mahalanobis and C.R. Rao), with a Foreword by M.W.M. Yeatts. *Sankhya*, Vol. 9: 89–304.

118. 1949. 'Report of the racial, serological and health survey of Gujarat; Part II Anthropometric status of castes and tribes of Gujarat', (Co-author A.R. Sen), *JGRS*, Vol. 11: 118ff.

119. 1949. 'The racial basis of Indian social structure', *The EA*, Vo. 2: 145–52.

120. 1949. Review of C. von Furer-Haimendorf's, The Raj Gonds of Adilabad, *The EA*, vol. 2: 171–73.

121. 1949. 'Racial elements in Gujarat', *JGRS*, Vol. 11: 188ff.

122. 1949. 'Anthropometry and crime', *MII*, Vol. 29: 46–58.

123. 1949. 'A study of height and weight of the castes and tribes of Gujarat', *MII*, vol. 29: 110–123.

124. 1949. 'Growth trends among aboriginal boys of Kolhan, Singhbhum, Bihar', *The EA*, Vol. 2: 201–4.

124.A* 1949. 'Notes and Comments', *The EA*, Vol. 3:1.

125. 1949. 'The changing canvas of tribal life', *The EA*, vol. 3: 40–47.

126. 1949. 'Hamari sanskriti ka vikas' (Hindi), *Prachya Manav-Vaigyanik*, Vol. 1: 21–35.

127. 1949. 'The social economy of the Bhotiyas', in K.S. Pangtey's, *Lonely Furrows of the Borderland*, Lucknow: The Universal Publishers, Ltd., pp. 1–XI.

127.A* 1949. 'Introduction' in *The Criminal Tribes* by B.S. Bhargava, Lucknow: Ethnographic and Folk Culture Society.

128. 1949–50. 'The racial status of the Nuniya, Nunera, Gola, Agaria, Shorgar, Kharwal, and similar castes of Etah, Mainpuri, and Farrukhabad, U.P.', *The EA*, Vol. 3: 101–9.

129. 1949–50. 'Review of R. Ruggles Gates', Pedigrees of Negro Familie', *The EA*, Vol. 3: 113.

130. 1949–50. Review of C. Kluckhohn and Henry A. Murray (eds) Personality in Nature, Society and Culture', *The EA*, Vol. 3: 113–14.

131. 1950. *The Affairs of a Tribe: A Study in Tribal Dynamics*, Lucknow: The Universal Publishers Ltd., IV–XXVI+376, 20 plates, Text Illustrations, Map, Bibliography.

132. 1950. *Race Realities in Cultural Gujarat*, Bombay: Gujarat Research Society, p. 24.

133. 1950. 'ABO blood among the Garos of Eastern Pakistan', *MII*, Vol. 30: 32–35.

134. 1950. 'Anthropology under glass', *The Journal of the Anthropological Society of Bombay*, 1–16.

135. 1950–51. 'The Sankha Banik of Dacca', *The EA*, Vol. 4: 98–103.

136. 1950–51. 'Review of Stephen Fuchs', The Children of Hari', *The EA*, Vol. 4: 112–13.

137. 1950–51. 'Review of A.V. Thakker's, Tribes of India', *The EA*, Vol. 4:116–17.

138. 1951. *Races and Cultures of India*, second edition, Lucknow: the Universal Publishers Ltd., VII–XIV+215.

138.A 1951. *Social Survey of Lucknow City*. Lucknow: Ethnographic and Folk Culture Society, UP.

139. 1951. 'Tribal rehabilitation in India', *International Social Science Bulletin*, Vol. 3: No. 4: 802–13.

140. 1951. 'Review of Cora du Bois', The People of Alor: A Social-Psychological Study of An East Indian Island', *The EA*, Vol. 4: 189–91.

141. 1951. 'Manav riti-vigyan tatha jan-sanskriti samiti Uttar Pradesh' (Hindi), *Prachya Manav Vaigyanik*, Vol. 2: 1–3.

142. 1951. 'Luniya, Nunera, Gola, Agaria, Shorgar, Tatha, Kharwal, Etah, Mainpuri, Farrukhabad, ki saman jatiyon ki jatiya-istihiti', (Hindi), *Prachya Manav Vaigyanik*, Vol. 2: 29–41.

143. 1951. 'Adim jatiya jivan men prayog', (Hindi), *Prachya Manav Vaigyanik*, Vol. 2: 72–93.

143.A* 1951–52. 'Anthropological study of Growth among School children in Lucknow', (co-author – S. Bahadur), *The EA*, Vol. 5: 1–26.

144. 1951–52. 'ABO blood in India' (Co-author: S. Bahadur). *The EA*, Vol. 5: 101–22.

145. 1951–52. 'Review of The International Journal of Sexology', *The EA*, Vol. 5; 139.

146. 1952. 'Review of Laura Thompson's Culture in Crisis: A Study of the Hopi Indians', *The EA*, Vol. 6: 90–92.

147. 1952. 'Adivasi jivan ki chunauti' (Hindi), *Aj-Kal*, Vol. 8: 15–18.

147.A* 1952. 'Review of Verrier Elwin's Bondo Highlanders (Bombay 1950)', *MII*, Vol. 32: 1: 43–46.

148. 1953. 'Children in a polyandrous society', *The EA*, Vol. 6: 177–89.

149. 1953. 'Review of Laura Thompson's, Theory and Practice of Social Case Work', *The EA*, Vol. 6: 211–12.

150. 1953. On 'Acculturation', *AAT*: 125–26.

151. 1953. On 'National character', *AAT*: p. 139.

152. 1953. On 'Prestige and food', *AAT*: p. 1.

153. 1953. On 'Anthropology and medicine', *AAT*: p. 175.

154. 1953. On 'Anthropology in government', *AAT*: p. 183–84.

155. 1953. On 'Cultural social anthropology', *AAT*: p. 222.

156. 1953. On 'Genetics and social selection', *AAT*: p. 272.

157. 1953. On 'Anthropology as a field of study', *AAT*: 343–45.

158. 1953. 'Tribal economy of the cis-Himalayas', *The Indian Journal of Social Work*, Vol. 14: 1–13.

159. 1953. 'The aboriginal tribes of Orissa', *March of India*, Vol. 6: 54–

160. 1953. 'Modern trends in anthropological research, Lucknow Orientation' (40th session), *Indian Science Congress Souvenir*: 23–37.

161. 1953. 'Racial survey of Uttar Pradesh', *The EA* Vol. 6: 94–106.

162. 1953. 'India, Pakistan and Ceylon', *International Directory of Anthropological Institutions*, (ed.) William L. Thomas, Jr. and Anna M. Pikelis, New York: Wenner-Gren Foundation for Anthropological Research, Inc., pp. 67–77.

162.A* 1953. D.N. Majumdar's paper in *The Handbook of World Resources for Research and Education in Anthropology* (referred to in Sol Tax, et al. (eds) *An Appraisal of Anthropology Today*, 1953: 344).

163. 1954. 'Status of women in patrilocal societies in South Asia', in A. Appadorai (ed.), *The Status of Women in South Asia*, Bombay: Oriental Longmans Ltd., pp. 99–115

164. 1954. 'Religious life of the Ho', *MII*, Vol. 34: 346–50.

165. 1954. 'Ethnic frontiers and caste distance in Uttar Pradesh', *The 31st All India Medical Conference Souvenir*, Vol. 19–33.

166. 1954. 'Caste and race', in *Professor Ghurye Felicitation Voume*, K.M. Kapadia (ed.). Bombay: Popular Book Dept., pp. 205–25.

166.A* 1954. 'Some Trends of Tribal and Caste demography', *Proceedings of the World Population Conference 1954*, Vol. VI. New York: The United Nations.

167. 1954–55. 'Family and marriage in a polyandrous society', EA, Vol. 8: 85–110.

168. 1955. 'Introduction', *Rural Profiles* Vol. I, D.N. Majumdar (ed.) Lucknow: Ram Advani, III–XV.

169. 1955. 'Demographic structure in a polyandrous village', *Rural Profiles*, Vol. 1: 32–44; also in *The EA*, Vol. 8: 161–72.

170. 1955. 'Inter-caste relations in Gohana-Kalan', (co-authors: M.C. Pradhan, C. Sen, and S. Mishra), *Rural Profiles*, Vol. 1: 63–86; also in *The EA*, Vol. 8: 191–214.

171. 1955. 'Review of J.J. Honigmonn's, Culture and Personality', *The EA*, Vol. 9: 63–67.

172. 1955. 'The dynamics of social change', Address of the sectional President (Anthropology), First Indian Sociological Conference, Dehradun, pp. 19; also in *Agra University Journal of Research* (letters), Vol. 3: 28–40.

173. 1955. 'The Chero tribe of Bihar', *The March of India*, Vol. 7: 39–43.

174. 1955. 'The eye and the anthropologist', *Journal of the Gandhi Eye Hospital and Aligarh Muslim University Institute of Ophthalmology, Aligarh*, (Silver Jubilee), Special Number: 65–69.

175. 1955. 'Samajik parivartan ka gatishastra' (Hindi), *Samaj*, Vol. 1: 166–80.

176. 1955–56. 'Rural analysis – problems and prospects', *The EA*, Vol. 9: 92–103; also in A. Aiyappan and L.K. Ratnam (eds) *Society in India*, (1956), Madras: S.S.A., pp. 134–48.

177. 1956. *An Introduction to Social Anthropology* (co-author: T.N. Madan), Bombay, Asia Publishing House, pp. V–X+304

178. 1956. 'What the sociologists can do, What They Must Do. How They Can Do and How They Should Do It?' Presidential Address, Second Indian Sociological Conference, Patna; also in *The EA*, Vol. 10: 130–43.

179. 1956. 'Educated Unemployment: Nature and Extent of unemployment among University students', (co-author: S.K. Anand), *The EA*, Vol. 10: 43–51.

180. 1956. 'Avadh ke ek gram men parivarik jivan', (Hindi), *Samaj*, Vol. 2: 525–36.

181. 1956–57. 'A Little Community: A polyandrous village Jadi in the Chakrata Tehsil, Dehradun District', *Sociologist: Journal of the Sociology Association*, Christ Church College, Kanpur, 1–4.

182. 1956–57. 'Anthropology and primitive medicine', *Manava: The Organ of the Anthropology Club*, Lucknow University, 1–4.

183. 1957. 'The functioning of school system in a polyandrous society in Jaunsar Bawar, Dehradun District, UP', (co-author; S.K. Anand), *The EA*, Vol.10: 182–210.

184. 1957. 'Rupkund in oral literature', *The EA*, Vol. 11: 36–41.

185. 1957. 'Bharat ke vikas men samaj-vaigyanikon ka dayitva', (Hindi) *Samaj*, Vol. 2: 703–16.

186. 1957–58. 'Caste as a process', *Manava-Darpana: Organ of the Anthropology Club*, Lucknow University, Vol. 2: 1–5.

187. 1958. *Races and Cultures of India*, Third edition, Bombay: Asia Publishing House.

188. 1958. *Caste and Communication in an Indian Village*, Bombay: Asia Publishing House.

189. 1958. *Bharatiya Sanskriti ke Upadan* (Hindi), Bombay: Asia Publishing House.

190. 1958. 'Rural life and communication', *The EA*, Vol. 11: 175–88.

191. 1958. 'Jati parivartan ke prakran men', (Hindi), *Samaj*, Vol. 3: 297–302 and 338.

192. 1958. 'Rupkund rahasya', (Hindi), *Prachya Manav Vaigyanik*, Vol. 3: 94–106.

193. 1958. 'Notes and comments', *The EA*, Vol. 12: 1–4.

194. 1958–59. 'A Village school in the context of tribal education in Jaunsar Bawar', *Manava-Darpana*, Vol. 3: 1–8.

195. 1959. 'Rupkund in prospect and retrospect', *Uttar Pradesh*, March 1959: 1–12.

196. 1959. 'Shramdan: An aspect of action anthropology', *Indian Sociologist*, Vol. 1: 1–12.

197. 1959. 'Indian anthropologists in action', *Journal of Social Research*, Vol. 2: 10–15.

198. 1959. 'The light that failed', *Journal of Social Research*, Vol. 2: 90–97.

199. 1960. Race elements in Bengal, (co-author: C.R. Rao), Bombay: Asia Publishing House.

200. 1960. *Social Contours of an Industrial City* (assisted by N.S. Reddy and S. Bahadur), Bombay: Asia Publishing House.

201. 1960. *An Introduction to Social Anthropology* (co-author: T.N. Madan), Third impression, Bombay: Asia Publishing House.

202. 1960. 'Shramdan: An aspect of action anthropology', *Rural Profiles* II, Lucknow: Ram Advani, 103–16.

203. 1960. 'Review of Thomas O. Beidelman's, A Comparative Analysis of the Jajmani System', *Man*, Vol. 60: 80 (No. 117).

204. 1960. 'Angrez' (Hindi), *Hindi Vishvakosh*, Vol. 1, Varanasi: Nagari Pracharini Sabha (*HV*), 13–14.

205. 1960. 'Ho', (Hindi) in L.P. Vidyarthi (ed) *Bihar Ke Adivasi*, Patna: College Centre, 111–125.

206. 1960. 'Adivasi aur unki samasyayen', (Hindi) in L.P. Vidyarthi (ed) *Bihar Ke Adivasi*, Patna: College Centre, pp. 180–96.

207. 1961. 'Foreword' in L.P. Vidyarthi's, *The Sacred Complex of Hindu Gaya*, Bombay: Asia Publishing House.

208. N.D. 'Vartaman Bharat ki adim-Jatiyon ki ek Jhalak', (Hindi), *HV*, Vol. 1: 239–43.

209. N.D. 'Madhya-Prant ke Gond', (Hindi), *HV*, Vol.1: 363–70.

210. N.D. 'Assam ke Kuki log', (Hindi), *HV*, Vol. 1: 639–47.

211. N.D. 'Singhbhum (ya Sinhabhumi) ki Ho jati', (Hindi) *HV*, Vol. 2: 773–80.

212. N.D. 'Chota Nagpur ki Kharia jati', (Hindi), *HV*, Vol. 2: 901–6.

213. N.D. 'Sanyukta Prant ki Korawa jati', (Hindi), *HV*, Vol. 2: 1043–48.

214. N.D. 'Jaunsar Bawar ki Khasa jati', (Hindi), *HV*, Vol. 2: 1155–62.

215. N.D. 'Orissa ki riyasanton men basanewali Juang jati', (Hindi), *HV*, Vol. 2: 1177–82.

216. N.D. 'Assam ki Garo jati', (Hindi), *HV*, Vol. 3: 1393–1402.

217. N.D. 'Karwal', (Hindi), *HV*, Vol. 3: 1725–31.

218. N.D. 'Dom-Sanyukta Prant ki ek aur jarayam pesha jati', (Hindi), *HV*, Vol. 4: 1949–55.

219. N.D. 'Bhil-jati (1)', (Hindi), *HV*, Vol. 4: 2155–60.

220. 1962. *Himalayan Polyandry*, Bombay: Asia Publishing House.

221. 1961. *Races and Cultures of India* (4th edition), Bombay: Asia Publishing House.

222. 1960. *Chhor ka ek Gaon*, (Hindi), Bombay: Asia Publishing House.

223. 1964. *Pragitihas*, (Hindi): (co-author: Gopala Sarana). Bombay: Asia Publishing House.

224. 'A Special Report on Teaching of Social Anthropology', H. Kabir et al. (eds), *Teaching Sciences in India*, Lucknow: The Universal Publishers.

225. 1968. 'Approach to Tribal Problems' in L.P. Vidyarthi (ed.) *Applied Anthropology in India*, Allahabad: Kitab Mahal.

226. 1990. *Pragitihas* (2nd revised edition in Hindi co-author Gopala Sarana). Delhi: Hindi Madhyam, Karyanavan Nideshalaya, Delhi University.

Notes

1. This bibliography is based on the bibliography appended to 1961. Sarana, Gopala: 'Dhirendra Nath Majumdar (1903–1960)'. *The EA*, XIV: 2: 113–21.

   Abbreviations used:

   AAT. *An Appraisal of Anthropology Today*, Sol Tax et al (eds) Chicago: The University of Chicago Press.

   EA. *The Eastern Anthropologist*, Lucknow.

   HV. *Hindi Vishva-Bharati*, Shrinarayan Chaturvedi (chief ed.) Lucknow: Educational Publishing Company Limited.

   JGRS. *Journal of the Gujrat Research Society*, Bombay.

   JPASB. *Journal and Proceedings of the Asiatic Society of Bengal*, Calcutta.

   MII *Man in India*, Ranchi.

   PISC *The Proceedings of the Indian Science Congress*, Calcutta.

   A*A*A* Sl. Numbers marked thus are additions to the bibliography (1961).

2. Serial No. 103 and 104 are parts of one running article.

References

Adhikari, A.K. and R.K. Bhattacharya. 1982. 'The Extremist Movement: An Appraisal of the Naxalite Movement with Special Reference to its Repercussions among Tribes', In K.S. Singh (ed.), *Tribal Movements in India,* Vol. 2. New Delhi: Manohar Publications.

Agrawal, B.C. 2009. 'Theory of Communication Alliance: An Asian Paradigm'. *The EA* Vol. 62: 1: 423–431.

Ansari, Ghaus. 1960. *Muslim Castes in Uttar Pradesh.* Lucknow: Ethnographic and Folk Culture Society.

Aiyappan, A. 1965. *Social Revolution in a Kerala Village: A Study in Culture Change.* Bombay: Asia Publishing House.

Appadurai, Arjun. 1986. 'Theory in Anthropology: Center and Periphery'. *Comparative Studies of Society and History,* 28(2), 356–374.

Arora, Vibha and N. Jayaram. (eds). 2013. *Routeing Democracy in the Himalayas: Experiments and Experiences.* New Delhi: Routledge.

Atal, Yogesh. 2003. *Indian Sociology: From Where to Where – Footnotes to the History of the Discipline.* Jaipur and New Delhi: Rawat Publications.

Atal, Yogesh. and Rajesh Misra (eds). 2004. *Understanding the Social Sphere: The Village and Beyond.* Jaipur and New Delhi: Rawat Publications.

Bailey, F.G. (ed.) 1957. *Caste and the Economic Frontier: A Village in Highland Orissa.* Manchester: Manchester University Press.

——. 1961. 'Tribe and Caste in India'. *Contributions to Indian Sociology,* 5 Paris and The Hague.

——. 1963. *Politics and Social Change.* London: University of California Press.

Bamshad, Michael. et al. 2001. 'Genetic Evidence on the Origins of Indian Caste Population'. *Genome Research.* www.genome.org.in.

Barnabas, A.P. 1969. *Social Change in a North Indian Village.* New Delhi: Indian Institute of Public Administration.

Basu, Swaraj. 2003. *Dynamics of a Caste Movement: The Rajbansis of North Bengal (1910–37).* New Delhi: Manohar.

B.B., P.R.C. and F.A.A.M. 1955. 'The World Population Conference, Rome, 1954'. *Journal of Indian Actuaries*: 81: 186–189.

Beals, Ralph L. 1951. 'Urbanism, Urbanisation and Acculturation'. *American Anthropologist* Vol. 53 No.1 January March, 1951.

——. 1953. 'Acculturation'. In Kroeber A.L. (ed.) *Anthropology Today.* Chicago: The University of Chicago Press.

Benedict, Ruth. 1946. *Patterns of Culture.* The New American Library.

Beteille, Andre. 1974. *Essays in Comparative Sociology.* Delhi: Oxford University Press.

——. 1996. *Caste, Class and Power: Changing Patterns of Stratification in a Tanjore Village.* New Delhi: Oxford University Press.

——. 2002. *Sociology: Essays on Approach and Method.* New Delhi: Oxford University Press.

Beteille, Andre and T.N. Madan. 1975. *Encounter and Experience: Personal Accounts of Fieldwork.* Delhi: Vikas Publishing House Pvt. Ltd.

Berger, Peter. 2012. 'Theory and Ethnography in the Modern Anthropology of India'. *HAU: Journal of Ethnographic Theory*: 2(2): 325–57.

Bhatt, G.S. 2004. *Between Anthropology and Sociology: An Anthropology of some Ideological Methodological Issues.* New Delhi: Jawahar Publishers & Distributors.

——. 2010. *Cult, Religion and Society: Polyandrous People of Western Himalaya.* New Delhi: Rawat Publications.

Bharagava, Bhawani Shankar. 1949. *The Criminal Tribes: A Socio-Economic Study of the Principal Criminal Tribes and Castes in Northern India*, Lucknow: Ethnographic & Folk Culture Society.

Bokil, Milind. 2002. 'De-notified and Nomadic Tribes: A Perspective', *Economic and Political Weekly* (January 2002), 148–154.

Bose, N.K. 1961. 'Foreword'. In Vidyarthi, L.P. edited *Aspects of Religion in Indian Society.* Meerut: Kedar Nath Ram Nath, p. iv.

——. 1967. 'The Hindu Method of Tribal Absorption' in *Culture and Society in India.* Bombay: Asia Publishing House.

——. 1968. *Calcutta: 1964 A Social Survey.* New Delhi: Lalvani Publishing House.

Bulsara, J.F. 1964. 'Foreword'. In Bulsara J.F. edited *Problems of Rapid Urbanisation in India.* Bombay: Popular Prakashan.

Cambridge University. 1935. *The Cambridge University Calendar for the year 1935–36.* London: University Press Cambridge.

Chacko, P.M. (ed.). 2005. *Tribal Communities and Social Change.* New Delhi: Sage Publications.

Chandra, Harish. 1975. 'Trafficking in Women and Prostitution in Jaunsar Bawar'. *Journal of LBS National Academy of Administration,* Vol. XX, No. 2. Mussoorie.

Chandra, Uday. 2013. 'Liberalism and Its Other: Politics of Primitivism in Colonial and Postcolonial Indian Law'. *Law and Society Review,* Vol. 47, No.1, 135–168.

Chauhan, B.R. 2009. *Rural Life: Grass Root Perspectives.* New Delhi: Concept Publishing Company.

Clinard, M.B. and J.R. Elder. 1965. 'Sociology in India: A Study in Sociology of Knowledge'. *American Sociological Review*: 30(4): 581–587.

Cohn, B.S. 1954. 'Review of *The Affairs of a Tribe* by D.N. Majumdar'. *American Anthropologist,* New Series, Vol. 56 No-3 (Jun 1954), 517–518.

——. (ed.). 1987. *An Anthropologist Among the Historians and Other Essays,* New Delhi: Oxford University Press.

Danda, Ajit K. 1995. *Foundations of Anthropology: India.* New Delhi: Inter-India Publications.

Dasgupta, Biplab. 1977. *Village Studies in the Third World.* Delhi: Hindustan Publishing Corporation.

Dasgupta, Somesh. 1995. 'The Evolution of the D^2-Statistic of Mahalonobis'. *Indian Journal of Pure Applied Mathematics* 26(6): 485–50.

Dasgupta, Sangeeta. 2010. 'Recasting the Oraons and the 'Tribe': Sarat Chandra Roy's Anthropology'. In *Anthropology in the East* (eds Patricia Uberoi, Nadini Sundar and Satish Deshpande). Ranikhet: Permanent Black, 132.

Deva, Indra. 1956. 'Modern Social Forces in Indian Folk-Songs', *Diogenes*, UNESCO, Paris.

——. 1966. 'Social Change in Asia and Its Impact on Folklore and Folk Culture', *Conspectus of Indian Society*, Agra, 350–364.

——. 1972. 'Folklore Studies: A Trend Report'. In *A Survey of Research in Sociology and Social Anthropology,* sponsored by Indian Council of Social Science Research. Bombay: Popular Prakashan.

——. 1978. 'Must Folk Culture Die'? *The Eastern Anthropologist,* Vol. 31, No. 4, pp. 575–587.

D' Souza, V.S. 1974. 'Urban Studies: A Trend Report'. In *A Survey of Research in Sociology and Social Anthropology.* Vol. 1. Bombay: Popular Prakashan.

Dube, S.C. 1947. *Field Songs of Chhattisgarh. Folk Culture Series* No. 2: 1–63, Lucknow: The Universal Publishers Ltd.

——. 1949. 'Some Aspects of the Tribal Problem'. *The Eastern Anthropologist* 3:1: 28–35.

——. 1955. *Indian Village.* London: Routledge and Kegan Paul.

——. 1972. 'The Changing Village'. In K.S. Mathur and S.C. Verma (eds) *Man and Society.* Lucknow: The Ethnographic and Folk Culture Society.

——. 1977, 'Indian Sociology at the Turning Point', *Sociological Bulletin* Vol. 26 No. 1

Dube, Saurabh. 2007. 'Ties that Bind: Tribe, Village, Nation, and S.C. Dube'. In *Anthropology in the East* (edited by Patricia Uberoi, Nadinin Sundar and Satish Deshpande). Ranikhet: Permanent Black, 444– 495.

Dumont, Louis. 1970. *Homo Hierarchicus: An Essay on the Caste System.* London: The University of Chicago Press.

Edward, Said. 1979. *Orientalism*, New York: Vintage Books.

Ekka, P. 1972. 'Revivalist Movements among the Tribals of Chotta Nagpur'. In Singh, K.S. (ed.), *Tribal Situation in India.* Shimla: Indian Institute of Advanced Studies.

Elwin, V. 1943. *The Aboriginals.* New Delhi: Oxford University Press.

——. 1960. *A Philosophy for NEFA.* Shillong: Government of Assam.

Epstein, T.S. 1977. 'Resurveys and Re-Studies of Rural Societies', in Biplab Das Gupta (ed.) *Village Studies in the Third World*, Delhi: Hindustan Publishing Corporation. p. 127.

Ellefsen, R. 'Review of *Social Contours of an Industrial City* by D.N. Majumdar'. *Journal of Asian Studies* Vol. 20 No-4 (Aug. 1961) 558–559.

E.R.L. 1946. 'Review of *The Fortunes of Primitive Tribes* by D.N. Majumdar'. *MAN*, Nos. 59, 60. May–June 1946. p. 67.

Evans-Pritchard, E.E. (et al.) 1954. *The Institutions of Primitive Society.* Oxford: Basil Blackwell.

——. 1965, *Theories of Primitive Religion.* London: Oxford University Press.

Firth, Raymond. 1951. *Elements of Social Organization.* London: Watts & Co.

——. (ed.). 1957. *Man and Culture: An Evaluation of the Work of Bronislaw Malinowski.* London: Routledge & Kegan Paul.

Fortes, M. 1953, *Social Anthropology at Cambridge Since 1900,* Cambridge: Cambridge University Press.

Fuchs, Stephen. 1992. *Godmen on the Warpath: A Study of Messianic Movements in India.* New Delhi: Munshiram Manoharlal Publishers.

Fuller, C.J. and Jonathan Spencer. 1990. 'South Asian Anthropology in 1980s'. *South Asia Research.* 10: 85–105.

Furer Haimendorf, C.Von. 1985. *Tribes of India: The Struggle for Survival.* Delhi: Oxford University Press.

Ganguly, P.G. 1958. *Growth of Jamshedpur and Some Aspects of Tribal Change:* Unpublished Master's thesis, Lucknow: Lucknow University.

Gandhi, Malli. 2013. 'Challenges of Livlihood, Dignity and Development of Denotified Communities'. *The EA* Vol. 66 No. 1 (January–March 2013), 121–144.

Gandhi, M. and V. Lalitha. 2009. *Tribes Under Stigma: Problem of Identity.* New Delhi: Serials Publications.

Geertz, Clifford. 1995. *After the Fact: Two Countries, Four Decades, One Anthropologist.* London: Harvard University Press.

Ghurye, G.S. 1943. *The Aborigines– 'So Called' – And Their Future.* Poona: Oriental Watchman Publishing House.

——. 1950. *Caste and Class in India.* Bombay: The Popular Book Depot.

Guha, R.C. 1999. *Savaging The Civilised: Verrier Elwin, His Tribals, and India.* New York: Oxford University Press.

Goodall, M.R. 1955. 'The Cornell-Lucknow Evaluation Studies of the Community Development Programme'. *Rural Profiles* (ed. D.N. Majumdar). Lucknow: The Ethnographic and Folk Culture Society.

Grierson, J.A. 1959. *Bharat ka Bhasha Sarvekshan. Vol. 1, Part 1.* (Hindi translation by Udayanarayan Tiwari). Lucknow: Uttar Pradesh: Prakashan Shakha, Suchana Vibhag.

Haddon, A.C. 1934. *History of Anthropology.* London: Watts & Co.

Hale, Sylvia M. 1984. *Decision Processes in Rural Development in India.* Lucknow: Ethnographic & Folk Culture Society.

Hasan, Amir. 1979. *The Buxas of the Tarai: A Study of their Socio-Economic Disintegration.* Delhi: B.R. Publishing Corporation.

——. 1987. 'Land Reforms in Tribal Areas and its Consequences', in H.S. Saksena et. al. (ed.) *Perspectives in Tribal Development: Focus on Uttar Pradesh,* Lucknow: Ethnographic and Folk Culture Society.

——. 1998. 'Reflections on Change among Tribes of Uttar Pradesh'. In H.S. Saksena et al. (eds) *Perspectives in Tribal Development: Focus on Uttar Pradesh,* 45–56.

Hasnain, Nadeem. 1982. *Bonded For Ever.* New Delhi: Prakashan Sansthan.

——. 2011. *An Anthropological Journey (Collection of D.N. Majumdar Memorial Endowment Lectures*), Lucknow: Department of Anthropology, University of Lucknow.

——. 2012. *Bonded For Ever.* New Delhi: Prakashan Sansthan.

Hogbin, H. Ian. 1957. 'Anthropology as Public Service and Malinowski's Contribution to it'. In Raymond-Firth (ed.) *Man and Culture: An Evaluation of the Work of Bronislaw Malinowski.* London: Routledge & Kegan Paul.

Hutton, J.H. 1946. *Caste in India: Its Nature, Function, and Origins (4th edition).* Delhi: Oxford University Press.

India, Government of. 1960–61. *Report of the Scheduled Areas and Scheduled Tribes Commission.* Vol. I. New Delhi: Manager of Publications.

——. 2008. *Development Challenges in Extremist Affected Areas* (Report of an expert group to Planning Commission). New Delhi: Planning Commission.

——. 1975. *Tribal Development in the Fifth Plan: Some Basic Policy Papers,* New Delhi: Ministry of Home Affairs.

——. 2006. *The National Tribal Policy* (A Policy for the Scheduled Tribes of India).

Iyer, L.A.K. (et al.). 1961. *Anthropology in India,* Bombay: Bhartiya Vidya Bhavan.

Jain, R.K. 1974. 'Social Anthropology of India: Theory and Practice'. In *Survey of Research in Sociology and Social Anthropology 1969–1974.* Vol. I. New Delhi: Satvahan.

Jodhka, S.S. 1998. 'From 'Book-view' to 'Field-view': Social Anthropological Constructions of the Indian Village'. *Oxford Development Studies,* Vol. 26, No 5.

——. 2000. 'Sociology/Anthropology, Nation and the 'Village Community'; Paper presented to IEG Delhi: National Workshop on Knowledge, Institutions, Practices: The Formation of Indian Anthropology and Sociology (April 2000).

——. 2012. *Caste.* Delhi: Oxford University Press. (305. 5 JOD – 42978)

——. (ed.) 2012. *Village Society*, New Delhi: Oriental BlackSwan.

Joshi, M.M. 1967. *Bastar India's Sleeping Giant.* Delhi: Peoples Publishing House.

Kapadia, K.M. 1952. 'The Criminal Tribes of India', *Sociological Bulletin*, Vol. I, No. 2.

Keesing, F.M. 1952. 'Review of *The Affairs of a Tribe: A Study in Tribal Dynamics.* By D.N. Majumdar'. *American Journal of Sociology*, Vol. 57, No. 4 (January 1952), p. 392.

——. 1953. *Culture Change: An Analysis and Bibliography of Anthropological Sources to 1952*. Stanford: Stanford University Press.

Kroeber, A.L. 1948. *Anthropology*. New York: Harcourt, Brace and Company.

——. (ed.) 1953. *Anthropology Today: An Encyclopedic Inventory*. Chicago: The University of Chicago Press.

Kroeber, Theodora. 1970. *Alfred Kroeber: A Personal Configuration*, London: University of California Press.

Kuper, A. (ed.) 1973. *Anthropologists and Anthropology*. London: Allen Lane.

Lakshmanna, C. 2012. 'Professor S.P. Nagendra Memorial Lecture 2012'. Lucknow: Department of Sociology, University of Lucknow.

Lambert, Claire M. (ed.) 1976. *Village Studies Data Analysis and Bibliography*, Vol. 1: India 1950–1975. Sussex: Bulky Epitomical Publication.

Leach, E.R. (ed.). 1960. *Aspects of Caste in South India, Ceylon and North-West Pakistan*, Great Britain: Cambridge University Press

Lieten, G.K. and Srivastava, R. 1999. *Unequal Partners: Power Relations, Devolution and Development in Uttar Pradesh*. New Delhi: Sage Publications.

Linton, Ralph. (ed.) 1945. *The Science of Man in the World Crisis*. New York: Columbia University Press.

Lok Sabha Secretariat, New Delhi. 1969, *The Scheduled Castes and Scheduled Tribes Orders (Amendment) Bill 1967 (Report of the Joint Committee)*. Delhi.

Lord, Raglan. 1949. *The Origins of Religion*. London: Watts & Co.

Lowie, Robert H. 1937. *The History of Ethnological Theory*. New York: Rinehart & Company, INC.

Madan, T.N. 1983. *Culture and Development.* New Delhi: Oxford University Press.

——. (ed.). 1992. *Religion in India*. Delhi: Oxford University Press.

——. 2011, *Sociological Traditions: Methods and Perspectives in the Sociology in India*. New Delhi: Sage Publications Ltd.

——. (ed.). 2013, *Sociology at the University of Lucknow: The First Half Century (1921–1975)*. Delhi: Oxford University Press.

Madan, Vandana (ed.). 2002. *The Village in India*. New Delhi: Oxford University Press.

Mair, Lucy P. 1939. 'Review of *A Tribe in Transition* by D.N. Majumdar'. *MAN*. Nos. 25–26. February 1939. p. 28.

——. 1957. 'Malinowski and the Study of Social Change'. In Raymond Firth edited *Man and Culture: An Evaluation of the work of Bronislaw Malinowski*. London: Routledge & Kegan Paul, 229–44.

Maiti, Sameera. 2004. *The Tharu: Their Arts and Crafts.* New Delhi: Northern Book Publishers.

Mandelbaum, D.G. 1972. *Society in India*. Bombay: Popular Prakashan.

Malinowski, B. 1926. *Crime and Custom in Savage Society*. London: Kegan Paul, Trench, Trubner & Co. Ltd.

——. (et al.). 1944. *A Scientific Theory of Culture and Other Essays.* New York: The University of North Carolina Press.

——. 1945. *The Dynamics of Culture Change: An Enquiry into Race Relations in Africa.* London: Oxford University Press.

Marret, R.R. 1938. Writing in the *Oxford Magazine*: 3: 3. Quoted by D.N. Majumdar in *Man in India*: 34: 4: 350, December 1954.

Marriot, McKim. 1955. *Village India: Studies in the Little Community.* Chicago: The University of Chicago Press.

Mathur, H.M. (ed.). 1977. *Anthropology in the Development Process*, New Delhi: Vikas Publishing House Pvt. Ltd.

Mathur, K.S. (et al. eds). 1972. *Man and Society.* Lucknow: Ethnographic & Folk Culture Society.

Mayer, A.C. 1960. *Caste and Kinship in Central India.* London: Routledge and Kegan Paul.

——. 1960. 'Review of D.N. Majumdar's *Caste and Communication in an Indian Village'.* *MAN* Vol. 60 (Jun 1960), p. 96.

Mehrotra, D.P. 2006. *Gulab Bai: The Queen of Nautanki Theatre.* New Delhi: Penguin Books.

Mencher, Joan P. 1975. 'Viewing Hierarchy From the Bottom Up'. In Beteille, A. and Madan, T.N. (ed.) *Encounters and Experience: Personal Accounts of Fieldwork.* Delhi: Vikas Publication.

Misra, K.K. 1987. *Social Structure and Change Among the Ho of Orissa.* Delhi: Gian Publishing House.

Mukerjee, Radhakamal and Baljit Singh. 1952. *A City in Transition: A Survey of Social Problems of Lucknow.* Lucknow: University of Lucknow.

Mukherjee, D.P. 1996. 'Some Anthropological Contributions of Biraja Sankar Guha: A Study in Retrospect'. In R.K. Bhattacharya and Jayanta Sarkar (eds) *Anthropology of B.S. Guha (A Centenary Tribute).* Kolkata: Anthropological Survey of India.

Mukerji, D.P. 1961. 'Indian Tradition and Social Change'. In R.N. Saksena (ed.) *Sociology and Social Research and Social Problems in India.* Bombay: Asia Pub. House.

——. 1962. 'Majumdar: Scholar and Friend'. In T.N. Madan and G. Sarana (ed.) *Indian Anthropology.* Bombay: Asia Publishing House.

Mukherjee, R. and Saroj Bandyopadhyay. 1964. 'Social Research and Mahalonobis's D^2'. In C.R. Rao (ed.) *Contributions to Statistic: Presented to Professor P.C. Mahalonobis on the Occasion of his 70th Birthday.* Calcutta: Statistical Publishing Society.

Mukherjee, R. 1965. *The Sociologist and Social Change in India Today.* New Delhi: Rentice-Hall of India (Private) Ltd.

——. 1979. *Sociology of Indian Sociology.* New Delhi: Allied Publishers Private Ltd.

Munshi, Indra, 2007. 'Partick Geddes: Sociologist, Environmentalist and Town Planner'. In Patricia Oberoi et al. (eds), *Anthropology in the East.* Ranikhet: Permanent Black, pp. 190–91.

Munshi, Indra. (ed.). 2012. *The Adivasi Question: Issues of Land, Forest and Livelihood.* New Delhi: Orient BlackSwan.

Murphy, R.F. 1971. *Dialectics of Social Life: Alarms and Excursions in Anthropological Theory.* London: Basic Books, INC Publishers.

Nadel, S.F. 1938. 'Social Symbiosis and Tribal Organization'. *MAN* Vol. XXXVIII.

——. 1953. *The Foundations of Social Anthropology.* Glasgow: The University Press.

Opler, Morris and Singh, R.D. 1950. 'The Division of Labor in an Indian Village'. In Carleton S. Coon (ed.) *A Reader in General Anthropology.* 464–496.

O' Reilly, Karen. 2005. *Ethnographic Methods.* London and New York: Routledge

Oommen, T.K. 1983. 'Sociology in India: A Plea for Contextualization'. *Sociological Bulletin* Vol. 32, No. 2, 111–136

——. 1995. *Alien Concept South Asian Reality: Responses and Reformulation.* New Del[illegible] Sage Publications.

——. (et al.). 1986. *Indian Sociology: Reflections and Introspections.* Bombay: Popular Prakashan Private Ltd.

Ortner, S.B. 1984. 'Theory in Anthropology since the Sixties'. *Comparative Studies in Society and History,* Vol. 26, No. 1 (January 1984), 126–166.

Parmar, Y.S. 1975. *Polyandry in the Himalayas.* Delhi: Vikas Publishing House Pvt. Ltd.

Patel, Sujata. (ed.). 2011. *Doing Sociology in India: Genealogies, Locations, and Practices.* New Delhi: Oxford University Press.

Penniman, T.K. 1935. *A Hundred Years of Anthropology.* London: Gerald Duckworth & Co. Ltd.

Peter Prince of Greece. 1963. Review of *Himalayan Polyandry* by D.N. Majumdar, *MAN* Vol. 63, October, p. 166.

Planning Commission. 1955. *Leadership and Groups in a South Indian Village,* New Delhi: PEO Publication, No. 9.

Powdermaker, H. 1940. 'Review of *A Tribe in Transition* by D.N. Majumdar'. *American Sociological Review,* Vol. 5, No. 5 (Oct. 1940), 794–795.

Pramanick, S.K. 2001. *Sociology of G.S. Ghurye.* Jaipur and New Delhi: Rawat Publications.

Radcliffe-Brown, A.R. 1952. *Structure and Function in Primitive Society: Essays and Address.* London: Cohen & West Ltd.

Radhakrishna, Meena. 2001. *Dishonoured by History 'Criminal Tribes' and British Colonial Policy.* Hyderabad: Orient Longman.

Ram, Kalpana. 2010. 'Anthropology as 'Ananthropology': L.K. Ananthakrishna Iyer (1861–1937), Colonial Anthropology, and the 'Native Anthropologist' as Pioneer'. In *Anthropology in the East* (eds). Patricia Uberoi, Nandini Sundar and Satish Deshpande). Ranikhet: Permanent Black.

Rao, M.S.A., Bhat C. and Kadekar L.N. 1991. *A Reader in Urban Sociology.* New Delhi: Orient Longman Ltd.

Rao, B. Shiva et al. 1968. *The Framing of India's Constitution: A Study.* New Delhi: The Indian Institute of Public Administration.

Redfield, Robert. 1955. *The Little Community: View points for the Study of a Human Whole.* Chicago: The University of Chicago Press.

Robb, Peter. (ed.) 1992. *Rural India: Land, Power and Society under British Rule.* Bombay: Oxford.

Roy Burman, B.K. 1974. 'Ethnicity in Chota Nagpur with Particular Reference to the Tribal Communities'. A Source Paper Prepared for a UNESCO Expert Committee on Race Relations in Asia and Oceania.

——. 1977. 'Village in the Census of India' in Biplab Das Gupta (ed.) *Village Studies in the Third World.* New Delhi: Hindustan Publishing Corporation.

——. 1994. *Tribes in Perspective.* New Delhi: Mittal Publications.

——. 2005. 'Meaning and Process of Tribal Integration in a Democratic Society'. In P.M. Chacko (ed.) *Tribal Conditions and Social Change.* New Delhi: Sage Publication.

Roy, S.C. 1912. *The Mundas and Their Country.* Calcutta: Logendranath Sarkar at the City Book Society.

Roy, S.C. 1933. *The Anthropology of Bihar and Patna.* Calcutta: Indian Science Hand Book.

Royal Anthropological Institute. 1960. *Note and Querries in Anthropology* (Revised edition) London.

Sachchidananda. 1978. *Builders of Indian Anthropology: Sarat Chandra Roy.* Varanasi: N.K. Bose Memorial Foundation.

——. 1988. *Social Change in Village India.* New Delhi: Concept Pub. Company.

Saksena, H.S. 1977. 'Uttar Pradesh Mein Vimukt Jatiyon ka Swaroop'. *Manav* Vol 5:1: 39–54.

——. 1981. *Safeguards for Scheduled Castes and Tribes: Founding Father's View: An Exploration of the Constituent Assembly Debates.* New Delhi: Uppal Publishing House.

——. 2004. 'Issues Concerning Vulnerable Groups: Vision 2020'. In *India Vision 2020 – The Report.* New Delhi: Planning Commission of India, 473–512.

——. 2006. 'Situating Chhor Ka Ek Gaon in the writings of D.N. Majumdar and Indian Village Studies'. In H.S. Saksena et al. (eds) *Scheduled Tribes and Development.* New Delhi: Serial Publications.

——. 2010. 'Has Anthropology Moved out of the 'Colonial' Woods?' In H.S. Saksena et al. (eds) *Anthropology in India.* New Delhi: Serials Publications, 75–84.

Saksena, H.S. and Chandra Sen. 1999. *Putting People Last: Tribal Displacement and Rehabilitation.* New Delhi: Inter-India Publications.

Saksena, R.N. 1962. *Social Economy of a Polyandrous People.* Bombay: Asia Publishing House.

Sanwal, B.D. 2005. *Rajrakshak Ki Ramkahani* (Hindi). Lucknow: Chaitanaya Prakashan.

Sarana, Gopala. 1961. 'Professor Majumdar and Anthropology of Indian Religion'. In Vidyarthi L.P. edited *Aspects of Religion in Indian Society.* Meerut: Kedar Nath Ram Nath, 1–12.

——. 1961 'Dhirendra Nath Majumdar: 1903–1960'. *The EA*: XIV: 2: 105–21.

——. 1983. *Sociology and Anthropology and Other Essays.* Calcutta: Institute of Social Research & Applied Anthropology.

Sarkar, R.M. 1991. 'Sarat Chandra Roy– The Architect of Indian Anthropology'. *Man in India* Vol. 71: 1.

——. (ed.) 2006. *Land and Forest Rights of the Tribals Today.* New Delhi: Serial Publications.

Shah, A.M. 2005. 'Sanskritization Revisited'. *Sociological Bulletin,* 54/2. Delhi: Indian Sociological Society.

Shah, Ghanshyam. 1990. *Social Movements in India: A Review of Literature.* New Delhi: Sage Publications.

Shah, Kantilal. 1955. *Thakkar Bapa* (Hindi). Delhi: Thakkar Bapa Smarak Samiti.

Shah, P.G. 1958. *The Dublas of Gujarat.* Delhi: Bhartiya Adimjati Sevak Sangh.

Sharma, B.D. 1976. *Planning for Industrial Development of the Tribal Areas.* New Delhi: Govt. Of India.

Sharma, K.N. (n.d.). *Institutions, Networks, and Social Change.* Shimla: Indian Institute of Advanced Study.

Simhadari, Y.C. 1979. *Ex. Criminal Tribes of India.* New Delhi: National Publishing House.

Singh, Indrajit. 1944. *The Gondwana and The Gonds.* Lucknow: The Universal Publishers Ltd.

Singh, K.S. (ed.) 1982. *Tribal Movements in India* Vol I and II. New Delhi: Manohar Publications.

——. 1989. 'Ethnography of L.K. Ananthakrishna Iyer and its relevance'. In Ajit K. Danda and Chakrabarti (eds) *L.K. Ananthakrishna Iyer-125th Birth Anniversary Tribute.* Calcutta: Anthropological Survey of India.

——. 1993. 'The Problems in Marginalised Tribals'. *Seminar.* 412: 1–7.

——. 1994. *The Scheduled Tribes.* People of India National Series Volume III. Anthropological Survey of India. Calcutta: Oxford University Press.

Singh, R.D. 1997. 'Majumdar, Dhirendra Nath (1903–60)'. In F. Spencer (ed.) *History of Physical Anthropology. An Encyclopedia.* New York and London: Garland Publishing Inc.

——. 1999. 'D.N. Majumdar as Physical Anthropologist', *The EA* Vol. 52 No. 4.

Singh, Y. 1973, 'The Role of Social Sciences in India: A Sociology of Knowledge', *Sociological Bulletin* Vol. 22, No. 1, 14–28.

——. 1986. *Indian Sociology: Social Conditioning and Emerging Concerns.* New Delhi: Vistaar Publications.

——. 2000. *Culture Change in India: Identity & Globalization.* Jaipur and New Delhi: Rawat Publications.

——. 2011. 'Discourses in Indian Sociology and Social Anthropology: Change and Continuities'. In Nadeem Hasnain (ed.) *An Anthropological Journey.* Lucknow: Department of Anthropology, University of Luckow.

Singer, M. and Cohn, B.S. 1996. *Structure and Change in Indian Society.* Jaipur: Rawat Publications

Sinha, S. 1965. 'Tribe-Caste and Tribe-Peasant Continuum in Central India', *Man in India.* Vol. XXXXV (1).

Sinha, A.C. 1999. 'Indian Social Anthropology and its Cambridge Connections'. *The EA*: 44: 4: 345–54.

Sol Tax (et al.). 1953. *An Appraisal of Anthropology Today.* Chicago: The University of Chicago Press.

Srinivas, M.N. 1952. *Religion and Society among the Coorgs of South India.* New Delhi: Oxford University Press.

——. (ed.). 1960. *India's Villages.* Bombay: Media Promoters & Publishers Pvt. Ltd.

——. (ed.) 1958. *Method in Social Anthropology: Selected Essays by A.R. Radcliffe-Brown.* London: The University of Chicago Press.

——. 1972. *Social Change in Modern India.* Delhi: Orient Longman Ltd.

——. 1976. *The Remembered Village.* Delhi: Oxford University Press.

——. 1997 'Practicing Social Anthropology in India'. *Annual Review of Anthropology*: 26: 1–24.

Srinivas, M.N. and M.N. Panini. 1973. 'The Development of Sociology and Social Anthropology in India', *Sociological Bulletin,* 22(2): 179–215.

Srinivashan, A. and Akhilesh Ranjan. 2006. 'Forntier Identity in the Tarai: The Tharu'. In H.S. Saksena et al. (eds), *Scheduled Tribes and Development.* New Delhi: Serials Publications. pp. 99–103.

Srivastava, S.K. 1958. *The Tharus: A Study in Cultural Dynamics.* Agra: Agra University Press.

Sundar, Nandini. 2007. *Subalterns and Sovereigns: An Anthropological History of Bastar (1854–2006).* New Delhi: Oxford University Press.

Thakkar, A.V. 1941. *The Problems of Aborigines in India.* Poona: Gokhale Institute of Politics and Economics.

——. 1949. 'Some Pressing Problems of Primitive Tribes'. *The EA* 1949: 3: 1–2.

Thompson, Stith. 1953. 'Advances in Folklore Studies'. In A.L. Kroeber (ed.) *Anthropology Today.*

Tripathi, C.B. 1962. 'Anuvadak ka Vaktavya'. In D.N. Majumdar's *Chhor Ka Ek Gaon.* Bombay: Asia Publishing House.

Turner, J.H. and Maryanski, A. 1979. *Functionalism.* London: The Benjamin/Cummings Publishing Company.

Upadhya, Carol. 2011. 'Colonial Anthropology, Law and Adivasi Struggle: The Case of Jharkhand'. In Sujata Patel (ed.) *Doing Sociology in India: Genealogies, Locations and Practices.* New Delhi: Oxford University Press.

Uberoi, Patricia. (et al.). 2007. *Anthropology in the East: Founders of Indian Sociology and Social Anthropology in India.* Ranikhet: Permanent Black.

Unnithan, T.K.N. (et al.). 1965. *Towards A Sociology of Culture in India.* New Delhi: Prentice-Hall of India (Private) Ltd.

Varma, S.C. (ed.) 1982. *Aspects of Society and Culture: An International Reader.* Lucknow: Ethnographic and Folk Culture Society.

Vidyarthi, L.P. 1968. *Applied Anthropology in India: Principles, Problems, and Case Studies.* Allahabad: Kitab Mahal.

——. 1969. *Cultural Configuration of Ranchi.* New Delhi: Planning Commission Publication

——. 1970. *Socio-Cultural Implications of Industrialization in India: A Case Study of Tribal Bihar.* New Delhi: Planning Commission Publication and Kitab Mahal Allahabad.

——. 1972. 'Social Anthropology in India since Independence'. In K.S. Mathur and S.C. Verma (eds) *Man and Society.* Lucknow: Ethnographic and Folk Culture Society.

——. 1978. *Rise of Anthropology in India: A Social Science Orientation* Vol. I and II. Delhi: Concept Publishing Company.

Vidyarthi, L.P. and B.N. Sahay. 1980. *Applied Anthropology and Development in India.* New Delhi: National Publishing House.

Visvanathan, Shiv. 2006. 'Officaial Hegemony and Contesting Pluralisms'. In Gustavo Ribeiro and Arturo Escobar (eds) *World Anthropologies.* Oxford: Berg.

Weiner, J.S. 1935. 'Physical Anthropology Since 1935: A Survey of Developments'. In T.K. Penniman (ed.) *A Hundred Years of Anthropology.* London: Gerald Duckworth & Co. Ltd. 376–412

Xaxa, Virginius. 2008. *State, Society and Tribes: Issues in Post-Colonial India.* New Delhi: Pearson Education.

Yugandhar, B.N. and Mukherjee Neela (ed.) 1991. *Studies in Village India: Issues in Rural Development.* New Delhi: Concept Pub. Company.

Index